BROKERING ACCESS

BROKERING ACCESS
Power, Politics, and Freedom of
Information Process in Canada

Edited by Mike Larsen and Kevin Walby

UBCPress · Vancouver · Toronto

21 20 19 18 17 16 15 14 13 12   5 4 3 2 1

Printed in Canada on FSC-certified ancient-forest-free paper
(100% post-consumer recycled) that is processed chlorine- and acid-free.

Library and Archives Canada Cataloguing in Publication

Brokering access : power, politics, and freedom of information process in Canada / edited by Mike Larsen and Kevin Walby.

Includes bibliographical references and index.
Issued also in electronic formats.
ISBN 978-0-7748-2322-7 (bound); ISBN 978-0-7748-2323-4 (pbk.)

1. Canada. Access to Information Act. 2. Freedom of information – Canada. 3. Freedom of information – Political aspects – Canada. 4. Government information – Canada. 5. Official secrets – Canada. I. Larsen, Mike, 1981- II. Walby, Kevin, 1981-

KE5325.B76 2012   342.71'0662   C2012-903444-4
KF5753.B76 2012

Canadä

UBC Press gratefully acknowledges the financial support for our publishing program of the Government of Canada (through the Canada Book Fund), the Canada Council for the Arts, and the British Columbia Arts Council.

This book has been published with the help of a grant from the Canadian Federation for the Humanities and Social Sciences, through the Award to Scholarly Publications Program, using funds provided by the Social Sciences and Humanities Research Council of Canada.

UBC Press
The University of British Columbia
2029 West Mall
Vancouver, BC V6T 1Z2
www.ubcpress.ca

We dedicate this book to Jessica and Seantel

Contents

List of Tables and Figures / xi

Foreword / xiii
ANN CAVOUKIAN

Acknowledgments / xvii

List of Abbreviations / xix

Introduction: On the Politics of Access to Information / 1
MIKE LARSEN AND KEVIN WALBY

Part 1: Access to Information, Past and Present

1 Sustaining Secrecy: Executive Branch Resistance to Access to Information in Canada / 35
ANN REES

2 Access Regimes: Provincial Freedom of Information Law across Canada / 68
GARY DICKSON

Part 2: Behind Closed Doors – Security and Information Control

3 Flying the Secret Skies: Difficulties in Obtaining Data on Canadian Airport Security Screening Tests Following 9/11 / 97
JIM BRONSKILL

4 Access to Information in an Age of Intelligencized Governmentality / 115
WILLEM DE LINT AND REEM BAHDI

5 Accessing Dirty Data: Methodological Strategies for Social Problems Research / 142
YAVAR HAMEED AND JEFFREY MONAGHAN

Part 3: Access to Information and Critical Research Strategies

6 The *Freedom of Information Act* as a Methodological Tool: Suing the Government for Data / 169
MATTHEW G. YEAGER

7 "He who controls the present, controls the past": The Canadian Security State's Imperfect Censorship under the *Access to Information Act* / 194
STEVE HEWITT

8 Beyond the Blue Line: Researching the Policing of Aboriginal Activism Using Access to Information / 209
TIA DAFNOS

9 Accessing the State of Imprisonment in Canada: Information Barriers and Negotiation Strategies / 234
JUSTIN PICHÉ

10 Accessing Information on Streetscape Video Surveillance in Canada / 261
SEAN P. HIER

Part 4: Dispatches from the Fourth Estate – Access to Information and Investigative Journalism

11 Access, Administration, and Democratic Intent / 287
FRED VALLANCE-JONES

12 Access to Information: The Frustrations – and the Hope / 314
       DAVID McKIE

13 The Quest for Electronic Data: Where Alice Meets Monty Python
       Meets Colonel Jessep / 335
       JIM RANKIN

       Postscript / 358
       SUZANNE LEGAULT

       List of Contributors / 363

       Index / 370

Tables and Figures

Tables

0.1 Canadian access to information regimes / 10

0.2 Selected international access to information laws / 14

9.1 Informal information requests, 2009 / 240

9.2 Formal information requests, 2009 / 243

9.3 Informal information requests, 2010 / 248

9.4 Scope of ongoing prison capacity expansion in Canada / 250

11.1 Extensions under the *Access to Information Act,* by fiscal year / 291

11.2 Number of extension complaints filed with the Information Commissioner of Canada, by agency, 2005-06 and 2008-09 / 292

11.3 Access to information requests received and fees collected by the federal government and the provinces, where available / 305

11.4 Average fees for requests for personal information and general records under the Ontario provincial and municipal acts / 306

Figures

8.1 Department of National Defence e-mail correspondence, 31 May 2007 / 225

11.1 Letter to reporter Jim Bronskill from Department of Justice Canada, 4 June 2009 / 293

11.2 Memo from Sébastien Togneri calling on ATIP manager to "unrelease" records, 27 July 2009 / 300

Foreword

ANN CAVOUKIAN

"We do not now and never will accept the proposition that the business of the public is none of the public's business."

These were the words of Ontario Attorney General Ian Scott when he introduced the province's first Freedom of Information law in 1985. They are words to remember for they underline the single, trenchant argument in favour of having freedom of information (FOI) or access to information (ATI) laws, namely, that for far too long, in jurisdictions around the world, governments appear to have accepted the proposition that the business of the public is none of the public's business.

As unacceptable as that may sound, this is not a new issue. Although the first ATI law was passed in Sweden in 1766, it was not an idea that caught on quickly. The next such law was not passed for another 187 years, this time in Finland in 1953. At that point the ball started rolling, with the United States following suit in 1966. Today some seventy-eight countries have laws supporting the public's right to request and receive information from their governments. The fact that many of these countries, in Eastern Europe and South and Central America, have emerged from totalitarian regimes and are passing these laws as part of that emergence shows how fundamental a principle of democracy is the public's right to know what government organizations are doing.

Here in Canada, the federal government passed the *Access to Information Act* in 1983 and since then every province and territory has introduced its own law. Since 1997, I have been the Information and Privacy Commissioner for the province of Ontario, overseeing the operation of the FOI and privacy laws introduced by Ian Scott. I believe passionately that citizens must be allowed to participate in the democratic process, and that in order to do so they must have timely access to the information held by their governments – essentially their own information.

In my time as commissioner, I have experienced enough setbacks and victories to understand that even in the fairest and most democratic societies, the road to information access makes for a long and bumpy ride. That is why this book is such a welcome addition to the literature on this subject. All of the contributors make it clear that although we have come a long way regarding access to information, we still have a long way to go.

In 1997, Supreme Court of Canada Justice Gérard La Forest spoke eloquently of the fundamental importance of access to information in a democracy in the case of *Dagg v. Canada (Minister of Finance)*:

> The overarching purpose of access to information legislation, then, is to facilitate democracy. It does so in two related ways. It helps to ensure first, that citizens have the information required to participate meaningfully in the democratic process, and secondly, that politicians and bureaucrats remain accountable to the citizenry. Parliament and the public cannot hope to call the government to account without an adequate knowledge of what is going on.

One of the frustrations for those of us in the business of upholding and promoting better access to information is the incongruence between what is stated and what is acted upon by our elected leaders. In 2004, Ontario Premier Dalton McGuinty echoed the words of Ian Scott in a memorandum to ministers and deputy ministers: "Our government should ensure that information requested of it should continue to be made public unless there is a clear and compelling reason not to do so." As my 2008 annual report to the Ontario legislature makes clear, I applauded the Premier's words and Ontario for achieving commendable results in providing timely responses to access requests. Ontario has also recently expanded its access laws to include publicly funded universities, announced plans to make the expense accounts of public officials available, and extended FOI to publicly funded hospitals.

Unfortunately, this commitment to the principle of access does not extend to the federal government. Despite promises to enhance government accountability, the federal Justice Minister has rejected recent recommendations of the House of Commons committee on access to information, privacy, and ethics that were aimed at improving access to information. Across Canada, the default position for far too many government agencies is to withhold information if at all possible.

We need look no further than the case of Maher Arar, the details of which are well known to most Canadians. The federal government refused to make public the so-called evidence against Mr. Arar, on the grounds of "national security." In the wake of Mr. Justice Dennis O'Connor's commission of inquiry into the affair, we now know that the real reason had far less to do with national security than with covering up bureaucratic incompetence. When a fundamental democratic value like public access to information can be set aside by the highest levels of government in order to disguise incompetence, and freedom of information can be obstructed through false claims of national security, we all need to ask ourselves – and our governments – how this reflects upon the nature of our democracy.

When we began passing FOI laws in this country, we collectively bought into the notion that government must be open, transparent, visible, accountable, and citizen-driven. Our governments accepted that the public perception and understanding of information sharing had changed – that receiving information from government should no longer be viewed as an occasional privilege that citizens were granted but rather as a right that they had been accorded under the laws of this land, one that they had every right to exercise.

Freedom of information is really about freedom, the preservation and advancement of which should be at the heart of all that we do. It is frustrating that books such as this still need to be published and hopefully read. But the fact that they *are* being published and read – and I would strongly encourage all Canadians to read this one – is a good sign. The road may indeed be a long one, and it may be bumpy along the way, but with every mile travelled and every obstacle overcome, our values are secured and our democracy is strengthened. May it grow steadily and may it in turn strengthen our freedom and liberty.

LEGISLATION CITED
Access to Information Act, R.S.C. 1985, c. A-1.

CASE CITED
Dagg v. Canada (Minister of Finance), [1997] 2 S.C.R. 403.

Acknowledgments

We would like to thank our contributors for their insights, commitment, and support. It has been a privilege to work collaboratively with so many active members of Canada's access community. We thank Jessica Ross for providing research assistance. We would also like to thank the anonymous reviewers who provided us with thorough feedback on the manuscript, as well as Randy Schmidt, Ann Macklem, and the editorial staff at UBC Press for seeing us smoothly through the review and production processes.

Royalties from *Brokering Access* have been donated to the BC Civil Liberties Association, in recognition of their sustained commitment to human rights, transparency, and government accountability.

Abbreviations

AFN	Assembly of First Nations
ART	Aboriginal Relations Team [Ontario Provincial Police]
ATI	access to information
ATIA	*Access to Information Act* [Canada]
CADORS	Civil Aviation Daily Occurrence Reporting System [Transport Canada]
CAIRS	Coordination of Access to Information Requests System [Canada]
CATSA	Canadian Air Transport Security Authority
CCAPS	Community, Contract, and Aboriginal Policing Services [RCMP]
CCCS	Coordinating Committee for Community Safety [London, Ontario]
CCTV	closed-circuit television
CFIA	Canadian Food Inspection Agency
CFNCIU	Canadian Forces National Counter-Intelligence Unit
CIA	Central Intelligence Agency [US]
CIC	Citizenship and Immigration Canada
CNA	Canadian Newspaper Association

CPC	Commission for Public Complaints Against the RCMP
CSC	Correctional Service of Canada
CSIS	Canadian Security Intelligence Service
CYFN	Council of Yukon First Nations
DEA	Drug Enforcement Administration [US]
DFO	Department of Fisheries and Oceans [= Fisheries and Oceans Canada]
DND	Department of National Defence [Canada]
ERT	Emergency Response Team [Ontario Provincial Police]
FBI	Federal Bureau of Investigation [US]
FIPPA	*Freedom of Information and Protection of Privacy Act* [Canadian provinces/territories]
FOI	freedom of information
FOIA	*Freedom of Information Act* [US]
IBET	Integrated Border Enforcement Team [RCMP]
ICT	information and communications technology
INAC	Indian and Northern Affairs Canada
INSET	Integrated National Security Enforcement Team [RCMP]
ITAC	Integrated Threat Assessment Centre [Canada]
LAC	Library and Archives Canada
LPS	London Police Service
LVMAC	Lions Video Monitoring Advisory Committee [Sudbury, Ontario]
MAF	Management Accountability Framework [Canada]
MCSCS	Ministry of Community Safety and Correctional Services [Ontario]
MFIPPA	*Municipal Freedom of Information and Protection of Privacy Act* [Ontario]
MLA	Member of the Legislative Assembly
NADDIS	Narcotics and Dangerous Drugs Information System [US Drug Enforcement Administration]
NGO	non-governmental organization
NSCI	National Security Criminal Investigations [RCMP]
NSG	National Security Group [Department of Justice Canada]

OIC	Office of the Information Commissioner of Canada
OIPC	Office of the Information and Privacy Commissioner [Ontario]
OMS	Offender Management System [Correctional Service of Canada]
OPC	Office of the Privacy Commissioner of Canada
OPI	office of primary interest
OPP	Ontario Provincial Police
PCO	Privy Council Office
PERT	Provincial Emergency Response Team [Ontario]
PMO	Prime Minister's Office
PSC	Public Safety Canada
SIRC	Security Intelligence Review Committee [Canada]
TRU	Tactics and Rescue Unit [Ontario Provincial Police]
VMAC	Video Monitoring Advisory Committee [Sudbury, Ontario]

BROKERING ACCESS

Introduction
On the Politics of Access to Information

MIKE LARSEN AND KEVIN WALBY

This book focuses on the workings of access to information (ATI) regimes in Canada. It explores the laws and practices that provide members of the public with the means to exercise a "right to know" about the work of government agencies. It also investigates the ways these same laws and practices act to maintain and legitimize secrecy, and the ways in which they are subverted and circumvented in the interests of information control. A key argument that appears throughout this volume is that access regimes emerge as sites of contestation situated between the public pursuit of transparency and the culture of secrecy in government. The various chapters engage with the politics of access at the level of policy and at the level of practice, where interactions between requesters and professional access brokers take place, negotiations ensue, and techniques of opacity are used.

Every citizen and permanent resident in Canada has the right to request information from federal, provincial, and municipal government agencies. At the federal level, under the *Access to Information Act (ATIA)*, this involves submitting a written request and a cheque for $5 to the access to information office at the agency in question. The *ATIA* came into force in 1983; the provinces and territories have adopted their own legislation, in the form of combined freedom of information (FOI) and privacy protection laws. There are municipal equivalents too. Most government agencies are listed as entities subject to the federal *ATIA* or to FOI acts at provincial and municipal levels.[1]

Brokering Access presents essays written by sociologists, journalists, and ATI advocates and professionals. Its purpose is to assess conceptual, political, and practical issues regarding the role played by ATI in government today, and how ATI can become part of a critical methodological strategy. Exploring the relationship between information, governance, secrecy, and security, the following chapters examine how ATI requests are crafted, how the request process is negotiated, how government employees bury the textual traces of their work, and how ATI results become part of media reporting.[2] We hope that this volume facilitates dialogue between the researchers, investigative journalists, administrators, and policy makers who are presently shaping the Canadian ATI community.

Our thoughts on ATI/FOI developed through our use of ATI in research on policing and national security in Canada (Larsen and Piché 2009; Piché and Walby 2010; Walby 2009; Walby and Larsen 2012; Walby and Monaghan 2010; Walby and Monaghan 2011). It struck us that the broader conceptual issues concerning ATI in Canada had yet to receive their due in sociology and political science. Most social scientists in Canada view ATI as something journalists use to break a big story rather than as a tool that can be utilized to produce qualitative and longitudinal data about government practices (Walby and Larsen 2012). Why, we wondered, are scholars with research interests similar to ours reluctant to use ATI? How can social scientists rethink research methods by incorporating ATI as a tool?

Several books have focused on government secrecy (see Bok 1989; Demac 1984; Helms 2003; Theoharis 1998), although few explore the relationship between secrecy and ATI in Canada; those that do focus on the federal level, overlooking provincial and municipal frameworks. The most thorough examination of ATI is *Blacked Out* (2006), by Alasdair Roberts. Roberts's research examines the role that political interference and bureaucratic resistance have played in delaying sensitive requests filed by journalists or political parties. Similar "information policing" operates at provincial levels (see Roberts 1999, 2002a, 2002b, 2004). Other than the work of Roberts, however, there is little literature on ATI processes in Canada. Recent contributions (such as Kinsman and Gentile 2010) are beginning to address the gap, but more conceptual work is needed. *Brokering Access* supplements Roberts's path-breaking analysis in four ways. First, we emphasize a two-pronged approach to ATI requests, using them systematically to seek out substantive information about the "backstage" of government practices while simultaneously studying ATI processes themselves as sites of information gatekeeping. Second, we include a consideration of provincial- and municipal-level ATI requests (see Chapters 2, 8, 9, and 10). Third, we include voices from numerous communities that have a stake in ATI, such as information advocates, ATI professionals, and investigative journalists. Fourth, we focus on policing, security, and war, as these areas are characterized by contestations over secrecy.

The chapters of *Brokering Access* are critical in tone, reflecting the frustrations of experienced researchers and transparency advocates who work within a Canadian ATI regime that is widely recognized as being outmoded, out of step with international trends, and subject to systemic delays (see Beeby 2011; Chase 2011; Hazel and Worthy 2010; Tromp 2008). This tone reflects a working personality characterized by a determination to work both within and against a flawed system. One thread connecting the chapters is a belief in ATI as a means of producing information of public interest. The corollary to this position is an implicit normative commitment to transparency in government as a public good (see Loader and Walker 2007). That the potential of ATI to facilitate transparency is often unrealized or deliberately inhibited is cause for concern, and this is an issue that the contributors to this volume take up in the form of critical accounts of opacity in government. Several contributors also remark on the need for comprehensive law reform. The 2011 Federal Court of Appeal decision that the Harper Conservatives have too often severed information in ways that contravene the *ATIA* was a progressive step. Our sense, however, is that broad law reform will come to fruition only as the result of agitation by an organized social movement. Certainly there are numerous committed and very active ATI and transparency advocates across the country; the question is how they can work together, and what key issues to focus on in mobilizing for an overhauled access regime in Canada.

One note on terminology is required before moving ahead. Although we use "ATI" to refer to requests at the federal level and "FOI" to refer to requests at the provincial and municipal levels, we insist on the phrase "access to information" over "freedom of information" to define the general process. Ideas of accountability, transparency, openness, and freedom can distract from understanding the complicated process of using ATI. "Freedom of information" is a prescriptive term reflecting the aspirations of the right-to-know movement, which calls for proactive disclosure of the vast majority of public sector information, with minimal interference in the form of redaction, delay, and exemption. By contrast, "access to information" more accurately describes the mediated processes that characterize the administration of the right to know in practice. Bok (1989) dismisses

the notion of a "right to know" itself as quixotic, since it glosses the intermediary actors and stages involved in the release, transmission, and acquisition of information, and risks implying a duty to inform that does not exist.
The public, she argues, does not have a right to information, "but at best to
access to information; and not to all information, but only to some" (258).
ATI processes have numerous built-in governance mechanisms, from the
design of software to the response tactics of ATI coordinators, in addition to
the limitations associated with current ATI laws. Some of the factors shaping ATI are tangible and visible – published guidelines and the precedents
set by court decisions in cases of contested access, for example – while
others, as Thomas (2010a, 15) notes, are submerged in "the overlapping political and administrative cultures of government." What we have is a legal
regime that allows for mediated record retrieval, which we refer to as brokered access. Access laws simultaneously facilitate transparency and circum-
scribe its limits.

The Live Archive and the Spectrum of Disclosure

Information plays a key role in all governance processes and government
agencies. Numerous social scientists have pointed to how governments rely
on information about people, places, and resources (see Dandeker 1990;
Foucault 1980; Giddens 1985; Higgs 2001; Maynard 2009). In Canada, when
scholars write about government, they often refer to federal, provincial,
and municipal agencies charged with providing essential services in various
jurisdictions. Government and the "state" are often conflated, and it is difficult not to invoke the notion of the "state" despite its shortcomings as a
concept. For all the effort put into trying to define the "state" (compare
Miliband 1973 with Poulantzas 1972, or Curtis 1995 with Rose and Miller
1992), social scientists still do not fully understand the work of political administration, for reasons we will elaborate on.

Abrams (1988) paints a picture of naïve sociologists who try to scrutinize the "state" but mistakenly study a preconceived idea of it because they
have no data about what government agencies do. The suggestion here is
that the state "is a spurious object of sociological concern" (63). There is no
"state" as such; a quick scroll down the list of departments to which one can
submit an ATI request at the federal level alone suggests that we are dealing
with a multitude of networked government agencies, each with specific missions, which also have a degree of autonomy from one another. Social scientists cannot say that they study state formation or government if they do not

develop an empirical understanding of what happens from day to day in government agencies. It is the manifold knowledge practices of government agencies that we must learn about in order to conduct a sociology of political administration.

Theorizing the state in general obscures otherwise knowable internal and external relations of political and governmental agencies. Where we part from Abrams (1988) is his suggestion that to escape from reification of the state we must resist what Elias (1987) has called the "retreat of sociologists into the present." It is not only historical documents that allow the internal and external relations of governmental agencies to become knowable. There is what we call the live archive (Walby and Larsen 2011), mounds of text detailing how governments do what they do, added to every day by civil servants, which we get at using ATI. Records pertaining to government policy and practices are created, stored, modified, and circulated – intra- and inter-institutionally, transnationally, and between sectors. Increasingly, this "deepening pool of information" (Roberts 2006, 218) is given structure through Electronic Document and Records Management Systems, a process that produces a new layer of organizational metadata (see Thomas 2010b). The networks between government agencies, the connections between different branches of the same government agencies, and the governance of citizens by these agencies are all enacted by texts. It is this textual trail we must investigate. The live archive is a dynamic system; it changes as researchers engage with it, so part of the ATI research process is to chronicle these changes in how ATI coordinators and other civil servants work with texts. The systematic use of ATI as a means of data production should involve critical reflections on the politics and practices of information brokering.

Information is always situated in a political context. The ability to access information and the power to control access to it depend in many ways on one's position in organizational hierarchies. The kind of information we discuss in this book is textual. Texts are the means by which government bureaucracies organize and communicate (Smith 1999). The idea of an information society (see Bell 1974; Webster 1995) also signals the importance of texts to understanding contemporary governance. Other commentators (e.g., Castells 1996; Poster 1990) have theorized the trend towards network governance and the pivotal role of information in government agencies today. Although governments have always relied on information about their citizenry, the role of information has shifted with the rise of so-called e-government. E-government is about supplying information (see Gil-Garcia, Chun, and Janssen 2009) as well as the careful management of disclosures. Information management requires new infrastructures of hardware and software. The move towards information management in government means that we should conceptualize "information as the primary input to, and product of, government activity" (Gil-Garcia, Chun, and Janssen 2009, 3). Information management also influences how governments interact with citizens. Workers are now expected to have information and communications technology (ICT) skills and also to manage more "sensitive" information, which requires an understanding of formal policy and a familiarity with the informal, unwritten "'rules of the game' for handling and disclosing information" (Thomas 2010b, 16).

Access to information confers a legal right to seek access to materials not already a matter of the public record. Yet the creation of formal information retention and disclosure mechanisms does not mandate government officials to be more accountable or transparent per se. The concept of accountability itself is the subject of considerable debate. Whitaker and Farson (2009, 4) suggest that a heuristic understanding of accountability is that "A is accountable to B when A is obliged to inform B about A's actions (or inactions) and decisions, to justify them as appropriate and proper and, in the case of misconduct, to suffer sanction." They are quick to note that this straightforward understanding belies the complexity of the concept; it makes more sense to speak of multiple and overlapping accountabilities that differ in their focus, intensity, and effects. Whitaker and Farson (2009, 6) also note that "processes of accountability might seem to imply a relationship of power or influence over those held to account [but] accountability importantly offers legitimacy to those persons or organizations held accountable."

From an accountability standpoint, the significance of the information that is disclosed is often, though not necessarily, tied to the means of disclosure. We find it useful to imagine a spectrum of means of disclosure. A mechanism's location on this spectrum is dependent upon the degree of control over the scope and timing of disclosure it affords to government officials. At the end of the spectrum characterized by maximum information control, we find coordinated and voluntary releases of official information. The opposite end of the spectrum, characterized by minimum official control over disclosure, is occupied by whistleblower exposés featuring the revelation of "dirty data" (see Marx 1984) and the mass publication of involuntarily leaked records. ATI mechanisms are located near the middle of the spectrum, in a zone defined by *rules*. They facilitate an uneven form of accountability, but also facilitate secrecy through exemption and provide a source of rhetorical legitimacy for governments.

By contrast, the work of the whistleblowing agency WikiLeaks is characterized by the transgression of rules governing information control and disclosure. Although information leaks are not the subject of this book, the broad impact of the WikiLeaks phenomenon is worth considering. As Slavoj Žižek notes, WikiLeaks represents a radical departure both from regulated disclosure processes and from what he characterizes as traditional investigative journalism, which remains tied to the logic of the bourgeois press: "Its [the bourgeois press's] ideology not only controls what you say, but even how you can violate what you are allowed to say. You [WikiLeaks founder and editor Julian Assange] are not just violating the rules. You are changing the very rules [governing] how we were allowed to violate the rules. This may be the most important thing you can do" (Democracy Now! 2011). *New York Times* editor-in-chief Bill Keller (2011, 3), whose newspaper was eager to capitalize on WikiLeaks's work, describes the organization as "a secretive cadre of anti-secrecy vigilantes." Keller (2011, 4) also notes that "by the end of the year, the story of this wholesale security breach had outgrown the story of the actual contents of the secret documents, and had generated much breathless speculation that something – journalism, diplomacy, life as we knew it – had profoundly changed forever." Precisely by transgressing them, the WikiLeaks disclosures revealed the scope of the rules governing the political management of information by governments. Keller's use of "wholesale security breach" to describe the disclosures is illustrative of the extent to which information control has become a central component of contemporary security politics (tellingly, US Vice President Joseph Biden described Assange as a "high tech terrorist").

This book is concerned with the same regimes of secrecy and politics of information control exposed by WikiLeaks, but our focus here is on everyday practices of transparency and opacity and the nature of the rules governing access.

A Short History of the Debate over ATI in Canada

Now that we have set the conceptual scene, we can get to the details of ATI. Canada has long operated with the British Westminster system of government, which offers little opportunity for citizens to learn about what officials are up to. Throughout most of the twentieth century in Canada, even if a person was allowed standing to view documents under the *Official Secrets*

Act, the "government [could] always assert its Crown privilege to deny access" (Rankin 1977, 12). Most courts would without question abide by a ministerial decision to veto information release. Thomas (1973, 160) suggested that Canada's "bureaucracy is sheltered from parliamentary control and supervision by the doctrines of Cabinet and Ministerial responsibility." Bazillion (1983, 382) likewise argued that "administrative secrecy is endemic in the Canadian political system, for reasons that are largely historical." One reason for secrecy is that ministers bear sole responsibility for department operations. Ministerial control in Canada has been reinforced by current Prime Minister Stephen Harper, who has intervened to prevent ministerial assistants from communicating with the media.

Whereas the United States enacted freedom of information legislation in 1966, there were delays in implementing ATI in Canada (see Table 0.1). A private member's bill recommending ATI was introduced in 1965. Conservative MP Gerald Baldwin introduced similar bills every year between 1969 and 1974. The October Crisis of 1970, with its allegations and revelations of police misconduct, was another step towards access. In June 1977, the Liberal government issued a Green Paper titled *Legislation on Public Access to Government Documents*. The Green Paper starts with the metaphor of a football huddle. These football players make a decision about an action to pursue in private, it is argued, because not to do so destroys the team's ability to enact the plan. This is the justification for barring access to cabinet confidences. "The Green paper frequently takes refuge in the convention of ministerial responsibility," argues Rankin (1977, 136).

A few years later, the *Commission of Inquiry Concerning Certain Activities of the Royal Canadian Mounted Police* was struck, headed by Justice D.C. McDonald. The commission published two reports (*Security and Information* in 1979 and *Freedom and Security under the Law* in 1981) arguing that the *Official Secrets Act* needed to be curtailed and used only in espionage cases. Then Joe Clark's Conservative government introduced draft ATI legislation as Bill C-15 in October 1979. Trudeau's Liberals replaced the Conservatives in February 1980, however, and in July of that year the Liberals introduced Bill C-43. The bills were similar. The two-tier system of appealing to an information commissioner and then Federal Court was introduced by Bill C-15 and is still part of the *Access to Information Act* today. Bill C-43 also introduced stringent exemptions concerning third-party information. Mandatory exemptions for cabinet documents were introduced at the final hour. One argument against ATI by numerous government officials was "maintenance of cabinet solidarity" (Bazillion 1980, 151). A second argument was that "the anonymity of public servants in a parliamentary system must be protected so that they may advise their ministers fully, frankly, and in confidence without involving themselves in the political process" (151). Riley (1977, 13) argued that ATI had "become a bit of a merry-go-round in Parliament."

Academics commented on these developments even before the law was passed. There was debate between Donald Rowat and K.W. Knight in the *Canadian Journal of Economics and Political Science*. An advocate of ATI, Rowat (1965, 480) questioned the information practices of Canada's federal government. He argued that Canada should adopt the publicity rule since it lets the "public have a chance to criticize and discuss proposals before decisions are made" (492). Knight (1966) responded that there would be practical limits to conferring a right to request information, arguing that "the civil servant may feel, too, that he [sic] must avoid placing on record anything which is likely to offend or cut across the interests of any individual or group in the community" (78). "Many officials, faced with open access, would seek to avoid completely the risks arising from the putting of pen to paper," he argued (79). Sadly, many of Knight's predictions have come true. Many in public administration see ATI as an unwelcome imposition on government.[3] For example, Donald Savoie (2003, 213), a proponent of the "traditional bargain" between anonymous career public servants operating in secret and providing advice to politically accountable ministers, has argued that ATI legislation contributes to a risk-averse culture in government, and that it "inhibits public servants from committing frank advice to paper for fear of embarrassing their ministers or compromising their political neutrality."

Access to information is a fairly new animal in some liberal democratic nation-states (see Table 0.2). It was only in 2000 that Britain moved towards a statutory right of access to official records. Numerous other countries have adopted ATI as a so-called accountability measure. For instance, Arko-Cobbah (2008) assesses some of the limits of access to information in post-apartheid South Africa. South Africa's *Promotion of Access to Information Act* from 2000 has been called one of the most progressive pieces of ATI legislation in the world. Yet there have been challenges in declassifying documents from the apartheid era, and reports of non-compliance. Where ATI laws have been implemented, differences arise concerning rules for redaction, the definition of personal information (which is also addressed in privacy law), third-party status, statutory compliance timelines, and the rate of charging schemes (Birkinshaw 1999). Access to information takes on a

TABLE 0.1

Canadian access to information regimes

Jurisdiction	Title of access law(s)	Year of adoption	Cost per request (initial)	Access commissioner	Commissioner has order-making power?
Canada (federal)	• Access to Information Act (ATIA) • Privacy Act	1983 (for both acts)	$5 for request	Information Commissioner of Canada	No
Newfoundland and Labrador	Access to Information and Protection of Privacy Act (ATIPPA)	Freedom of Information Act of 1981 replaced by ATIPPA, 2005	$5 for request + 2 hours search time, $15 per hour after; $0.25 per page for copies; "actual cost" for other formats	Information and Privacy Commissioner of Newfoundland and Labrador	No
Prince Edward Island	Freedom of Information and Protection of Privacy Act (FOIPPA)	2002	Free for personal information, copy fees apply; $5 for public records + $10 per half-hour search time and computer time + copy and associated costs	Information and Privacy Commissioner of Prince Edward Island	Yes
New Brunswick	Right to Information and Protection of Privacy Act	Right to Information Act, 1978 repealed and replaced in 2010	$5 for request + 2 hours search time, $15 per half-hour after; $0.25 per page for copies	Access to Information and Privacy Commissioner of New Brunswick	No

Province	Legislation	Year	Fees	Oversight Body	
Nova Scotia	• Freedom of Information and Protection of Privacy Act (FOIPOP) • Municipal Government Act	*Freedom of Information Act,* 1977 replaced by FOIPOP in 1994	$5 for request; $15 per hour may be charged for compiling; $0.20 per page for copies + various format fees	Review Officer	No
Québec	*An Act Respecting Access to Documents Held by Public Bodies and the Protection of Personal Information*	1982	Free request; copy fees only	Commission d'accès à l'information (5 commissioners and 1 chair)	Yes
Ontario	• *Freedom of Information and Protection of Privacy Act (FIPPA)* • *Municipal Freedom of Information and Protection of Privacy Act (MFIPPA)*	1987	$5 for request, personal or otherwise; copy and additional search time fees apply	Information and Privacy Commissioner of Ontario	Yes
Manitoba	• *Freedom of Information and Protection of Privacy Act (FIPPA)* • *Personal Health Information Act (PHIA)*	1997	Free for *FIPPA* application + 2 hours search time, $15 per hour after; copy fees apply	• Access and Privacy Division of Manitoba Ombudsman • Information and Privacy Adjudicator	No

▼ TABLE 0.1

Jurisdiction	Title of access law(s)	Year of adoption	Cost per request (initial)	Access commissioner	Commissioner has order-making power?
Saskatchewan	• *Freedom of Information and Protection of Privacy Act (FOIP)* • *Local Authority Freedom of Information and Protection of Privacy Act (LAFOIP)*	1992	Free for personal information but copy fees may apply; first 2 hours free, $15 per hour after	Information and Privacy Commissioner of Saskatchewan	No
Alberta	• *Freedom of Information and Protection of Privacy Act (FOIP)* • *Health Information Act (HIA)*	1995	$25 for request	Information and Privacy Commissioner of Alberta	Yes
British Columbia	*Freedom of Information and Protection of Privacy Act (FIPPA)*	1993	Free for personal information and search time up to 3 hours, $30 per hour after; copy fees apply	Information and Privacy Commissioner for British Columbia	Yes

Nunavut	*Access to Information and Privacy Protection Act (ATIPP)* (an amended form of the NWT act)	*NWT ATIPP adopted under the Nunavut Act 1999*, pending new legislation	Free for personal information, with possible copy fees; $25 fee per request for public records	Access to Information and Privacy Commissioner of Nunavut	No
Northwest Territories	*Access to Information and Protection of Privacy Act (ATIPP)*	1996	Free for personal information; $25 for other	Information and Privacy Commissioner of the Northwest Territories	No
Yukon	*Access to Information and Protection of Privacy Act (ATIPP)*	1984	Free request; retrieval and processing fees $25 per hour + copying expenses over $10	Information and Privacy Commissioner of the Yukon	No

TABLE 0.2

Selected international access to information laws

Country	Title of access law	Year adopted
Sweden[a]	*Freedom of the Press Act*	1766/1945/1976[c]
Denmark	*Access to Public Administration Files Act*	1965/1970/1985
United States	*Freedom of Information Act*	1966
Norway	*Freedom of Information Act of 1970*	1970
France[a]	*Law on Access to Administrative Documents*	1978
Australia	*Freedom of Information Act*	1982
New Zealand	*Official Information Act*	1982
Philippines[b]	*Code of Conduct and Ethical Standards for Public Employees*	1987
Spain	*Law on Rules for Public Administration*	1992
Ukraine	*Law on Information*	1992
Ireland	*Freedom of Information Act*	1997
Thailand	*Official Information Act*	1997
Israel	*Freedom of Information Law*	1998
South Africa	*Promotion of Access to Information Act*	2000
Pakistan[b]	*Freedom of Information Ordinance 2002*	2002
Mexico[a]	*Federal Law of Transparency and Access to Public Government Information*	2002
Zimbabwe	*Access to Information and Privacy Protection Act (AIPPA)*	2002
Angola	*Law on Access to Administrative Documents*	2002
Croatia[a]	*Act on the Right of Access to Information*	2003
Turkey	*Law on Right to Information*	2003
India[a]	*Right to Information Act*	2005
United Kingdom	*Freedom of Information Act*	2005
Germany	*Act to Regulate Access to Federal Government Information*	2006
China[b]	*People's Republic of China Ordinance on Openness of Government Information (OGI Regulations)*	2008
Chile	*Law on Access to Public Information*	2008
Russia[a]	*Law on Providing Access to Information on the Activities of State Bodies and the Bodies of Local Self Government*	2009

▶

◄ TABLE 0.2

Country	Title of access law	Year adopted
Liberia	*Freedom of Information Act*	2010
Nigeria	*Freedom of Information Bill*	2011

Notes: Access provisions can take a variety of forms: stand-alone legislation, administrative regulations, and/or jurisprudence and constitutional rights. The following are some examples.

a These countries have constitutional provisions for access to information or high court rulings that a right to information is necessary to the interpretation of certain constitutional rights.

b While China's *OGI Regulations,* the Philippine *Code of Conduct and Ethical Standards for Public Employees,* and the Pakistani *Freedom of Information Ordinance 2002* are not acts, they do provide some legal basis for rights to information.

c Sweden's *Freedom of the Press Act* (1766) is the world's first freedom of information act. The dates indicate the enactment and two major amendments.

different tenor in each country. Byrne (2003), for instance, discusses how the focus on "transparency" in the former Soviet bloc means something different than in western nation-states due to vestiges of the communist apparatus.

The events of 11 September 2001 led to substantial changes for ATI in Canada and the United States. As Relyea (2009, 315) argues, "these events prompted rethinking, as well as continuing concern, about ... the public availability of information [deemed to be] of potential value to terrorists for either the commission of their acts or forewarning them of ways of their being detected." The *Federal Advisory Committee Act (FACA)* and the *Critical Infrastructure Information Act (CIIA)* were passed as part of the *Homeland Security Act* of 2002; both led to greater secrecy. The CIIA prohibits the disclosure of "critical infrastructure information" by the Department of Homeland Security (Shapiro and Steinzor 2006, 124). Numerous groups filed ATI requests after 9/11 only to see these denied unjustifiably. The Coalition of Journalists for Open Government were vocally defiant (Kirtley 2006).

All this raises questions about whether Canada is modelling itself after the US in the post-9/11 quest for continental security. Anti-terrorism has a digital infrastructure – it depends on up-to-the-second intelligence accessible in numerous sites (Roy 2005). This requires "interoperability," or the ability to share information across space and time. Post-9/11, Canada was accused by Homeland Security directors of having an outdated digital infrastructure. It responded by creating Public Safety and Emergency Preparedness Canada (now Public Safety Canada) soon after. Reflecting on the post-9/11 context, Pozen (2010, 266) offers a theory of government secrecy, with secrets being organized "on a continuum running from maximally opaque to maximally intelligible." The "depth" of a given secret is determined by the number of people within government who know the secret, the types of actors who are in the know, and the extent of the secret known by each of these actors (see Hinson 2010). Deep secrets are the province of a small group of authorized knowers, and they correspond to the Rumsfeldian concept of "unknown unknowns" – things that we don't know that we don't know. Shallow secrets, by contrast, are those things that we know that we don't know. A given secret can be simultaneously shallow and deep, relative to different audiences, and its depth can change over time, given the expansion of the network of actors "in the know" and the proliferation of the textual trail.

Much of the information in the live archive is clustered at the shallow end of the spectrum. Other information is classified as secret, and subject to official efforts to increase control over its dissemination (see Chapter 4). The circulation of secret information within and between networks increases the likelihood that it will become more knowable to others. Relatively shallow and accessible records often reference other documents, such that sustained research using ATI can reduce the depth of secret practices. Yet the flow of information between agencies can be an impediment to formal ATI processes, as multiple stakeholders are often consulted prior to the release of records, creating delays and backlogs (see Walby and Larsen 2011).

There are barriers that accompany access law. In Canada, successive Information Commissioners have reported on systemic issues facing the federal access regime (on access regimes, see Chapter 2). Access loopholes caused by broad exemption clauses in ATI laws, quasi exemptions (see Chapter 11) such as chronic delays, and prohibitive fee estimates are efforts to keep decisions "off the record" and disconnected from the live archive. Each chapter in this book engages with the limitations of ATI. While we support the notion that ATI can facilitate democratic accountability, we conceptualize ATI as a field of contestation, a site for struggles over what can be known about government actions.

Our position as users of access law and as proponents of increased government transparency is that the federal access regime is in need of major law reform. The problem facing the Canadian access regime is not a lack of well-researched, principled solutions to current dilemmas or detailed plans for ATI modernization. Instead, the problem exists at the level of implementation. Successive governing parties have capitalized on the rhetoric of transparency while presiding over a dysfunctional ATI regime and refusing to undertake comprehensive reform efforts. The dysfunctionalities of the current ATI framework are by no means reducible to problems with the law; as we discuss below, "techniques of opacity" are tied to political and administrative cultures. Nonetheless, the federal access law anchors the access regime and defines its scope and limitations. It is hard to imagine a meaningful solution to problems such as chronic delays and denials without a new act. There is no shortage of ideas for law reform, including mandatory periodic review of the legislation; the granting of order-making powers to the Information Commissioner; radical limitations on cabinet confidence exemptions; limitations on exemptions, extensions, and consultation-related delays; clearer guidelines for the delegation of authority for ATI decisions; and commitments to principles of open government. Translating these ideas into a legislative mandate will require an organized social movement that can effectively connect moments of secrecy and opacity to the (dys) functioning of the ATI regime.

Bureaucracy and Information Brokers

ATI can provide social scientists with a more nuanced understanding of how government agencies do what they do. Yet access is contingent on the intensity of "information management" in any government agency, the political contentiousness of the request, the limits of the Canadian ATI law and oversight mechanisms, and the complexities of requester-agency interactions and request wording. Thus, ATI is a source of both opportunity and constraint for the researcher (Gentile 2009). We use the term "access brokering" to describe the range of interactions involved in the filing and processing of ATI requests. Access brokering is an interactive, mediated process. Several factors are key. The effective framing of initial requests, such that the language used fits closely with the specialized jargon of government agencies, is crucial. Understanding this process and the actors, interests, and technologies involved is not simply a means to the end of gaining information. "Brokering" itself is an important subject of inquiry (Walby and Larsen 2012).

Users of ATI mechanisms often interact with ATI analysts many times over the life cycle of a request; these encounters can involve the negotiation of request wording and scope, discussions about time extensions and delays, and contestation over the accessibility of records. Inexperienced requesters can find themselves talked into making concessions that drastically alter the outcome/disclosure. Questions such as "Can we interpret this part of your request to mean *xyz?*" or "Can I ask why you are looking for this information?" can help coordinators to assist requesters, but they can also steer requests away from more contentious texts. Experienced users of ATI requests are not immune to this steering.[4] When the brokering process results in opacity, this may not reflect a commitment to keeping certain records secret but instead may signal an access regime that is disproportionately concerned with procedural measurements of compliance. A brokering process that narrows a request so as to render it manageable within a deadline avoids the production of a "deemed refusal" statistic – the primary unit of measurement for many access oversight processes (see Thomas 2010a). The invocation of extension clauses and the chronic delays that characterize some ATI regimes contribute to decisions to restrict the date range or complexity of requests. An understanding of government information management processes, careful request follow-up, and the asking of probing questions by ATI researchers can lead to more effective brokering.

This complex process of brokered access raises questions about the powers and activities of government ATI analysts and coordinators. Former Assistant Information Commissioner of Canada Bruce Mann (1986) argued that access coordinators represent the "meat in the sandwich," occupying a role unlike any other in the federal government. The uniqueness of this role is due to the position of the ATI coordinator within the "pyramidal hierarchy of government," where the coordinator maintains "multiple working relationships" of both a hierarchical and lateral nature (580). According to Mann, ATI coordinators are positioned between a suspicious requesting public and a distrustful bureaucracy, and are further positioned in a confrontational role with oversight bodies such as the Office of the Information Commissioner. By foregrounding the competing interests in play within and between government agencies, however, Mann creates a certain distance between ATI coordinators and the agencies in which they are embedded.

Brokering access is political and, at present, inextricably linked to the management of public perceptions through government communications efforts. In using the metaphor of brokerage, we do not mean to imply that analysts and coordinators occupy the neutral position of a mediator or the proverbial honest broker between two parties with competing claims. For this to be the case, we would have to ignore the location of ATI workers within government agencies as well as the influence of overarching cultures of secrecy on the information disclosure process (Hazell and Worthy 2010).

We would also have to make assumptions about the neutrality of access law itself, including that it effectively operates according to a principle of presumptive disclosure and that it empowers ATI workers to apply balancing tests when disclosure is contested. And we would have to ignore inequalities in the exercise of power between the two parties – the requester and the government – whose interests are being brokered.

This is not the picture we paint. We use the term "brokering" to highlight the contingent and mediated nature of the ATI process, to foreground the position of ATI workers as the point of contact between the requesting public and government agencies, and to recognize the role that discretion and negotiation play. We are not implying that ATI workers possess a uniform set of motivations that serve to inhibit access, or that they necessarily work to advance secrecy. Our interest is in the *position* that ATI workers occupy within the machinery of government. We could just as easily speak about negotiated access, mediated access, or the gatekeeping of information within a secretive system. Access coordinators certainly play a gatekeeping role, not only through the negotiations that characterize access brokering but also through the discretionary application of exemption clauses under the *ATIA*. Journalist Dean Beeby (2011) argues that "overworked [ATI] bureaucrats largely focus on the technical application of legal loopholes to withhold information," a position that echoes the perspectives of many of the contributors to this book. In the federal access regime, high rates of personnel turnover, coupled with the lack of a full devolution of authority from senior departmental bureaucrats to access coordinators, mean that ATI offices are unable to develop the institutional memory or independence that would enable them to operate as the proverbial meat in Mann's information sandwich. Willem de Lint (2003, 386), in his study of police as brokers of access to sites and individuals, argues that knowledge work and the negotiation of access "cannot simply be decoupled from the question of 'for whom?' or 'in whose interests?'" These questions are central to the study of access brokering and ATI as well.

The brokering of access also has a technological component. The quintessential image of an access-brokered document remains the white page with blacked-out sections of redacted text. In Canada, the hands-on production of blacked-out texts is becoming a thing of the past, as more government agencies switch to specialized software systems such as *ATIPflow* and the more advanced *AccessPro Case Management*. While the "where, when, and why" of redaction are established by discretion, law, and, at the federal level, regulations issued by the Treasury Board, agencies are free to develop in-house policies around the "how" of redaction. This has led to an uneven access field, with many of the large agencies using state-of-the-art software and others not. These new programs, developed by the Ottawa-based software company Privasoft to meet the needs of Canada's access regime, allow for the real-time management and tracking of all aspects of the ATI process, from filing to the tasking of requests to offices of primary interest (OPIs), to standardized correspondence, to redaction – which now appears as blank white space – and release package approval. They also offer tools for the stonewalling of sensitive requests through amber lighting and red filing. Amber lighting refers to the tagging of a request or a requester as politically contentious. Red filing refers to requests that are stonewalled by the minister or by the Prime Minister's Office, who receive a weekly inventory of tagged requests.

Roberts (2005) contends that internal routines and technological developments ensure that ATI laws do not effectively break down governmental secrecy. Arguing that "special procedures for handling politically sensitive requests are commonplace in major departments" (4), Roberts discusses the way government departments try to mitigate the potential fallout of disclosing information. Over half of the requests in some departments (the Department of National Defence, for example) are amber lighted. Media lines and house cards are then prepared prior to the release of request packages so government spokespersons can field questions. There are various other techniques that ATI officers use to stall or stunt requests, some specific to certain types of agencies. The Canadian Security Intelligence Service (CSIS) ATI office has a policy of citing the sections of the *ATIA* it has invoked to exempt or redact information in a release package, but refusing to indicate which portion of the document the exemption clause has been applied to. This is explained as necessary to protect national security, lest unauthorized knowers glean information about state secrets by using exemption clauses as clues to missing content. Our favourite response from CSIS is, "We neither confirm nor deny the existence of such records."

We use the term "techniques of opacity" to encompass the range of formal and informal attributes of access regimes that can effectively inhibit timely and comprehensive access to information. Some techniques of opacity stem directly from ATI law, in the form of exemption and redaction clauses. Others are more informal. Rigid and narrow interpretations of requests and efforts to steer requesters away from particular parts of the live archive through negotiation are techniques of opacity, for example. Many of the contributors to this book express frustration over the systemic delays that characterize the Canadian access regime. The chronic delay problem certainly constitutes a technique of opacity, in that it inhibits timely access. In Canada, techniques of opacity are enshrined in access laws, institutional cultures, and technology. In Chapter 11, Fred Vallance-Jones describes the routine failure of ATI regimes to realize their own ideals of disclosure as the product of a range of "quasi exemptions."

In making sense of opacity, we have found it useful to draw on the work of Ericson (2007), who argues that western societies have come to be governed through the problem of uncertainty. This shift in focus has caused many agencies to reorganize their work around precautionary measures and the identification and pre-emption of potential sources of harm or insecurity. We suggest that the idea of governing – and governing through – uncertainty and the ascendance of precautionary logics are helpful in thinking about the politics of ATI in the contemporary context. From the perspective of government, ATI mechanisms are often viewed as a pervasive source of uncertainty and political risk (see Savoie 2003; Thomas 2010b). Requests that seek potentially embarrassing records can destabilize carefully crafted and centrally controlled messaging efforts (see Roberts 2006), with unpredictable results. Seen in this light, the range of techniques of opacity employed by access brokers, the creation of communications products in anticipation of the publication of ATI records, and the broader cultures of secrecy within governments emerge as attempts to manage uncertainty, pre-empt surprises, and consolidate control. The intersection of this preoccupation with uncertainty and the ongoing expansion of the information society creates a paradox in which the circulation of information within the live archive is simultaneously a source of power and a potential source of insecurity for government agencies. As Ericson (2007, 217) notes, "the problem of uncertainty creates the urge to hunker down, avoid risk, and limit the freedom of others in the name of security." It is this defensive hunkering down that has given rise to a federal ATI regime in Canada that is "sluggish, unresponsive and obstructionist" (Chase 2011).

Yet not all delays with ATI stem from the government agencies supplying the information. Drapeau (2009) has commented on the inability of the Office of the Information Commissioner (OIC) to investigate complaints concerning non-compliance, leading some government departments to exploit this impotence (see also Roberts 2002b; Rosner 2008). Information Commissioner Robert Marleau, who served from 2006 to 2009, is credited with spearheading a compliance campaign based on a business model of managing OIC investigations. Drapeau, however, accuses Marleau of

replacing knowledgeable OIC executives with new assistant commissioners with no expertise. Drapeau claims that more emphasis has been placed
on the OIC ATI report cards, without any teeth being given to OIC
enforcement.

To circumvent these techniques of opacity and to deal with complica-
tions stemming from OIC management of the federal access regime, researchers should consider ATI research as part of an information production
feedback loop. The production and circulation of information within the
live archive is shaped by an awareness of the potentiality of its release
through ATI (see Chapter 8 of this book). ATI offices routinely inform government officials of the content of requests, and this information can influence changes in substantive practices and in the production of talking points
and media lines. We find it fruitful to file requests for records pertaining to
the management of previous requests. Adopting this stance demands a
heightened commitment to reflexivity by the ATI researcher, and raises
questions about how ATI requests as a form of data production can supplement existing social scientific research strategies.

Coda: Access to Information as a Tool for Critical Social Science

The access to information process appears to have a tenuous relationship
with the social sciences (Walby and Larsen 2011, 2012). There is a prejudg-
ment among most scholars that ATI requests are something used by journalists and lawyers, which means that systematic ATI research is an
underdeveloped methodological approach in the social sciences. Those who
wish to incorporate ATI into their research tend to learn through trial and
error.

Haggerty (2004) has compared the knowledge production of social scientists and journalists. He suggests that journalists are comparatively free
from the scrutiny of research ethics protocols that stifle researchers in social
science. Academic research is often "comparatively less robust and critical
than investigative journalism that can and does 'name names'" (409). There
is a need for social scientists to break away from "the path of least institutional resistance" (413) or letting ethical review boards govern the topics
and methods of our research. There are clear rationales for using ATI/FOI
instead of and in addition to conventional research methods. Journalists
prefer ATI data because interviews with public officials are unreliable by
comparison. If our goal in using ATI is to understand how government
agencies do what they do, even the experience of being amber lighted, red
filed, and stonewalled is important to write about (see Chapter 8).

ATI/FOI can play a key data production role in reinvigorating critical social science. Used systematically and with attention to key moments of reflexivity, ATI/FOI can provide researchers with invaluable access to back-stage government texts. Additionally, and crucially, by treating the ATI/FOI process itself as an object of research, as opposed to an unexamined means to an end, we can study the interplay between practices of secrecy and information management in government agencies (Walby and Larsen 2012). We want this book to push social scientists beyond studying rhetoric and towards muckraking sociology. What we have called the live archive needs to be opened up. We are not suggesting that ATI can provide a "true" account of government – the results of ATI requests are more like acquiring small pieces of an always-shifting puzzle. There is a time and place for studying official discourse (Burton and Carlen 1979), but we also need access to the kinds of "dirty data" (Marx 1984) that are out there if we want a more comprehensive picture of the internal and external relations of political and governmental agencies.

Overview of the Chapters

This book is organized into four thematic sections. Part 1 sets the stage with two chapters on the history of ATI mechanisms and key features of ATI in Canada today.

In Chapter 1, Ann Rees argues that political opposition to access among party leaders and senior civil servants is the central problem facing ATI in Canada. This state of affairs is tied to the makeup of the *ATIA*, which includes broad exemption clauses for cabinet confidences and other sensitive executive branch records. Rees argues that the *ATIA* is as much about the codification of secrecy as it is about the facilitation of transparency, particularly given the ascendancy of security as a motif in government. Despite the political, legal, and bureaucratic forces operating to reduce transparency, Rees argues that ATI is essential to democracy. She concludes with several recommendations intended to rebalance the current equation of state secrecy and public interest access.

In Chapter 2, Gary Dickson, Information and Privacy Commissioner of Saskatchewan, provides an account of the historical development of provincial ATI laws in Canada. He makes a valuable contribution to the literature on ATI in Canada, which has predominantly focused on the federal level. Dickson introduces the concept of "access regime," which encompasses the various legal, bureaucratic, oversight, and political mechanisms, actors, and decisions that collectively shape ATI in a given jurisdiction. Focusing on provincial access regimes, he identifies the factors that contribute to the unevenness of access across Canada.

Part 2 contains three chapters on security and information control. These chapters examine the use of security as an organizing framework for government activity, concomitant with moves to entrench mechanisms of secrecy and techniques of opacity, and the idea of "dirty data" (see Marx 1984).

Chapter 3, by journalist Jim Bronskill, explores the securitization of Canadian airport security screening tests in the post-9/11 context. Reconfigurations of security politics have led to this information being considered extremely sensitive. Bronskill discusses his efforts to obtain information about aviation security, the nature of the opposition he has encountered, and the ways in which government actors have gone about framing this material as a source of risk and a subject of secrecy. The chapter then addresses the implications of the securitization of information, discussing what this trend poses for ATI in Canada.

In Chapter 4, Willem de Lint and Reem Bahdi build on the theme of the securitization of information by providing an account of information control in the Canadian national security field. The unchecked flow of information is viewed by national security agencies as a source of risk. Opposition to this flow takes the forms of discourses of exceptionalism, efforts to procure public trust against a dynamic media backdrop, and attempts to challenge the loyalties of those who would contest secrecy. De Lint and Bahdi argue that efforts to consolidate information control also produce opportunities for resistance and contestation.

Chapter 5, by Yavar Hameed and Jeffrey Monaghan, focuses on strategies for push-back against information control. Their goal is to advance a social problems research agenda informed by opposition to injustice by gaining access to dirty data: "information which is kept secret and whose revelation would be discrediting or costly in terms of various types of sanctioning" (Marx 1984, 79). Hameed and Monaghan discuss strategies for getting at dirty data, unpacking these approaches through two case studies. Monaghan's experience using civil litigation to gain access to data otherwise denied under ATI and *Privacy Act* requests has yielded significant results. In contrast, Hameed, working on the case of Abousfian Abdelrazik, has found that litigation can lead to a defensive tightening of information control, as evidenced by a comparison of pre- and post-litigation flows of information. The chapter argues for the use of multiple methods in search of disparate pieces of a puzzle that can later be combined.

Part 3 includes five chapters that illustrate how the use of ATI as a method of data production in the social sciences can assist in understanding government practices. Each chapter includes an account of techniques of opacity and a discussion of the formal and informal tactics that can be used to push back and obtain data. Chapter 6, by Matthew Yeager, discusses the merits of ATI requests as components of a research methodology. He focuses on request follow-through, complaints, and civil litigation as components of a conflict criminology approach. Originally published in the *Canadian Journal of Criminology and Criminal Justice* in 2006 and reprinted here with permission, this chapter represents one of the first pieces of Canadian criminological scholarship to focus on ATI. Yeager has revised the piece to include reflection on his recent experiences with suing the government for data. By responding to the denial of access by taking information brokering to its logical (and legal) extreme, Yeager argues that elite and state interests control disclosure.

In Chapter 7, historian Steve Hewitt reflects on eighteen years of using the *ATIA* in research on the Canadian security state. He reviews the exemption and redaction clauses used to withhold information from researchers, and considers the relationship between these exclusionary practices and broader political agendas. One of the strategies that Hewitt employs is to seek access to records that are held by multiple agencies, and to compare the release packages and note the differential redacting of information. Hewitt moves on to discuss the implications of the existence of multiple versions of the same document for historical researchers and the ongoing trend towards reduced disclosure of security-related material, even of a historical nature.

In Chapter 8, Tia Dafnos discusses her research on the policing of Canadian Aboriginal activism using ATI. Outlining the access barriers and forms of opposition she has encountered, she reviews the successes and failures she has experienced using ATI to conduct research on the policing of the reclamation of Caledonia and the blockades of Tyendinaga. Dafnos observes that the policing of Aboriginal activism is characterized by an awareness of the potentiality of ATI requests, which in turn has shaped information management practices at the agencies in question. Her chapter is informed by a normative commitment to transparency as a means of ensuring accountability in public policing.

In Chapter 9, Justin Piché discusses his use of multi-jurisdictional formal and informal ATI requests in a study of contemporary Canadian prison expansion. He recounts a three-stage research strategy that moved from the collection and analysis of publicly available information to a series of informal requests, and finally to the filing of federal ATI and provincial FOI requests. He discusses the various brokering processes he has developed, and the techniques of opacity that he encountered. The chapter concludes by considering the policing of criminological knowledge through access restrictions, and the importance of transparency for informed participatory politics.

Chapter 10, by Sean Hier, continues the discussion of methods. Hier's focus is the development of policy concerning streetscape surveillance cameras in Canada. Through the cultivation of informal relationships with government managers (essentially the individuals who would be considered the offices of primary interest in a formal ATI request), he gained access to extensive sets of documents. The analysis of these texts has contributed to a more nuanced understanding of the forces influencing streetscape surveillance, enabling the revision of hypotheses developed during earlier phases of the research project and providing insights into the role of the privacy sector in streetscape video surveillance policy diffusion. Hier concludes by contrasting the tendency of researchers to adopt a conflict approach to ATI methods (see Chapter 6) with an argument for informal rapport building.

Many ATI researchers in the social sciences have been influenced by investigative journalists, who have helped shape the Canadian access regime by publishing the results of ATI research and challenging denials through litigation. Part 4 of this book includes chapters from some of Canada's most prominent journalistic users of ATI. Given the fluid format of contemporary news media and the push towards instant reporting, timeliness of access emerges as a key issue. For journalists, access delayed is access denied.

Chapter 11, by Fred Vallance-Jones, is based on an exploration of what he describes as quasi exemptions – regulatory provisions within ATI laws beyond formal exemption clauses that can be used to block or delay the release of information. Disregard for statutory time limits for the processing of requests emerges as the most prominent quasi exemption, but prohibitive processing fees are also discussed. Based on interviews with veteran users of ATI, Vallance-Jones discusses the tensions between openness and secrecy as well as the implications of barriers at the bureaucratic, oversight, and legal levels. He argues that the current focus on incremental administrative reforms will not address quasi exemptions, and that legislative reform is necessary.

In Chapter 12, the Canadian Broadcasting Corporation's David McKie argues that the Canadian federal access regime currently faces endemic issues that arise from its organization. McKie argues that the absence of political will to enact reforms or enforce compliance is the central problem facing the Canadian access community. The chapter is based on a case study of ATI research and reporting in the context of the 2008 Ontario listeriosis crisis. McKie notes the ways in which endemic access problems contributed to the media's inability to convey information to the public in a timely fashion. Despite the pitfalls, reporting using ATI enables journalists to break stories of great public worth. The chapter concludes by exploring key resources and strategies for research success.

Chapter 13, by Jim Rankin of the *Toronto Star*, elaborates on lessons learned through data-based investigative reporting, and speaks directly to both journalistic and academic audiences. This chapter explores the idea that access to information is actively opposed by government agencies that have vested interests in the preservation of exclusive control over information. Rankin argues that ATI researchers must develop a particular skill set to effectively broker access, suggesting that proactive approaches based on knowledge of information management systems and persistent follow-up with ATI analysts are necessary. The chapter closes with reflections on the relationship between data-based journalism – currently the province of a small cadre of reporters – and traditional news media structures, and the prospects of moving towards an online, interactive reporting format.

ACKNOWLEDGMENTS
We thank the anonymous reviewers at UBC Press, as well as Sean Hier and Chris Hurl.

NOTES
1 One of the flaws with the Canadian federal ATI regime is that government departments and agencies can be brought under its authority only by being added to Schedule I of the *Access to Information Act*. This must be done either at the time that an agency's own enabling legislation is created or amended, or in an omnibus fashion, as occurred following the passage of the *Federal Accountability Act* (2006). There is no presumption of inclusion, which means that some government agencies and Crown corporations "fly under the radar" of the act.
2 One of the only revelations as it concerns the pre-emptive information policing in government departments comes from Kelly (2006), who discusses his work as a government employee under the Mike Harris government in Ontario. Kelly discusses systematic methods of obstructing requests. First, requests can be obstructed by

taking a literal reading of request wording instead of helping to facilitate the search. It is easy to respond that "no such records exist" when a literal reading of the request is taken; only the provided key words are searched for. Second, Kelly discusses the way that cabinet briefing notes are covered under "Advice to Minister" or "closed meeting" clauses. Third, orders were given to destroy information. Twice, Kelly writes, he was advised to destroy all documents concerning Ipperwash and the murder of Dudley George by the Ontario Provincial Police.

3   Relyea (2009) argues that, similar to Canada, when ATI was introduced in the United States there were few government agencies that supported it. The Canadian provinces beat the federal government to the punch with regard to access law (see Rowat 1982, 177). Nova Scotia became the first jurisdiction in the British Commonwealth to establish a public right of access when in 1977 it passed a *Freedom of Information Act*. New Brunswick followed in 1978.

4   One of us filed a request with the RCMP for "documents and records" related to information-sharing arrangements between partners of the Integrated Security Unit in charge of the 2010 G20 Summit. The analyst in charge noted that the request was broad in scope and, for the sake of avoiding delays, recommended that its wording be amended to seek memoranda and letters of understanding only. This proposal sounded expedient, and was accepted. The RCMP responded by noting that no such MOUs or formal letters existed, closing the file.

REFERENCES

Abrams, P. 1988. "Notes on the Difficulty of Studying the State." *Journal of Historical Sociology* 1 (1): 58-89.

Arko-Cobbah, A. 2008. "The Right of Access to Information: Opportunities and Challenges for Civil Society and Good Governance in South Africa." *IFLA Journal* 34 (2): 180-91.

Bazillion, R. 1980. "Access to Departmental Records, Cabinet Documents and Ministerial Papers in Canada." *American Archivist* 43 (2): 151-60.

–. 1983. "Freedom of Information: A Canadian Dilemma." *Round Table* 288: 382-94.

Beeby, D. 2011. "Canada Ranks Last in Freedom of Information: Study." *Globe and Mail*, 9 January. http://www.theglobeandmail.com/.

Bell, D. 1974. *The Coming of Post-Industrial Society: A Venture in Social Forecasting*. London: Heinemann.

Birkinshaw, P. 1999. "Proposals for Freedom of Information in the United Kingdom." *Government Information Quarterly* 16 (2): 93-109.

Bok, S. 1989. *Secrets: On the Ethics of Concealment and Revelation*. Toronto: Vintage Books.

Burton, F., and P. Carlen. 1979. *Official Discourse: On Discourse Analysis, Government Publications, Ideology and the State*. London: Routledge and Kegan Paul.

Byrne, M. 2003. "Freedom of Information in the Post-Communist World." *Problems of Post-Communism* 50 (2): 56.

Castells, M. 1996. *The Rise of the Network Society*. Oxford: Blackwell.

Chase, S. 2011. "Can Access to Information Be Fixed?" *Globe and Mail*, 15 January, A4.

Curtis, B. 1995. "Taking the State Back Out: Rose and Miller on Political Power." *British Journal of Sociology* 46 (4): 575-89.

Dandeker, C. 1990. *Surveillance, Power, and Modernity: Bureaucracy and Discipline from 1700 to the Present Day.* New York: St. Martin's Press.

De Lint, Willem. 2003. "Keeping Open Windows: Police as Access Brokers." *British Journal of Criminology* 43 (2): 379-97.

Demac, D. 1984. *Keeping America Uninformed: Government Secrecy in the 1980s.* New York: Pilgrim Press.

Democracy Now! 2011. "Watch: Full Video of WikiLeaks' Julian Assange and Philosopher Slavoj Žižek With Amy Goodman," *Democracy Now!* 5 July. http://www.democracynow.org/blog/.

Drapeau, M. 2009. "A Commentary from Canada: Canada's Access to Information." *Open Government: A Journal of Freedom of Information* 5 (1). http://www.opengovjournal.org/.

Elias, N. 1987. "The Retreat of Sociologists into the Present." *Theory, Culture and Society* 4 (2): 223-47.

Ericson, R. 2007. *Crime in an Insecure World.* Cambridge: Polity.

Foucault, M. 1980. "The Politics of Health in the Eighteenth Century." In *Power/Knowledge: Selected Interviews and Other Writings, 1972-1977,* ed. by C. Gordon, 166-82. New York: Pantheon.

Gentile, P. 2009. "Resisted Access? National Security, the *Access to Information Act,* and Queer(ing) Archives." *Archivaria* 68: 141-58.

Giddens, A. 1985. *The Nation-State and Violence: Volume Two of a Contemporary Critique of Historical Materialism.* Cambridge: Polity Press.

Gil-Garcia, J., S. Chun, and M. Janssen. 2009. "Government Information Sharing and Integration: Combining the Social and the Technical." *Information Polity: The International Journal of Government and Democracy in the Information Age* 14 (1/2): 1-10.

Haggerty, Kevin. 2004. "Ethics Creep: Governing Social Science Research in the Name of Ethics." *Qualitative Sociology* 27 (4): 391-414.

Hazel, R., and B. Worthy. 2010. "Assessing the Performance of Freedom of Information." *Government Information Quarterly* 27: 352-59.

Helms, H. 2003. *Inside the Shadow Government: National Emergencies and the Cult of Secrecy.* Los Angeles: Feral House.

Higgs, E. 2001. "The Rise of the Information State: The Development of Central State Surveillance of the Citizen in England, 1500-2000." *Journal of Historical Sociology* 14 (2): 175-97.

Hinson, Christopher L. 2010. "Negative Information Action: Danger for Democracy." *American Behavioral Scientist* 53 (6): 826-47.

Keller, Bill. 2011. "The Boy Who Kicked the Hornet's Nest." In *Open Secrets: WikiLeaks, War, and American Diplomacy,* ed. by Alexander Star, 3-24. Toronto: HarperCollins.

Kelly, Paul. 2006. "Information Is Power." *Open Government: A Journal of Freedom of Information* 2 (1). http://www.opengovjournal.org/.

Kinsman, G., and P. Gentile. 2010. *The Canadian War on Queers: National Security as Sexual Regulation.* Vancouver: UBC Press.

Kirtley, J. 2006. "Transparency and Accountability in a Time of Terror: The Bush Administration's Assault on Freedom of Information." *Communication Law and Policy* 11 (4): 479-509.

Knight, K. 1966. "Administrative Secrecy and Ministerial Responsibility." *Canadian Journal of Economics and Political Science* 32 (February): 77-84.

Larsen, M., and J. Piché. 2009. "Exceptional State, Pragmatic Bureaucracy, and Indefinite Detention: The Case of the Kingston Immigration Holding Centre." *Canadian Journal of Law and Society* 24 (2): 203-29.

Loader, I., and N. Walker. 2007. *Civilizing Security.* New York: Cambridge University Press.

Mann, B. 1986. "The Federal Information Coordinator as Meat in the Sandwich." *Canadian Public Administration* 29 (4): 579-82.

Marx, Gary. 1984. "Notes on the Discovery, Collection, and Assessment of Hidden and Dirty Data." In *Studies in the Sociology of Social Problems,* ed. by J. Schneider and J. Kitsuse, 78-113. Norwood, NJ: Ablex.

Maynard, S. 2009. "Police/Archives." *Archivaria* 68: 159-82.

Miliband, R. 1973. "Poulantzas and the Capitalist State." *New Left Review* 82: 83-92.

Piché, Justin, and Kevin Walby. 2010. "Problematizing Carceral Tours." *British Journal of Criminology* 50 (3): 570-81.

Poster, M. 1990. *The Mode of Information: Poststructuralism and Social Context.* Cambridge: Polity Press.

Poulantzas, N. 1972. "The Problem of the Capitalist State." In *Ideology in Social Science,* ed. by R. Blackburn. Glasgow: Fontana Collins.

Pozen, David E. 2010. "Deep Secrecy." *Stanford Law Review* 62 (2): 257-339.

Rankin, M. 1977. *Freedom of Information in Canada: Will the Doors Stay Shut?* A research study prepared for the Canadian Bar Association.

Relyea, H. 2009. "Federal Freedom of Information Policy: Highlights of Recent Developments." *Government Information Quarterly* 26 (4): 314-20.

Roberts, A. 1999. "Retrenchment and Freedom of Information: Recent Experience under Federal, Ontario, and British Columbia Law." *Canadian Public Administration* 42 (4): 422-51.

–. 2002a. "Is There a Double Standard on Access to Information?" *Policy Options* (May-June): 49-55.

–. 2002b. "Administrative Discretion and the *Access to Information Act*: An 'Internal Law' on Open Government?" *Canadian Public Administration* 45 (2): 175-94.

–. 2004. "Treatment of Sensitive Requests under British Columbia's Freedom of Information Law." *Freedom of Information Review* 10 (9): 2-4.

–. 2005. "Spin Control and Freedom of Information: Lessons for the United Kingdom from Canada." *Public Administration* 83 (1): 1-23.

Roberts, Alasdair. 2006. *Blacked Out: Government Secrecy in the Information Age.* Cambridge: Cambridge University Press.

Rose, N., and P. Miller. 1992. "Political Power beyond the State: Problematics of Government." *British Journal of Sociology* 43 (2): 173-205.

Rosner, C. 2008. *Behind the Headlines: A History of Investigative Journalism in Canada.* Oxford: Oxford University Press.

Rowat, D. 1965. "How Much Administrative Secrecy?" *Canadian Journal of Economics and Political Science* 31 (November): 479-98.

–. 1982. "The Right of Public Access to Official Documents." In *The Administrative State in Canada,* ed. by O. Divivedi, 151-76. Toronto: University of Toronto Press.

Roy, J. 2005. "Security, Sovereignty and Continental Interoperability: Canada's Elusive Balance." *Social Science Computer Review* 23 (4): 463-79.

Savoie, D. 2003. *Breaking the Bargain: Public Servants, Ministers, and Parliament.* Toronto: University of Toronto Press.

Shapiro, S., and R. Steinzor. 2006. "The People's Agent: Executive Branch Secrecy and Accountability in an Age of Terrorism." *Law and Contemporary Problems* 66: 98-129.

Smith, D. 1999. *Writing the Social: Critique, Theory and Investigations.* Toronto: University of Toronto Press.

Theoharis, A. 1998. *A Culture of Secrecy: The Government versus the People's Right to Know.* Lawrence: University Press of Kansas.

Thomas, P. 1973. "The Issue of Administrative Secrecy in Canada." In *Bureaucracy in Canadian Government,* ed. by W. Kernaghan, 160-64. Toronto: Methuen.

–. 2010a. *Advancing Access to Information Principles through Performance Management Mechanisms: The Case of Canada.* World Bank Institute Governance Working Paper Series. Washington, DC: International Bank for Reconstruction and Development.

–. 2010b. "Who Is Getting the Message? Communications at the Centre of Government." In *Public Policy Issues and the Oliphant Commission: Independent Research Studies,* ed. by C. Forcese, 77-136. Ottawa: Minister of Public Works and Government Services Canada.

Tromp, S. 2008. "Fallen Behind: Canada's *Access to Information Act* in the World Context." http://www3.telus.net/index100/report.

Walby, K. 2009. "'He Asked Me if I Was Looking for Fags ... ': Ottawa's National Capital Commission Conservation Officers and the Policing of Public Park Sex." *Surveillance and Society* 6 (4): 367-79.

Walby, K., and M. Larsen. 2012. "Access to Information and Freedom of Information Requests; Neglected Means of Data Production in the Social Sciences." *Qualitative Inquiry* 18 (1): 31-42.

–. 2011. "Getting at the Live Archive: On Access to Information Research in Canada." *Canadian Journal of Law and Society* 26 (3): 623-34.

Walby, K., and J. Monaghan. 2010. "Policing Proliferation: On the Militarization of Police and Atomic Energy Canada Limited's Nuclear Response Forces." *Canadian Journal of Criminology and Criminal Justice* 52 (2): 117-45.

–. 2011. "Private Eyes and Public Order: Policing and Surveillance in the Suppression of Animal Rights Activists in Canada." *Social Movement Studies* 10 (1): 21-37.

Webster, F. 1995. *Theories of the Information Society.* New York: Routledge.
Whitaker, R., and S. Farson. 2009. "Accountability in and for National Security." *IRPP Choices* 15 (9): 2-51.

LEGISLATION CITED

Access to Information Act, R.S.C. 1985, c. A-1.
Critical Infrastructure Information Act, 6 U.S.C. (2002).
Federal Accountability Act, S.C. 2006, c. 9.
Federal Advisory Committee Act, 5 U.S.C., Appendix 2 (1972).
Freedom of Information and Protection of Privacy Act, 1993, c. 5, s. 1.
Homeland Security Act, Pub. L. 107-296, 116 Stat. 745 (2002).
Official Secrets Act, R.S.C. 1970, c. O-3.
Promotion of Access to Information Act No. 2 of 2000 (South Africa).

PART 1

ACCESS TO INFORMATION, PAST AND PRESENT

Sustaining Secrecy
Executive Branch Resistance to Access to Information in Canada

ANN REES

American duties on the export of British Columbia's giant cedar and Douglas-fir trees might seem like an unlikely topic for national headlines. In the summer of 2006, however, the softwood lumber dispute, as it came to be known, was big news. It was a David-and-Goliath story, with the big American lumber industry using its political muscle to have the Bush administration impose duties that would drive up the price of cheaper Canadian lumber, critically wounding the crucial lumber industry in British Columbia and Québec in the process. The story also had a political dimension. The stakes for Canada's lumber industry were so high that the recently elected Conservatives convinced the former Liberal minister responsible for softwood negotiations to change parties, join the Conservatives, and continue his work. It was the kind of story that not only drew the attention of the daily media but also raised behind-the-scenes questions for more indepth analysis of how the Conservatives would operate under pressure. The way to get to that story was through the *Access to Information Act (ATIA)*, the disclosure law that allows individuals to request government records that would otherwise remain secret.

Among the many access to information (ATI) requests filed that summer for inside information on the Conservative handling of the softwood lumber dispute was my request to the Privy Council Office (PCO), which is the administrative arm of the Prime Minister's Office (PMO). The request was received by the PCO on 17 July 2006 (A-2006-00073/RS). I had filed it to the

PCO rather than the PMO because the executive branch of government in Canada is exempt from disclosure law. It operates in complete secrecy. The PCO is as close as anyone using ATI can get to opening the door on PMO policies and decisions. As a PhD student in Communication, my interest was in political communication practices in the PMO. Its staff of around one hundred people consists entirely of partisan political appointees, most of whom are strategic political communication specialists. The high-profile, high-stakes softwood lumber dispute appeared to provide an opportunity to examine the influence of PMO partisan communication practices on public policy, albeit at a distance through the PCO. My request was simple: "I am seeking copies of all PMO/PCO Communication records concerning the softwood lumber agreement." The records were requested from the time the Conservatives won office on 20 January 2006 until the request was received on 17 July. It would take forty-four months for my request to be completed, and then only partially. Records were finally mailed to me on 22 March 2010, just under four years after I filed my request.

The story about softwood lumber had long grown cold and was no longer news, but the records were still of interest. The length of the delay suggested that political interference in ATI was as alive in the Conservative PMO as it had been under the previous Liberal governments (Rees 2003). A follow-up request for a log of activities on the file, known as the *ATIPFlow* log, would confirm suspicions. The *ATIPFlow* log received in June 2010 (ATI request PCO A-2010-00020/PF) showed clear evidence of inappropriate political interference in the ATI process by the PMO. The final step before mailing the records to me was to transmit them to William Stairs, then Senior Advisor to the Prime Minister. Stairs and other political staff have no legit-imate role to play in the processing and handling of the ATI requests. Yet my file was delayed in his office for a week, from 9 March until 16 March 2010, before it was returned for release by the ATI official handling the file in the PCO. It was a clear case of political interference.

The *ATIPFlow* log of the activities over the forty-four months also showed that the political interference was ongoing, beginning on the day the request was received. The log shows that it was immediately flagged as a "Red File," a code word used to alert strategic political communications staff in govern-ment that an ATI request may be of interest to them and should be mon-itored throughout the processing of the requested records (Rees 2003). The request was subsequently bounced back and forth between ATI officials, whose job it is to handle ATI requests in accordance with the law, and PMO communication staff, whose interest in the file is political.

The requested records were reaching final approval stage when on 9 April 2009 the file was reassigned to a different ATI officer in the PCO, according to the log. Within days, the new ATI officer arbitrarily rewrote the wording of the request and narrowed the scope of records requested. There was no consultation and no permission obtained to rewrite the request. Now instead of requesting "all PMO/PCO Communication records" as I had intended, the request targeted only "records involving the exchange of communications on softwood lumber policy between policy makers and political communications officials." That change led to the removal of 438 pages from the file – reducing the number of records slated for release from 654 pages to 126 pages. The radically reduced package was processed by the ATI section but was not yet ready for release. First, it would have to meet the approval of the political staff in the PMO.

On 28 April 2009, the file was transmitted to top-ranking PMO political staffer Jenni Byrne, at the time a top strategic political communication advisor to Prime Minister Stephen Harper. Byrne wielded tremendous power and influence as the director of PMO Issues Management, the group trusted to monitor and manage political risk issues for the Conservative government. As further evidence of her political pedigree and loyalty, in February 2011 she was appointed to run the next federal election campaign for the Conservative Party (Taber 2011). Nobody in government was a more partisan actor than Byrne. And it was her job to review my request before it could be released. According to the log, the file was "due" on 4 May 2009 but was actually "completed" by the high-ranking political PMO staffer on 3 June.

Byrne wasn't the only member of the PMO political staff to be involved in reviews of the long-overdue request. A copy of the "Red File" category request was transmitted on 9 March 2010 to William Stairs, who at the time was Senior Advisor to the Prime Minister and had also recently replaced Byrne as Director of Issues Management, which is the most powerful and influential partisan political communications unit in government. Stairs "completed" his review of the file on 16 March 2010, according to the *ATIPFlow* log, which also shows that the revised and substantially reduced package of documents was finally released and sent to me on 22 March 2010.

There is no question that the political interference caused delays on the softwood request. The extent of the delays and other negative impacts on the request that resulted from the political interference will be up to Information Commissioner Suzanne Legault to determine. She is investigating the file following my complaint to her office in April 2010. Whatever the determination on this file, it is not an isolated case.

Political interference in the ATI process started as soon as the *Access to Information Act* was introduced in Parliament in 1982. The executive branches of every government since its passage into law have continued to resist the transparency and public accountability of government intended by the disclosure law. It is not enough that the executive branch operates in secret and outside of the *ATIA*. What governing parties refuse to accept are the limits ATI places on control of information by the executive branch of government. Governments resist ATI because by increasing government transparency and limiting secrecy, it effectively limits the ability of executive branches to strategically control political communication between government and the people.

The *ATIA* is the breach in the secrecy wall that for more than a century has not only protected legitimate state secrets but also served to protect the political interests of government in managing the flow of information between government and citizens. ATI poses a risk to the political interests of the party in power, first by limiting its control over information about governance, and second because requesters – particularly media and members of opposition parties – often use ATI to target contentious records that are intended to hold government accountable and potentially cause political damage. It is a political risk that successive governments have proven unwilling to accept. The *ATIA* challenges the normative Canadian governance paradigms of secrecy and information control, a limit on the powers of office that the executive branch continues to resist.

Canada was just the eighth country in the world to guarantee citizens the right to request secret government records in accordance with disclosure law when it passed the *ATIA* on Canada Day, 1983. The *ATIA* was an important but limited victory for transparency and open government, with the executive branch ensuring that it would be largely exempt from the law's jurisdiction and scope. The *ATIA* was first introduced in Parliament in 1982, the same year that Canada implemented the *Canadian Charter of Rights and Freedoms*. ATI was not enshrined as a Charter right of citizens that would be forever guaranteed, however. Instead, and perhaps as a result, the law has been resisted and undermined by successive governments since it was introduced.

Passage of the *ATIA* into law was delayed for a year until the governing Liberal Party of Pierre Elliott Trudeau secured the exclusion of cabinet from *ATIA* jurisdiction (section 69). Even this watered-down version of the law would prove a greater challenge to the powers of public office than successive executive branches of government were prepared to accept. Resistance to the *ATIA* has taken a number of forms: successful court challenges of ATI jurisdiction over records in the offices of the prime minister and cabinet ministers, and the introduction of supposedly temporary anti-terrorism amendments that eight years later still provide ministers with the right to veto the release of records that otherwise qualify to be made public. In addition to limiting the scope of the law, the federal government has also succeeded in limiting access rights through political interference in the processing of ATI requests. The ongoing campaign to restore executive branch powers of secrecy by attacking ATI has succeeded in weakening the law, and has left Canadians with fewer access to information rights today than on that promising Canada Day almost three decades ago.

The key question concerning the status of federal access to information rights in Canada is not whether the law has been weakened by the executive branch. That is a matter of public record. Every government since 1982 has resisted the *ATIA*. The question that is the focus of this chapter is why successive governments in Canada have worked to restrict the public's right of access to government information under the *ATIA*. The answer lies in the threat that ATI poses to the once-unchallenged right of the executive branch to control the dissemination of information, and thereby to control what the public is allowed to know about how the powers of public office are exercised. The *ATIA* challenges executive branch information control by allowing citizens to legally request otherwise secret government records that may result in public scrutiny and accountability, regardless of the political damage that might ensue. The only legal requirement for release of information is that the records requested be qualified to be made public under the *ATIA*. This does not mean that every secret record can be obtained under ATI. Far from it. Records related to national security or other public interests will be denied, and will remain secret. Qualified records, however, must be released upon request in accordance with the law, rather than in accordance with the wishes of the executive branch. This puts the *ATIA* in direct conflict with the historical right of Canada's executive branch to control government information.

Resisting Access to Information Rights

Canada's *ATIA* is intended to serve as a counterbalance to secrecy laws such as the Canadian *Official Secrets Act* of 1939, which had replaced previous *Official Secrets Acts* adopted in whole from Britain. The *ATIA* did not end secrecy laws, and in fact protected the core principles of existing secrecy laws. As a result, issues of national security and international affairs are among the many areas that remain secret and are exempt from the *ATIA*. The law did, however, make one profound difference to the powers of the executive branch by limiting its ability to apply secrecy provisions without challenge. Prior to the *ATIA*, the executive branch had an absolute right of government information control. This meant that in addition to using secrecy provisions to protect the public's interest in issues such as national security, the executive branch could also use secrecy to censor and suppress any government information that might not serve its own political interests. The *ATIA* set legal limits on secrecy – too many limits in terms of making the executive branch exempt – but at least secrecy was determined by the law.

According to Donald Rowat, the federal disclosure law was also intended to address growing calls from academics and members of the public for more "participatory democracy [which] ... implies a better-informed public with greater access to information" (cited in Roberts 2006b, 282). Trudeau told Parliament that the law would result in "effective participation of citizens and organizations in the taking of public decisions" (cited in Roberts 2006b, 87). The Liberals, however, insisted on adding extensive secrecy protections for the executive branch prior to passing the law. In his review of the legislation twenty years later, Information Commissioner John Reid, who was a cabinet minister in the Liberal government at the time the *ATIA* was passed by Parliament, complained that the changes made by the Trudeau government had in effect allowed the executive branch to continue to work in secret. The law does not apply to cabinet confidences, nor would the Information Commissioner have the right to intercede if cabinet records were denied. Section 69 of the *ATIA* also excludes memos that "present proposals or recommendations ... discussion papers the purpose of which is to present background explanations, analysis of problems or policy options ... agenda or records recording deliberations" as well as briefings for ministers or records of "communications or discussions between ministers." The only exception to this exclusion concerns decisions of cabinet made in public, or decisions where at least four years have passed (Reid 2003).

From the outset, Canada's disclosure law was flawed by excessive secrecy protections for the executive branch. K.G. Robertson (1999, 130) describes the ATIA as a light and less effective version of the American *Freedom of Information Act (FOIA)*, introduced in 1966:

> The Canadian elite did not have a uniform attitude to the introduction of
> FOI [freedom of information] and demanded a degree of "protection," for

the process of government, hence the exclusion of consultative and cabinet papers, for the core political process. We can see that Canada has implemented a version of "freedom of information" but by no means the full, radical vision, contained in ideals such as open government ... the way in which Canada implemented the ideal is very much conditioned by its history and circumstances.

Although the government could not turn back the tide of public opinion in favour of greater transparency in government, the executive branches – in particular the PMO – of every government since 1983 has worked to strengthen the executive branch "immunity" (McCamus as cited in Robertson 1999, 130) from ATI. This effectively prevents public scrutiny of those who occupy Canada's highest elected offices. The result has been described by John McCamus as "the most secretive executive privilege rules to be found in the western world" (Robertson 1999, 130).

Despite its serious limitations, ATI represented a radical departure from Canada's history of official secrecy laws that had previously provided the executive branch with absolute control over what information would be made public and what information would remain secret. The *ATIA* offered the only challenge other than the courts to the otherwise absolute powers of the executive branch to determine which records remain confidential. It did so by forcing the release of requested information based on the law, rather than depending on the goodwill or political agenda of government officials. In practice, however, the law does little to break the right of executive branches to act, through secrecy laws, as the sole arbiter in government of what information can be made public.

This is all the more the case following the 13 May 2011 Supreme Court of Canada decision in *Canada (Information Commissioner) v. Canada (Minister of National Defence)*, which finally declared the executive branch – PMO and ministers' offices – excluded from the ATIA. The ruling was ten years in the making and stemmed from an opposition party researcher's request under ATI to examine the daily agendas of then Liberal Prime Minister Jean Chrétien. Rather than turn over the agendas, which would have shown who met with the prime minister on a daily basis, Chrétien turned to the courts. The court battle would move through five levels of courts, including the Federal Court and the Federal Court of Appeal, before finally being heard by the Supreme Court of Canada. Each level of appeal was supported by the prime minister of the day. Following Chrétien, who led the fight to have the executive branch exempted from the law, the court appeal was carried on by his successor, Liberal Prime Minister Paul Martin. Following his election in 2006, Conservative Prime Minister Stephen Harper also chose to continue the appeal. The decision was all the more cynical given that it was a researcher for Harper's then Reform Party who had filed the original ATI request for the agendas when the party was in opposition. Protecting the executive branch from public scrutiny under ATI clearly becomes a priority once any party is in power.

In what may well be one of its most puzzling rulings, the Supreme Court agreed with lower court rulings that under the language of the *ATIA*, "the PMO and the relevant ministerial offices are not part of the 'government institution' for which they are responsible" and were therefore excluded from the act. The law requires that records be in the possession of a government agency in order to be covered by the disclosure law. If the PMO and minister's office are not government institutions, then records from those offices are not covered and are therefore not accessible through ATI. When I interviewed him in Ottawa on 1 June 2011, former Information Commissioner John Reid, who initiated the court case when the request for the agendas was denied, said that the decision seriously weakened and undermined Canada's federal disclosure law by creating a "black hole" for government information by denying access to any records held in a minister's office or in the PMO:

> This is a rollback. And it is a rollback that is serious because what it does by taking the head of an institution out of the loop and making it all but impossible to get into that office; it means that the head of the institution is separated from the body. It means that the Act only now applies to the deputy minister down. So once you take the head out of the equation and you give the head immunity, in effect, you have created an enormous black hole.

Mr. Reid said that excluding the executive branch from ATI meant that Canada had the dubious distinction of standing alone among nations that had passed disclosure laws: "We are now on our own. I think of all the regimes that exist, we are the only one that excludes the cabinet or senior officials." As a cabinet minister in the Trudeau government who helped draft the legislation while serving as a Liberal Member of Parliament, Reid fully understood the implications of exempting the executive branch from transparency through ATI: it would allow the government to control the flow of information out of the executive branch. Controlling the information agenda was the prerogative of the executive branch prior to the *ATIA*, and with the help of the Supreme Court of Canada the executive branch is once again in control of what it will allow the public to know about government, in particular the PMO and ministers' offices, and how it governs. The old order of secrecy has been restored.

The Old Order: A Legacy of Secrecy

Secrecy is an old and welcome friend of the executive branches of government in Britain and in Canada, which simply adopted and replicated British secrecy laws during the late nineteenth century and through most of the twentieth century. The laws strengthened executive branch authority and control over what information would be secret. This privilege has long served as a key mechanism for the centralization of power under the control of the prime minister and cabinet (Robertson 1982, 51-52). The *Official Secrets Acts* in Canada and Britain were amended and strengthened by Britain several times between 1889 and 1920, further consolidating political control of government information and expertise by making the civil service answerable only to the minister, thus helping to establish the principle of ministerial responsibility. Canada followed Britain's example in requiring all public servants to swear an oath of secrecy as a condition of employment, requiring that they keep confidential all knowledge of government gained through their employment.

Robertson (1982, 54) argues that the secrecy policies were a deliberate political strategy on the part of the executive branch to limit the power of high-profile bureaucrats who had begun to challenge government authority in the press. Once bureaucrats had been rendered silent through secrecy laws and confidentiality oaths, they could no longer embarrass the government by speaking out about policies and practices with which they disagreed. They were therefore no longer a political threat and instead were limited to providing expertise and advice internally. With the advent of official secrecy laws, the party in power had sole authority over government information, and could withhold damaging information to prevent opposition and dissent. It could also release information that it believed would shed a positive light on government and encourage positive public opinion. Robertson (1982, 51-52) argues that secrecy allowed the party in power to use government information as a means of maintaining political power: "The consequence of this is that information is not simply a neutral commodity linked to rational decision-making, but a part of the political process, an element of victory and defeat. One would therefore expect that the greater the element of party government, the more secrecy one would find. The Official Secrets Act starts when party politics becomes finally dominant."

Similarly, British historian Ann Rogers (1997) links secrecy and executive branch power in the British government. Revisions to the *Official Secrets Act* in 1911 – adopted in whole by the Canadian Parliament – were aimed as much at ending government leaks to the press as at preventing espionage. A key provision was to extend the leaks section to cover "recipients as well as disclosers of information, a provision that would directly affect the press. In a wide departure from normal legal practice, the burden of proof was thrown upon the individual ... and the power of search was introduced" (23). The implications of this section continue to challenge freedom of the press in Canada today.

The consequences for Canadian journalists were evident on 11 January 2004 when the RCMP raided the home and office of *Ottawa Citizen* reporter Juliet O'Neill seeking leaked information they believed she had obtained concerning the deportation to Syria and subsequent torture of Canadian citizen Maher Arar. Sections of the *Security of Information Act* that sanctioned such raids were struck down by the Superior Court of Justice of Ontario in October 2006. In her ruling, Justice Lynn Ratushny found that the sections infringed O'Neill's *Charter* rights of "freedom of expression" and "freedom of the press," according to a press release issued by the Canadian Journalists for Free Expression on 19 October 2006.

Rogers argues that the 1911 revisions were intended to legalize the secrecy regime that had always existed on a more informal cultural basis within the British government – in effect, to bolster the elites who held power and ensure that their hold on power would not be threatened by a dissenting press and public. Previously, a gentleman's agreement between the upperclass males who held public office was understood to imply that matters of governance would stay between those who governed and were not for public consumption. But broadening enfranchisement from those considered to belong to lesser classes, increasing partisanship, and a growing and powerful professional bureaucracy threatened the self-imposed code of silence. The risk of public exposure for misconduct and incompetence in office grew real as opposing parties and ambitious bureaucrats increasingly leaked damaging information to the thriving press as a means of making the case against government with the public. Near the end of the nineteenth century, a new secrecy law would make this practice a crime.

With these new policies in place, the transition from an economy of secrecy based upon a shared culture and values to one of formal legal-rational control had begun. The British Citizen now lived in a state where disclosure of any official information without express authorization was an offence; where the accused was guilty until proven innocent; where the "right to know" resided only at the centre of the state; and where decisions about loyalty and threat could be taken by the elites – this at a time when alternative political discourses were emerging that had as their objective empowerment of the demos ... The effect was to maintain strict control of official information, to prevent its falling into hostile hands – hands that could belong to its own electorate as easily as a foreign power. (Rogers 1997, 23-24)

While bureaucrats created, managed, and distributed information within government, they did not decide what information to make public. That task was entirely the prerogative of the prime minister and members of cabinet, who often turned to the advice offered by the partisan political staff they appointed as their team of advisors in the executive branch.

Official secrecy laws in effect rendered the non-political public service silent outside of government, deliberately leaving political communication between government and its public to the often-partisan decisions of the executive branch (Robertson 1982, 1999; Rogers 1997). The effect of official secrecy and subsequent secrecy laws in Canada from 1890 until the implementation of the *ATIA* in 1983 was to allow the executive branch of the federal government to hold the exclusive and absolute authority (Martin 2003) to determine what information would remain secret (Roberts 2006b, 65).

In his study "Cabinet Secrecy," Nicholas d'Ombrain (2004) argues that, if anything, the introduction of the *ATIA* tightened secrecy, particularly as it applied to what were referred to in section 69(1) of the act as "Confidences of the Queen's Privy Council for Canada." As a result, the documents excluded from ATI included "Cabinet agendas, memoranda, minutes and decisions" (343). The same exclusions were also added to the *Canada Evidence Act*, and in combination with the identically worded section of the *ATIA* served to provide "absolute immunity for claims of cabinet secrecy made by a minister" (344). A "confidence" was "declared ... to be anything that resided in particular classes of papers used by the cabinet in the transactions of its business – agendas, memoranda and so on." The codification of specific classes of excluded information prompted routine claims of "privilege (now restyled by the courts as 'public interest immunity') for any paper that fell into one of these classes, regardless of content" (344). The de facto result was blanket secrecy for this class of documents:

> There has been no exercise of discretion: all records covered by the acts are routinely withheld. This does not mean that the privilege is being claimed inappropriately, still less carelessly or mendaciously. It means simply that the law is being applied as Parliament prescribed. In effect, the old order of governing under a regime of secrecy was restored. (d'Ombrain 2004, 344)

A New Order: Transparency as a Democratic Right

Sweden passed the first freedom of information law, called the *Freedom of the Press Act,* in 1766. It introduced the principle of open government, or "offentlighetsgrundsatsen" (Banisar 2006, 141-43). The law, however, applied only to public sector records and not to the political records of government. One important principle was that all records that are secret must be specified as such by law. This approach means that secrecy becomes the exception, that it must be justified, and that the records that are secret are identified as such. Harvard political philosopher Dennis Thompson (2002, 185) argues that while secrecy is in some circumstances necessary, the process of determining secrecy must be open: "Secrecy is justifiable only if it is actually justified in a process that itself is not secret. First-order secrecy (in a process about a policy) requires second-order publicity (about the decision to make the process or policy secret)."

The American *Freedom of Information Act (FOIA)* is considered to be the first modern disclosure law because it covers all areas of government unless they are specifically excluded for reasons such as security. The American law was introduced in 1966 following years of pressure from journalists, primarily the Associated Press Managing Editors Association, which led to the establishment of a Congressional subcommittee on government secrecy and manipulation of government information for propaganda purposes (Foerstel 1999, 39). American journalists also protested obvious media manipulation techniques employed by the Kennedy administration in the early 1960s, prompting a prominent *New York Times* columnist to complain just weeks before President John F. Kennedy's assassination in 1963: "News management policy not only exists, but ... has been enforced more cynically and boldly than by any previous Administration" (Foerstel 1999, 39). *FOIA* was passed three years later. It provided a mechanism for accessing otherwise secret government information and, just as important, it established citizens' access to government information as a democratic right: "The Freedom of Information Act of 1966 established a right to information held by government agencies, articulated a presumption that government documents should be publicly accessible, and provided methods for compelling officials to comply with its requirements" (Roberts 2006a, 14).

FOIA was strengthened by several amendments during the 1970s in response to the loss of public trust over the unpopular war in Vietnam and President Richard Nixon's resignation over Watergate. The American disclosure law was "recognized globally as trailblazing legislation" (Roberts 2006b, 14) that for the first time gave citizens a measure of control over the release of government records, and in so doing set a standard of open and accountable government as a hallmark of modern democracy. Certainly, the enactment of *FOIA* put pressure on politicians in Ottawa to pass similar legislation, albeit reluctantly and almost two decades after the first American *FOIA*.

FOIA, which remains the most influential model for modern disclosure acts, is grounded in the Enlightenment and American Revolutionary ideals of John Locke, John Adams, and James Madison as they relate to the rights and duties of the individual as a citizen in a democratic society. Herbert Foerstel's history of the American FOI movement quotes an essay written in 1765 by Adams in which he describes the need for "a knowledgeable citizenry as the most effective opposition to British rule" (Foerstel 1999, 3). Adams's position is consistent with the Enlightenment belief in empowerment through knowledge, which remains a central premise in defending access to state information as an individual's right: "The people have a right, an indisputable, inalienable, indefeasible divine right to that most dreaded and envied kind of knowledge, I mean of the characters and conduct of their rulers. The preservation of the means of knowledge among the lowest ranks is more important than all the property of all the rich men in the country" (cited in Foerstel 1999, 3, from an unsigned essay written by John Adams and published in the *Boston Gazette*).

Of all the American influences in favour of public disclosure, Madison may be the most important and is certainly most often quoted. Although the right to know is not specified in the US Constitution, the principle of the public's right to know is implied by the First Amendment that Madison helped write: "A popular Government, without popular information or the means of acquiring it is but a Prologue to a Farce or a Tragedy; or, perhaps both. Knowledge will forever govern ignorance: And a people who mean to be their own Governors must arm themselves with the power that knowledge gives" (Foerstel 1999, 11).

John Dunn sees unwarranted secrecy in government, combined with the manipulation and censorship of information for political purposes, as a violation of the bargain of accountability between voters and those they elect to power as their representatives:

> Governmental seclusion is the most direct, and also the deepest subversion
> of the democratic claim, sometimes prudent, but never fully compatible
> with the literal meaning of the form of rule. The more governments control
> what their fellow citizens know, the less they can claim the authority of
> those citizens they rule. The more governments withhold information from
> their fellow citizens, the less accountable they are to those who give them
> their authority. Even to fit its own name, modern representative democracy
> would have to transform itself very radically in this respect. (Dunn 2005,
> 185-86)

An informed and empowered citizenry must sit at the core of a successful democracy. Transparency is justified in a democracy as a means for citizens to understand governance: first, in order to assert their right and duty to hold those who govern to account, and second, as a means of making government both answerable and responsive to citizens. Ann Florini (2007, 3) links transparency and democracy because "the essence of democracy is informed consent, which requires that information about governmental practices and polices be disclosed." Based on this core premise, Florini offers a broad "working definition" of transparency as "the degree to which information is available to outsiders that enables them to have informed voice in decisions and/or to assess the decisions made by insiders." The purpose of transparency in a democracy is therefore to enable "citizens to gather information on the policies and behavior of governments" in order that they may "hold decision makers accountable and have informed say in decisions" (5). By this definition, transparency implies a governmental responsibility to provide citizens with authentic information that is relevant to the decision-making process and that also informs citizens to such a degree that they have the ability to adequately judge the risks, benefits, and consequences involved. Only then do citizens have the ability to grant their informed consent.

The literature on disclosure rights in a democracy invariably and inextricably links transparency and accountability. Christopher Hood (2010,

989) defines transparency in relation to accountability as it applies to governance and citizenship. He first defines accountability, which "broadly denotes the duty of an individual or organisation to answer in some way about how they have conducted their affairs." He then defines transparency as "the conduct of business in a fashion that makes decisions, rules and other information visible from outside." Hood's definition of transparency is similar to Florini's. Both scholars also tie together the principle of transparency and the right to information that makes those who govern answerable to citizens. "Accountability in the sense of answerability necessarily implies the answerers sharing information with those to whom they are answerable" (Hood 2010, 991). Hood notes that there can be accountability "of a certain sort" inside government without public transparency, as is the case when civil servants answer to their deputy minister or to the minister responsible (991). There can, however, be no transparency as defined without accountability.

David Heald (2006, 25) defines transparency in a democracy as "when the 'ruled' can observe the conduct, behaviour, and/or 'results' of their 'rulers.'" Transparency by this definition is central to voters' ability to legitimate their representation in a democracy, by scrutinizing their rulers' actions and holding them to account. Since transparency is linked to accountability, there is a need for voters to have sufficient information about government to critique its performance. The volume of information produced by a government is in no way an indication of transparency; rather, the information must provide meaningful insight in order for authentic political transparency to exist. Against this backdrop, government transparency, to be at all meaningful, must take on a qualitative rather than quantitative dimension, and must be tied to the potential for accountability. From this perspective, disclosure law, which like Parliament facilitates the dissemination of dissenting information, serves as a mechanism for the legitimation of state power.

Hood characterizes the relationship between transparency and accountability as dependent on the attitudes of the government actors who risk being held to account by citizens through transparency. Depending on the actor or party perspective, the relationship between transparency and accountability ranges from compatible and inseparable to contentious and adversarial. Hood's colourful description has the relationship varying between "'Siamese twins,' not really distinguishable; as 'matching parts' that are separable but nevertheless complement one another smoothly to produce good governance; and as 'awkward couple,' involving elements that are potentially or actually in tension with one another" (2010, 989). The problem,

Hood explains, lies in the need for political parties to avoid being blamed by the public, and instead to present a positive image that will allow them to continue in power. The awkward-couple analogy best describes the relationship between transparency and accountability in the Canadian government experience.

Managing the Political Risks of Transparency: A Hierarchy of Information Access and Control

The executive branch, comprising the prime minister, cabinet, and the president of the Treasury Board of Canada Secretariat, is ultimately in control of information access and dissemination. The members of the executive branch rely on the advice of politically appointed staff, who act as their advisors. The partisan employees are known as "exempt staff" because they are not part of the public service and do not belong to the Public Service Alliance of Canada, which represents career bureaucrats. Their jobs depend on the government's tenure in office and their interests are therefore tied to the interests of the party in power, even if these are in conflict with the public's interest in being adequately and accurately informed. Both the professional mandate and personal interests of exempt staff lie in promoting the fortunes of the party to which they owe their personal security. Unlike career public servants, they are out of work when the government loses power. Despite their uncertain tenure, however, as political advisors and managers exempt staff are among the most powerful agents inside government. In many cases, they are assigned to monitor and direct the public service in order to ensure that the latter operates in sync with the political agendas of the executive branch. It is their job to promote and enforce the party line not only with the public but also with the supposedly politically neutral public service. Often they do so with little expertise in the area in which they are assigned to provide direction. In an article written for the Commission of Inquiry into the Sponsorship Program and Advertising Activities (the Gomery Commission) titled "The Prime Minister, Ministers and Their Exempt Staff," Liane Benoit (2006, 1.1) points to the unusual degree of power and influence granted to the politically appointed executive branch staff, including the right to direct ministers and interfere with the work of far more experienced bureaucrats:

> Though unelected, often uneducated in the theory and operation of the machinery of government and regularly devoid of professional qualifications

relevant to the ministries with which they are involved, these individuals, by virtue of their political relationship with the party in power and/or the minister they serve, are well placed to influence both the bounce and bobble of bureaucratic-political interface and the pace and progress of public policy in Canada.

The prime minister and cabinet ministers have open access to government information as needed in the performance of their duties – a privilege which is extended to political staff to varying degrees, and entirely at the discretion of the prime minister or the cabinet minister to whom they answer. It is clear that their high-level access to information, and influence in the control and public dissemination of information make the exempt staff, particularly in the PMO and ministers' offices, primary agents in any discussion about the public's right to know.

What they do with that information depends on both their mandate and their perspective on whether transparency and accountability are a matter of public interest or an issue to be managed in the best interests of the party they represent. In a 2007 article titled "What Happens when Transparency Meets Blame-Avoidance?" Hood argued that although transparency and accountability may be taken outside of government as a "normative doctrine for the conduct of governance," it is at odds with government praxis of "blame avoidance ... that is often said to underlie much of political and institutional behavior in practice" (192). In effect, politicians in particular seek to avoid negative accountability, and rather seek to build credibility with and gain support from voters by showcasing positive aspects of their decisions and policies. The result is a conflict of interests – the public's interest in transparency and accountability, and the political interest in avoiding blame through transparency and accountability. Blame avoidance, Hood argues, acts as "as driver of political and institutional behaviour" (193). He cites Roberts's studies of political interference in ATI in Canada as an example of how blame-avoidance strategies serve to limit transparency:

According to Alasdair Roberts (2006) ... government responses to freedom of information laws, typically involve more active and defensive central management of information than before, to lower political risks of blame ... the result is likely to be at least jeopardy and, in Roberts' argument, perversity. His central claim is that, while FOI measures are almost invariably introduced with the promise that they will produce a new culture of openness in executive government, the effect in practice tends to be the opposite, in the form of a climate of tighter central management of politically sensitive information.

In Canada, blame-avoidance strategies and information control are determined at the highest level of government: the Prime Minister's Office. With the exception of the Clerk of the Privy Council, the entire staff of the PMO are political appointees. Many of the appointees are strategic political communications experts, often referred to as spin doctors, whose mandate is to represent the interests of the governing party as a political entity that needs to be sustained in power. Little is known about the individuals hired to work in the PMO, in large part because the PMO does not fall under the *ATIA*. Nor are exempt staff required to meet the transparency guidelines of civil servants, whose resumes, job descriptions, and salaries are all a matter of public record. Occasionally members of the media provide insight into the world of the powerful political staff who surround the prime minister. In February 2011, when former Issues Management Director Byrne was promoted to head the Conservative national election campaign, *Globe and Mail* political columnist Jane Taber (2011) wrote a profile of the top political advisor:

> She is 34 years old. Described by colleagues as possessing a volcanic temper with a penchant for yelling at cabinet ministers, staffers and senior bureaucrats alike, Ms. Byrne is fiercely loyal to the Prime Minister, his decisions and the small "c" Conservative brand ... it was her stint at the PMO as director of issues management that cemented her reputation as tough but effective. The job involved daily damage control; she started at 6:30 a.m. with a conference call to ministerial staffers, gauging the issues, troubleshooting and helping to frame the government's response. "She turned issues management into a tiger operation," says a former colleague.

It is evident from her ability to gain promotion after "yelling at cabinet ministers" and bureaucrats that the political staff are powerful and highly partisan actors within the executive branch. Their influence on the political communication process cannot be overestimated. Power in a democracy depends entirely on achieving and maintaining public support, and information control is a primary mechanism for elected officials and political parties to contain dissent and promote public approval and support. In a democracy, all negative information about governance has at least the potential to pose a political risk and therefore damage the government's public image. On the government side, positive information about governance in the form of news releases and political ads are churned out for media and public consumption by the partisan public relations professionals on staff in the PMO and by those working for cabinet ministers. Their mandate is to show government in a positive light in order to win public favour and political support, not to provide the public with a balanced view of government. The manipulation of information for partisan purposes relies on the ability to control what the public knows about government.

The second tier inside government is the public service, which has access to government information as necessary in the performance of its work. Bureaucrats are prevented by secrecy laws and by oaths of confidentiality from making government information public, unless they are so directed by the executive branch or in accordance with ATI. The Clerk of the Privy Council Office (PCO) and the deputy ministers in each department are bureaucrats who serve as liaisons between the public service and the executive branch. While they are privy to all levels of information, they do not have the right to decide what information is made public. Nor do they speak for their departments in public. That is the responsibility of the minister or the prime minister.

Although elected to represent constituents, MPs have no special status in terms of access to information. While the governing party may choose to make certain privileged information available to its own backbench MPs, this is entirely at the discretion of the executive branch. Opposition party MPs have no more information access rights in Canada than any other citizen and must rely on ATI to obtain records that the government is holding in secret. Therefore, even in the open forum of Parliament, opposition parties are far less persuasive than the governing party because they lack access to information, including even basic background reports used in the decision-making process. Under Canada's Westminster model of government, opposition parties are denied access to expertise on issues that the public service provides exclusively to the governing party. The executive branch's exclusive right to policy advice is a direct consequence of confidentiality oaths and official secrets laws that prevent it from making public, even to opposition MPs, any information that has not been authorized for release by the executive branch.

Transparency of Governance as a Right
Fears about the politically damaging potential of ATI are not without

foundation. Disclosure laws are designed to question and challenge the political status quo by allowing citizens to scrutinize government and hold it to account. The democratic function of Canada's 1983 *Access to Information Act* was best defined by Supreme Court Justice Gérard La Forest in an often-quoted judgment in the 1997 *Dagg v. Canada (Minister of Finance)* decision: "The overarching purpose of access to information is to facilitate democracy. It does so in two related ways. It helps to ensure first, that citizens have the right to information required to participate meaningfully in the democratic process, and secondly, that politicians remain accountable to the citizenry."

La Forest's judgment was reinforced in 2006 by Justice John Gomery, who noted the importance of disclosure law in a democracy: "An appropriate access to information regime is a key part of the transparency that is an essential element of modern democracy" (Gomery 2006, 136). His final report on the Liberal government's Sponsorship Scandal, in which hundreds of millions of taxpayers' dollars went missing, centred on improving government accountability, which he defined as "the requirement to explain and accept responsibility for carrying out an assigned mandate in light of agreed upon expectation" (9). Gomery recommended that the *ATIA* be significantly strengthened as a means of achieving greater accountability of government. His recommendations, as with all previous recommendations to strengthen ATI, have been ignored. Meaningful transparency, it would seem, may not be in the political interest of governments. Transparency of government is very much in the public's interest, however, and is in fact a right in a democracy.

Despite government's resistance to transparency, the public's right to know how those they elect exercise power as their representatives is increasingly accepted as a fundamental right of citizenship in a democracy. The legal right to request and receive qualified government information is a manifestation of that right. Patrick Birkinshaw (2006a, 48) argues that legal public access to government records is a right that is fundamental to all other human rights, and should be enshrined along with other human rights. He cites the 1946 United Nations General Assembly resolution that states: "Freedom of Information is a fundamental human right and is the touchstone for all freedoms to which the United Nations is consecrated" (United Nations 1946). Birkinshaw points out that "in Britain [as in Canada, which wholly adopted the British secrecy laws] official secrecy was protected by draconian laws as a matter of culture." Canada evolved as a country in a governance "culture of secrecy" and citizen exclusion from government decision making, as opposed to the government openness and public accountability that is the purpose of transparency laws.

For Birkinshaw, accountability is dependent on transparency, which relies on the right of the public to obtain and discuss meaningful and uncontrolled government information. He lists the public-access arguments for open government (2006b, 183):

> Information is used in the public interest; ... information is a necessity for accountability – accountability is based upon reliable information; ... reliable information is a prerequisite to establish effectiveness and efficiency in government; ... information is a necessary right of citizenship; ... information is power and its exclusive possession especially so; secrecy is a cloak for arbitrariness, inefficiency, corruption and so on: FOI reciprocates the trust that people place in government.

Access laws assume citizens' participation in the democratic process of legitimation of government as a core principle. The public right to know as a political communication right of citizens is intended to shift the unequal balance of power between society and the state, to make the state more accountable to citizens for its actions and decisions.

Transparency versus Spin

The well-documented trend in advanced democracies is towards increased politicization of governance communications processes under partisan public relations marketing professionals who are appointed by, and work for, the executive branch. This is certainly the case in Canada, where political appointees dominate the PMO staff, primarily working as political advisors on various aspects of public communication and media relations. Political communication between the executive branch and the public is therefore increasingly partisan and strategic (Franklin 1994; Morgan 1986; Rose 2000; Scammell 1999). The intent of politically mediated communications is to win favourable public opinion in the public sphere through information selection, promotion, and control. The goal is distinctly not to induce transparency and accountability. This penchant for censorship and information control by executive branches of successive governing parties is enabled in Canada by the disproportionate strength of secrecy laws and by the corresponding weakness of the *Access to Information Act,* which has failed to shift the central secrecy paradigm of Canadian governance towards greater transparency and openness in government.

The *ATIA* has from the outset excluded the executive branch from public scrutiny, a reality that has only been strengthened through court challenges and amendments over the decades since it was introduced. The *ATIA* is as much about the codification of secrecy and executive branch control of government information as it is about granting the public, including parliamentarians, access to government records. In defining what the public may know, the *ATIA* also defines what the public may not know, with the scales heavily weighted in favour of the latter. Government propaganda and public relations campaigns do not meet the criterion for government transparency, namely, to meet the information needs of citizens engaged in legitimating governance through processes of deliberative democracy. "Under deliberative democracy, the essence of democratic legitimacy should be sought ... in the ability of all individuals subject to a collective decision to engage in authentic deliberation about that decision. These individuals should accept the decision only if it could be justified to them in convincing terms" (Dryzek 2000, v).

As important as the need for meaningful and accurate information is the need to recognize that the call for government transparency is never a demand for full disclosure of government information. There are limits on what can be made public, and these limits are clearly defined in disclosure laws. Although disclosure laws are intended to give citizens access to "uncontrolled information" about government (Roberts 2006a), records are excluded from release by law if release of the information would harm the public's interest, including personal privacy rights. For example, few would argue that it would serve the public's interest to release detailed floor plans for nuclear plants. Under disclosure laws, such information remains secret because secrecy in this case is in the public's interest. Every disclosure law contains extensive exemptions and exclusions that prevent the release of records that would harm such things as national security, public health and safety, and even the personal right to protection of privacy. That said, the underlying assumption of transparency and disclosure laws is that state secrecy, except when it is clearly in the public interest, is bad for democracy because it impedes accountability, and therefore impedes the ability of voters to legitimate their representation.

The public right of access is very much concerned with the role of citizenship in a democracy, particularly the role played by citizens in the self-regulation process of democracy. The debate therefore borrows from larger debates on democratic theory, communication and citizenship rights, and the role of information and the public sphere and deliberative dialogue in a democracy, and also the relationship of media to the state and to the public sphere. The concept of openness in government is central to the idea of access to meaningful information that allows citizens to scrutinize government and hold it to account.

Political Interference in Access to Information

Perhaps the most obvious and contentious example of executive branch information control in Canada is systematic political interference in the processing of ATI requests. Over ten years in office ending in 2003, the Liberal government of Jean Chrétien established a government-wide system of surveillance of so-called sensitive ATI requests that were monitored and reviewed by political communications staff reporting to the Prime Minister's Office. All requests from media, members of opposition parties, and other contentious requesters were flagged by strategic political communications advisors, using secret internal communications branch codes such "amber light" and "Red Files" (Rees 2003). Besides tracking and reviewing of the requests, the requested records were not released to the requester until copies had been sent to the government's spin doctors. The Privy Council Office and the Prime Minister's Office communication departments played a key role in overseeing the political surveillance process. All ministries and departments of government reported to executive branch communications when they received a contentious request (Rees 2003). The requests were logged and monitored by political appointees working in the strategic communications offices of the executive branch.

In 2003, Roberts was interviewed about the practice for a *Toronto Star* series on the *ATIA* (Rees 2003). He pointed out that singling out certain types of requesters such as journalists for different and delayed processing of requests was the equivalent of unequal treatment under the law. His own research showed that requests from journalists and other contentious requesters such as opposition MPs were subject to longer processing delays than other types of requests. "Everyone is entitled to equal protection and treatment under the law," he said when interviewed for the *Toronto Star* story. "There is no provision in the law that says that journalists and politicians get second-class treatment." In a 2005 article, Roberts warned that the "lessons from Canada are sobering." He pointed to damaging political interference in ATI by the executive branch through the amber light and Red Files monitoring systems:

The promise of increased openness has been undercut by the development of administrative routines designed to centralize control and minimize the disruptive potential of the FOI law. Special procedures for handling politically sensitive requests are commonplace in major departments. Information technology has been adapted to ensure that ministers and central agencies are informed about difficult requests within days of their arrival. Communications officers can be closely involved in the processing of these requests, developing "media lines" and other "communications products" to minimize the political fallout of disclosure. These practices are largely hidden from public view. Nevertheless, they play an important role in shaping the substance of the right to information.

Systematic political interference under the amber-light process was condemned as "wrong" in 2003 by Stephen Harper, who was then leader of the opposition Canadian Alliance party. When asked for comment on amber lighting, Harper, who is now the prime minister, said that such practices violated the spirit of the *ATIA* (Rees 2003): "My understanding, and the public's understanding, is that this is not how it is supposed to work ... This entire super-process ... blurs the line between the statutory public service functions of the civil service, and political reporting. That to me is really wrong in principle and there is no doubt that this is not in the spirit of the act."

As my softwood lumber request confirms, however, following his rise to power Prime Minister Harper has changed his view. In government, his party has implemented an even more comprehensive communication surveillance process for ATI requests, particularly for requests made to the Privy Council Office, which is the administrative arm of the Prime Minister's Office and is therefore targeted by requesters for information about the PMO. The practice of political interference in ATI requests appears to have become even more sweeping and made the process even more laborious than under the Liberals. For example, under the Liberals only politically sensitive requests for information were designated as Red Files for communications branch clearance. My recent research has confirmed that under the Conservatives, every ATI request received by the PCO is referred to the PMO for political oversight prior to release.

The change may have been a reaction to criticisms that the amber-light process singled out certain requesters, particularly the media and members of opposition parties, for different and therefore unequal treatment under the law. The result is hardly an improvement, however, as contentious requests are still submitted to the PMO/PCO for political communication reviews, and the dramatic increase in delays means that it may take years to receive information requested from the PCO.

Similar PCO delays are routine and are cited as a "Key Performance Related Challenge" in a report by former Information Commissioner Robert Marleau (2009) titled "A Dire Diagnosis for Access to Information in Canada." Although resistance to ATI is partisan and political, it is not a single-party issue. Every executive branch since the *ATIA* was passed has taken steps to limit its potential to negatively impact their tenure in office.

Information Commissioners: Transparency Watchdogs

> *A key fact of downgrading democracy campaigns has got to*
> *be cutting off access to information – so much so that you leave*
> *the Information Commissioner appalled, especially with*
> *stonewalling at the Privy Council Office.*
>
> – Globe and Mail *political columnist Lawrence*
> *Martin, 17 December 2009*

The most consistent and effective critics of the limits of the *ATIA* have been the Information Commissioners, who serve as ombudsmen for ATI and are required to report to Parliament annually on the state of access in Canada. Information Commissioner John Grace was highly critical of what he termed "the culture of secrecy" (Grace 1996) in government during the 1990s. Chiefly, Grace was concerned with the unwillingness of the bureaucracy to embrace the idea of public access to government records that had previously been entirely under their control and that of the executive branch. In particular, Grace pointed to what he termed "a traditional culture within ND/CF [the Department of National Defence and Canadian Forces] of secrecy and suspicion of those seeking information" (18).

Prior to the *ATIA*, civil servants were part of an inside elite who, unlike the public, were trusted because of their professionalism and expertise to handle sensitive government information. These same bureaucrats were being asked to hand over information with which they had previously been entrusted and required to keep in confidence, in effect to protect the information from the public. British social historian David Vincent (1998, 85) provides some valuable insight into public servants' perceptions of confidentiality as an indication of trust and therefore as an honour: "The honour of the civil service was seen as both the means and the end of the maintenance of secrecy ... 'official confidence' had a double charge. It referred at once to the confidentiality of the information, and to the faith the public vested in the discretion of officials." Allowing the public access to the type of information that had once been entrusted only to bureaucrats was, in some eyes, a show of disrespect for the professionalism of the civil service, and was therefore resented.

The more fundamental problem, however, was that the executive branch, including the PMO, offices of cabinet ministers, and the Treasury Board Secretariat, which oversees administration of the *ATIA*, failed to set an example and tone that made it clear to the bureaucrats processing the requests that this was a priority. From the outset, Information Commissioners have complained about inadequate funding and staffing levels. The resources to do the job in a timely manner have never been provided. The message that underfunding sent to the public service was that the *ATIA* was not a government priority. Grace noted this failure. He reported that bureaucrats responsible for processing the requests were not encouraged to consider ATI as "a core function, and [it] may thus be given a low priority" (Grace 1996, 18).

Information Commissioner John Reid, who succeeded Grace, has been the harshest critic of the secrecy provisions of the *ATIA*. The act contains thirteen exemptions that prevent the release of any records related to national security, policing, or other issues the release of which might harm public health and safety. It also prevents the release of information concerning advice to cabinet, as well as all cabinet records. In 2000, the federal government commissioned a task force consisting almost entirely of federal bureaucrats to review the *ATIA* and make recommendations for amendments. The task force received submissions from most of the major stakeholders and from several scholars in the area of public administration. Most of the submissions recommended that many of the mandatory exemptions be either dropped entirely or made discretionary, meaning that in some cases the government could choose to release the information. Several submissions and a special report on the task force tabled by Reid (2002) called for an amendment of the *ATIA* that would include a "public interest override," similar to clauses already included in several of the provincial freedom of information laws, including British Columbia's *Freedom of Information and Protection of Privacy Act*. The override would state that the public interest was paramount and acted to supersede all other sections of the act. Reid (2002) explained the need for the override as follows:

The absence in the federal Act of a general public interest override is a serious omission which should be corrected. Again, with the exception of the personal privacy exemption, the Act should require government to disclose, with or without a request, any information in which the public interest in disclosure outweighs any of the interests protected by the exemptions.

The decision, according to several submissions and a subsequent report by Reid, would be based on whether or not the release of the information was in the public interest, and whether or not the release of the information would result in harm, which was contrary to the public interest. This was an important and reasonable test that would determine that secrecy was justified only if it served the public's interests. Records could therefore be denied only on the grounds that their release would harm the public interest. Secrecy essentially would be decided on the basis of a public harms test – if it was harmful to the public interest to release information, then the information would remain secret.

Despite the recommendations, however, the task force recommended that the number of exemptions be almost doubled – from thirteen to twenty-five, with eight of the new ones being mandatory. The recommendations were roundly dismissed by scholars, stakeholders, and the Information Commissioner as an attempt by the bureaucracy to retrench secrecy practices within government. Reid produced a special report for Parliament that took the government to task for attempting to shift the already uneven balance of disclosure and secrecy. The bureaucratic task force failed to recommend a public interest override, but it was a moot point. The terrorist attacks of 11 September 2001 resulted in an increase in secrecy and delivered a severe blow to public access to information in Canada.

Securing Secrecy: Anti-Terrorism Law Trumps Access to Information

Although an increased level of concern is clearly justified after 9/11, security has also been appropriated by the government in order to challenge disclosure laws and expand the scope of secrecy laws. The balance tipped dramatically in favour of secrecy and executive branch control of information as part of Canada's *Anti-terrorism Act,* which was rushed through Parliament on 15 October 2001, just over a month after the 9/11 attacks on New York and Washington. The most important amendment in terms of limiting public access rights allowed a minister to issue a certificate vetoing the release of a record that would otherwise qualify for release under the

ATIA. The ministerial override could not be challenged by the Information Commissioner, whose role as ombudsman was to mediate and rule on disagreements between government and the requester. Nor was there any avenue for appeal to the courts. Although it was deemed essential at the time, in the eight years since the *Anti-terrorism Act* was passed not one certificate has been issued. Nonetheless, the power of cabinet to overrule the act and the commissioner remains law.

Another significant aspect of the *Anti-terrorism Act*'s section 13 amendment of the *ATIA* provides a mandatory refusal to release information involving other governments, both domestic and foreign. The *ATIA* already contained a discretionary provision – meaning that it was up to the bureaucrats to decide – concerning the release or refusal of information that involved other governments. Other governments would be consulted as part of the discretionary process and, in practice at least, any objections that they raised would usually be grounds for refusal, but it was still occasionally possible to get information from the federal government that also involved another government. Following the intergovernmental restrictions on accessing records, this potential no longer exists.

The government argued that the *Anti-terrorism Act* amendments were necessary in a post-9/11 world. The justification was that the terrorist attacks were the impetus for the restrictions on public access. This does not appear to have been the case, however. Roberts used ATI to obtain a confidential Privy Council memo (although the PMO is currently exempt from the *ATIA*, the PCO is not) written months prior to 9/11 that called for the amendments on intergovernmental records that were passed as part of the anti-terrorism amendment package. In an 8 October 2002 article in the *Winnipeg Free Press,* Roberts wrote that the memo "written in May 2001 suggested that the access law created a growing problem for security and intelligence officials. The end of the Cold War had led to 'the development of more bilateral intelligence relationships' and 'a more complex set of sensitivities regarding protection of information provided in confidence'" (A3). Eight years later, the restrictions on the public right of access introduced as temporary emergency measures under Canada's *Anti-terrorism Act* still stand as law.

Sidney Shapiro and Rena Steinzor (2006, 99) point to the increase in government secrecy since 9/11 as challenging and undermining the checks and balances system of accountability in the US Constitution. Transparency plays an important role in the "constitutional system of checks and balances, not least because it is the condition precedent for a free press." They point to the risk of "information asymmetries" in which "the agent [in this case the executive branch] is often in control of the information the principal [individuals who comprise the voting public] needs to judge that person's performance" (110). Not only does it make it more difficult to monitor the agent's performance but it also opens the door to the potential for propaganda methods – the promotion of false information or half-truths and withholding of negative information – to mislead the public into supporting the party in power. It is therefore essential to define transparency as access to meaningful information, which enables citizens to accurately scrutinize and assess government's actions and decisions in order to hold it to account.

Security increasingly takes precedence over freedom of information, and as a result secrecy remains the dominant and normative governance paradigm. There was a stage in the late 1990s when there appeared to be global momentum for the public right of access. Since 1966, more than sixty countries have implemented FOI legislation, admittedly with varying degrees of effectiveness. In countries such as Canada and the United States that were leaders in the FOI movement, however, the public right of access has been curtailed in response to 9/11.

Conclusion

Disclosure law is essential to ensure government transparency and accountability. It is difficult for a democratically elected government to argue against accountability, and none do. Accountability is an issue that has wide public support. There is an understanding that government lacks sufficient accountability in Canada, as pointed out by Justice John Gomery (2006, 1: 8), who held the PMO directly responsible in his report on how weak accountability resulted in the disastrously secretive Liberal sponsorship program: "A general lack of transparency about government spending, and a reluctance by the public service to call attention to irregularities because of the increased concentration of political power in the PMO, are the weaknesses in the present-day system of Canadian government."

The lack of meaningful "uncontrolled" information about governance is as apparent in Canada as are the consequences for its democratic system. The PMO has become a partisan public relations operation more inclined towards managing the message as a means of promoting its own political interests than towards providing meaningful information that promotes the public's interests in scrutinizing government and holding it to account. Excessive secrecy enables the executive branch to manage, limit, and control both Parliament's and the public's right to know, which as a result ceases to be a right.

Fundamental to any shift from the current secrecy and information control paradigm to one of openness and accountability is the need to set a test or parameters for information access. It is true that governance requires a considerable degree of secrecy in areas such as national security, criminal investigations, and even the protection of personal privacy. What is becoming increasingly clear, however, is that secrecy, if unchecked, can threaten the very basis of democracy by diminishing or even extinguishing the public's ability to scrutinize those whom they elect as their representatives. Democracy therefore requires a significant degree of both secrecy and transparency. The balance must be determined in and by the public's interest. If it is in the public's interest for certain records to be held in secrecy, then secrecy is justified. If it is in the public's interest for information to be made public – as in cases of risks to public health or safety – then secrecy is not justified. Even when secrecy can be justified, the processes of secrecy need to be transparent. Citizens have a right to know what sort of information is being withheld and why (Thompson 1999).

There needs to be a re-evaluation of how elected representatives are informed or, as in the case of opposition MPs, excluded from any meaningful opportunity to be briefed about government policies and decisions. Currently, opposition MPs, who are elected with the same duty to represent their constituents as government MPs, have no more right to access unpublished government records than members of the public. This leads to an impoverishment of debate in the House of Commons, where the government holds all the information cards. Not even the most basic background reports produced by bureaucrats specifically for the government, including for bureaucrats and for the executive branch, can be released to MPs without the permission of the executive branch. The expertise of Canada's massive federal bureaucracy is currently restricted to advising the executive branch alone, including unelected political advisors who have far greater access to secret information than elected MPs.

While some information will always be restricted to those who hold government office, a better-informed Parliament would no doubt elevate the level of debate, and might even lead to a less adversarial discussion between informed participants, all of whom are stakeholders in the public's interests. The deliberate poverty of information for opposition parties is also a loss for the public. The open forum of Parliament is an important opportunity to inform the public from both the government perspective and that of the opposition parties. Although essential elements of secrecy laws must always apply, if MPs were granted access to such things as background reports – compiled by politically neutral bureaucratic experts to inform the executive branch in its decision-making process – the public would subsequently also gain access to meaningful information about governance practices and policies.

It is evident that the historical governance paradigm of secrecy is still the normative mode of operation for the executive branch of Canada's federal government. The PMO has consistently resisted the *ATIA* as an infringement on the executive branch's traditional right to decide what the public is allowed to know about how it is represented in government. Canada's PMO is a closed shop, staffed primarily by spin doctors and political strategists hired specifically to take advantage of the cloak of secrecy to control and manipulate the public's perspective of what happens in that secret world. There must be a re-evaluation of the current practice of blanket secrecy for Canada's highest office and elected officials. What is clear is that secrecy for political purposes alone has no place in the democratic process of government. Determining whether secrecy is in the public's interest would be one way to approach the re-evaluation process. What is required is a paradigm shift from a historical sense of an executive entitlement to control information through secrecy, to an understanding and acceptance of the notion that the price of the right to represent is public accountability. The central premise must be that if it is in the public's interest to have information, then the information should be made available to the public. Only when it is against the public interest to release information is secrecy justified. This paradigm shift would both enable and encourage the public service to be more proactive in providing the public with information that it is in the public's interest to have.

REFERENCES

Banisar, D. 2006. *Freedom of Information around the World 2006: A Global Survey of Access Records Laws.* London: Privacy International. http://www.privacy international.org/.

Benoit, L.E. 2006. *The Prime Minister, Ministers and Their Exempt Staff.* Ottawa: Public Works and Government Services.

Birkinshaw, P. 2006a. "Transparency as a Human Right." In *Transparency: The Key to Better Governance?* ed. by C. Hood and D. Heald, 47-57. Oxford: Oxford University Press.

–. 2006b. "Freedom of Information and Openness as a Fundamental Human Right." *Administrative Law Review* 58 (1): 177-218.

d'Ombrain, N. 2004. "Cabinet Secrecy." *Canadian Public Administration* 47 (3): 332-59.

Dryzek, John S. 2000. *Deliberative Democracy and Beyond: Liberals, Critics, Contestations.* Oxford: Oxford University Press.

Dunn, J. 2005. *A History of Democracy.* Toronto: Penguin Canada.

Florini, A., ed. 2007. *The Right to Know: Transparency for an Open World.* New York: Columbia University Press.

Foerstel, H.N. 1999. *Freedom of Information and the Right to Know: The Origins and Applications of the Freedom of Information Act.* Westport, CT: Greenwood Press.

Franklin, B. 1994. *Packaging Politics: Political Communications in Britain's Media Democracy.* London: Edward Arnold.

Gomery, C.J. 2006. *Commission of Inquiry into the Sponsorship Program and Advertising Activities: Restoring Accountability – Recommendations.* http://publications.gc.ca/.

Grace, J. 1996. *Annual Report Information Commissioner 1995-1996.* Ottawa: Minister of Public Works and Government Services. http://www.oic-ci.gc.ca/.

Heald, D. 2006. "Varieties of Transparency." In *Transparency: The Key to Better Governance?* ed. by C. Hood and D. Heald, 25-43. Oxford: Oxford University Press.

Hood, C. 2007. "What Happens When Transparency Meets Blame Avoidance?" *Management Review* 9 (2): 191-210.

–. 2010. "Accountability and Transparency: Siamese Twins, Matching Parts, Awkward Couple?" *West European Politics* 33 (5): 989-1009.

Marleau, R. 2009. "A Dire Diagnosis for Access to Information in Canada." http://www.oic-ci.gc.ca/.

Martin, Lawrence. 2009. "Democracy Canadian-style: How Do You Like It So Far?" *Globe and Mail,* 17 December, A23.

Martin, R. 2003. *Media Law Essentials of Canadian Law.* Toronto: Irwin Law.

Morgan, D. 1986. *The Flacks of Washington: Government Information and the Public Agenda.* Westport, CT: Greenwood Press.

Rees, A. 2003. "Red File Alert: Public Access at Risk." *Toronto Star,* 1 November, A32.

Reid, J. 2002. *Response to the Report of the Access to Information Review Task Force: A Special Report to Parliament.* http://publications.gc.ca/.

–. 2003. Annual Report 2002-2003: Twentieth Anniversary Year in Review: The Assertion of Cabinet Confidence to Justify Secrecy. http://www.oic-ci.gc.ca/.

Roberts, A. 2002. "Canadian Officials Use September 11 as Excuse to Restrict Access to Information." *Winnipeg Free Press,* 8 October, A19.

–. 2005. "Spin Control and Freedom of Information." *Public Administration* 83 (1): 1-23.

–. 2006a. "Two Challenges in Administration of the *Access to Information Act.*" In *Commission of Inquiry into the Sponsorship Program and Advertising Activities: Restoring Accountability – Recommendations.* Ottawa: Public Works and Government Services Canada.

–. 2006b. *Blacked Out: Government Secrecy in the Information Age.* New York: Cambridge University Press.

Robertson, K.G. 1982. *Public Secrets: A Study in the Development of Government Secrecy*. London: Macmillan.

–. 1999. *Secrecy and Open Government: Why Governments Want You to Know*. London: Macmillan.

Rogers, A. 1997. *Secrecy and Power in the British State: A History of the Official Secrets Act*. London: Pluto Press.

Rose, J.W. 2000. *Making "Pictures in Our Heads": Government Advertising in Canada*. Westport, CT: Praeger.

Scammell, M. 1999. "Political Marketing: Lessons for Political Science." *Political Studies* 47: 718-39.

Shapiro, S.A., and R.L. Steinzor. 2006. "The People's Agent: Executive Branch Secrecy and Accountability in an Age of Terrorism." *Law and Contemporary Problems* 69 (3): 99-129.

Taber, J. 2011. "Young Harper Aide Shatters Glass Ceiling to Run Election Campaign." *Globe and Mail*, 4 February. http://www.theglobeandmail.com/.

Thompson, D. 1999. "Democratic Secrecy." *Political Science Quarterly* 114 (2): 181-202.

United Nations. 1946. General Assembly, First Session, Resolution 59(1). "Calling of an International Conference on Freedom of Information," 14 December. http://daccess-ods.un.org/access.nsf/Get?/.

Vincent, D. 1998. *The Culture of Secrecy in Britain, 1832-1998*. New York: Oxford University Press.

LEGISLATION CITED

Access to Information Act, R.S.C. 1985, c. A-1.

Anti-terrorism Act, S.C. 2001, c. 41.

Canada Evidence Act, R.S.C. 1985, c. C-5.

Canadian Charter of Rights and Freedoms, Part 1 of the *Constitution Act, 1982*, being Schedule B to the *Canada Act 1982* (U.K.), 1982, c. 11, s. 6.

Freedom of Information Act, 5 U.S.C. s. 552 (1966).

Freedom of Information and Protection of Privacy Act, R.S.B.C. 1996, c. 165.

Freedom of the Press Act (Sweden, 1766)

Official Secrets Act 1911 (1 & 2 Geo. 5 c. 28).

Official Secrets Act 1939 (2 & 3 Geo. 6 c. 121) (adopted by Canada).

Security of Information Act, R.S.C. 1985, c. O-5; 2001, c. 41.

CASES CITED

Canada (Information Commissioner) v. Canada (Minister of National Defence), 2011 SCC 25, [2011] 2 S.C.R. 306.

Dagg v. Canada (Minister of Finance), [1997] 2 S.C.R. 403.

2

Access Regimes
Provincial Freedom of Information
Law across Canada

GARY DICKSON

The first provincial freedom of information (FOI) law in Canada was proclaimed in 1977 in Nova Scotia. Much has changed in the treatment of freedom of information at the provincial/territorial level in the intervening thirty-five years. In the period between 1977 and 2002, access to information (ATI) laws were enacted in every other Canadian province and territory.

The purpose of this chapter is to consider major developments in access to records over the last two decades at the provincial/territorial level. While the relevant statutes have been revised and updated in some jurisdictions, this chapter will focus more broadly on the "access regime" in each province or territory. The access regime captures not only the statutes but also the machinery that governments and public bodies create to meet their obligations. These features include those officers within executive government tasked with meeting statutory access requirements (often referred to as FOIP, or Freedom of Information and Privacy, coordinators, since most provinces have a statute with two parts, access to information and the protection of privacy, and officers have responsibility for both access and privacy protection) and the extent to which they are supported and resourced as well as the kinds of tools and training developed to assist them in their key role. The access regime also includes the decisions, practices, and procedures of oversight bodies. In fact, given that the legislation tends to consistently be written in broad terms that can be applied to a very wide range of organizations, there is an important role for the interpretation of the statutes by those oversight bodies. Finally, the access regime also includes the executive and management levels of leadership within government and the extent to which value is assigned to complying with access legislation. Freedom of information law alone will not achieve robust transparency in the operations of government, but needs to be accompanied and reinforced by a range of measures to support that law.

A practical challenge with any survey of provincial/territorial access to information regimes is the sheer number of public bodies that are subject to the legislation. In contrast to the scope of the federal *Access to Information Act (ATIA)* and its application to federal government agencies, provincial and territorial laws usually apply not only to provincial government agencies but also to thousands of local government agencies such as library boards, regional health authorities, municipalities, schools, universities, and colleges. In most jurisdictions, the provincial-level coordinating agencies as well as oversight agencies are small and resources for coordination or oversight are usually very limited. Current statistics with respect to compliance with access laws for all public bodies at the provincial/territorial level are incomplete, and in some jurisdictions not available. As a result, any overview of the statutory compliance efforts of so many entities will be imperfect and must be considered with some caution.

The Freedom of Information Statute

The freedom of information statute is obviously a key element of any jurisdiction's access regime. There are a number of excellent resources that review the specific provisions in the freedom of information laws in Canadian provinces and territories in a comprehensive fashion that is not possible in this chapter (see McNairn and Woodbury 2009). There is value, however, in highlighting some interesting features in different statutes.

Generally speaking, the mechanics of how an individual makes an access request are similar at both the federal level and throughout provincial and territorial regimes. The Supreme Court of Canada has held that this kind of law is of a special nature and is "quasi-constitutional."[1] One of the reasons for this elevated status is that provincial and territorial access legislation is generally made paramount to other legislation. Before a paramountcy provision can be applied, there has to be a determination that there is a genuine conflict. This would effectively require that to comply with one law would mean a violation of the other. Generally in Canadian jurisdictions, whenever there is a conflict between the access law and another provincial law, the access law prevails unless a statute explicitly makes the other law paramount.

The Supreme Court of Canada has gone further in its decision in *Ontario (Public Safety and Security) v. Criminal Lawyers Association* by declaring that there is a *prima facie* case that section 2(b) of the *Canadian Charter of Rights and Freedoms* requires disclosure of documents in government hands where it is shown that, without the desired access, meaningful public discussion and criticism on matters of public interest would be substantially impeded.

The exemptions, sometimes described as exceptions, are quite similar from one jurisdiction to another. It is common that there are three or four mandatory exemptions and then seven or eight discretionary exemptions. The mandatory exemptions usually include cabinet confidences, third-party business information, and personal information of third parties. The discretionary exemptions usually include advice from officials; solicitor/client information; disclosure harmful to individual or public safety; confidential evaluations; disclosure harmful to law enforcement; disclosure harmful to intergovernmental relations; disclosure harmful to economic and other interests of a public body; testing procedures, tests, and audits; and disclosure harmful to conservation of heritage sites. Ideally, exemptions should apply only where there is a risk of substantial harm to the protected interest and where "that harm is greater than the overall public interest in having access to the information" (Report of the Special Rapporteur, Promotion and Protection of the Right of Opinion and Expression, UN Doc. /CN4/2000/63, 18 January 2000, para. 14). Although access best practices would require that freedom of information laws be guided by the principle of maximum disclosure, a number of the provincial/territorial laws fail to reflect that principle. Particularly in some of the older freedom of information laws, there are a number of exemptions that are class-based and do not require a "harms" test.

Critics of freedom of information laws frequently point to the number of mandatory and discretionary exemptions and suggest that such statutes are more about authorized secrecy than they are about greater transparency (also see many of the chapters in this book). In several jurisdictions, the statute incorporates a general type of "public interest override" that, at least potentially, provides a measure of balance that would otherwise not be available in assessing whether a particular record should or should not be released. Ontario's act was the first in Canada to incorporate a mandatory public interest override. This was limited, however, to only certain exemptions. A narrow type of discretionary override is also found in the Québec, Nova Scotia, Manitoba, and Saskatchewan legislation.

The concept of a mandatory public interest override was adopted and expanded to apply to all exemptions in British Columbia, Alberta, Prince Edward Island, and Newfoundland. In these four jurisdictions, the obligation to disclose exists regardless of whether a formal access request has been submitted for that information. On its face, the imposition of a positive duty on the head of a government agency to disclose information where health or safety is at risk or some environmental hazard is at hand may provide reassurance to those skeptical of just how much transparency the statute mandates. In practice, the public interest override is approached quite cautiously both by the heads of public bodies and by oversight offices.[2] In Ontario, however, there have been significant orders from the Information and Privacy Commissioner that directed disclosure on the basis of the public interest override. It may have some persuasive value in nudging the heads of public bodies to disclose where they might not otherwise be prepared to do so, but it has rarely been found by a commissioner that it applies after a head of a public body determined that it did not.

A positive duty to assist[3] applicants can be found in the freedom of information statutes in British Columbia, Alberta, Manitoba, Newfoundland and Labrador, Nova Scotia, Prince Edward Island, Northwest Territories, Nunavut, and Yukon. An example would be section 6 in the British Columbia *Freedom of Information and Protection of Privacy Act (FIPPA)*: "6(1) The head of a public body must make every reasonable effort to assist applicants and to respond without delay to each applicant openly, accurately and completely." This duty to assist is similar to features in the access legislation in the United Kingdom, Australia, New Zealand, and the United States. The Ontario act includes a more limited duty to "offer assistance in reformulating" a request that does not comply with the act.

For those jurisdictions that have empowered the commissioner to issue binding orders, there is the question of practically how such an order can be enforced. Curiously, only three jurisdictions appear to have addressed this in their legislation. There is a feature in the Alberta *Freedom of Information and Protection of Privacy Act* providing that a copy of an order made by the Information and Privacy Commissioner may be filed with a clerk of the Court of Queen's Bench and, after filing, the order is enforceable as a judgment or order of that court. The British Columbia and PEI statutes now have an equivalent provision.

Since a freedom of information access request has the effect of capturing only records in existence as of the date of receipt of the access request, applicants are often placed in the position of sending in requests at different intervals if they are interested in records that capture information subsequent to the date of receipt of the last access request. Ontario and Alberta permit a "continuing access request." Such a continuing request remains in effect for up to two years after it is submitted to the public body.

The most commonly cited exemptions across jurisdictions appear to be third-party personal information, advice from officials, and third-party business information. Considerable interpretative material has been produced dealing with all these major exemptions. If one considers the body of orders of the Ontario Information and Privacy Commissioner dealing with third-party business information and the evolution of access practices of Ontario public bodies over the last ten or fifteen years, it appears that the proposition that records relating to the transfer of public funds to a private business generally warrant disclosure seems to be well established and respected in that jurisdiction.

The "advice from officials" exemption is an example of a frequently used exemption that has attracted a lot of attention from oversight offices and from the courts. This also provides an excellent example of different approaches to interpreting a major discretionary exemption. The British Columbia Court of Appeal has interpreted this exemption very broadly. On the other hand, the Ontario Court of Appeal has taken a much narrower interpretation of this exemption consistent with the orders issued by the Ontario commissioner and recommendations from the commissioners in British Columbia and Saskatchewan.

In 2005, the Ontario Court of Appeal concluded in *Ontario (Ministry of Northern Development and Mines) v. Ontario (Assistant Information and Privacy Commissioner)* that the suggestion that mere information or intelligence in the possession of a public body may qualify as "advice from officials" and can therefore be withheld from access requesters is incompatible with a freedom of information law. On 13 April 2006, the Supreme Court of Canada refused leave to appeal from that Ontario Court of Appeal decision.

A further conspicuous omission from a number of the older laws is whistleblower protection for government employees who alert the oversight office to actions contrary to the legislation. Only Alberta and Prince Edward Island offer such protection.

Political Leadership

When the various access regimes across Canada are surveyed, it is apparent that some are much more strongly entrenched within their jurisdiction than others. An excellent example is the situation in Alberta. In the year before the 1993 provincial general election, the leader of the opposition Liberal party had campaigned specifically on the promise of more transparency, and according to polls was poised to possibly displace the Conservative government. A cornerstone of the Liberal platform was the introduction of a strong and modern freedom of information law. Premier Ralph Klein, who had just won a Conservative Party leadership contest, announced shortly before the general election that, if his party was re-elected, the first bill he would introduce in the new Legislative Assembly would be a freedom of information act. Mr. Klein prevailed and, as promised, introduced an access to information bill as his first piece of legislation. He also created an all-party panel to travel the province, receive submissions, and make recommendations on revision of his Bill 1. The consultation led directly to the development of a new bill, the *Freedom of Information and Protection of Privacy Act* that was passed in 1994 and proclaimed in 1995. When training materials for Alberta public sector employees were prepared in advance of proclamation, Premier Klein personally provided a video introduction stressing the importance of this new law to him and his government. The message to all in that government was clear. His personal endorsement of the new law was also reflected in generous funding of the office within government that would be responsible for implementation and administration, as well as the new independent Office of the Information and Privacy Commissioner. It is no surprise that overall, Alberta has in the intervening seventeen years achieved one of the strongest access to information regimes in the nation. This observation is consistent with the conclusion of Alberta Information and Privacy Commissioner Frank Work in his *Annual Report 2007-2008:* "The bottom line is that the access and privacy laws of [Alberta] work well in the majority of cases" (Alberta Information and Privacy Commissioner 2008).

As Ontario Information and Privacy Commissioner Ann Cavoukian observed in her 2005 annual report: "A key message is that leadership on openness and transparency must come from the top. Public servants are more apt to disclose information without claiming inapplicable exemptions if they feel that their decisions will be supported by both the politicians and senior executives who lead their ministry, agency, board, commission or local government" (Ontario Information and Privacy Commissioner 2006). In 2004, Commissioner Cavoukian had urged the newly elected provincial government to ensure that a central message promoting open, transparent government be delivered to all levels of Ontario government. In response, Premier Dalton McGuinty issued a memorandum to all ministers and deputy ministers urging them "to strive to provide a more open and transparent government." In September 2010, Premier Brad Wall of Saskatchewan issued a memorandum to all employees of the Saskatchewan government that underscored the importance of compliance with freedom of information and protection of privacy legislation, urging extra efforts to protect the information rights of citizens.

Other kinds of political leadership are needed as well. The experience in most jurisdictions is that access and privacy responsibility is assigned to a ministry with broad responsibilities for cross-government issues, such as a ministry of "government services," or in some cases to the ministry responsible for the administration of justice. In either case, the minister nominally responsible for FOIP may simply not devote enough time or attention to the "FOIP file." The opposition "shadow cabinet" rarely includes a critic with specific responsibility for FOIP. The history of Alberta's Legislative Assembly in the mid-1990s suggests that designating a specific opposition Member of the Legislative Assembly (MLA) with responsibility for FOIP can be an effective way of raising its profile in the legislature. This, in turn, requires the responsible minister to become better informed on FOIP issues.

The political reality is that transparency in the operation of government can be a very attractive issue for electors of all political persuasions. Specific examples of a government that appears to be secretive may be only a short-lived wedge issue. On the other hand, a perception of systemic secrecy on the part of a government and a lack of accountability can significantly impact elections. This was certainly the experience in the campaign preceding Alberta's 1993 general election.

Role of Provincial Ministries

As noted earlier, in each of the Canadian provinces and territories, one ministry is tasked with responsibility for administration of the FOIP act. In most provinces, this has resulted in the creation of a dedicated office within the ministry. Such an office becomes a vital part of the access regime in that jurisdiction. To the extent that the office is adequately resourced, has strong leadership, and is respected within executive government, the jurisdiction's overall FOIP regime will almost always be much stronger. In provinces with stronger access and privacy regimes, administrative responsibility is assigned to a ministry that provides a broad range of support services to the rest of the executive branch. This is the Ministry of Government Services in Ontario, the Ministry of Labour, Citizens' Services and Open Government in British Columbia, and Service Alberta in Alberta. In a number of other jurisdictions – Newfoundland and Labrador, Saskatchewan, Prince Edward Island, Nova Scotia, and the Northwest Territories – administrative responsibility is often assigned to the ministry responsible for justice. Such assignment can be awkward, since it is the same justice ministry that normally advises public bodies when an appeal is taken to the oversight agency. This sets up an area of potential conflict between the oversight agency and the arm of government responsible for training, development of tools, and provision of legal advice and advocacy to those public bodies. It may also be seen as a signal that access and privacy law is so complicated that it should be primarily the purview of those who are legally trained instead of a law that should be accessible to all citizens regardless of whether they have legal representation. It may also discourage public bodies from assigning administrative responsibility to non-lawyer employees even when that may be the most appropriate way to handle the work.

Such access and privacy offices are responsible for ensuring that all ministries are properly organized to meet FOIP responsibilities, that staff are properly trained, and that appropriate forms and manuals are available, as well as for generally supporting all branches of executive government insofar as FOIP is concerned. Further, the access and privacy office with overall responsibility for FOIP administration commonly collects statistics from public bodies that are consolidated in an annual report on FOIP compliance. Such a report is useful in understanding the extent of access to information activity in government. The Canadian experience is that jurisdictions with a stronger regime will typically feature a collaborative relationship between the responsible office within the executive branch and the oversight agency. Conflict between those two key offices leads to contradictory messages and confused guidance to public bodies, and also fuels adversarialism.

In each jurisdiction, responsibility for freedom of information is vested by statute not in the executive branch as a collective but in each individual ministry and public body. Although the minister is often the head of the public body for FOIP, he or she usually delegates to a FOIP coordinator specific operational responsibility for FOIP compliance. In larger departments or ministries, a number of persons may work in support of and under the direction of the FOIP coordinator. Most jurisdictions will have a

government website managed by the access and privacy branch that includes links to the legislation, to the information and privacy commissioner's website, and to a variety of tools.[4] In most jurisdictions, a detailed
manual has been published that provides practical granular information for
FOIP coordinators, including decision trees, sample forms, checklists, and
plain language descriptions of the various mandatory and discretionary
exemptions. One of the best examples may be the *FOIP Guidelines and
Practices Manual 2009* published by Service Alberta. Most of the jurisdictions have produced a number of training tools for FOIP coordinators and
senior managers. Most of these are available online. The Access and Privacy
Branch in the Saskatchewan Ministry of Justice and Attorney General has
developed an online training course[5] to provide general information to
government employees, and this has now been adapted for employees of
Saskatchewan local authorities. These offices also commonly organize periodic workshops for in-service training of FOIP coordinators. Directors of
these provincial and territorial access and privacy offices typically meet on
an annual basis to share experiences and resources.

Any jurisdiction's success in building a strong freedom of information
regime is determined by the extent to which these offices achieve their goals
of training, preparation of resources, and statistical tracking. Perhaps most
importantly, it is essential that the deputy minister responsible for the administration of FOIP genuinely embraces the importance of government
transparency and accountability.

Role of the FOIP Coordinator

In his *Annual Report 2007-2008,* Commissioner Work observed that since
the rollout of the freedom of information legislation in Alberta, "there has
grown a body of knowledgeable and dedicated professionals who are employed to administer these laws" (Alberta Information and Privacy Commissioner 2008). A major difference across Canada is the variation in the
role of the FOIP coordinator. In jurisdictions with strong access regimes,
such as Ontario, British Columbia, and Alberta, this role is well defined.
FOIP coordinators in these jurisdictions tend to be more senior in their organization's hierarchy. They oversee their organization's response to requesters, but this usually requires only a modest portion of their time. They
usually spend a good deal of time providing training for new hires and in-
service training for other staff. They frequently provide advice to senior
management with respect to proposed programs or legislation that may

impact the access and privacy interests of either the public or staff. They are also actively engaged in the preparation of educational materials, contracts governing outsourcing arrangements, and auditing of the organization's information practices. In jurisdictions with weaker access regimes, the FOIP coordinator's role is narrower and reactive, and is usually filled by a very junior employee. In such jurisdictions, the actual decisions on providing or denying access to an applicant will often be made by middle or senior managers with little or no FOIP training or experience. Not surprisingly, such decisions often do not reflect transparency, best practices, or even legislative requirements in the particular jurisdiction. Furthermore, inexperienced and undertrained FOIP coordinators are unlikely to champion within their organization open government and proactive disclosure to the public.

An important and welcome development has been the creation by the University of Alberta's Faculty of Extension of a certificate program for access and privacy professionals. This distance learning program has been strongly supported by oversight offices and a number of provincial governments. Many of those who have completed the program work as FOIP coordinators in public bodies or investigators in oversight offices. This has contributed to the development of a more professional and learned approach to compliance with freedom of information laws.

Role of Information and Privacy Commissioners

The Canadian experience is that jurisdictions with a part-time commissioner (Saskatchewan prior to 2003, Nunavut, Northwest Territories, and Prince Edward Island), or where the provincial ombudsman (Manitoba, Yukon, New Brunswick) has been tasked with access and privacy oversight in addition to other substantial responsibilities under an ombudsman statute or other legislation, the FOIP regime is weaker. This will likely result in lower levels of public awareness about access and privacy laws and rights. This is not surprising since the activities and the awareness-raising efforts of ombudsman offices will not be focused exclusively on "information rights." The remarkable thing is just how much access and privacy work has been done in jurisdictions such as Manitoba, Yukon, and New Brunswick despite the ombudsman's far broader mandate in these jurisdictions. In jurisdictions that have relied on a part-time commissioner, the experience is that a lawyer in private practice is contracted to primarily do the reactive work of responding to requests for review of access denials, but there are simply not the resources to enable the commissioner to discharge the other parts of the mandate.

Communication and Collaboration

Ten years ago, the resources available to information and privacy commissioners were very limited, with some notable exceptions. The larger offices of the Ontario commissioner and the Québec commission, along with the British Columbia and Alberta commissioners' offices were active in all parts of their mandate. This entailed producing an array of publications and tools, publishing orders and investigation reports on their office websites, and undertaking public education about their statutes. The smaller offices in Manitoba, Yukon, and Nova Scotia were also active in dealing with appeals from the public regarding decisions of public bodies to deny access to records. There was only a part-time commissioner in Saskatchewan until late 2003, and no commissioner in Newfoundland and Labrador until 2005. In New Brunswick, the ombudsman acted as the access oversight official but with a modest office that also served as Children's Advocate and an appeal office under the *Civil Service Act.* Prince Edward Island had no legislation and no commissioner prior to 2001. The Northwest Territories had a part-time commissioner who was also given responsibility for Nunavut when Nunavut became a separate territory. What communication and information sharing did occur among commissioners was largely informal. Today, the office of the Newfoundland and Labrador commissioner has approximately ten staff and that of the full-time Saskatchewan commissioner has seven staff. There is a commissioner in Prince Edward Island, and in 2010 New Brunswick appointed its first full-time information and privacy commissioner.

The commissioners now meet formally at least once a year. These annual meetings typically result in joint resolutions on access and privacy issues. In 2004, the commissioners created a closed listserv available only to commissioners and staff designated by them. This has proven to be an efficient and effective means of sharing experience and resources among all offices, and smaller offices benefit from the research capabilities of the larger offices. An intranet has also been created to archive e-mail exchanges and to facilitate the sharing of internal resources.

For four successive years starting in 2005, the Office of the Privacy Commissioner of Canada organized an intensive workshop for investigators from every provincial and territorial commissioner's office. In 2009 and 2010, the Information Commissioner of Canada became a co-sponsor. This workshop provided a unique opportunity for investigators from all jurisdictions to develop and refine the skills required by an access oversight office.

As a result of these developments, a much higher level of information sharing and collaboration occurs among Canada's provincial and territorial commissioners and their respective offices. Generally, most freedom of information oversight offices at the provincial or territorial level have four primary functions: review decisions made by public bodies to deny access; investigate alleged privacy breaches by public bodies; provide detailed advice to public bodies on statutory compliance; and educate the public and public bodies. For the purposes of analysis, I will consider development across the nation relative to each of these primary functions except for the "protection of privacy" component.

Review of Access Decisions
Information and privacy commissioners have order-making power in five Canadian jurisdictions: Québec, Ontario, British Columbia, Alberta, and Prince Edward Island. The initial iteration of this order-making model was the Ontario *Freedom of Information and Protection of Privacy Act.* Unlike the earlier access statutes in Nova Scotia, New Brunswick, Newfoundland and Labrador, and Manitoba, the statute created by the Ontario Legislative Assembly assigned order-making power to the commissioner. The statute was a response to the report of the Ontario Commission on Freedom of Information and Individual Privacy (1980; the "Williams Report"). This Royal Commission considered the experience in Sweden, the United States, New Brunswick, and Nova Scotia before concluding that the officer responsible for oversight "should be empowered to investigate the circumstances of the dispute, seek a reconciliation of the differences between the parties, and in the event that the dispute cannot be satisfactorily resolved, make an appropriate order with respect to the matter after giving both parties an opportunity to make representations" (361). This feature of the Ontario model was adopted by the British Columbia Legislative Assembly in that province's *Freedom of Information and Protection of Privacy Act,* which came into force in 1993. The following year, the Alberta Legislative Assembly adopted the same model when it enacted its *Freedom of Information and Protection of Privacy Act,* which came into force in 1995. The Legislative Assembly of Prince Edward Island followed suit with its own *Freedom of Information and Protection of Privacy Act,* which was proclaimed in 2002. Québec has used a similar model since 1982.

In contrast to the model in these five jurisdictions, the oversight agency in the other provinces and territories has the powers of an ombudsman. In

Manitoba, New Brunswick, and Yukon, responsibility for access oversight was assigned to the ombudsman (although in 2010 FOIP oversight responsibilities were transferred from the New Brunswick ombudsman to a full-time information and privacy commissioner). This means broad powers to review all records responsive to an access request that may be in the custody or control of a public body; the power to take evidence under oath; and the mandate to attempt to find a mediated settlement of the file and, if that is not feasible, to issue a report with findings and recommendations for the public body. In most jurisdictions, an aggrieved applicant who is dissatisfied with the public body's response to the commissioner's recommendations can appeal to the court on a *de novo* basis for a binding order. Given the extensive experience we have in Canada with both models, is one superior to the other? On the one hand, there is evidence that some public bodies have paid little attention to requests for documents and submissions from ombudsman-like commissioners and are very slow to respond to communication from the oversight office. There is also some evidence that public bodies generally will recognize the risks of failing to cooperate with an oversight office that has order-making powers and may organize themselves to expedite the handling of access requests. This may not be the case when the commissioner has a mandate to make recommendations only. As well, unless an applicant has the resources to initiate an appeal to the courts, a public body may see little advantage in accepting the recommendation from the commissioner to release the record to the applicant. In such a case, the only negative outcome for the public body might be public criticism of its actions in the commissioner's report. On the other hand, most disputes over access to records are resolved through mediation and informal resolution and would not require an order in any event. Even the five offices with order-making powers place a great deal of emphasis on mediation and informal resolution, and view the order as an instrument of last resort. Indeed, the Williams Report observed that "we anticipate that expeditious considerations of the disputed cases by the [oversight officer] would lead to satisfactory resolution of the vast majority of disputes. We hope that the responsibility of this office would be assumed by an individual of such stature that efforts at conciliation would normally result in a resolution of the conflict acceptable to both parties," and this has been borne out by the experience of Canadian provinces and territories.[6] It can be said that for the vast majority of cases, the process by the oversight office to informally resolve a dispute in British Columbia or Alberta (where the commissioner can issue orders) would not look very different from what takes place in Saskatchewan (where the commissioner can only issue recommendations). In addition, since the commissioner's offices with order-making power constitute "administrative tribunals," they are bound to a certain formality and rigour in their processes leading up to an order. This necessary formality associated with administrative tribunals stands in contrast to the flexibility common to ombudsman-type offices that can, without very much difficulty, examine additional issues that are uncovered in the course of a formal review and can efficiently consolidate matters as they determine appropriate.

A further consideration is that one of the biggest challenges to an effective freedom of information regime is adversarialism. This has been described by Alasdair Roberts (2006, 117) as an attitude and approach that is a product of the conflict over government records that is "often precisely that – a conflict precipitated by the clash of sharply opposed interests. Disclosure laws regulate this conflict, and aim to change the terms of engagement in favour of non-governmental actions; but they cannot bring an end to conflict itself. On the contrary, experience suggests that government officials and non-governmental actors become more adept in developing strategies that exploit or blunt the opportunities [for denying access] created by [the federal *Access to Information Act*]." In this context, the commissioner who arrives at the door of the head of a public body may be seen as an adversary to be viewed with caution and suspicion. Rather than fostering a discussion that leads to informal resolution, this may cause the public body to focus on aggressively defending its original decision. A significant challenge for commissioners such as those in Ontario, British Columbia, and Alberta is the increasing frequency of judicial review applications to the courts. These are attempts by aggrieved public bodies to overturn an order from the commissioner. Such judicial review applications are expensive and time-consuming for the commissioner's office. A discussion of adversarialism must be qualified, however, with the observation that this is evident most often with a fairly small proportion of all requests for access – those seeking politically sensitive records that may cause discomfort to the government of the day. The experience at the provincial/territorial level is that most access requests are submitted by businesses or individuals and do not involve politically sensitive material. This is not surprising when one considers the large role of provincial governments in providing direct service such as education, health care, social services, or environmental protection.

Finally, useful commentary on this question is provided by Supreme Court Justice Gérard La Forest in his analysis of the two federal offices of Information Commissioner and Privacy Commissioner in 2005. In discussing the two different models for the oversight office, La Forest (2005) observed:

> Commissioners in most of these provinces [Québec, Ontario, British Columbia, Alberta, and Prince Edward Island] use this power sparingly, preferring whenever possible to resolve complaints through conciliation, mediation, and other informal means. They nonetheless consider the existence of this power, which provides a strong incentive to the parties to settle on reasonable terms, to be essential to their effectiveness. In practice, this model could be described as an "ombudsman with a stick." By and large, claims are settled in a manner satisfactory to the parties.

My conclusion is that a jurisdiction where the premier issues and periodically reinforces strong messages to his or her government that freedom of information is a bedrock commitment of that government and that public records should be released in a timely way wherever appropriate may be further ahead with the ombudsman-type model. Ideally, in such a scenario the adversarialism that can be a problem with complicated or politically sensitive requests would be mitigated. Indeed, there would be little value added by conferring order-making powers, and possibly some prejudice to positive working relationships between the oversight office and the public bodies. In the absence of that kind of strong, clear commitment to open government from the premier of a province or territory, there would be value in following the order-making model for the oversight office. Unfortunately, it is not possible to design access laws to complement the disposition of the occupant of the premier's office. We are then left with recommending an order-making model for the oversight office, but with the qualification that there must be an ongoing commitment on the part of the oversight body to build positive relationships with public bodies.

Body of Orders, Reports, and Recommendations
Initially it was only the Ontario, British Columbia, and Alberta commissioners who produced full-text orders and reports that were published on their websites. They were followed by the Nova Scotia Freedom of Information and Protection of Privacy Review Officer in 1997 and the Manitoba Ombudsman in 2001, who began publishing summaries of their reviews on their respective websites.

In 2004, the Saskatchewan commissioner commenced publication of full-text reports on that website, followed in 2005 by the Newfoundland and Labrador commissioner. For ombudsman-type offices such as those in Saskatchewan and Newfoundland, the decision to produce not a summary but the full text of the report was made because of their educational value for other public bodies as well as the public. In 2006, the New Brunswick Ombudsman commenced publishing summaries of access reviews on that office's website.

There is now a substantial body of orders, reports, and recommendations from eight different offices across Canada. In all of these reports or case summaries, the identity of the citizen is masked to respect his or her right of privacy, but in the interests of public accountability the identity of the public body is typically disclosed. Most of these reports are now available on the Canadian Legal Information Institute (CanLII) website (http://www.canlii. org/) as well as other legal resources such as QuickLaw. Given the many similarities in freedom of information legislation across Canada, this larger body of orders and reports provides a useful resource to public bodies and the public in understanding how these laws and particularly the mandatory and discretionary exemptions are being interpreted. To assist public bodies and the public to access that body of orders and reports, an annotated section index is now available on the websites of the commissioners in British Columbia, Alberta, Saskatchewan, Ontario, and Newfoundland.

One of the challenges in jurisdictions without a strong FOIP regime is that those government employees who are processing access requests may be overwhelmed by the sheer volume of information described above. These employees may feel less competent to make decisions on the processing of access requests and on the application of exemptions. It is not uncommon to find staff who, when confronted with a request for access, feel that it must be referred to their organization's lawyer because the compliance require-ments appear too complicated. This challenge underscores the critical im-portance of providing the staff and the public with simple, easy-to-use tools to promote transparency. This would include more aggressive use of routine disclosure and active dissemination of information by government agencies. Unfortunately, these very tools constitute one of the conspicuous gaps in the immature access regime.

Detailed Advice and Commentary to Public Bodies

Provincial access oversight offices have produced a variety of tools and re-sources for the public bodies they oversee and the public they are accountable to, including detailed instructions and advice on the process for requesting a review of a decision by a public body that denies access to a record. This material also informs public bodies of the review process, how to search for responsive records, how to meet the duty to assist, how to communicate with requesters or applicants, how to prepare a record, and how to sever.

In addition to these process materials, most provincial and territorial commissioners are mandated to provide substantive advice on freedom of information issues to government and to public bodies. Much of this advice is sought by public bodies with respect to proposed programs or legislation.[7] It is customary that this advice is viewed as an important function by oversight offices and given priority.

The challenge for the oversight office is to ensure that it provides only general, non-binding advice when consulted by public bodies. The practice in most provincial and territorial oversight agencies is to caution the public body seeking advice that it cannot compromise its independence and neutrality since it may at some future date be required to address a specific request for review or appeal and then must deal with and dispose of that matter on the basis only of the evidence, submissions, and relevant law.

Public Education

Another major activity of commissioners' offices is providing information to the public about freedom of information rights and issues. This is typically done through materials on office websites, through brochures, posters, and other materials, and through public presentations. This also includes the use of newsfeeds, blogs, and social networking sites to electronically distribute information, orders, and recommendations produced by oversight offices. Copies of presentations and speeches by commissioners and their staff are routinely made available to the public through their websites. A number of commissioners' offices produce newsletters or e-newsletters that may be distributed monthly or quarterly. They are usually targeted at both those in the access and privacy community and members of the public. The Right to Know Week activities discussed below constitute a major annual public education initiative.

Evaluating the Oversight Agency

More research is needed to find an objective way to measure the performance of access and privacy oversight bodies. As noted by Malcolm Crompton (2004), the former Federal Privacy Commissioner for Australia, "the focus is often on the nature of the legal structures and the economic incentives they create as opposed to whether, within the bounds of the law and surrounding environment, the regulator itself has performed well or badly." This issue was also considered by Bennett and Raab (2003). More recently, France Houle and Lorne Sossin (2010) produced a report for the Office of the Privacy Commissioner of Canada titled *Powers and Functions of the Ombudsman in the* Personal Information Protection and Electronic Documents Act: *An Effectiveness Study.* Given the imperative that commissioners be credible and provide valuable service in their respective jurisdictions, this kind of analysis should be adapted and expanded to provincial and territorial oversight offices in Canada.

Managing Access Requests

Typically, the two most significant barriers to freedom of information are delay and cost.

Delay

There are two major areas where delay becomes an issue. One is the length of time it takes the public body to respond once it receives a proper access request. In most jurisdictions, the time period is thirty calendar days, with provision to extend this period up to sixty days in limited circumstances. In some provinces, there is explicit provision for the sixty-day period to be further enlarged. Normally the performance of public bodies in this respect is documented in annual reports produced by provincial and territorial governments.

To address concerns about delay by public bodies, the former British Columbia commissioner implemented a program of compliance report cards for ministries. He had described this as an "annual exercise intended to gauge ministry performance against published criteria that measure the timelines of ministry access requests" (British Columbia Information and Privacy Commissioner 2009a). In the 2008-09 fiscal year, almost one-third of government responses to information requests in British Columbia exceeded the thirty-day time limit, and half the responses to political parties were late, on average, by three times the time limit permitted by the *Freedom of Information and Protection of Privacy Act*. The commissioner's office has also developed a new procedure for deemed refusals and an early intervention program to attempt to reduce delays at the review stage. Former commissioner David Loukidelis issued a comprehensive report in early 2009 focusing on delay by public bodies in responding to access requests (British Columbia Information and Privacy Commissioner 2009). He made a number of recommendations for action if the problem of delay was to be seriously addressed. One recommendation was that government cease using any kind of sensitivity rating, whether applied to the types of requesters or to complex or otherwise difficult requests (7).

The other area of delay is the time from the point that an appeal or review is initiated with the oversight agency until the appeal or review is concluded. In a number of provinces, there is a prescribed deadline for the appeal or review to be completed. The Commission d'access a l'information in Québec must reach a decision within three months unless the chair extends the time. The New Brunswick commissioner must complete his or her review within ninety days, the same deadline as in Newfoundland and Labrador and Manitoba. There is no deadline in Saskatchewan and Nova Scotia. A number of the provincial and territorial offices are relatively small and often overwhelmed by the volume of requests for review or appeals. This is particularly problematic in jurisdictions where the oversight agency reflects the ombudsman model and an aggrieved applicant must, after learning that the public body has refused the recommendations from the oversight body, then appeal to the court. Delays in completion of work by the oversight agency are prejudicial to the applicant seeking to expedite a court hearing. This has led to a number of different strategies by oversight agencies to expedite their work.

Perhaps one of the most successful strategies was that created and implemented by former Alberta Commissioner Frank Work, who adopted a six-point action plan to address the substantial backlog of inquiries (Alberta Information and Privacy Commissioner 2008). The results were dramatic. In fiscal year 2007-08, his office issued eighty-one orders, up from fifty-three orders during the previous fiscal year. On 1 April 2007, fifty-eight cases awaited disposition by inquiry and order; by the end of the fiscal year, only four orders were still to be issued. Most orders are now being issued within three to six months from the date that the inquiry is held. In some cases, this has meant classification and staging of work on the basis of explicit criteria; in others, a kind of triaging is done internally. Some of the variables that the oversight office might consider are the number of persons affected by the review, the conduct of the public body, or the novelty of the issue for the oversight office.

Other oversight offices have also developed special procedures to expedite processing of access decision appeals or reviews. For example, in Newfoundland and Labrador, a new "banking policy" was developed to deal with requests for review when the Office of the Information and Privacy

Commissioner is already dealing with five files from the same applicant (see Newfoundland and Labrador Information and Privacy Commissioner 2009): additional requests from the same applicant may be placed in a "bank." This decision is discretionary but is based on four different factors, including current caseload of the office, matters of urgency, and the potential for early informal resolution.

Costs

Fee schedules vary among provinces and territories. Some jurisdictions prescribe an application fee ranging from $5 to $25; others, including British Columbia and Québec, do not charge an application fee. Additional fees are permitted in most jurisdictions, including fees for search, preparation of the record, and photocopying. An excellent survey of the fee regimes in Canadian provinces can be found in the research paper done for the Access to Information Review Task Force in November 2001 (Denham 2001). This survey includes an outline of criteria for fee waivers and a fee schedule comparison by jurisdiction.

Most jurisdictions provide for a fee waiver in certain circumstances. Generally, such provisions permit a fee waiver when the request is for personal information of the applicant or where the request for general information is "in the public interest" or where the applicant is impecunious. An excellent discussion of public interest in the context of fee waivers can be found in the 2002 decision of Justice T. McMahon acting as an independent adjudicator under Alberta's *Freedom of Information and Protection of Privacy Act* (Alberta Information and Privacy Commissioner 2002). The decision dealt with two requests for access to documents relating to the settlement of a defamation suit brought against Stockwell Day, then a senior cabinet minister in the Alberta government. The requests were made by an opposition MLA and by the *Globe and Mail.* In each case, the estimate of fees was approximately $60,000. Justice McMahon determined that both the MLA and the newspaper were acting in a public, not personal, interest capacity. He stated: "When the beneficiaries of the release of records of public interest are the public at large, then the public purse should primarily bear the costs." He went on to conclude:

> Access to the requested records would be of benefit to the Alberta public in a pursuit of openness and accountability in government affairs and the management of public funds. The records relate to a matter of public interest as described in s. 93(4)(b). The fees demanded of both applicants should

be reduced or waived, except for the application fee of $25.00 if it was paid. I emphasize that the burden of proving a public interest is an onerous one. It will neither be frequently nor easily met. It has been met here in the unique factual circumstances of this case.

In the end, the fees were reduced to $500 for the opposition MLA and $2,500 for the *Globe and Mail.*

Role of Civil Society

In general, Canadian citizens are not motivated to demand a stronger access regime in those Canadian jurisdictions with a decidedly weak regime. This can be attributed to several factors. It may be difficult for citizens to gather sufficient information to feel competent to catalogue the flaws in their jurisdiction's access regime. Information and privacy commissioners may not have been effective in acting as the public watchdog, highlighting problems with freedom of information that warrant remedial action, or they may have simply been ineffective in communicating their observations and recommendations to citizens. There is certainly evidence of strong reaction by the public from time to time to a perception that their government is hiding information from them. This strong reaction tends to be episodic and of relatively short duration. It tends not be sustained, yet without sustained public pressure the goal of achieving greater transparency and accountability may be exceedingly difficult to achieve. A cynical view is that greater transparency is readily championed by opposition parties who, upon forming a government may feel obligated to legislate open government principles yet soon set out to devise strategies to undercut the law for fear of adverse political consequences to themselves that may result from greater transparency.

Colin Bennett (2008, x), in his book *The Privacy Advocates: Resisting the Spread of Surveillance,* describes the kinds of organizations and individuals in civil society "who have consciously and purposefully attempted to advance the cause for privacy protection." Can we identify and catalogue a community within Canada that can be seen as consciously and purposefully attempting to advance the cause of open government? Leaving aside opposition legislators, the media, and information and privacy commissioners, it is difficult to identify a significant number of advocates of open government in this country. At different times, university researchers, environmental groups, taxpayer advocacy groups, civil liberties and human rights organizations, academics, lawyers, librarians, and archivists will challenge the secrecy practices of public bodies and articulate the need for more transparency. Historically these groups rarely act in concert and are often narrowly focused on a particular document or report; hence their advocacy tends to be for the most part episodic and not sustained. The few examples of Canadian organizations that purposefully and consistently advocate for open government include the Canadian Newspaper Association, the Canadian Bar Association, the Freedom of Information and Privacy Association (FIPA), Democracy Watch, the Sheldon Chumir Foundation for Ethics in Leadership, the Right to Know Coalition of Nova Scotia, and the Canadian Taxpayers Federation.

A relatively recent development has been the collaborative work undertaken in Canada to observe annually a Right to Know Week at the end of September. Although conceived by information and privacy commissioners in Canada, it has grown quickly and now involves a much broader network of individuals, agencies, and organizations. Internationally, Right to Know had its start on 28 September 2002 in Sofia, Bulgaria, at an international meeting of access advocates. The Office of the Information Commissioner of Canada hosts a national website that publishes information about events across Canada and related information about the public's right to know. This kind of nationally coordinated public awareness campaign that focuses on providing information to citizens about how to access public records is an attempt to raise the importance of access to information in the eyes of both legislators and the Canadian public.

Legislative Reform Initiatives
Many provincial/territorial laws governing access to information are based on a model that is approximately thirty years old. It is trite to say that there have been major changes in government recordkeeping, data sharing between ministries and governments, advances in e-government, a proliferation of portable computing devices, and an explosion in the use of e-mail for intra-ministry communication (see Reid 2004). The move to e-government is very much premised on viewing executive government as a single entity and not the multiple silos that represent the foundation for existing provincial and territorial access laws. Accountability that is so fundamental to FOIP laws is focused on the responsibility of the minister or the head of a government agency. How can accountability be ensured in a web of networks and information-sharing practices that will be opaque to most citizens? There is a compelling need to undertake periodic reform of Canadian

access laws so that they will be adequate for the existing and projected information and communications technology and the emerging e-government model.

There is a large body of recommendations from Canada's information and privacy commissioners for amendment of freedom of information laws. This includes changes to procedural requirements and substantive changes to the exemptions, responsibilities, and timelines. The annual reports of these commissioners are replete with suggestions to remedy identified problems in different jurisdictions and to better achieve the goals of heightened transparency. The response by governments, however, can perhaps best be described as spotty.

With the benefit of hindsight, one of the most significant features of the Ontario *Freedom of Information and Protection of Privacy Act* that came into force in 1988 was the statutory requirement that a comprehensive review be initiated within three years for the purpose of making recommendations to the Legislative Assembly for amendment of the statute. As a direct result, a long list of amendments was recommended by a Standing Committee of the Legislative Assembly in early 1991. A subsequent parallel review of the *Municipal Freedom of Information and Protection of Privacy Act* in 1994 yielded an equally long list of recommendations for amendment. This model of a statutory deadline for a formal review of the access legislation has been followed in a number of other jurisdictions, including Manitoba, British Columbia, Alberta, Newfoundland and Labrador, and, more recently, Prince Edward Island. Even in those jurisdictions, however, there is a question of how many of those recommendations result in legislative or policy change. In his latest annual report, the former British Columbia commissioner observed that "it has been more than five years since the last all-party review of *FIPPA*, yet some of the amendments unanimously recommended by the Legislative Assembly committee that reviewed the law continue to languish" (see British Columbia Information and Privacy Commissioner 2009a, 5).

Several different trends can be discerned in legislative reform activities across the nation. In provinces that have a legislated statutory review requirement, there has been a good deal of consultation, public input, and legislative study but only modest actual legislative reform. This trend is apparent in Nova Scotia, British Columbia, Alberta, and Ontario. In Newfoundland, there is a mandatory review provision but it has not yet been triggered. Some legislative reform has been undertaken in the Yukon, Manitoba, Québec, Nova Scotia, and New Brunswick even in the absence of a statutory review requirement, although the legislation in question is generally older. In most provinces and territories without such a review requirement – such as Saskatchewan, the Northwest Territories, and Nunavut – there has not even been a formal review of existing legislation. Prince Edward Island would have fallen into this last group but for the fact that amendments of the province's freedom of information law in 2005 included a three-year review requirement.

It is difficult to generalize from the experience with legislative reform in different jurisdictions, but it is safe to say that in jurisdictions with a stronger access regime, there is markedly more activity leading to legislative reform than in jurisdictions with much weaker access regimes. It may be that where there are more senior civil servants who have some experience with and investment in a jurisdiction's access regime, it is less likely that the need for legislative reform will be ignored for long periods.

Conclusion

The Canadian landscape of provincial and territorial access regimes is rich and diverse. While this may make it difficult to determine clear trends and confidently predict future directions, there is at least one inescapable conclusion. No jurisdiction will succeed in achieving a strong and robust regime unless a package of elements exists, consisting of modern, comprehensive legislation, strong political and administrative leadership, and properly resourced FOIP coordinators and oversight agencies. Advocates of stronger access to information would do well to consider more durable strategies to promote the development of such an access regime. This will in turn require the mobilization of a focused civil society that will sustain the demand for reform.

NOTES

1 See *Nautical Data International Inc. v. Canada (Minister of Fisheries and Oceans)*, 2005 F.C. 407 at para. 8; *Canada (Attorney General) v. Canada (Information Commissioner)*, [2004] 4 F.C.R. 181 at para. 20, 255 F.T.R. 56, 15 Admin. L.R. (4th) 58, 32 C.P.R. (4th) 464, 117 C.P.R. (2d) 85, 2004 F.C. 431, rev'd (2005), 253 D.R.R. (4th) 590, 335 N.R. 8, 40 C.P.R. (4th) 97, 2005 F.C.A. 199, leave to appeal to SCC requested; *Canada (Attorney General) v. Canada (Information Commissioner)*, [2002] 3 F.C. 630 at para. 20, 216 F.T.R. 247, 41 Admin. L.R. (3d) 237, 2002 F.C.T. 128, 3430901; *Canada Inc. v. Canada (Minister of Industry)*, [2001] 1 F.C. 421 at para. 102, 45 Admin L.R. (3d) 182, (2001) 14 C.P.R. (4th) 449, 2001 F.C.A. 254, leave to appeal to SCC refused, [2001] S.C.C.A. No. 537 (Q.L.); *Lavigne v. Canada (Office of the Commissioner of Official Languages)*, [2002] 2 S.C.R. 773, 2002 SCC 53 at para 25;

R. v. Dyment, [1988] 2 S.C.R. 417; *R. v. Mills*, [1999] 3 S.C.R. 668; *Dagg v. Canada (Minister of Finance)*, [1997] 2 S.C.R. 402; *R. v. Plant*, [1993] 3 S.C.R. 281; *R. v. Duarte*, [1990] 1 S.C.R. 30; *R. v. Edward*, [1996] 1 S.C.R. 128; *Canada (Information Commissioner) v. Canada (Commissioner of the Royal Canadian Mounted Police)*, [2003] 1 S.C.R. 66, 2003 SCC 8.

2 In Alberta, the public interest override has been frequently cited as authority for the disclosure of personal information about a "dangerous" inmate about to be released from a correctional facility at the end of a custodial sentence.

3 In Saskatchewan, the commissioner has found that there is an implied "duty to assist" in FOIP and the *Local Authority Freedom of Information and Protection of Privacy Act* (LA FOIP), which requires public bodies to respond openly, accurately, and completely to applicants (Saskatchewan Information and Privacy Commissioner 2004).

4 A good example would be the 2008 revisions to the website maintained by the Information and Privacy Policy Secretariat, a division of Manitoba Culture, Heritage and Tourism. This includes a "Members of the Public" portal and a "Public Bodies" portal.

5 Saskatchewan Justice, Access and Privacy Branch, Access and Privacy Training Course for Saskatchewan Executive Government, and Access and Privacy Training Course for Saskatchewan Local Authorities, available online at http://www.justice.gov.sk.ca.

6 See, for example, the statistic that 88 percent of cases of the Alberta Information and Privacy Commissioner in 2007-08 were resolved by mediation/investigation and only 12 percent by order (Alberta Information and Privacy Commissioner 2008, 37). See also the commentary on this question by Ed Ring, the Newfoundland and Labrador Information and Privacy Commissioner (2009, 6).

7 In 2008, the Ontario commissioner offered commentary on two provincial bills, undertook two major municipal consultations, and produced three major submissions/special reports. In 2008-09, the British Columbia commissioner undertook 127 reviews of proposed legislation and completed 114 of them. See also Alberta Information and Privacy Commissioner 2009, 10. In the much smaller office of the Saskatchewan Information and Privacy Commissioner in 2009-10, 82 detailed advice and commentary projects were undertaken for public bodies and trustees.

REFERENCES

Alberta Information and Privacy Commissioner. 2002. Adjudication Order #2, 24 May 2002, Review Numbers 2170 and 2234. http://www.oipc.ab.ca/.

–. 2008. *Annual Report 2007-2008.* Edmonton: Office of the Information and Privacy Commissioner.

–. 2009. *Annual Report 2008-2009.* Edmonton: Office of the Information and Privacy Commissioner.

Bennett, Colin J. 2008. *The Privacy Advocates: Resisting the Spread of Surveillance.* Cambridge, MA: MIT Press.

Bennett, Colin J., and Charles Raab. 2003. *The Governance of Privacy: Policy Instruments in Global Perspective.* London: Ashgate Publishing.

British Columbia Information and Privacy Commissioner. 2009a. *Annual Report 2008-2009.* Victoria: Office of the Information and Privacy Commissioner.

–. 2009b. *Timeliness of Government's Access to Information Responses – Report for Calendar Year 2008.* Victoria: Office of the Information and Privacy Commissioner.

Crompton, Malcolm. 2004. *"Light Touch" or "Soft Touch": Reflections of a Regulator Implementing a New Privacy Regime.* Canberra: Office of the Federal Privacy Commissioner, Australia.

Denham, Elizabeth. 2001. "Issues and Options Regarding Fees under the *Access to Information Act*." Ottawa: Access to Information Review Task Force. http://www.atirtf-geai.gc.ca/.

Houle, France, and Lorne Sossin. 2010. *Powers and Functions of the Ombudsman in the* Personal Information Protection and Electronic Documents Act: *An Effectiveness Study.* Ottawa: Office of the Privacy Commissioner of Canada.

La Forest, Gérard V. 2005. *The Offices of the Information and Privacy Commissioners: The Merger and Related Issues. Report of the Special Advisor to the Minister of Justice.* Ottawa: Department of Justice Canada. http://www.justice.gc.ca/.

McNairn, C., and C. Woodbury. 2009. *Government Information Access and Privacy.* Toronto: Carswell.

Newfoundland and Labrador Information and Privacy Commissioner. 2009. *Annual Report 2008-2009.* St. John's: Office of the Information and Privacy Commissioner.

Ontario Commission on Freedom of Information and Individual Privacy. 1980. *Public Government for Private People: Report of the Commission on Freedom of Information and Individual Privacy.* Toronto: The Commission.

Ontario Information and Privacy Commissioner. 2006. *Annual Report 2005.* Toronto: Information and Privacy Commissioner/Ontario.

Reid, J. 2004. "Holding Governments Accountable by Strengthening Access to Information Laws and Information Management Practices." In *E-Government Reconsidered: Renewal of Governance for the Knowledge Age,* ed. by L. Oliver and L. Sanders, 79-88. Regina: Canadian Plains Research Center.

Roberts, Alasdair. 2006. "Two Challenges in Administration of the *Access to Information Act.*" In R*estoring Accountability, Research Studies,* vol. 2, *The Public Service and Transparency,* Commission of Inquiry into the Sponsorship Program and Advertising Activities.

Saskatchewan Information and Privacy Commissioner. 2004. *Review Report 2004-003: Saskatchewan Government Insurance.* Regina: Office of the Information and Privacy Commissioner.

Service Alberta. 2009. *Freedom of Information and Protection of Privacy (FOIP) Guidelines and Practices Manual 2009.* Edmonton: Alberta Queen's Printer.

LEGISLATION CITED

Canadian Charter of Rights and Freedoms, Part 1 of the *Constitution Act, 1982,* being Schedule B to the *Canada Act 1982* (U.K.), 1982, c. 11, s. 6.

Civil Service Act, S.N.B. 1984, c. C-5.1.

Freedom of Information and Protection of Privacy Act, R.S.A. 2000, c. F-25.

Freedom of Information and Protection of Privacy Act, R.S.B.C. 1996, c. 165.

Freedom of Information and Protection of Privacy Act, R.S.O. 1990, c. F.31.

Freedom of Information and Protection of Privacy Act, S.P.E.I. 2002, c. F-15.01.

Local Authority Freedom of Information and Protection of Privacy Act, S.S. 1990-91, c. L-27.1.

Municipal Freedom of Information and Protection of Privacy Act, R.S.O. 1990, c. M.56.

CASES CITED

Ontario (Ministry of Northern Development and Mines) v. Ontario (Assistant Information and Privacy Commissioner), [2005] S.C.C.A. No. 564.

Ontario (Public Safety and Security) v. Criminal Lawyers Association, 2010 SCC 23, [2010] 1 S.C.R. 815.

PART 2

BEHIND CLOSED DOORS – SECURITY AND INFORMATION CONTROL

Flying the Secret Skies
Difficulties in Obtaining Data on Canadian Airport Security Screening Tests Following 9/11

JIM BRONSKILL

For a journalist, writing about government is much like trying to explore an iceberg. One easily sees the shimmering mass of ice above the water, but nothing below the murky surface. The federal government sends out news releases, stages announcements, and publishes content on departmental websites – the proverbial tip of the iceberg. The *Access to Information Act* *(ATIA)* is a useful tool for the intrepid reporter intent on getting a look at the submerged portion. This has long been the case for this author, a reporter who has covered security and intelligence issues, among other subjects in the federal political sphere, since 1995. My experience with the *Access to Information Act* dates from 1989.

The *ATIA*, enacted in 1983, gave journalists and other citizens a formal means of applying to see government files, including those held by the various federal security agencies. I have used the act to obtain Canadian Security Intelligence Service (CSIS) briefs on the possible threat from online hackers, Royal Canadian Mounted Police (RCMP) criminal intelligence studies on smuggling, reports by the watchdog over Communications Security Establishment Canada – Canada's electronic eavesdropping agency – as well as internal records on terrorist financing, police taser use, espionage cases, and the security of radiological materials. Access to information laws are a mixed blessing, in that they allow such records to become public by virtue of the fact that passages deemed too sensitive to disclose are excised prior to release (also see the Introduction and Chapter 1 of this book). In effect, it is half a loaf, but arguably better than no loaf at all. For this reason, the *ATIA* remains an important tool for journalists writing about security and intelligence issues, a means of lifting the veil of secrecy to provide a glimpse, if not a full look. It is akin to trying to do a jigsaw puzzle while blindfolded: one has only a vague sense of the overall picture, and little notion of its component pieces.

The events of 11 September 2001 have led to increased efforts by the Canadian government to control information related to national security. One example of this trend is Transport Canada's refusal to release the results of airport security screening tests, which were accessible prior to the attacks. These restrictions coincide with heightened public interest in security-related information, placing demands upon the government to adapt to new circumstances. Transport Canada, however, has thus far withstood these pressures through its adherence to long-standing – and rather cautious – approaches to information management, the inadequacies of Canada's access to information regime, and a relatively immature system of national security review pertaining to data disclosure (see, for example, Whitaker and Farson 2009). As a result, there is little reason to believe that the federal approach will change appreciably in the foreseeable future, which effectively denies the public access to vital information about airport security screening and similar security issues.

In the remainder of this chapter, I discuss some pressing issues concerning access to information at the federal level in Canada and how it relates to aviation security. Although my claims are shaped by my experiences as a journalist and my background investigating and writing about national security issues, my argument draws from Roberts's claim (2004) that national security and information disclosure are not antithetical but in fact can be complementary. I begin by discussing some of the challenges I have faced in trying to obtain information about aviation security, and then I broaden the focus to discuss limitations of the current federal access to information regime.

Flying the Secret Skies

Following 9/11, the Canadian government has intensively tried to control information related to national security in general and defences against political extremism in particular (see also Chapter 1). In the most formal sense, these measures have flowed primarily from the *Anti-terrorism Act* approved by Parliament in December 2001, as well as subsequently enacted regulatory provisions. The legislation allows the government to issue certificates denying the release of specified records for fifteen years in the interests of national defence, international affairs, or national security. Such a certificate could also effectively halt an investigation by the Information Commissioner into a federal refusal to disclose material under the *ATIA* should it be considered sensitive to one of these areas. The umbrella legislation also introduced the *Security of Information Act,* a reworking of the antiquated *Official Secrets Act,* creating a class of individuals in various federal agencies who are, to quote, "permanently bound to secrecy" about aspects of their security and intelligence work. It was initially believed that this restriction of the *Security of Information Act* would affect some six thousand past and present officials, especially in the national security and intelligence field. As of early 2011, the number stood at more than twelve thousand.

Other federal measures to restrict the release of information considered potentially sensitive were less formal and introduced only temporarily. For instance, following 9/11, the federal Privy Council Office (PCO), which provides advice to the prime minister, directed that disclosures of security information by federal agencies under the access law be vetted by PCO authorities. In another case, the Canadian Nuclear Safety Commission withdrew, then restored, the documentation library on its Internet website. Some tightening of information disclosure has occurred on a discretionary basis by agencies interpreting the provisions of the *Access to Information Act.*

There have been few quantitative studies of the effects of 9/11 on the amount or nature of information released under the access law. Among the most instructive is Darcy-Anne Wintonyk's study of Transport Canada (2006), which found that between 2000 and 2002 there were "drastic changes in the processing and effectiveness of media requests" at the agency:

> Media outlets were denied information based on security exemptions in a higher number of cases and a significantly higher percent of information was withheld on the basis of National Security, Law Enforcement and Defence ... the number of days before requests were abandoned reflects the struggle for resources within Transport Canada during 2000 and, more so, 2002. Lengthy extensions were applied to media requests, even more so in 2002, causing delays and frustrations gaining information under the Access Act.

In the case at hand, Transport Canada began concealing the results of airport security screening drills. In what are known as infiltration or

penetration tests, department inspectors have long gauged the effectiveness of security at Canadian air terminals by trying to slip materials by staff
responsible for searching passengers and carry-on baggage. In various exer-
cises conducted from 1996 through 2001, inspectors had succeeded in
sneaking items, including simulated handguns, knives, and bombs, past security personnel. Overall failure rates in the tests ranged from 6 percent to
19 percent (see Bronskill 2002). Transport Canada had released the statistics to the media under the *Access to Information Act* and, on at least one
occasion, informally. In 2001, CTV News obtained documents showing
that inspectors smuggled weapons, including disabled grenades, dynamite
sticks, explosives, pipe bombs, knives, and phony guns past airport security
staff 18 percent of the time. The documents said that sixty-nine screeners
were suspended and retrained before resuming work (Saunders 2001). The
importance of such tests would soon become apparent.

On 11 September 2001, terrorists armed with box cutters overpowered
pilots and flew commercial aircraft into the World Trade Center towers and
the Pentagon. Another hijacked plane crashed in rural Pennsylvania. The
assaults, carried out by Osama bin Laden's network of extremists, had a
profound effect on the security apparatus of the western world, prompting
billions of dollars in spending on new initiatives, including changes to airport procedures. Transport Canada continued to carry out security screening infiltration tests; however, the results of these drills would no longer be
publicly disclosed. In response to a request that Southam News filed under
the access law, Transport Canada acknowledged in March 2002 that "similar
records may have been released on a previous occasion, however the decision to withhold has changed because the injury in disclosure has increased
as a result of the events of Sept. 11, 2001" (Transport Canada 2002). The
department invoked sections of the *ATIA* that allow government agencies
to refuse to release records concerning: the detection, prevention, or suppression of subversive or hostile activities; investigative techniques or plans
for specific lawful investigations; the vulnerability of particular buildings,
structures, or systems; and consultations or deliberations involving federal
employees, a minister, or their staff. A department spokesperson contacted
by the news agency declined to elaborate on the reasons for withholding the
records. The rationale, however, was clear enough: the federal department
contends that information about weaknesses in airport security screening
could be misused by those determined to do harm.

The decision to discontinue release of test results coincided with a period
of intense interest in airport security measures following the 9/11 attacks.

At least one other Canadian journalist, David McKie of the Canadian Broadcasting Corporation, was similarly denied access to results of air security screening tests. Alasdair Roberts, a public policy specialist and expert on the Canadian access law, argued that although there may be a good reason for withholding information about particular security weaknesses at specific airports, the department could have released national statistics in aggregate form, as it had done in the past (Bronskill 2002). The Standing Senate Committee on National Security and Defence, which had been engaged with the security file prior to 9/11, conducted an extensive examination of airports. Witness Chuck Wilmink, a consultant and former corporate security manager for Canadian Airlines, advised the senators that the public should be made aware of the results of screening tests and other data even if they pointed to weaknesses, saying: "The terrorists know the holes. Hiding that information is not going to help" (Standing Senate Committee on National Security and Defence 2002a). The committee's subsequent report called for better screening of checked baggage and parcels, stricter terminal security, and improved training for employees. The Senate panel, which was denied access to the screening test results, also criticized the government for "unreasonable secrecy" about safety problems at air terminals given the difficulties in obtaining information relevant to its inquiry. Added the panel: "Loose lips are unlikely to sink ships when anyone who takes time to scrutinize security systems at airports – and terrorists do take the time – quickly sees glaring holes" (Standing Senate Committee on National Security and Defence 2003).

Transport Canada has remained steadfast in its refusal to release screening test results. Although a new agency, the Canadian Air Transport Security Authority (CATSA), became responsible for airport security screening, its parent department, Transport Canada, retained oversight and policy functions. In February 2003, the department invoked grounds previously relied upon to again bar disclosure to the media, and also cited two new ones: exemptions for personal information about individuals, and for testing or audit procedures, if release "would prejudice the use or results of particular tests" (Bronskill 2003). Colin Kenny, then chairman of the Standing Senate Committee on National Security and Defence, said that concealing the test data from the public "hides incompetence, hides inefficiencies and I think it allows the system to proceed without any proper checks. And we have a system that depends on regular checks." Kenny also insisted that taxpayers "have a right to know if their money is being wisely invested and if they're getting some value for it" (Bronskill 2003). In a December 2004 report, the committee insisted that it was "possible to provide transparency without undermining security." It proposed that infiltration test data be released after a delay of twelve to eighteen months, giving the government the necessary opportunity to fix any problems while keeping the public informed (Standing Senate Committee on National Security and Defence 2004).

Federal spending on anti-terrorism measures since 9/11 topped $10 billion by 2005, with funds allotted for myriad initiatives, including improved transportation security, expanded police and intelligence services, technological advances, and emergency preparedness. The expenditures attracted the attention of then federal auditor general Sheila Fraser, who undertook a series of studies. In her April 2005 report to Parliament, Fraser noted that the security of passenger air travel is based on a number of measures, including the gathering of intelligence, law enforcement by police, questioning by ticket agents, primary screening of passengers, secondary screening of some passengers, use of protective officers on some flights, and fortification of the flight decks of aircraft. The auditor general said that Transport Canada had not analyzed the overall effectiveness of its security systems, and that the infiltration tests constituted the only performance indicator. Upon detecting a failure in CATSA's procedures, Transport Canada issues an enforcement letter to the agency. Fraser was not impressed with the two bodies:

> Neither Transport Canada nor CATSA adequately tracked action taken in response to individual enforcement letters. Neither organization had a complete and accurate inventory. The numbers of letters on file at Transport, CATSA, and in the Transport database did not agree. Neither agency could find responses to all the enforcement letters. We could not find responses to about 12 per cent of enforcement letters related to infiltration tests and to 16 per cent of letters addressing other deficiencies. (Office of the Auditor General of Canada 2005)

Fraser also took special note of the fact that although she had access to the infiltration test data, she could not include the figures in her report because Transport Canada had chosen to classify them: "How can Parliament scrutinize the spending and performance of security and intelligence activities if key information must be kept secret? How will members of Parliament conduct an informed debate about security and intelligence matters?" To make her point, she specifically cited the secrecy of infiltration tests:

For example, passenger screening at airports involves weighing considerations such as how much security is desired, how long passengers are willing to wait, how intrusive a screening process they are prepared to accept, and what costs passengers and the rest of society are prepared to pay. While decisions on how to balance these questions are up to the government, it is up to Parliament to hold the government accountable for those decisions on behalf of Canadians.

She suggested creation of a parliamentary committee bound by secrecy that could receive information from security and intelligence agencies, the auditor general, and the Security Intelligence Review Committee (SIRC), the watchdog over CSIS.

Similar committees have long performed this role in Britain and the United States. Fraser encouraged the government to move expeditiously since security and intelligence had become "a significant part of the federal government's activities and should receive the informed attention of Parliament." Plans for a revamped national security committee of parliamentarians were still being discussed as of early 2012. In a special examination of CATSA, Fraser concluded that the authority "did not have reasonable assurance that screening operations were conducted economically, efficiently, effectively, and in the public interest" (Office of the Auditor General of Canada 2006). She cited the limited number of authority managers to oversee screening operations, shortages of screening officers, and high turnover rates. Fraser also noted "weaknesses in the oversight of infiltration tests." In fact, performance had declined since her 2005 report. Even though she could not publish infiltration test results, it is through extraordinary agents such as the auditor general, House of Commons committees, Royal Commissions on security issues, and court proceedings that the media and, in turn, the public have learned much of what they know about the inner machinations of national security since 9/11. Such agents, though not immune from federal reluctance to disclose sensitive data, have considerable powers to compel the release of, analyze, and, within legal limits, make public a certain amount of national security–related information. If we are operating with the understanding that there is a relationship between transparency resulting from the public disclosure of information and democratic accountability, however, it is important to consider the full implications of relying on review and oversight bodies or ad hoc fact-finding commissions that are themselves bound to secrecy. There is a great deal of discretion and uncertainty involved in the work of these agents. What I am suggesting is that the strictures of official secrecy have created an information void, and the federal access to information regime is rather ill-suited to fix the problem.

While recent Canadian screening data continue to be kept under wraps, even from parliamentarians, there have been occasional indications since 9/11 that similar tests in the United States uncovered serious deficiencies. Test data from the US, like Canadian figures, are not officially disclosed. Information leaked in March 2002, however, revealed that screeners at thirty-two American airports missed hundreds of knives, guns, or simulated explosives during tests in the months after the terrorist attacks on New York and Washington (Morrison 2002). In May 2005, the Canadian Senate committee called for "regular publication of statistics in both Canada and the United States to allow citizens to track whether genuine improvements are being made to airport security" (Standing Senate Committee on National Security and Defence 2005). The committee cited two recent US reports, one by the US Government Accountability Office (2005), the other by the Department of Homeland Security Office of the Inspector General (2005), that found security at American airports wanting, based in part on infiltration test results. The classified figures were not included in the reports. During a trip to Washington, DC, however, the Canadian senators had met with Senator Ted Stevens, a Republican from Alaska and chair of the Commerce, Science and Transportation Committee, who told them he was "appalled at the results" (Standing Senate Committee on National Security and Defence 2005).

Transport Canada officials have publicly indicated that the reason for concealing screening data is to ensure that the information is not used to plan an attack. There has been, however, no explanation of how such information might assist criminals or of the reasons for ruling out a compromise such as delaying disclosure of data until problems might be corrected, as suggested by the senators. During an appearance before the Standing Senate Committee on National Security and Defence (2002b), then CATSA president Jacques Duchesneau said that it "would be very counterproductive for me to say things that would help other people try to do a crime. I have a problem with that. I always did have a problem with that." On the other hand, it is not clear why an informed public need be considered a potential risk by CATSA. In early 2003, Transport Canada spokeswoman Jacqueline Roy said that officials decided following 9/11 that release of the data could "compromise security" by putting "ideas in people's heads" about certain air terminals. "The events of Sept. 11 sort of changed the world forever," she said. "For reasons of security, there are some things that we're not able to discuss publicly" (Bronskill 2003). In effect, the argument here is that disclosing such data would help would-be terrorists and is of little relevance to the flying public. Notably, CATSA has released annual figures detailing the number and types of actual prohibited items, including guns and explosives, detected by airport screeners. When it was suggested that making the infiltration test data public would provide some indication as to the percentage of prohibited items that do make it onto aircraft, Transport Canada spokeswoman Vanessa Vermette said that disclosure of the numbers would "compromise the security of our aviation system," adding that "at this point we don't see the advantage of releasing those numbers" (Bronskill 2005a). The commission of inquiry into the 1985 Air India bombing said in its 2010 report that generally screening officers who fail an infiltration test receive additional training, and are penalized in some cases. "The evidence before the commission did not clearly demonstrate a need to disclose the failure rates of infiltration tests," the report concluded. "Instead, the experts who testified at the commission placed greater importance on ensuring that deficiencies are identified and corrected" (Commission of Inquiry into the Investigation of the Bombing of Air India Flight 182 2010). As Roberts (2004, 71) points out, there is a tendency in government to see national security as a trump card that eliminates any right to information: "This is a dangerous fallacy. National security is important interest, but it must always be weighed against legitimate interests that will be harmed if information is withheld. An impartial calculation about the costs and benefits of disclosure must always be made." Brian Flemming, former chairman of the CATSA board of directors, said in a 2004 speech that infiltration test results "have improved substantially since CATSA got up and running." Without data to analyze, what can we do but take his word? All of this begs some perspective: while public discussion of efforts to keep the skies safe has focused on passenger screening, critics denounce the preboarding examinations as "security theatre" – a mere illusion of increased safety. One reason for this skepticism – the failure to properly screen cargo loaded onto aircraft – was highlighted by the Air India inquiry (2010). "Air cargo is neither routinely searched prior to loading, nor subjected to adequate screening measures," said the inquiry's key findings. "Its vulnerability, which has been understood by the government for decades, makes it a serious potential target for sabotage."

So far, the Canadian government has been able to withstand pressures for disclosure of screening test data due to several factors, including adherence to entrenched approaches to information management, the inadequacies of the access regime (see Chapter 2), and a relatively underdeveloped system of national security review pertaining to data disclosure. A number of the *Access to Information Act* provisions invoked to shield infiltration test data from release are discretionary exemptions, meaning that the agency that controls the records "may refuse to disclose" them but is not bound to do so, as with some exemptions under the law. In declining to make records public, however, an agency is not necessarily obliged to explain its rationale beyond citing the relevant sections of the law applied. Dissatisfied requesters may complain to the federal Information Commissioner about any aspect of how their application has been handled by an agency, including the failure to release records. The commissioner has the power to investigate complaints through examination of the records, with the exception of cabinet confidences, and to interview officials who processed the request. Upon completion of his or her investigation, the commissioner can either uphold the department's decision or recommend, but not order, that some or all of the disputed records be disclosed. Southam News lodged two complaints about Transport Canada's refusal to release infiltration test data in 2002 and 2003, respectively, but the complaints, which appeared to make little headway, were abandoned in 2004. As of early 2012, the Canadian Press continued to pursue the matter with the commissioner, however.

The Relevance of Access to Aviation Security Information for Broader Debates

The question of whether Canada's Information Commissioner should have the power to order the release of records has been debated in the context of possible reforms to the access to information regime. Scrutiny of the *ATIA* has also focused on the nature of exemptions to the act, specifically the extent to which federal agencies should be required to explicitly consider and document whether release of information would be likely to cause injury to the government. Certain exemptions used to deny the release of air security tests, though discretionary, contain an "injury test" – a direction to weigh possible harm to relevant government interests. A federal task force on reform of the *Access to Information Act* noted in 2002 that "heads of government institutions (or their delegates) do not always consider all relevant factors in exercising their discretion, nor do they articulate clear reasons for withholding information." The task force concluded that the challenge was to find ways to bring the practice more in line with the intent of the law:

We believe that institutions should consider whether an identifiable harm could result from disclosure, regardless of whether a particular exemption includes a specific injury test. We also believe that, in exercising discretion, institutions should consider the fact that information usually becomes less sensitive over time. The most productive reform would be to find a way to ensure that discretion is exercised only after such consideration. An exemption would then be claimed only where good reasons can be articulated for withholding information. The application of exemptions should not be a matter of intricate legal reasoning, but of basic questions asked consistently at all stages in the process: Are there good reasons for withholding the information in this case? How soon can it be made available without causing harm to one of the interests protected by the Act? (Access to Information Review Task Force 2002)

The task force suggested that the Treasury Board of Canada Secretariat, which has since become the lead agency responsible for administration of the *ATIA*, work with the federal Information Commissioner to develop user-friendly guidelines aimed at helping government agencies determine how to apply discretionary exemptions. The rationale for these was clearly spelled out by University of Toronto law professor Lisa Austin (2010): "Who has strong political incentives to prevent the disclosure of potentially embarrassing and damaging information despite the public interest? The government."

Despite even these mild nudges towards reform, there is little reason to believe that the federal approach will change appreciably in the foreseeable future, with the possible exception of disclosure of some classified information to select parliamentarians who submit to an oath of secrecy. A chronic lack of interest in information reform on the part of senior government leaders, internal federal pressures to tighten – not loosen – the reins on records, and a culture of caution reinforced by the events of 9/11 have contributed to this malaise. Although it has been a decade since the Access to Information Review Task Force issued recommendations, the government has yet to act on the vast majority of them. Bureaucrats within the Justice Department and Treasury Board Secretariat have been reviewing the access law since the mid-1990s, generating thousands of pages of reports and memos.

Former Information Commissioner John Reid's oft-repeated laments about a culture of secrecy pervading the federal bureaucracy and a lack of political will to address the problem fell largely on deaf ears (see also Chapter

12). Planned legislative reforms have been driven in substantial measure by the efforts of Members of Parliament, particularly former Liberal MP John Bryden, to bring forward private bills to overhaul the access law. Instead of embracing these independent initiatives, the former Liberal government signalled its intention to introduce its own legislation. Reid expressed concern, however, that the federal amendments under consideration would do more to curb existing access rights than to usher in new ones (Department of Justice 2005; Bronskill 2005b). In the 2005-06 federal election campaign, the Conservative party promised to enact reforms put forward by Reid that would make a wider range of records available and enhance the Information Commissioner's powers. The platform included specific pledges to provide "a general public interest override for all exemptions, so that the public interest is put before the secrecy of the government," as well as to ensure that "all exemptions from the disclosure of government information are justified only on the basis of the harm or injury that would result from disclosure, not blanket exemption rules" (Douglas, Hurtubise-Loranger, and Lithwick 2006). Following the election, the government of Stephen Harper brought more federal agencies, including several Crown corporations, under the *Access to Information Act* but broke its pledge to modernize the law by ushering in the other planned changes. As is too often the case, election promises have not been fulfilled. Unfortunately, access to information is used as a ploy in the federal party system to gain political points with voters.

In June 2009, the House of Commons Standing Committee on Access to Information, Privacy and Ethics (2009) largely endorsed Information Commissioner Robert Marleau's proposed twelve quick fixes to the access law, which included giving the commissioner order-making power for administrative matters and bringing cabinet confidences under the scope of the access law, making them subject to the commissioner's review. In a letter of response to the committee, Justice Minister Rob Nicholson showed little enthusiasm for amending the act, calling it "a strong piece of legislation." He argued that "amendments must be examined in the context of administrative alternatives, such as enhanced guidance and training that can be equally effective to realize continued improvements" (Minister of Justice and Attorney General of Canada 2009).

There would be little sign of administrative improvement, however. A germane illustration of this is the snail's pace at which my October 2009 request to Transport Canada for infiltration test data proceeded. It took Transport Canada more than eighteen months to respond with a refusal to release the figures, even in aggregate form. The department would say only that it conducted a total of 1,090 infiltration tests from January to the beginning of December 2009. Interim Information Commissioner Suzanne Legault reported in April 2010 that delays in answering queries from the public were getting worse and threatened to scuttle the right to know. Thirteen of the two dozen key departments studied by Legault's office received below-average marks. She gave Transport Canada a grade of D, noting that "the agency faced serious human resource problems in 2008-2009, when approximately half of the staff in its access to information office departed" – largely because of poor office morale (Information Commissioner of Canada 2010). "Delays are eroding Canadians' right to know," Legault told a news conference (Bronskill 2010). Departments are allowed to take extensions to answer requests, but agencies that lack enough staff to process applications are "using extensions as an administrative measure to cope with heavy workloads." Legault, since confirmed as an appointee to the commissioner's post, cited other chronic or "systemic" issues, including "multiple layers of review and approval" within agencies, which slowed processing, as well as lengthy consultations with other departments before records are released. Stockwell Day, then Treasury Board president, acknowledged the problem, expressing a desire for government to do better. The government's tepid pronouncements on access to information contrast sharply with those of US President Barack Obama, who on his first day in office breathed new life into the country's *Freedom of Information Act*. Obama said that all agencies should "adopt a presumption of disclosure" and, furthermore, "take affirmative steps to make information public. They should not wait for specific requests from the public." The directive effectively reversed notices from the former Bush administration that saw declassification of federal records slow to a virtual crawl (Kaplan 2009). What I suggest is not that Obama will fix everything but that we should pay attention to what is going on with access to information in other countries to ensure that best practices take root here in Canada. There had been no Canadian signals remotely comparable to those of Obama, Legault noted. Unlike the United States, Canada lacks a strong national movement pushing for greater access to information. An attempt in the early part of the last decade to model a body along the lines of the US National Freedom of Information Coalition sputtered due to lack of money and staff. The short-lived Open Government Canada, of which I was a founding member, succeeded in temporarily bringing journalists, librarians, historians, lawyers, and democracy watchdogs together in the fight against unwarranted secrecy. But these professions have since largely been limited to sporadic, individual efforts. The absence of a united voice for greater openness has made it easier for the federal government to ignore the occasional call for reforms.

Conclusion

Recent government policy on access to information has not entirely stymied investigative journalism but has arguably made it more challenging for reporters to uncover all key elements of a story. As such, in many cases the access law has allowed only a partial view – or disparate glimpses – of the submerged portion of the iceberg. For example, records obtained under access to information helped fuel reporting on the federal sponsorship scandal, the RCMP's use of taser stun guns, and the Canadian military's transfer of detainees in Afghanistan, bringing to light various aspects of these important public policy issues. The journalistic narratives shared a common thread in that the media's fight to obtain information, and the transparency of the relevant federal agencies, became a significant part of the stories. Official inquiries into these topics by parliamentarians and other watchdogs would also later highlight the tussles between media and government agencies over federal records. The rare instance in which the struggle for access to information becomes the focus of a national policy issue paradoxically results in greater public attention by prompting the question "What is government trying to hide?" While such unintended scrutiny can foster accountability, the goal of obtaining access to vital information remains elusive. Even in cases where there are no great secrets to shield from the public, the vacuum is often filled with rumour, speculation, and half-truths, none of which help the government dispel controversy or better inform citizens about the reality of the issues.

The events of 9/11 have prompted the government to enhance the arsenal of federal legislative tools to shield information from disclosure. In her 2010-11 annual report, Legault said that the percentage of exemptions claimed for national security had increased threefold since 2002-03 (Information Commissioner of Canada 2011). Yet some believe that this approach may ultimately be self-defeating, cutting the intelligence apparatus off from the lifeblood of broad public support. In his 2001 comments as part of the Access to Information Review Task Force, Wesley Wark (2001), a University of Toronto historian, argues that it is in the security and intelligence community's enlightened self-interest to ensure a reasonable flow of information about its activities to the public, noting that there is "a demonstrable link between high levels of public knowledge about security and intelligence issues, which can only be fostered by systematic information release, and the perceived legitim-acy and real capabilities of the community itself." In this vein, Alasdair Roberts (2004, 82) contends that government leaders and security agencies may see only the short-term risk to security in disclosing information:

> What may be less evident are the ways in which disclosure can actually improve security. An informed public can help policymakers to formulate better policy, monitor the readiness of national security bureaucracies and act independently to preserve security. An information-rich environment is one in which citizens and front-line government employees are better able to make sense of unfolding events and respond appropriately to them.

Access to information, then, is the handmaiden of accountability. Armed with information about which airports had the poorest infiltration test rates, even if it were data tabulated months earlier, passengers could choose to patronize those facilities in which they had the most confidence (although this is admittedly a bit of speculation on my part). Publication of test data would also put pressure on Transport Canada and CATSA to improve infil-tration test results at facilities that lagged in performance. In the case of air security, however, the government's efforts to engage the public have been limited primarily to informing people about the sorts of items barred from aircraft and commissioning opinion polls on perceptions of air travel safety. A revamped national security committee of parliamentarians could provide a forum for disclosure of data, including air security test results. These fig-ures, however, would still be beyond the reach of the group most affected: the flying public.

REFERENCES

Access to Information Review Task Force. 2002. "Access to Information: Making It Work for Canadians." http://www.atirtf-geai.gc.ca/.

Austin, Lisa. 2010. "Canada's Access Axis." *Globe and Mail*, 20 April. http://www.theglobeandmail.com/.

Bronskill, Jim. 2002. "Air Security Tests Kept Secret." *Ottawa Citizen*, 9 March, A3.

–. 2003. "Transport Won't Release Airport Security Results." *Ottawa Citizen*, 5 February, A1.

–. 2005a. "Hundreds of Explosive Items among Objects Confiscated at Airports." Canadian Press, 10 February.

–. 2005b. "Information Watchdog Pans Federal 'Pro-Secrecy' Proposals for Access Law." Canadian Press, 12 April.

–. 2010. "Access Denied: Federal Delays Stymie Information Requesters, Watchdog Says." Canadian Press, 13 April.

–. 2011a. "Government Keeps Mum on Airport Security Test Scores 10 Years after 9-11." Canadian Press, 3 June. http://ca.news.yahoo.com/.

–. 2011b. "Info Watchdog Calls for Updates to 'Out of Touch' Access Law." Canadian Press, 16 June. http://ipolitics.ca/2011/.

Commission of Inquiry into the Investigation of the Bombing of Air India Flight 182. 2010. *Air India Flight 182: A Canadian Tragedy.* Vol. 4, *Aviation Security.* Ottawa. http://epe.lac-bac.gc.ca/.

Department of Homeland Security, Office of the Inspector General. 2005. *Follow-up Audit of Passenger and Baggage Screening Procedures at Domestic Airports (Unclassified Summary).* Washington, DC: Department of Homeland Security. http://www.dhs.gov/.

Department of Justice. 2005. "A Comprehensive Framework for *Access to Information* Reform: A Discussion Paper." http://www.justice.gc.ca/eng/.

Douglas, Kristen, Élise Hurtubise-Loranger, and Dara Lithwick. 2006. "The *Access to Information Act* and Recent Proposals for Reform." Ottawa: Parliamentary Information and Research Service, Library of Parliament. http://www2.parl. gc.ca/.

Gordon, James. 2005. "Senator Urges Disclosure of Airport Security." CanWest News Service, 9 May.

House of Commons Standing Committee on Access to Information, Privacy and Ethics. 2009. "The *Access to Information Act*: First Steps towards Renewal." http://www2.parl.gc.ca/.

Information Commissioner of Canada. 2002. "Response to the Report of the Access to Information Review Task Force: A Special Report to Parliament." Ottawa. http://dsp-psd.pwgsc.gc.ca/.

–. 2010. *Out of Time: A Special Report to Parliament by Suzanne Legault, Interim Information Commissioner of Canada.* Ottawa: Minister of Public Works and Government Services Canada. http://www.oic-ci.gc.ca/.

–. 2011. *Paving the Access Ramp to Transparency: Annual Report of the Information Commissioner of Canada.* Ottawa: Minister of Public Works and Government Services Canada. http://www.oic-ci.gc.ca/.

Kaplan, Fred. 2009. "A Presumption of Disclosure: Obama Revives the *Freedom of Information Act*." *Slate*, 23 January. http://www.slate.com/.

Mayeda, Andrew. 2006. "Air Security Boss Concedes Gaps in Agency's Coverage." CanWest News Service, 31 October.

Minister of Justice and Attorney General of Canada. 2009. "Government Response: Tenth Report of the Standing Committee on Access to Information, Privacy and Ethics, 'The Privacy Act: First Steps Towards Renewal.'" http://www2.parl. gc.ca/.

Morrison, Blake. 2002. "Weapons Slip Past Airport Security." *USA Today*, 25 March.

Office of the Auditor General of Canada. 2005. *Report of the Auditor General to the House of Commons. Chapter 2, National Security in Canada – The 2001*

Anti-Terrorism Initiative. Air Transportation Security, Marine Security, and Emergency Preparedness. Ottawa: Office of the Auditor General of Canada. http://publications.gc.ca/.

–. 2006. *Canadian Air Transport Security Authority: Special Examination Report.* Ottawa: Office of the Auditor General of Canada. http://acsta.gc.ca/.

–. 2008. *Report of the Auditor General of Canada to the House of Commons. Chapter 8, Special Examination of Crown Corporations – An Overview.* Ottawa: Office of the Auditor General of Canada. http://www.oag-bvg.gc.ca/.

Roberts, Alasdair. 2004. "National Security and Open Government." *Georgetown Public Policy Review* 9 (2): 69-85.

Salter, Mark B. 2007. "In Airport Security, Sometimes a Knife Is Just a Knife." *Ottawa Citizen*, 7 August.

Saunders, John. 2001. "69 Dummy Weapons Got Past Security at Canada's Airports." *Globe and Mail*, 18 September.

Standing Senate Committee on National Security and Defence. 2002a. "Proceedings of the Standing Senate Committee on National Security and Defence. Issue 1 – Evidence, November 4, 2002." http://www.parl.gc.ca/.

–. 2002b. "Proceedings of the Standing Senate Committee on National Security and Defence. Issue 1 – Evidence, November 25, 2002." http://www.parl.gc.ca/.

–. 2003. *The Myth of Security at Canada's Airports.* Fifth Report, 21 January 2003. http://www.parl.gc.ca/.

–. 2004. *Canadian Security Guidebook: An Update of Security Problems in Search of Solutions.* http://www.parl.gc.ca/.

–. 2005. "Testing Airport Security: The Right to Know." News release, 3 May. http://www.parl.gc.ca/.

Transport Canada. N.d. "Inspection Activities by Calendar Year: Deficiencies by Type of Enforcement Action." Ottawa.

–. 2002. "Correspondence from Kathy Wesley to Jim Bronskill." Access to Information file no. A-2001-00223/kf. Ottawa, 7 March.

US Government Accountability Office. 2005. *Aviation Security: Screener Training and Performance Measurement Strengthened, but More Work Remains.* Washington, DC: US Government Accountability Office. http://www.gao.gov/.

US Subcommittee on Aviation of the House Committee on Transportation and Infrastructure. 2004. *A Review of the Airport Private Security Screening Pilot Program.* Washington, DC: Government Printing Office.

Ward, John. 2005. "Auditor Finds Security Policy Flaws." *London Free Press*, 6 April.

Wark, Wesley K. 2001. *The Access to Information Act and the Security and Intelligence Community in Canada.* Ottawa: Access to Information Review Task Force. http://www.atirtf-geai.gc.ca/.

Whitaker, R., and S. Farson. 2009. "Accountability in and for National Security." *IRPP Choices* 15 (9): 2-51.

Wintonyk, Darcy-Anne. 2006. "Hide and Seek: The Relationship between National Security and Open Government at Transport Canada since September 11, 2001." *Media* (Spring): 12. http://caj.ca/wp-content/.

LEGISLATION CITED

Access to Information Act, R.S.C. 1985, c. A-1.
Anti-terrorism Act, S.C. 2001, c. 41.
Freedom of Information Act, 5 U.S.C. s. 552 (1966).
Security of Information Act, R.S.C. 1985, c. O-5; 2001, c. 41.

Access to Information in an Age of Intelligencized Governmentality

WILLEM DE LINT AND REEM BAHDI

In national security, access to information is everything; information must be shared with allies but kept from enemies. Canada's *Access to Information Act (ATIA)*, like other legislation governing access to information, exempts national security from the principle that "government information should be reviewed independently of government" (sections 2[1] and 16[1]). Although national security agencies carefully guard the authority to broker access to information, they have also repeatedly violated basic human rights, including the prohibition on torture. These violations can be traced back to agency management of information flow and have precipitated renewed scholarly, community, and policy interest in the relationship between access to information and access to justice.

The O'Connor and Iacobucci inquiries, mandated to examine the role of Canadian officials in the overseas torture of Canadian, Arab, Muslim men, and several recent Supreme Court of Canada decisions have reinforced the need to check agency discretion over information flows in favour of fundamental human rights. Advocates, frustrated by agency resistance to disclosure and accountability through traditional litigation procedures, have crafted creative responses to agency resistance, including successfully leveraging the *ATIA* as a litigation tool. After the O'Connor commission released its report, the Royal Canadian Mounted Police (RCMP) and other national security agencies undertook to change their information-sharing protocols and practices with the promise of greater accountability. Scholars have

debated the significance and efficacy of these developments – with an eye
to securing better access to information through procedural innovations –
and governments have promised reforms – with an eye to maintaining
public trust.

These developments, debates, and reforms are welcome. There are at
present multi-faceted strategies that incorporate federal and provincial access to information regimes, and these are directed at government disclosure. Our focus, however, is not on access to information regulation per se,
and like many of our fellow contributors to this book, we sound a note of
caution. We focus attention on the strategic instruments and frames that
stipulate access to information in the national security context. We argue
that recent reforms consolidate rather than ease agency control over information exclusivity. We begin by framing the backdrop against which modern information control practices are played out: media, shifting bureaucratic
structures, and documentation or note-taking protocols. We then identify
strategies adopted by national security agencies to secure information exclusivity while simultaneously implementing changes purporting to respond
to concerns over an insufficiently qualified information regime. These strategic instruments include the centralizing and silencing of the information
flow and documentary record. Such finessing of reform is achieved by link-
ing it to discourses of exceptionalism and risk, and also by taking proactive
measures to attract public trust on the one hand and by questioning and
validating loyalties and thwarting official oversight on the other. We contend that while national security agencies use these mechanisms, they also
generate diametric opportunities for push-back from the margins. Finally,
we contextualize discretion and accountability in information control
against the larger sociological frame of networked agents finessing institutional and ideological resources in support of exclusionary systems.

The Margin of Exclusion – Information Control

Foucault's "systems of exclusion" refers to the variety of practices that maintain a particular body of knowledge or govern the will to knowledge
(Foucault 1971).[1] This includes the mechanisms that protect the base assumptions or founding affirmations and the institutional and professional
self-understandings that maintain institutional knowledge forms. It also includes internal rules that arrange principles of classification, ordering, and
distribution of texts and the distinction between primary and secondary
texts (Foucault 1971, 12-13). In outlining the function of disciplines,

Foucault noted the priority of building criteria, or an endless supply of fresh propositions that fit into and reinforce the hierarchical order of a given field over meaning or hermeneutics (17). Thus, "disciplines constitute a system of control in the production of discourse, fixing its limits through the action of an identity taking the form of a permanent activation of the rules" (16). In addition, Foucault noted what conditions must be met for subjects to be qualified to speak, a phenomenon he referred to as "rarefaction." Finally, discourses require "fellowship," or the preservation and reproduction of stipulations on circulation and in the maintenance of their truth claims. How propositions are allowed to shape a field, who is qualified to speak and make claims, and how claims and claims makers are vouched for by others in a community of peers are significant to understanding the power relations of governmental rationalities.

Building criteria, rarefaction, and fellowship are visible in and maintained through information management systems and in the normalization of intelligence or intelligencization into regular or routine bureaucratic practices.[2] Wilsnack (1980) argues that information control is accomplished through mastery of persuasion, secrecy, espionage, and evaluation. The transformation and consolidation of intelligence into intelligencization depends on the maintenance of the exclusivity of what passes as knowledge or actionable information and simultaneously serves to validate exclusive action capabilities with their founding affirmations and principles of classification, ordering, and distribution. Such information control permits practices that exploit this structural availability of actionable information (see Holquist 1997, 423).[3]

Misinformation and spin-doctoring alongside deliberate silencing of the documentary record are both declarative and constitutive of agency sovereignty. In the post-Arar era, a focus on generating accountability for information flow and what gets said across or between agencies has generally eclipsed the equally important antecedent issue of what does not get documented and shared internally within the agency in the first place. As a function of expert claims making, trust, and monitoring, information control turns just as much on the silences or the unsaid as on the documents or the said. Our goal is to refocus attention on intra-agency silences and the role of the unsaid, because what gets left out can be just as important to agency sovereignty and accountability as what gets passed around.

The power of this mode of governmentality resides in how information is rendered a commodity of politics. Security apparatuses transmit that power

through, for instance, the elaboration of the precautionary and the revitalization of the exceptional (Aradau and van Munster 2009). They vigorously
add and subtract information to supplement the vitality of the sovereign or
to produce the effect of a secure order. While the sovereign and sovereign
discretion must be vital, this vitality must not staunch the fertility of economy, most particularly neoliberal entrepreneurial relations. Accordingly,
the keenest exercise of decision-making authority may be anticipated at the
overlapping juncture of state and market vitalities or public and private industry (see Donzelot 2008). "Telling it like it isn't," ideologically or by more
crude forms of information repression and suppression, assists reputedly
democratic governments to push unpopular and unjust economic choices
for elites (see, for example, Klein 2008).

Information is translated into a commodity of politics primarily through
three modalities: use of media to perpetrate a message, the redefinition of
information flows according to new governance structures, and note-taking
practices that buttress agency discretion over national security messaging.
These modalities have become central to information control policing and
security, but they extend beyond these sites and threaten to displace the
legal regime with an information regime.

Media and Information Flow

Information control is built up as a security apparatus, differentiated, and
reconnected with agency objectives through mass corporate media, the
principal conduit for the dissemination of actionable information. Security
actionable information is made ready for what Walter Lippmann (1922, 17)
called "sound public opinion" in large part through the management of mass
corporate media sources and distributions. Lippmann identified three elements to public opinion formation, including the subsumption of political
communication under the economics of mass media, the creation of an "objectivity" culture within journalism, and the construction of a system of organized intelligence in elite administrative cycles (16). The news editor is
an intermediary between mass opinion (and mass hysteria) and corporate
government objectives. The better the organization of information by security and police, the greater the precision in reporting to the public and
the clearer the message regarding the requisite political choices.[4]

Cognizant of media's role in defining actionable information, Canadian
national security agencies selectively leak information to mass corporate
media to buttress agency credibility and decision making while casting
critics as national security threats. For instance, Jasminka Kalajdzic notes

how "unnamed Canadian government officials" falsely told CTV News in October 2003 that Abdullah Almalki was one of four Canadians "linked to an al Qaeda cell." A month later, "unnamed Canadian officials" described him to the *Ottawa Citizen* as "the main target" of terrorist investigation (Kalajdzic 2009). After Seymour Hersh wrote in the *New Yorker* that Syria had, according to George Tenet, helped avert a "suspected bomb plot against an American target in Ottawa" (Hersh in Pither 2008, 259), the *National Post* and *Ottawa Citizen* placed a front-page story based on unnamed official sources that was titled "Tipoff from Syria Bears Fruit," the fruit being the mitigation of an attack on Marines guarding the US Embassy in Ottawa, a story probably based on a chain-link of bad intelligence greased by torture. A commission of inquiry later debunked the claim that Almalki represented an imminent threat. And, in efforts to derail the Arar inquiry, government officials "leaked classified information" intended to discredit Maher Arar, using the media "to put a spin" on the case (O'Connor 2006, 257).

Shifting Bureaucratic Frameworks

Agencies deploy information control through a shifting organizational context of the intelligencized bureaucracy. This structure is no longer the traditional modernist hierarchy that encompasses relatively clear lines of accountability and discrete mandates. It is rather a "new governance" network (Salamon 2001, 2002) characterized by dynamic fusions and mobile, fluid loci of command. In the modernist bureaucracy, the paper trail and the ability to monitor the trail through a relatively clear organizational hierarchy offered some measure of protection from improper state action. But once decisions and knowledge are generated within liquid, flexible, and makeshift networks – often struck up around projects or problems rather than established bureaucratic lines – traditional forms of inquiry and oversight prove less effective.

Justice Dennis O'Connor addressed the challenges to oversight presented by the rise of new governance within the national security context by suggesting that a new national security review body, the Independent Complaints and National Security Review Agency for the RCMP, be established (O'Connor 2006, 317, 342). Unlike the existing Commission for Public Complaints Against the RCMP (CPC) or the Security Intelligence Review Committee (SIRC), whose mandates limit them to overseeing the RCMP and the Canadian Security Intelligence Service (CSIS), respectively, O'Connor proposed that the new body be constituted to follow the information chain across agency borders. Only then can an oversight agency effectively audit for compliance with policies and human rights standards. Forcese (2008), Sheptycki (2004), and Whitaker and Farson (2009) make similar recommendations in policy documents focused on intelligence accountabilities. However sensible such reforms may be, they may well need to extend beyond domestic inter-agency links because the intelligencized network is one in which information is linked and controlled transnationally and thus may not be captured by a reconstituted oversight body that is deterred from following the information chain outside national borders.

Most fundamentally, oversight is hampered by limitations to discovery given the foundation tenets of intelligence that have proliferated into routine governmental operations: ORCON, or the principle that the ORiginator of a piece of intelligence or information has the right to CONtrol further distribution; and "need to know," or the principle that dissemination of information should be restricted to those who are deemed to need the information. Thus buttressed, information-filtering techniques control information within bureaucracies. As illustrated in the next section, evidence of trends within and across the RCMP, Citizenship and Immigration Canada (CIC), the Department of Foreign Affairs and International Trade (DFAIT), and CSIS suggests that an intelligencized network fosters the compartmentalization of information and thus contributes to sovereign vitality.

Non-Documentation

Inasmuch as they represent the executive function and the "petty sovereign," policing and security agencies operate at the intersection of discretion and constraints on discretion. At the "low" register of policing, for example, the documentary burden (note taking and report writing) on police is heavy. Police officers' field notes are pivotal and there are requirements that an officer's note taking be complete and accurate and kept secure. These notes form the basis of the documentary record that supports prosecution. At a higher register of "political policing," notes form the basis of risk or threat assessments that in turn support security certificates or other government actions. Constraints come from the need to develop an evidentiary trail that enables prosecutions and other legal proceedings, from the accountability of police to the legal order and the public, and from the validity and reliability of police or security information for the transfer of liabilities (Ericson and Haggerty 1997). The presence or absence of a documentary record within and between police and security agencies enables or curtails both discretion and accountability.

While law regulates information dissemination,[5] police and intelligence services generally retain significant discretion over who sees or admits to seeing the record and how information is shared. National security agencies such as CSIS have long maintained the "verbal handshake" practice: when another agency requests sensitive information, intentions may be vetted informally without initiating a paper trail. "Informal" person-to-person contacts also help agencies clarify their mutual interests while avoiding committing intentions to a documentary record prior to mutual clarification. Even where information is shared in writing, ORCON dictates that information be given in confidence and not be further shared without the explicit consent of the party that provided it, thereby giving the originating agency discretion over who gets to see the information. That consent is further stipulated according to the "need-to-know" convention: that the requesting agency or agent makes a case that they need to know the specified information.

Information Control in Policing and Security after the O'Connor Commission

In Canada and elsewhere, especially after the events of 11 September 2001, there has been much greater fusion of the agencies and agents carrying out the mandate of internal public safety and policing and those that traditionally have been oriented to look outward to counter threats to national security. One consequence is that transnational intelligencized networks that combine law enforcement, military and defence, and security and intelligence agencies have been created or extended to provide a more seamless interoperability to counter "all-source" threats. This has placed a strain on the local and national mandates of policing and security, however. In assembling exclusive networked power-knowledges in such fusions, the agency/agency rather than sovereign/subject relationship forms the vital and fertile ground for discretionary authority, thus downplaying citizenship, rights, and individual privacy. In the process, operational decision making shifts from the front lines to the command centre through real-time monitoring and shaping of the information chain, particularly the production of documents at those intersections, conduits, and interfaces with competing systems. An examination of post-Arar RCMP information flow practices reveals the extent to which discretion is maintained and control is exercised through centralization and the power play of silences. These same techniques of centralization and silencing also mark the work of other national security agencies and highlight the extent to which brokering access to information has become both the means and mark of sovereignty.

RCMP

The 9/11 attacks led to a relaxation of information exchange protocols between law enforcement and security intelligence agencies, even across borders. "Caveats were down" because in the new "information paradigm" (Swire 2006), "it was not practical or desirable to adhere to policies on screening information shared with the United States" (Iacobucci 2008, 83). Bolstered by the common misconception that a cautious approach to information sharing contributed to the events of 9/11, the new information paradigm was reflected in Canada's National Security Policy and articulated by the US Director of Central Intelligence. It stipulated a move from "need to know" to "need to share," or a maximum degree of information exchange (Inge and Findlay 2006).

High-ranking RCMP officials claimed that a new information paradigm did not extend to front-line discretion and required a centralizing of discretionary decision making and an intelligencization of the law enforcement mandate. Senior officers blamed junior officers for the wholesale dumping of caveat-free information in relation to Maher Arar. Since the publication of the final reports by Justices O'Connor and Iacobucci, there has been a dramatic redirection of RCMP resources to national security (with as much as a third of the National Security Criminal Investigations [NSCI] budget coming from the allocations to the rest of the force), a tenfold increase in information flow on national security, a substantial resource injection to stimulate the municipal and local level of the national security mandate (including Integrated National Security Enforcement Teams [INSETs]; see RCMP NSCI 2009), and the firming up of the role of the RCMP as junior partner to CSIS in the determination of national security strategic priorities.

In March 2009, the RCMP reported on measures taken to implement the O'Connor recommendations, led by the NSCI unit and with fifty-seven staff positions explicitly tasked with implementation. The measures included a Joint National Counter-Terrorism Strategy, "the goal of which is to promote a thorough understanding of the RCMP/CSIS mandates by those involved in national security activities" (RCMP NSCI 2009). In addition, a Memorandum of Understanding (MoU) between CSIS and the RCMP that was entered into in September 2006 ostensibly outlines the respective counterterrorism roles of the RCMP and CSIS. The RCMP "takes its lead" and the NSCI devolves its priorities from CSIS's assessment of the nature of threats. Priorities "are now guided by the CSIS National Strategic Priorities." There is also an MoU template "to ensure compliance of the RCMP with NSCI policy and Ministerial direction, the Ministerial Direction on National

Security and Related Arrangements and Cooperation" (November 2003). The RCMP and CSIS have monthly meetings to "identify investigations of mutual interest" and to "engage in a de-confliction process" (RCMP NSCI 2009). At the same time, and arguably because of the tension in mandates, the RCMP has redesigned its National Security Criminal Investigators course, placing an emphasis on differences between the agencies.

Justice O'Connor recognized the trend towards intelligence-led delivery of police services but stipulated that the RCMP place "controls" on national security investigations in accordance with the law enforcement mandate of prevention, investigation, and prosecution of crimes. The RCMP interpreted this recommendation as requiring centralized control of national security (NS) investigations. It adopted a governance framework that places accountability and responsibility for the NS program with the Assistant Commissioner NSCI. According to the RCMP NSCI, the National Security Criminal Operations Branch (NSCOB) headquarters "monitors every NS file," particularly "with respect to information sharing, sensitive sectors, NS-related foreign travel, and relations with foreign agencies." The RCMP NSCI has centralized real-time access to ongoing investigations, has implemented a national secure electronic case management system, and supports a Common Framework for National Security adopted by the Canadian Association of Chiefs of Police.

Justice O'Connor's sternest recommendation focused on securing the integrity of information that forms the basis of linkages between agencies. Interconnectivity involves a "nexus of security, technology, and democracy" (Roy 2005, 463), and recent research has found that security authorities are exploiting interoperability requirements to widen information control mandates (Roy 2005, 463; Shapiro and Steinzor 2006). The RCMP has divided its national security information requirements into outgoing and incoming streams. A Sensitive Information Handling Unit (SIHU) staffed by four people manages incoming information. Referred to as a "new beast post-O'Connor" or "lead-lined box," the SIHU is empowered "to receive, review, centrally control and disseminate information from foreign security and intelligence agencies and the Communications Security Establishment Canada" (RCMP NSCI 2009). The SIHU is also mandated with section 38 applications and the attachment of sufficient caveats. This means, according to the RCMP, that there is "no direct relationship with RCMP and US people": the information transfer must be screened at headquarters.

SIHU's counterpart, the NSCOB, oversees cooperation and information sharing with foreign law enforcement. In early 2009, there were four extraterritorial investigations ongoing, and about thirty major projects monitored by the branch. The number of active files is "in the hundreds," however, and has grown considerably in the past five years (National Security Criminal Investigations 2009). The NSCOB at RCMP HQ screens outgoing information or information sharing with foreign law enforcement agencies and with other domestic and federal departments or agencies for "relevancy, reliability and accuracy." Domestic national security law enforcement inter-agency information sharing (provincial and municipal partners) is reviewed and approved by the Division Criminal Operations Officer or the Assistant Criminal Operations Officers carrying the national security responsibility. In addition, the INSETs and the Integrated Border Enforcement Teams (IBETs) have been expanded while their intelligence, law enforcement personnel, and mandates have been laterally and vertically fused and reconfigured.[6]

During a workshop on national security organized by the RCMP NSCI (National Security Criminal Investigations 2009), RCMP representatives explained that the adoption of CSIS "analysis" leadership and the necessity of producing section 38–ready prosecutions supported the use of parallel or duplicate investigations: "We deployed a team that duplicated all the circumstances of a prior CSIS investigation to run them consecutively or concurrently. The duplication can then be used for a criminal investigation in court" (National Security Criminal Investigations 2009). With respect to sharing information with countries with a record of torture, the current response is that the Assistant Commissioner "must approve of all sharing of information" with such countries, and "awareness and policy surrounding the sharing" of such information "forms an integral part of the NS Criminal Investigators Course" (RCMP NSCI 2009).

While there has been much movement since O'Connor, accountability for information sharing remains unfinished business. Most importantly, the review by an arm's-length body of the RCMP's information-sharing practices still consists only of a Commission for Public Complaints Against the RCMP and the Auditor General of Canada, although the RCMP is on record as "supporting the concept of review" of its national security activities.

One might be tempted to applaud the post–Arar Report reforms, but more careful review reveals that this activity will not generate accountability for two main reasons. First, the RCMP's focus has been on developing protocols for information sharing with other agencies, but it has not directly and explicitly addressed the fundamental question of how and when the agency itself documents information that is to be shared. Second, the RCMP reforms have clearly centralized decisions over information exchange, and thus centralized control over information. These are precisely the kinds of information control practices that facilitate non-production of documents and ultimately undermine accountability.

Courts and successive RCMP Public Complaints Commissioners have commented on national security agencies' persistent and misguided resistance to information disclosure. In *Canada (Royal Canadian Mounted Police) v. Canada (Attorney General)*, the Federal Court of Appeal criticized the RCMP Commissioner for withholding relevant information based on the faulty argument that the Complaints Commission chair had no need to consider relevant materials from confidential sources. Noting the frequency with which information is vetted without notice or explanation, former Complaints Commissioner Shirley Heafey commented: "It's like putting the fox in charge of the chicken coop: they would get to decide what I would see or what I would not see" (House of Commons Standing Committee on Public Safety and National Security 2009).

Whereas Heafey's complaints focus on the refusal to share information, her successor observed the general refusal of the RCMP to document its decision making in the first place. Commenting on the "sub-standard note-taking" practices of RCMP officers in his investigation of the taser death of Robert Dziekanski at the hands of RMCP officers at Vancouver International Airport, Commissioner of Public Complaints Paul Kennedy observed that poor note taking constitutes a systemic agency failure that clearly frustrates oversight of the RCMP but it is tolerated by agency leadership that has not clearly, explicitly, or directly responded to this problem (Commission for Public Complaints Against the RCMP 2009, 19).

Other Agencies: CIC, DFAIT in Afghanistan, CSIS

Like other national security agencies, including CIC, DFAIT in Afghanistan, and CSIS, the RCMP has demonstrated a reluctance to keep a paper trail or document the reasons that animate its decision making. This failure to keep notes has been acknowledged and asserted in legal fora. The trend across agencies suggests that Canadian government agencies may at times be more proactive in exerting information control through strategies of non-documentation as opposed to denial of access. For example, the Canadian government, through the CIC, offers the following in its statement of defence to explain why immigration officials failed to document the reasons for and circumstances under which Algerian refugee claimant Benamar Benatta was handed over to American authorities as a 9/11 suspect:

CIC did not complete the usual form, or otherwise record on paper the "direct back" which occurred. Such recording in CIC's computer system and completion of the applicable form are in fact administrative, not legal requirements. Such failure is attributable to the overwhelming circumstances of the day. In any event, any such failure is not causative of any problems experienced by the plaintiff after his return to the United States. (Statement of Defence, *Benamar Benatta v. The Attorney General of Canada et al.* at para. 22)

Government lawyers argue that government officials, whose authority flows only from their enabling statutes, are not required to document decisions with life-and-death consequences and that documentation failures prove relatively trivial in the shadow of 9/11. One wonders about an intelligencized Department of Justice. American officials, for their part, acknowledged the existence of the information pertaining to Benatta but claimed national security confidentiality over it.

During the Arar inquiry, government counsel overclaimed national security confidentiality and forced Justice O'Connor to seek a court order permitting disclosure of contested documents (O'Connor 2008). Perhaps the lessons that government officials drew from the battle over redactions is that censorship of comments before they are committed to writing proves more effective than censorship through redaction. Silence, after all, leaves even fewer traces than the redacted word. Government preferences for silence over redaction as a mode of information control surfaced in diplomatic letters between Canadian diplomat Richard Colvin and Ottawa, which record Colvin's several attempts to attract attention and resources to the procedures of handover of Afghan detainees to Afghan authorities. In particular, Colvin's letter to David Mulroney in a year-end report of 24 October 2007 remarks on the centralization of information flow according to terms defined by HQ and points out the emerging policy, a secretive "information control" protocol including restrictions on internal reporting and writing things down.

The expansion in Ottawa has been accompanied by a greater emphasis on information control ... Discussion of detainee issues has since been restricted to a very small group of people, which does not include essential embassy staff (i.e. the head of the political section, the pol/mil officer). Reporting on detainees from the post is now virtually impossible – HQ has made clear that it wants nothing in writing. This hyper-secrecy is conducive to information control but not to effective management of this critical issue ...

I have never before in my 15-year career been told that, internally, we must lie to each other. A similar message was delivered when it was recommended that we be "very careful" about what we put into our next human-rights report. This all adds up, in my opinion, to a very troubling politicization of reporting. (BC Civil Liberties Association 2009, 125)

During the period that Richard Colvin was in Afghanistan, when there was a heavy flow of information and intelligence, DFAIT developed "new, secretive information protocols" emphasizing "information control" over effective issue management and clear policy guidelines or instructions to the diplomatic mission's political section head. This new "information control" emphasis resulted in the "politicization of reporting," as evidenced by the pressure not to commit truthful observations to paper and the concentration "of information in the hands of a very small number of officials. Any onward distribution was strictly at their discretion. The change also eliminated any record of who had actually seen a given report" (Colvin 2009, 11).

CSIS has also been criticized over information management. In *Charkaoui v. Canada (Citizenship and Immigration)*, the Supreme Court of Canada found that information from CSIS was "erroneously" withheld, thus improperly denying Charkaoui his procedural rights at trial. In the case of Hassan Almrei *(Re Almrei)*, the Federal Court under Justice Mosley ruled on the reasonableness of the security certificate that held that Almrei was inadmissible to Canada on security grounds. The court once again stressed that CSIS had improperly withheld information, including "surveillance and intercept reports that contradicted human source reports on which the Service and the Ministers relied" (para. 502). The court reminded CSIS of its "responsibility to fairly consider and present the information in their possession" (para. 502), and emphasized that the agency's tendency to edit out exculpatory information from its reports breached "its duties of utmost good faith and candour" (para. 500). Justice Noel made a similar observation about CSIS's "institutional failure(s)" around disclosure (para. 44) when the Federal Court learned that three CSIS witnesses had failed to inform the court about the unreliability of CSIS's key human source (*Harkat [Re]* at para. 62). The failure to document and disclose cuts across agencies, suggesting a trend, if not a policy, of accountability suppression through the creation of information gaps, and more generally the manipulation of access conduits.[7]

Push-Back or Brokering Access

Today, politically actionable information is a commodity that slips into and
out of the margins through the security intelligence sieve. In what Elmer
and Opel call the "survivor society," political discourse (or talk about action-
ability) is powerful because it takes place "without documentation of
threats" (Elmer and Opel 2006, 481). Quests for centralization and lack of
documentation also create opportunities for push-back in the same sites,
however, and through the same mechanisms adopted by agencies to consolidate their control. Information control practices are open to counter-
measures built along the lines of building criteria, rarefaction, and fellowship.
Agency claims are met with counterclaims, trust and loyalty assertions are
countered with questions and detractions, and measures to exclude and
make information rare are greeted with measures to bring "sunshine" and
accountability to the national security agenda. In this section, we follow the
rendering of information into a commodity of politics and note the push-
back against systems of exclusion.

Claim and Counterclaim

In the past twenty years, and especially since 9/11, Schmittian political philosophy and the notion that openness renders liberal democracy vulnerable
has resurged. Governmentality today deploys decisionism and risk precaution to structure reasonable claims. Exceptionalism and risk discourse or
a precautionary approach to public policy support information control.
Precautionary risk management, where the "decision on the enemy is expanded into decisions on catastrophic contingency" (Aradau and van
Munster 2009, 11) posits the necessity of pre-emptive action in the avoidance of risks that "exceed the limits of the insurable" (Ewald 1993, 222, cited
in Aradau and van Munster 2009). The discourse of precaution and risk
management has become virtually a prerequisite of policy discussions, and
this discourse has further pushed exceptionalist information control impera-
tives and the enemy/friend binary into the heart of political articulations.

There is push-back, however. A robust literature (e.g., Ashworth and
Zedner 2008; Elmer and Opel 2006; McCulloch and Pickering 2009; Mythen
and Walklate 2006; Neocleous 2006; Pape 2003; Walker 2008) demonstrates,
first, that the precautionary agenda and catastrophic or endemic risk mitigation and information control by national security agencies are not logic-
ally interdependent. On the contrary, information control serves other ends
as connections between information control and resource or risk distributions are developed to serve the antecedent commitment to an exclusionary

social and political economy. For example, the representation of persons as terrorists before they can act promotes the popularization of ideological violence for a particular configuration of state authority. Second, the signifier of national security seems to have its strongest foundation as a method of an anticipatory claim or precautionary risk management rather than established fact. Validation of the authority of the claimant and not the claim itself takes centre stage. The popularization of decisionism and its narrative has uncoupled claim and fact in Baudrillardian simulations that blur illusion and reality and defy the firm grounding of knowledge.

The lack of grounding between exclusive systems contributes to fanciful claims that often turn on "recipe knowledge" (Ericson 1982), or the intuitive "street smarts" of police and security professionals. In counterterrorism cases, efforts have been made to intelligencize the courts, or substitute the court's evidence pool with intelligence knowledge stipulations, such as ORCON and "need to know," and to alter the demands of disclosure through intelligence allusions to precaution, risk aversion, and mosaics.[8] For instance, in *Canada (Citizenship and Immigration) v. Mahjoub* (2009), the CSIS witness was asked repeatedly how the agency had determined the probability that Mahjoub would use violence and direct others to violence. Focusing on the authority of the claimant rather than the efficacy of the claim itself, the witness focused on

> the experience of many persons – operational, analytical – and their access to classified information, their ability to consult with each other, to compare the information of past analysis, to consult with a variety of subject matter experts, to synthesize the work of many who have come before them, to analyze the work of different sources of information, to put it together into a coherent package and produce a document such as this.[9]

As painstakingly clarified by Mahjoub's lawyers, the intelligence agency prefers to provide no vehicle by which to externally assess the reliability or predictive accuracy of CSIS claims. The claim to authority is maintained even though the threat assessment was, as CSIS freely admitted, made in the shadow of falsification, without peer review, and was "not based on science."[10] Where cases involving access to information have successfully made their way before them, the courts thus far have at least partially reintroduced transparency and access to justice as considerations. In *Charkaoui v. Canada* (2008), for instance, the Supreme Court of Canada found that CSIS "compromised the judicial system," violated section 7 *Charter* rights, and breached section 12 of the *Canadian Security Intelligence Service Act* when, in keeping with its internal policy of retaining only summaries, it destroyed operational notes of CSIS interviews with Charkaoui (BBC News 2009).

Trust and Distrust

National security claims making facilitated by establishment corporate media and government agencies relies on trust commitments that may be vulnerable where agencies have abused those commitments (Tilly 2004). If as Lippmann (1922) claims, the *organization of information* by security and police packages precise reporting to the public directed at creating clear messages on political choices, the disorganization of information through unofficial countermessage leaks and disclosures can confuse agency messaging and undercut agency attempts to direct policy choices.

For example, when Kerry Pither wrote *Dark Days,* documenting the role of government officials in the torture of three Muslim Canadians in secret Syrian and Egyptian prisons, she offered an accessible counternarrative to government claims making. Her account invites a larger question: what else might they be hiding from us (Pither 2008)? When half of New Yorkers polled express the belief that "some leaders had prior knowledge" of 9/11 and "consciously failed to act" (Zogby International 2004), their responses reveal a trust gap that is ripe for exploitation by alternative conspiratorial narratives.[11] Indicatively, major WikiLeaks exposures of US State Department cables and internal military communications on the war in Afghanistan were front-page stories throughout the world in the spring and fall of 2010. The relatively tame response to revelations of government duplicity by the corporate mass media was countered by a wellspring of support for WikiLeaks director Julian Assange, who was named the Reader's Choice for *TIME's* Person of the Year for 2010. When investigative reporters follow a story beyond the public relations messaging and government claims making to suggest an ulterior motive, the integrity of the sovereign and its instruments become targets of correction. The disorganization of information thus negatively impacts sovereign claims to discretionary information control.

Loyalty and Counter-Loyalties

Anxiety over fulfillment of Canada's transnational obligations in the international security network feeds on the premise that substitution of fact for claim can make the "national" of national security measures weak because the insistence on facts dilutes the prevention side of the mandate and hence frustrates agency ability to keep the nation safe. Given the routine intersection of law and security agents in transnational commitments and given that foreign representations are formalized in explicit language protecting against release of information to the public, where do the international claims overcome the indigenous claims to national security? If the language of catastrophic contingency is to be preferred, what is included and excluded from how risk claims are made? And who is doing the claiming? Is it the national or the international?

At the Arar inquiry, government lawyers representing James Gould, then deputy director of DFAIT's Foreign Intelligence Division, used the phrase "out of an abundance of caution" to claim national security confidentiality and avoid disclosing whether his agency shared information with foreign intelligence agents (O'Connor Commission 2005, 10398-99). The release of information about Arar to the United States that contributed to Arar's extraordinary rendition was a decision that represented the will of the sovereign, but did it emanate from the marginal space between sovereign entities?

The interjection of transnational security mandates and targets into national, regional, and local law enforcement was formerly a source of much inter-agency tension and two-way information obstructionism, especially where agencies lacked sufficient socialization against nurtured differences in priorities, values, and missions. Now, transnationalism has become the desired norm. Amply socialized to the intelligencized network, agents' reference to such differences has itself come to represent the core obstacle to be overcome. Where formal ties do not permit sufficient information exchange, the pressure is to demonstrate due diligence in working around the legal obstruction. In the meantime, the lateral circulation of personnel between agencies ensures that officers will adapt to an organizational culture that privileges interoperabilities. This also fertilizes a habitus or outlook that increasingly substitutes the parochial with the superior mandate of an intelligencized law enforcement cosmopolitanism (see, for example, Bigo 2001).

CSIS Director Richard McFadden publicly railed against NGOs, journalists, and lawyers after the abandonment of the security certificate against Charkaoui (MacLeod 2009). Commenting on the court's requirement for enhanced disclosure, McFadden emphasized that the disclosure demand

> pushed us beyond what we could accept ... We were faced with a dilemma:
> to disclose information that would have given would-be terrorists a virtual

road map to our tradecraft and sources; or to withdraw that information from the case, causing a security certificate to collapse ... We chose the path that would cause the least long-term damage to Canada and withdrew the information. We did this because an intelligence agency that cannot protect its sources and tradecraft cannot be credible or effective. (MacLeod 2009)

That "long-term damage to Canada" referred to Canada's place within and commitment to a higher (and for all *we* know, treacherous) loyalty, the transnational security intelligence network. Canada's shortsighted NGO-led advocacy journalism and a misdirected judiciary together, according to McFadden, constitute a dangerous sovereign constitutional protectionism, a source of anxiety because of its insistence on its own system of exclusion.

Richard Colvin's testimony and the release of his reports demonstrate that agency information control strategies are being countered by revealing them in their calculated specificity. Colvin's appeal to the counter-loyalty in the traditions of Canada's diplomatic services, to the *Canadian Charter of Rights and Freedoms,* to the *Convention against Torture and Other Cruel, Inhuman or Degrading Treatment or Punishment,* and to other "higher" loyalties is a direct rebuke to the information control policy of DFAIT and other agencies. In *Canada (Justice) v. Khadr* (2008), the Supreme Court found against the loyalty substitution offered by the Minister of Justice and affirmed human rights over unfettered information control. It held that "the principles of international law and comity of nations, which normally require that Canadian officials operating abroad comply with local law, do not extend to participation in processes that violate Canada's international human rights obligations" (para. 2).

Rarefaction and Countermeasures (Monitoring)

Canada's policing and security practices at home and abroad have adapted by establishing protocols and procedures that are suspicious of external review and accountability, viewing these as sources of weakness, particularly where they protect individual rights and liberties and demand standards of proof focused on the known or provable instead of the unknown and hypothesized.

Our review of the post-O'Connor reforms that were ostensibly designed to enhance review of the government's national security mandate indicates that significant human resources have been deployed to centralize oversight within executive information control direction. The RCMP and other government agencies have created or adapted mechanisms capable of filtering information precisely to avoid the documentary chain that Justice O'Connor proposed be traced and checked by inter-agency review. Consistent with an intelligencized bureaucracy, these avoidance measures include claiming that information need not be disclosed because it is not relevant or, alternatively, that the information does not exist because decisions were not documented.

While government agencies experience some success with their strategies for information-filtering, the tide may be turning as even courts have pushed back against the intelligencized bureaucracy's information control practices. For example, a master in the Ontario courts created "the Benatta remedy" in requiring government counsel to certify the integrity and completeness of the disclosure provided by government agencies. Federal Court judges have struck down several security certificates because the information provided by national security agencies did not meet the demands of the rule of law (see *Re Almrei*). Although access to information remains a major impediment to the legal process as the torts claims of Benamar Benatta, Abdullah Almalk, and others wind their ways through Ontario's courts, more creative doctrines to address agency attempts to manipulate information may yet be fashioned.

Ramifications for Sovereignty, Liberalism, and Governmentality

There is an ongoing contest between the law's knowledge claims and practices and the knowledge claims and practices of national security agents and agencies, with frequent skirmishes for and against the substitution of the law's truth for the intelligencized truth of the sovereign. This involves the production (and non-production) of information through principles of classifying, ordering, and distribution. The law's truth is predicated, in part, on the notion of an adversarial system that stipulates that information is cross-checked by contesting parties in front of a third party representative of the polity, whose role is to maintain the production of information according to evidentiary rules. National security's truth is predicated, in large part, on the principle that the most vital or actionable information must be accessible only to agents of the sovereign, and that the production and dissemination of information must strengthen the sovereign's discretionary vitality and not betray strategic or tactical advantages to "the enemy."

The protection of information control and the systems of exclusion on which it depends is consistent with the transition to societies of control. As Deleuze (1992) theorized, in societies of control, the unique and distinct status of the individual in relation to the social body is supplanted by "dividual" subjects no longer recognized in their distinctness or indivisibility but instead posited as governable in terms of the fluid information packets that stream into positions, roles, or "agents." The traditional contest between sovereign subjects and authorities is reflected in arguments by government officials in defence of a regime of information control that include reference to existential fears and risks and to the need for forthrightness in action and candor in policy discussions. Even this traditional stipulation of parties (and authorities) is increasingly besieged, however, as less and less of law's light enters the court to illuminate the truths that maintain and regenerate its system of exclusion, including, of course, the indivisibility of the sovereign subject him- or herself.

Even at the higher registration, the notion that sovereign subjects in the great game of the international system must be able to return to the play remains an uncontested fact. We are familiar with the view of sovereignty as the existential precondition, and the nostrum that its capacity requires an absence of limits or regulation; the sovereign is the threshold "on which violence passes over into law and law passes over into violence" (Agamben 1995, 32); according to decisionism,[12] the sovereign agency is aggrandized through exceptions and exclusions, with the final say not dictated by law or rule. If the measure of sovereign discretion is taken at the boundary of violence and law, it is maintained through the control of actionable information. For the sovereign the salient question is: "What information can make a difference to my unrestricted freedom or my place in the game?" Discretion in the exclusive power to broker information access defines and perpetuates sovereignty.

There is more, however. In today's information society, sovereign exceptionalism and neoliberalism are practised through the production and dissemination of information, through its flows and its controls. Systems of exclusion underwrite the knowledge claims and governabilities at the back of *neoliberal* governmentality, in which the discursive basis and object is also the *homo œconomicus,* or the entrepreneur him- or herself. According to Donzelot (2008, 132), liberalism (and neoliberalism) places emphasis on the limit of rule to foster productive capacities. Under neoliberal governmentality, the state is restricted to stimulating the conditions in which the entrepreneurial self may play the game while sufficiently maintaining system credibility. In Donzelot's terms (2008, 129), neoliberalism stipulates that "everything must be done to avoid some players being definitively excluded from the game, otherwise it loses its sense and credibility. One should therefore see to it that those who find themselves on the borders of

the game can return to it." To avoid welfarism's failure as a game of inclu-
sions without limits, (neo)liberalism's rules simultaneously define the terms
of participation, regulate some to the margins, and put out the promise that
a return to full participation is possible.

At first glance, then, it might appear that in addition to the clash between
the claims of law rooted to natural justice and the claims of the sovereign
buttressed by security intelligence, there is a clash between neoliberalism
and its entrepreneurial actors and sovereignty and its political agents: the
economy of society versus the economy of sovereignty. Indeed, we do see
the outlines of a stark opposition: the preservation of the vitality of the economic root and an umpire's discretion to produce sufficient deregulation of
the market; the expansive possibility of politics within the political and an
umpire's reaffirmation of rule by or after the exception. Where neoliberal
game changes align with the emergent geopolitical norms (as to limits, exchanges), however, there is no clash. It is only where sovereign and economic vitalities diverge that the discourses on economic and collective
security will show these tensions.[13] For example, Maple Leaf Foods has a
workforce of temporary foreign workers fast-tracked into the country
through Manitoba's nominee program; according to its negotiated contract
with employees, it is accountable for helping these workers gain citizenship (CBC News 2010). Here, the *neoliberal* sovereign is at work: decision-
making agency is contracted out to entrepreneurs because corporate and
state vitalities align.

Institutionally, information control is relatively autonomous of competing entreaties that require bright lines of inclusion and exclusion; it embod-
ies and extends the battle between discretion and rules of play; it acts to
provide space to buffer the vitalities of the sovereign and *homo œconomicus*
in their distinction and competition.[14] It may be argued that information
control policing and security is the latest attempt to crack open the liberal
identity in the context of the maintenance of trade and commerce or in
the desire not to extinguish (economic) vitality by (political) constriction.
Through practices of information control, law is enabled as governmentality, or as that complex form of power "which has population as its main
target and apparatuses of security as its essential technical instrument"
(Foucault 2007, 108).

Conclusion

Information control factors into the struggle between discretion/rules,
outside/inside, chaos/stability, and so on, and how this plays itself out in

attempts by national security agencies to broker access to information about their own conduct and the targets they are tailing. Information control is not merely an element of the security apparatus; the play of information reconceptualizes targets and knowledge forms, so that discretion is not acting on populations so much as constituting actionable entities. The battle over accountability and the rule of law is precisely the battle over information flow and who gets to broker access. Ultimately, however, brokering access is not about reproducing political economy but charting the deployment of the nostrums of neoliberalism against those of sovereign exceptionalism and other discourses.[15]

Information control does not mean that all the conduits of politically actionable information are managed centrally according to a defined policy agenda. Rather, an assembly of relations is intelligencized or made *differentially accessible* to exceptional interests of corporate government elites. The discretion to differentiate, however, turns on trust, claims, and loyalties, each of which can generate counters and resistance. Information control thus involves efforts to mitigate resistance while also seeking to exploit it for further refinement. Thus, for example, if there are leaks, there are also plumbers to fix the leaks and those who leak alongside analysts who draft pre-emptions against further leaks. And, as we have shown, if documentary release has come to pose a problem for intelligencization silence and centralization have emerged as tools that facilitate information control and dosing.

NOTES

1 Foucault identified the "three great systems of exclusion" that govern discourses as prohibited words, division of madness, and the will to truth.
2 Some prominent recent conceptualizations of the conduct of conduct more or less follows the double-bind of the Foucauldian diagram.
3 Peter Holquist (1997, 423) refers to the implementation at the beginning of the twentieth century in "large scale" of a particular type of modern governmental politics called the national security state through, among other devices, various techniques of "patriotic instruction" called "enlightenment activity."
4 Hugh Wilford's *The Mighty Wurlitzer: How the CIA Played America* (2008) recently presented the extent to which establishment corporate media and government agencies, including the *New York Times*, the Central Intelligence Agency (CIA), and the Rendon Group share Lippmann's view of public opinion management; there may be few who are in a position to decipher when and where the "mighty Wurlitzer" is being played.

5 The Department of Justice routinely cites a number of documents in support of
   Canada's information-sharing obligations. See, for example, *Almalki et al. v. Attorney
   General of Canada et al.* at para. 11.

6 With respect to the IBETs initiative, federal and provincial authorities are deployed
   to the local community level and are conducting "cold" interviews of persons fre-
   quenting ports, harbours, train stations, etc., and asking for information on suspicious activity at the same time as they are taking tombstone data (name, age, address,
   citizenship, licence and passport numbers, travel companions, and information regarding enforcement actions taken and the results of inquiries) in order to "check on
   warrants." In this way, they are deploying national security with law enforcement
   authority (collecting names and birthdates of persons they happen to interview) and
   expanding both the local crime catchment and the intelligence web through border
   enforcement synergies.

7 After this article was written, the *Hill Times* reported that Prime Minister Harper
   "plans to extend his notorious personal control over government affairs into a surprising arena – the oversight of national security and intelligence gathering by a
   range of military and civilian agencies and departments." As the article explained,
   the Prime Minister established "an entirely new committee of Cabinet ministers
   responsible for overseeing national security and intelligence agencies, even intelligence and information gathered through delivery of Canadian aid programs. It will
   be only the second of two Cabinet committees now chaired by the Prime Minister"
   (Naumetz 2011). Pursuant to sections 69(1)(2) and (3), the *Access to Information Act*
   does not apply to "confidences of the Queen's Privy Council for Canada," which includes documents of cabinet and committees of cabinet. Section 69(3)(a) states that
   this exemption does not apply to cabinet confidences that have existed for more than
   twenty years.

8 In a US case, Judge Gladys Kessler ruled that the government had failed to establish
   a case against Alla Ali Bin Ali Ahmed. Instead of accepting the government's conten-
   tion that the court should accede to the intelligence experts and their mosaic theory,
   Kessler subjected it to a test of court-based evidence and made a mockery of the
   government's case.

9 Transcript of Proceedings, Monday, 26 October 2009, *Canada (Citizenship and
   Immigration) v. Mahjoub,* 2009 F.C. 439, Docket: DES-7-08, at 15.

10 Ibid.

11 A 2008 Ipsos-Reid Poll found that one-third of Canadians believed that the US government allowed the attacks to happen and 16 percent believed that the US government made the attacks happen (Humphreys 2008).

12 "Decisionism describes the view that, in politics, sovereign power is defined by having the final say ... The decisionist ruler must be the source of law, as diktat" (Lazar
   2006, 257).

13 For instance, in a recorded message to employees, Delta Air Lines CEO Richard
   Anderson expressed disappointment that international screening and passenger
   watch lists didn't prevent the attempted Christmas bombing of a Northwest Airlines
   flight from Amsterdam to Detroit. He reportedly said that Delta officials plan to

"make our points very clearly in Washington" as the Obama administration reviews the bombing attempt and air travel security procedures (Siemaszko 2010).

14 It is not clear that vitality is found wholly in what the individual may or may not be able to contribute. On the contrary, since at least the invention of the corporate legal subject, support for vitality is often support for corporate entities despite what such support might mean for individuals.

15 How population and population productivities are known and measured (in terms of threat, resource) depends on instruments that may be crafted as much for the productive negations of the *homo sacer.*

REFERENCES

Agamben, G. 1995. *Homo Sacer: Sovereign Power and Bare Life,* trans. D.H. Roazen. Stanford, CA: Stanford University Press.

Aradau, C., and R. van Munster. 2009. "Exceptionalism and the 'War on Terror': Criminology Meets International Relations." *British Journal of Criminology* 49 (5): 686-701.

Ashworth, A., and L. Zedner. 2008. "Defending the Criminal Law: Reflections on the Changing Character of Crime, Procedure, and Sanction." *Criminal Law and Philosophy* 2: 21-51.

BBC News. 2009. "Appeal over Torture Claim Ruling." http://news.bbc.co.uk/.

BC Civil Liberties Association. 2009. Richard Colvin documents. http://www.bccla. org/antiterrorissue/ColvinDocs3.pdf.

Bigo, D. 2001. "Liaison Officers in Europe: New Officers in the European Security Field." In *Issues in Transnational Policing,* ed. by J. Sheptycki, 67-99. London: Routledge.

CBC News. 2010. "Hog Workers Approve Contract that Aids Foreign Workers: Deal with Maple Leaf Foods Helps Fast-Track Immigration Status." CBC News Manitoba, 5 January. http://www.cbc.ca/.

Colvin, Richard. 2009. "Further Evidence of Richard Colvin to the Special Committee on Afghanistan, December 16, 2009." CBC: http://www.cbc.ca/.

Commission for Public Complaints Against the RCMP. 2009. *Report Following a Public Interest Investigation into a Chair-Initiated Complaint Respecting the Death in RCMP Custody of Mr. Robert Dziekanski.* http://www.cpc-cpp.gc.ca/.

Deleuze, G. 1992. "Postscript on the Societies of Control." *October* 59 (Winter): 3-7.

Donzelot, J. 2008. "Michel Foucault and Liberal Intelligence." *Economy and Society* 37: 115-34.

Elmer, G., and A. Opel. 2006. "Surviving the Inevitable Future: Preemption in the Age of Faulty Intelligence." *Cultural Studies* 20 (4-5): 477-92.

Ericson, R. 1982. *The Ordering of Justice: A Study of Accused Persons as Dependents in the Criminal Process.* Toronto: University of Toronto Press.

Ericson, R., and K. Haggerty. 1997. *Policing the Risk Society.* Toronto: University of Toronto Press.

Forcese, D. 2008. "The Collateral Consequence of Collaboration: The Consequence for Civil and Human Rights of Transnational Intelligence Sharing." Draft paper presented to the Conference on Intelligence Sharing, Oslo.

Foucault, M. 1971. "Orders of Discourse." *Social Science Information* 10 (2): 7-30.

Holquist, P. 1997. "'Information Is the Alpha and Omega of Our Work': Bolshevik Surveillance in Its Pan-European Context." *Journal of Modern History* 69 (3): 415-50.

House of Commons Standing Committee on Public Safety and National Security. 2009. "Evidence, Tuesday, March 24, 2009" (print version). http://www.parl.gc.ca/.

Humphreys, Adrian. 2008. "9/11 Skeptics Resurface." *National Post,* 20 October.

Iacobucci, Frank. 2008. *The Internal Inquiry into the Actions of Canadian Officials in Relation to Abdullah Almalki, Ahmad Abou-Elmaati and Muayyed Nureddin.* Ottawa: Queen's Printer.

Inge, J., and E. Findlay. 2006. "North American Defense and Security after 9/11." *Joint Force Quarterly* (40): 23-28.

Kalajdzic, J. 2009. "Access to Justice for the Wrongfully Accused in National Security Investigations." *Windsor Yearbook of Access to Justice* 27: 171-205.

Klein, N. 2008. *The Shock Doctrine: The Rise of Disaster Capitalism.* Toronto: Vintage.

Lazar, N.C. 2006. "Must Exceptionalism Prove the Rule: An Angle on Emergency Government in the History of Political Thought." *Politics and Society* 34 (2): 245-75.

Lippmann, W. 1922 [1997]. *Public Opinion.* New York: Free Press Paperbacks.

MacLeod, Ian. 2009. "New CSIS Director Tees Off on Critics of Anti-Terrorism Fight." *CanWest News Service.*

McCulloch, J., and S. Pickering. 2009. "Precrime and Counter-Terrorism: Imagining Future Crime in the 'War on Terror.'" *British Journal of Criminology* 49 (5): 626-45.

Mythen, G., and S. Walklate. 2006. "Criminology and Terrorism: Which Thesis? Risk Society or Governmentality?" *British Journal of Criminology* 46 (3): 379-98.

National Security Criminal Investigations. 2009. Workshop, RCMP NSCI, RCMP HQ, Ottawa, 16-17 January (all references made under the Chatham House Rule).

Naumetz, Tim. 2011. "Harper Extending Personal Control to Oversight of National Security and Intelligence Gathering." *Hill Times* Online. http://hilltimes.com/.

Neocleous, M. 2006. "From Social to National Security: On the Fabrication of Economic Order." *Security Dialogue* 37 (3): 363-84.

O'Connor, Dennis. 2006. *Commission of Inquiry into the Actions of Canadian Officials in Relation to Maher Arar.* Ottawa: Canadian Government Publishing.

–. 2008. *Report of the Events Relating to Maher Arar,* ADDENDUM Disclosure of Information Authorized by the Federal Court of Canada in Accordance with Sections 38.04 and 38.06 of the *Canada Evidence Act.*

O'Connor Commission (Commission of Inquiry into the Actions of Canadian Officials in Relation to Maher Arar). 2005. "Public Hearing, Wednesday, August 24, 2005" (transcript of proceedings). http://www.stenotran.com/commission/maherarar/2005-08-24%20volume%2041.pdf.

Pape, R. 2003. "The Strategic Logic of Suicide Terrorism." *American Political Science Review* 97 (3): 1-19.

Pither, K. 2008. *Dark Days: The Story of Four Canadians Tortured in the Name of Fighting Terror.* Toronto: Viking.

RCMP NSCI. 2009. "Report of the Events Relating to Maher Arar: The RCMP's Response to Recommendations." National Security Criminal Investigations Workshop, Ottawa, 16-17 January.

Roy, J. 2005. "Security, Sovereignty and Continental Interoperability: Canada's Elusive Balance." *Social Science Computer Review* 23 (4): 463-79.

Salamon, L.M. 2001. "The New Governance and the Tools of Public Action: An Introduction." *Fordham Urban Law Journal* 28: 1611-74.

–. 2002. *The Tools of Government: A Guide to the New Governance.* New York: Oxford University Press.

Shapiro, S., and R. Steinzor. 2006. "The People's Agent: Executive Branch Secrecy and Accountability in an Age of Terrorism." *Law and Contemporary Problems* 66: 98-129.

Sheptycki, J. 2004. "Review of the Influence of Strategic Intelligence on Organized Crime Policy and Practice." Development and Statistics Directorate Special Interest Paper No. 14. London: Home Office Research.

Siemaszko, Corky. 2010. "Delta CEO Says Don't Blame Attack on Northwest Airlines Flight 253 – Blame the Feds." *New York Daily News,* 1 January 2010. http://www.nydailynews.com/.

Swire, P. 2006. "Privacy and Information Sharing in the War on Terrorism." *Villanova Law Review* 51: 951-80.

Tilly, C. 2004. "Trust and Rule." *Theory and Society* 33 (1): 1-30.

Walker, C. 2008. "Know Thine Enemy as Thy Friend: Discerning Friend from Foe in Anti-Terrorism Laws." *Melbourne University Law Review* 32: 275-301.

Whitaker, R., and S. Farson. 2009. "Accountability in and for National Security." *IRPP Choices* 15 (9): 2-51.

Wilford, H. 2008. *The Mighty Wurlitzer: How the CIA Played America.* Cambridge, MA: Harvard University Press.

Wilsnack, R. 1980. "Information Control: A Conceptual Framework for Sociological Analysis." *Social Problems* 8 (4): 467-99.

Zogby International. 2004. "Half of New Yorkers Believe US Leaders Had Foreknowledge of Impending 9/11 Attacks and 'Consciously Failed' to Act." Zogby International press release. http://www.911truth.org/.

LEGISLATION CITED

Access to Information Act, R.S.C. 1985, c. A-1.

Canadian Charter of Rights and Freedoms, Part 1 of the *Constitution Act, 1982,* being Schedule B to the *Canada Act 1982* (U.K.), 1982, c. 11, s. 6.

Canadian Security Intelligence Service Act, R.S.C. 1985, c. C-23.

CASES CITED

Almalki et al. v. Attorney General of Canada et al. (4 May 2009), Court File No. 06-CV-035416 (Ont. Sup. Ct.).

Benamar Benatta v. The Attorney General of Canada et al. (4 November 2008), Court File No. 07-CV-336613PD3 (Ont. Sup. Ct.).

Canada (Justice) v. Khadr, 2008 SCC 28, [2008] 2 S.C.R. 125.

Canada (Royal Canadian Mounted Police) v. Canada (Attorney General), 2005 F.C.A. 213.

Charkaoui v. Canada (Citizenship and Immigration), 2008 SCC 38, [2008] 2 S.C.R. 326.

Harkat (Re), 2009 F.C. 1050, [2010] 4 F.C.R. 149, Docket: DES-5-08, 15 October 2009.

Canada (Citizenship and Immigration) v. Mahjoub, 2009 F.C. 439.

Re Almrei, 2009 F.C. 1263.

INTERNATIONAL AGREEMENT CITED

Convention against Torture and Other Cruel, Inhuman or Degrading Treatment or Punishment, 10 December 1984, 1464 U.N.T.S. 85 (entered into force 26 June 1987).

Accessing Dirty Data
Methodological Strategies for Social Problems Research

YAVAR HAMEED AND JEFFREY MONAGHAN

Like a river, researchers follow the path of least resistance.
Or, perhaps better, like immigrants, we tend to go where, if we
are not necessarily welcomed, we are at least tolerated. Often,
of course, this is at the bidding (or at least with the resources)
of the very elites who sit atop mountains of dirty data.

– Gary Marx

There is no consensus on what it means to study "social problems."[1] For those of us who research issues of social injustice, it involves looking up hierarchies of power to demand how an increasing number of intolerable conditions can be tolerated. Invariably, researching the construction and/or management of "social problems" includes consideration of the contentious decisions made and practices carried out by governmental actors and agencies. Curious social problems researchers are rarely welcomed by those agencies they seek to research, however. In Canada, a common tool for accessing behind-the-scenes governmental decision-making processes is the *Access to Information Act (ATIA),* but the toothlessness of current non-binding oversight agencies limits the reliability of access to information (ATI) as a research method.[2] The greatest concern facing ATI users is that the adjudication of requests has become an institutional process that is, according to a host of critics, reliably unreliable.

It has been over twenty-five years since Gary Marx outlined the methodological challenges that face researchers wanting to access "dirty and hidden data." These are the evidentiary trails produced and hidden by government. According to Marx (1984, 79) dirty data is "information which is kept secret and whose revelation would be discrediting or costly in terms of various types of sanctioning." Marx argued that social problems researchers face a variety of measures that impede the release of dirty data, and he issued a challenge intended to spark a discussion about strategies to uncover these hidden gems. The government's impetus for controlling the outflow of information can arise from a range of objectives, from the banality of risk management, to partisan objectives that are associated with the control of sensitive issues, to the suppression of illegality or corruption. Despite the breadth of importance, there is a small literature on dirty data research issues. Despite Marx's calls for increased scholarship on the subject, there has been a lack of interest within fields of methodological research to debate and expand on his work. Contributing to Marx's conceptual and methodological work, this chapter explores two contemporary case studies of dirty data research within the Canadian legal/juridical context. In particular, the cases of Jeffrey Monaghan and Abousfian Abdelrazik highlight how researchers can utilize the *ATIA,* the *Privacy Act,* and litigation as tools to access dirty data.

We begin by further outlining Marx's description of dirty data. We then explore the current barriers to information access in Canada. After reviewing the literature on dirty data and the challenges facing ATI users, we present two cases that include a number of ATI strategies and tactics. The case of Jeffrey Monaghan demonstrates the contrast between the use of *ATIA* and *Privacy Act* methods and civil litigation, and suggests that lawsuits are, despite their economic inaccessibility, a useful methodological tactic when researching particular subjects. In contrast, the case of Abousfian Abdelrazik suggests that contentious litigation with federal government departments produces a defensive and ethically questionable suppression and/ or delay of information disclosure in both the litigation process and parallel *ATIA* and *Privacy Act* requests. In *Abdelrazik v. Canada (Minister of Foreign Affairs), Privacy Act* requests conducted pre- and post litigation were markedly different. This material offers empirical evidence for what Marx (1984, 89) termed "giveaways," where "persons do not realize they are revealing dirty data." Both *Monaghan v. Canada (Attorney General)* and *Abdelrazik* highlight broader dilemmas facing ATI users and social problems researchers: namely, how can we pierce the secrecy that so often surrounds subjects that are perceived as potentially contentious, damaging, or illegal? This chapter explores two cases that utilize diverse strategies for accessing dirty data, with an emphasis on *Privacy Act* requests and civil litigation.

In Canada, access to information has been a subject of debate for at least four decades (see Knight 1966; Roberts 2005). We position Marx's conceptual framework within the current crisis facing ATI processes in Canada. As described below in the section on current barriers to information access, recent controversies have sparked a renewed critical interest in the subject. The sponsorship scandal, the widespread disappointment of stakeholders over the ill-constructed *Federal Accountability Act,* Canada's shameful record on rendition cases, the four-year-and-counting Afghan torture cover-up, increasingly vocal conflicts between the federal Information Commissioner(s) and federal departments, and a host of examples of boondoggled ATI files have highlighted systemic failings endemic to Canada's ATI practices. The common thread among these examples is that they are all highly contentious files that present a risk to ruling governments. These are the conditions that give rise to dirty data.

As frequent users of both federal and provincial access and privacy legislation, we believe that the challenge of uprooting contentious material requires researchers to develop methodological strategies that adapt to – and even pre-empt – the capacities of governments to limit released material. Despite the small literature on dirty data research issues, this chapter highlights possibilities of inquiry and action for social problems researchers in the hope of strengthening our capacities and knowledge base in the use of existing tools. As a method of doing so, we appropriate a term used by the courts on issues of national security – the "mosaic effect." This refers to information released in portions that, when collected and analyzed, reveals more than its parts in isolation. Through enculturating a strategy of research mosaics, we demonstrate that dispersed tapestries of data can be woven into empirical material for users of the *ATIA* and litigation processes. As we argue, a strategy that utilizes "mosaic effects" can engage multiple access avenues, premised on an understanding that concealment and suppression practices may be successful in stymieing the outflow of information but that these efforts cannot be complete.

The Dirty Data Problem

The challenge of uprooting contentious material held by government departments has been called the "hidden or dirty data problem" (Marx 1984, 78). Marx discusses the means by which some social problems researchers confront this problem in their attempts to procure dirty data "which insiders wish to keep secret and whose revelation would be discrediting or costly in terms of various types of sanctioning." Through various means of collection – experiments, accidents, whistleblowing, coercive institutionalized discovery practices, and so on – these hidden gems can be produced. For Marx, the existence of dirty data is more than an inability to properly fulfill institutional duties of transparency. It reveals deliberate forms of data hiding by governmental powers.

As Marx (1984, 81) explains, dirty data are produced where "the vested interest in maintaining secrecy may be much stronger because illegal or immoral actions are involved and the costs of public disclosure very high." The desire for insiders to maintain a veil of secrecy can stem from a number of reasons, although the most relevant to social problems researchers are related to actions that breach the legal and moral expectations of government. Marx (1984, 80) writes: "Issues of hidden and dirty data are likely to be involved to the extent that the study of social problems confronts behaviour that is illegal, the failure of an agency or individual to meet responsibilities, cover-ups, and the use of illegal or immoral means." Accessing information held by the government enables researchers to scrutinize the actions of these agencies. Inquiries are initiated because researchers are alerted to the general existence of material, normally as a result of government practices. Dirty data are thus less about the information per se than about the actions that become detailed through texts and communications. Trails of dirty data name names, provide details, and offer explanations of contentious issues of public interest that governments seek to suppress.

The purpose of the *ATIA* is to fulfill a commitment to transparent processes. Governments are less forthcoming in practice, however, especially as researchers – in their attempts to understand the motivations and contexts of decisions – advance up the hierarchies of power. This is magnified in the case of contentious files, where opposition groups, concerned individuals, and victims are directly impacted by the actions of government. The question facing social problems researchers is how can we pierce these spaces of contentious information? Considering more specifically those working on uprooting material on particular, contemporary issues, how can we get access to material that government agencies are opposed to revealing? Finally, how can we do this in a timely fashion, so that the products of our research are "actionable" in terms of these debates? These questions are instrumental for improving our abilities to challenge the practices of government (see also Chapters 9 and 13).

ATI and freedom of information (FOI) legislation has emerged as one among many tools for challenging the bureaucracy's power over these stores of hidden knowledge. As Shapiro and Steinzor (2006, 100) note, the spirit of freedom of information legislation speaks to "the democratic principle that people have a right to know about business transacted in their name." In Canada, the media have been especially active users of ATI methods to investigate stories, but not without criticism and frustration (Bronskill 1999; Chapters 11 and 12). The *ATIA* has been a subject of heated political debate in Canada. The most notable aspect of this debate is the gulf between rhetoric and substantive reform. Before discussing the case studies, it is important to contextualize our discussion of the *ATIA, Privacy Act,* and litigation strategies within the current problems plaguing Canada's ATI system.

Current Barriers to Access in Canada

During the 2006 federal election, the Conservative Party made accountability a central element of its platform, seizing the ethical high ground in the wake of the sponsorship scandal.[3] In the lead-up to the election, Stephen Harper pledged radical changes to the way in which ATI works in Canada. He wrote in an op-ed: "Information is the lifeblood of a democracy. Without adequate access to key information about government policies and programs, citizens and parliamentarians cannot make informed decisions, and incompetent or corrupt governance can be hidden under a cloak of secrecy" (Harper 2005). During the election campaign, he pledged a major overhaul, including expansion of the Information Commissioner of Canada's powers, reduction of the scope of cabinet-confidence exclusion, and procedures to prevent officials from dodging the access law through record-avoidance strategies.[4] Following the 2006 election, the Conservatives made access to information and transparency central themes of Canadian political discourse. In contrast to this rhetoric, however, the only significant improvement to ATI processes made by the Harper government has been the opening up of Crown corporations to access requests (Whittington 2008). On the other hand, the Harper government has compiled a sizable record of broken promises and mechanisms to protect government secrecy.

These began with the deceptively named *Federal Accountability Act.* As an indication of the dramatic shortcomings of the act, then Information Commissioner John Reid was one of the proposed legislation's most vocal critics. Only three months after the Conservatives were sworn in, Reid released an "emergency report" that coincided with the act's presentation to Parliament. He declared that "no previous government has put forward a more retrograde and dangerous set of proposals" with respect to the amendments to the *ATIA* (McMurdy 2006). Reid's term ended in September 2006. His replacement, Robert Marleau, continued the office's vocal criticisms of the Harper record.[5] The first report he wrote as commissioner condemned the *Federal Accountability Act:* "A government's access reform bill might weaken access, not strengthen it! From a government's perspective, reform might entail making it easier to justify secrecy, making it more expensive to use the *Act,* weakening the power of oversight, removing classes of records from the *Act*'s coverage, and so forth" (Aubry 2007). The following year, he warned that, contrary to Harper's pledge to make the federal government more transparent, a "fog over information" has crept across the bureaucracy (Greenaway 2008). The following summer, simmering tensions over a series of 150 "severally delayed" requests boiled over when Marleau threatened to "walk into PCO next week ... for files they didn't give us." In an interview, he added: "We're going to take them and they can't stop us" (Campion-Smith 2009).

In another highly visible conflict, Marleau publicly condemned what he described as a "communications stranglehold" over the bureaucracy. This occurred after Justice Minister Rob Nicholson quietly posted on the website of the House of Commons Standing Committee on Access to Information, Privacy and Ethics that he was not taking any action on Marleau's twelve-point proposal on access reform. Nicholson's decision was at odds with the fact that the wide-ranging recommendations had been unanimously confirmed by the committee, which included Conservative Members of Parliament (*Saskatoon StarPhoenix* 2009). In his public comments, Marleau explicitly connected the Harper government's control over government communications with the inability to access information through ATI mechanisms (Campion-Smith 2009). Instead of forthright ATI reforms, the Harper government has gone to absurd lengths to protect information. The Tories have gone so far as to defend the government's practices against a lawsuit initiated by themselves – as the Canadian Alliance – over former Liberal Prime Minister Jean Chrétien's refusal to hand over portions of his agendas. The Tories went to the Federal Court of Canada – and won – to ensure that notes made by cabinet ministers (and their offices) are not subject to the *ATIA* (Clark 2008).

These attacks on ATI processes are symptoms of an ill system, with ailments that certainly predate the transparency-averse Harper Tories. In 2005, the Canadian Newspaper Association presented evidence to the Office of the Information Commissioner describing a federal government policy of "amber lighting" or "red flagging" that had been detailed by investigative journalist Ann Rees (2003a). Roberts (2005) and Rees (2003a, 2003b) describe "amber lighting" as "a highly sophisticated, government-wide access to information surveillance system" (Rees, 2003a). It allows political and communications officials "to view sensitive records, to question access and FOI staff about what they intend to release, and to delay release until they are satisfied that they have identified all troublesome issues and prepared their political masters with a soothing public response" (Rees 2003a). Although the process of politically screening potentially "sensitive" requests had been long suspected, Rees catalogued and described its systematic practice within the federal bureaucracy. Despite denials about the existence of such programs, subsequent research has confirmed the use of amber lighting as a term and a practice in the federal government. According to an e-mail dated 12 June 2006, from Citizenship and Immigration Canada access coordinator Heather Primeau, the government is "amber lighting" access requests that are considered to be more politically sensitive (Thompson 2006). The purpose of amber lighting is clearly defined at the bottom of the e-mail: "The amber light process is a heads up process to advise senior management of upcoming access to information releases that may attract media or political attention" (Thompson 2006).

Amber-lighting policies are methods of systematically guarding against the release of dirty data. They identify the likely categories of dirty data researchers and, through formal and informal channels, delay and/or omit the release of sensitive material. This practice has predominantly targeted media and political parties (Rees 2003a; Roberts 2005), but its impacts affect all users of the ATI system. Roberts (2005, 10) discusses how data management software used by federal departments and agencies supports the "task of communications management."[6] There are also forms of bureaucratic culture that produce "informal laws" when processing potentially sensitive ATI requests (Mashaw 1983; Roberts 2002a, 2002b). Under sometimes intense pressure, ATI bureaucracies have produced practices that go against the spirit of access legislation. Roberts (2005, 1) describes these measures by explaining that the *ATIA* was initially intended to "constrain executive authority, but officials developed internal routines and technologies to minimize its disruptive potential."

Besides barriers within federal bureaucracies, the Harper government – displaying its distrust of public servants in general – has used amber-lighting protocols to ensure that all potentially sensitive requests are sent to the Privy Council Office (PCO) and Prime Minister's Office (PMO) for review

(Galloway 2010). As Gary Marx notes, however, efforts to contain the release of dirty data cannot be flawless. Often with contentious issues a number of individuals and departments are implicated. These issues are complex, further increasing the scope of contact and information production within the bureaucracy. The task facing social problems researchers lies in developing a repertoire of strategies and tactics that can probe and pry dirty data from the grip of these government bodies that conceal contentious information. As ATI users, we hope to contribute to these discussions through our two case studies, which utilize combinations of *ATIA* and *Privacy Act* requests. We also compare and contrast these ATI methods with litigation, highlight the advantages and disadvantages that arise in particular contexts, and demonstrate how these multiple strategies can be used in tandem during different dirty data campaigns.

The *Monaghan* Case

Our first case is that of Jeffrey Monaghan. *Monaghan v. Canada (Attorney General)* is a lawsuit over violations of the *Canadian Charter of Rights and Freedoms* that arose in a hastily organized (but highly publicized) criminal investigation. Unlike litigation that is explicitly focused on the release of data (see Yeager 2006), this lawsuit was in part initiated in an effort to discover whether data existed in the first place. In *Monaghan*, the material we sought was secondary to the actual argumentation over *Charter* violations by the RCMP, but the process of litigation was integral in procuring the data needed to validate the arguments advanced in the proceedings.

The particular aspects of institutional deviance in this case are somewhat minor but, in the context of the actions, garnered a greater degree of public attention because of a number of interrelated contentious issues. The case centres on the allegations that Monaghan, a low-level temporary worker at Environment Canada, leaked the Conservative government's "green plan" two weeks ahead of the highly anticipated, long-overdue, and carefully crafted official rollout. After Monaghan was arrested at his workplace, the RCMP participated in a highly politicized public relations campaign that, according to the plaintiff's argument, had little interest in anything to do with Monaghan but was undertaken in an attempt to intimidate and discipline the public service more broadly.[7]

A key strategy in *Monaghan* was to unearth dirty data that identified communications and coordination of the arrest and publicity campaign between political officials, department authorities, and the RCMP. To do so, we initiated a tiered ATI approach. First, we tried a general access request with the RCMP under a colleague's name, not invoking the *Privacy Act*. This request was made immediately following the arrest. Predictably, nothing in addition to media lines, transcripts, and news clips were released. It is worth mentioning that the overall number of documents, including withheld material, was substantially less than that released under subsequent *Privacy Act* requests. This could have been due to two possibilities. One was that the time frame could have allowed for more material to be produced. This was considered unlikely, however, after cross-referencing of dated material released under the subsequent request. The other possibility was that the first request could have had withheld information, through one process or another, a potential conclusion that we have no means of evaluating but that is nonetheless of interest.

As noted, the second request under the *Privacy Act* resulted in a significantly greater volume of material. Although the *Privacy Act* request was intended only to release materials redacted for privacy exceptions in the original ATI request, it in fact produced a much greater number of records. The additional materials were also very useful, but took almost a year and a half to produce. Departmental e-mails that were not included, or marked as redacted from the initial request, showed clear lines of communication between police and the bureaucracy in the process of staging the arrest. There was no information pertaining to the RCMP investigation and several files were still omitted from the material.[8] One element of the investigation that was revealed was an open and quickly closed investigation by the Integrated National Security Enforcement Team (INSET), the Mounties' anti-terrorism squad. As a result of media investigation into Monaghan's political involvements, INSET spent a couple of days googling Monaghan's anarcho-punk band and analyzing lyrics for potential threats to national security. As any rational mind might assume, the investigation did not produce much more than a couple of hours of anti-terror wages for INSET desk cops. The importance of the INSET investigation, however, is that it was likely another factor in the delay of the request. The addition of the national security agency added political sensitivity to the file. This played out after the media made light of the INSET investigation (Thompson 2008). The case offers an empirical demonstration of what scholars have noted (see Kirtley 2006 and Shapiro and Steinzor 2006) as an environment of hyper-secrecy on issues of national security (despite this case having nothing to do with terrorism). It also speaks to a history within Canadian security agencies of *producing* perceived threats to the national imagination (see Kinsman, Buse, and Steedman 2000).

Following the production of slightly improved data as a result of our tiered ATI strategy, we initiated a civil suit as our final stage. First, it should be noted that lawsuits as a data-gathering tool are not very accessible. Yeager (2006, 502) notes that limitations to using litigation as a data-gathering tool can include the costs, the commitment of time, and the delays involved. There is also a professionalization barrier. Unless individuals have the connections, training, education, and so on needed to research, write, and file a claim, it can be very onerous. Despite these barriers, *Monaghan* was successful in generating additional data. It is worth noting the sheer difference in volume of material between the *Privacy Act* request and the evidentiary disclosures in *Monaghan*. The former totalled 182 pages (including redactions), while the lawsuit produced more than a thousand pages of material. Much of this material was not included in, or was noted as an omission from, the original RCMP request. It included interviews with potential witnesses – despite assurances of anonymity in the interview process – and a final report of the investigation. It also produced a number of important internal communications not covered in previous requests, raising further questions about the contents of the first and second requests and the reliability of the *ATIA* measures when searching for key documents.

The lawsuit resulted in disclosure of an extraordinary quantity and quality of information, but there are also questions that arise when dealing with the reliability and honesty of evidentiary disclosure. Although the litigation was terminated by mutual agreement before trial, it should be noted that there are two additional issues to consider when using this tactic. First, as Yeager (2006) demonstrates, a researcher using litigation can positively influence the legal landscape with a friendly judgment. Besides compelling the production of important records, court findings can become incorporated into legal regulations. Positive decisions can potentially result in favourable rulings becoming cemented – temporarily, perhaps – within the case law (Yeager 2006, 509). On the other hand, negative decisions can also become difficult legal precedents for other researchers attempting to access dirty data. Besides these jurisprudential issues, litigation can also be very costly (Yeager 2006).

Unlike Yeager (2006), this case is not explicitly a lawsuit over data. It is a lawsuit concerning governmental activities, but accessing particular data is integral to demonstrating the course of these actions. Like other cases over the abuse of governmental powers, the imbalance of resources between individuals and government agencies is dramatic. As Rubin notes, it seems like a David-versus-Goliath battle, in which the odds are stacked against the citizen (Rubin 1986a, 1986b, 1990, quoted in Yeager 2006, 513). *Monaghan* demonstrates that ATI can be useful in uncovering data when researchers have a strong inclination about where those data are located. In addition, it demonstrates that litigation can force substantially larger volumes of information to the surface, ensuring that data previously unreleased – through questionable circumstances – are reviewed by Crown agents who are unconnected with the ATI division and the amber-lighting measures of the PCO/PMO. This extra oversight is particularly useful for social problems researchers because litigation provides an additional layer of accountability in terms of information review. Litigation also complements data collection efforts by subjecting a lens of scrutiny over the actions reflected in the data. For actors who are implicated in the particular subject of research, civil litigation also provides a useful means of redress in the face of governmental transgression. In this sense, *Monaghan* demonstrates that civil redress through litigation provides both dirty data and just desserts.

The *Abdelrazik* Case

Our second case study, *Abdelrazik v. Canada (Minister of Foreign Affairs),*[9] relates to a Federal Court application pursuant to section 6 of the *Charter* (i.e., the mobility right of Canadian citizens to enter and leave Canada) to repatriate Abousfian Abdelrazik, a Canadian citizen, to Canada. Abdelrazik had been detained by Sudan at Canada's request in 2003, and for six years was prevented by the Canadian government from returning to Canada because he was listed under a United Nations travel ban. The Federal Court determined, however, that the UN travel ban did not impede Abdelrazik's right of return to Canada, and the government was forced to order him back to Canada on 4 June 2009. *Abdelrazik* provides an interesting strategic counterpoint to *Monaghan,* in that highly significant information in *Abdelrazik* was obtained through pre-litigation *Privacy Act* requests, rather than disclosure received through procedural rules governing civil litigation. *Monaghan* highlights significant omissions in the government's responsiveness to *Privacy Act* and *ATIA* requests for information, compared with the relatively more expansive information disclosed through pre-trial discovery. In *Abdelrazik,* however, the process of civil litigation, mired in national security considerations, effectively heightened the latent censorship mechanisms. The different results that can be observed through information disclosure in *Abdelrazik* and *Monaghan* are instructive in terms of contextualizing Yeager's empirical research on data gathering within the broader context of the litigation of contentious legal and political cases where data disclosure per se is not the objective of the litigation.

Initial *Privacy Act* requests were submitted in 2005 through Abdelrazik's wife at the time. During this period, the Department of Foreign Affairs and International Trade (DFAIT) was constantly reassuring both Abdelrazik and his family that his case was being treated as a "normal" consular case.[10] Although this reassurance belied a complex network of political and bureaucratic interference aimed at preventing Abdelrazik's return, internal communications within DFAIT revealed the opinion that Abdelrazik's case would not receive the same kind of public exposure as that of Maher Arar, and would not cause similar outrage among Canadians.[11] In the shadows of a case that was intended to neither see the light of day nor stir public sentiment, *Privacy Act* material was presumably processed without an added layer of political sensitivity. Interestingly, DFAIT's early public relations strategy on *Abdelrazik* represents an inversion of the strategy employed in *Monaghan*. DFAIT displayed a passive approach towards suppressing the development of a media campaign, rather than a proactive media strategy that aimed to frame a media-oriented debate. Animating both cases, however, was the anticipation of public sentiment as the litmus test for transparency.

One of the key documents referred to in the Federal Court decision that ordered the Harper government to repatriate Abdelrazik is an internal undated memo stamped "CSIS." The document states that Abdelrazik was detained "at ... our request."[12] It was largely on the strength of this document, which remained uncontradicted through direct evidence during the course of the application, that Justice Russell Zinn concluded that Abdelrazik had been detained in Sudan at the request of the Canadian Security Intelligence Service (CSIS).[13] It is difficult to know whether this document would have been redacted by DFAIT had the profile of Abdelrazik's case already reached national headlines, but in subsequent *Privacy Act* requests and other litigation-based discovery, few documents proved to be as revealing as this and other information released through the initial *Privacy Act* request. Significantly, whereas the initial request was processed shortly after it was submitted, *Privacy Act* requests on behalf of Abdelrazik made to DFAIT in 2008 were not released until 2011.[14]

Canada Evidence Act Exemptions

As Yeager (2006) points out, the costs and administrative bureaucracy surrounding litigation act as significant disincentives to the use of lawsuits as a data-gathering process. Besides the cost barrier, *Abdelrazik* has unfolded under the haze of "national security," which provides the government with numerous ways to block, delay, or limit disclosure of information. Section 38 of the *Canada Evidence Act*, for example, allows the government to object to material being produced on the basis of potential injury to international relations, national defence, and/or national security. The section 38 *Canada Evidence Act* process does not technically arise from a specific objection. It can be triggered by a notice by counsel for the federal government to the Attorney General. Although the decision on whether to disclose information subject to this privilege claim must be made by the Attorney General within ten days of receiving the notice,[15] in practice the court does not enforce this requirement; instead, there is a complex process by which a specialized branch of the Department of Justice known as the National Security Group (NSG) vets all information.[16]

Were this a simple process of elimination arrived at by analyzing discrete pieces of information, the initial vetting would perhaps occur efficiently. The vetting process occurs, however, through overlapping and simultaneous comparisons of different pieces of information to verify whether partial disclosure placed in the context of other publicly available information or other sensitive and potentially privileged information would render information injurious to national security. National security agencies have termed this the "mosaic effect," whereby information that in isolation appears meaningless or trivial could, when fitted together, permit a comprehensive understanding of the information being protected.[17] The "mosaic effect" magnifies the degree of scrutiny and includes complex in camera proceedings to determine whether the privilege claim asserted is legitimate. Several national security cases have seen the Crown's use of the "mosaic effect" argument as a basis for stopping disclosure of evidence being held in secret against defendants. In Maher Arar's attempts to force the government to disclose certain redacted portions of the public report issued by the Commission of Inquiry into the Actions of Canadian Officials in Relation to Maher Arar, Justice Noel warned that merely invoking the claim of "mosaic effect" does not grant a carte blanche to the government: "At minimum, [the Crown] will have to provide some evidence to convince the Court that disclosure would be injurious due to the mosaic effect. Simply alleging a 'mosaic effect' is not sufficient" [*Canada (Attorney General) v. Canada (Commission of Inquiry into the Actions of Canadian Officials in Relation to Maher Arar)*, 252].

In *Abdelrazik*, the government's broad assertion of privilege under section 38 of the *Canada Evidence Act* was challenged by way of a Federal

Court application. The section 38 litigation process (a litigation within a litigation) was discontinued in this case, however, in view of the release of 208 highly redacted documents by the NSG (after a review of approximately five months). None of the redactions or any of the undisclosed documents were pursued, in the interest of expediting the hearing date.[18] It should be recalled that during the course of litigation before the Federal Court, which lasted fourteen months, Abdelrazik was living in difficult and humiliating circumstances in the Canadian Embassy in Khartoum (Aly 2008). In the interests of time, the record in support of his application was finalized on the basis of the 208 documents disclosed in conjunction with previous information obtained through *Privacy Act* requests, without further challenge to the broad-based national security privilege claims of the government.

Section 41 *Privacy Act* Applications

In cases of contentious litigation, the normal reluctance of the government to release potentially embarrassing information is compounded by other political interests, which make the process of information release untenable through direct negotiation with the government. In this context, the courts are positioned to play a useful role in adjudicating dispute over information access. For example, under the *Privacy Act,* at certain junctures within the *Abdelrazik* litigation other parallel applications were made to expedite the process of disclosure that had been dragging on for several months.[19] Simultaneous *Privacy Act* applications were made to numerous other government departments, each of which participates in controlling the international travel of persons in a national security context. Under section 14 of the *Privacy Act,* each department has thirty days to respond to a request for information. In certain instances, however, no response was provided. These matters were immediately referred to the Privacy Commissioner of Canada for a finding that the government was in violation of the *Privacy Act.* A finding of violation then provided the basis for an application to Federal Court authorized by section 41 of the *Privacy Act.* Under such applications, the Federal Court may order disclosure of information; more than likely, however, it may simply declare that there has been a violation of the act and impose a timetable for disclosure. The threat of judicial sanction worked in *Abdelrazik* to elicit some useful information from the government; however, the fact that other litigation needed to be initiated to make the government comply with its statutory obligations, even after a finding of violation of the act by the Privacy Commissioner, is illustrative of the kind of illegal and politically obstinate behaviour that frustrates *Privacy Act* disclosure during the process of litigation. Significantly, a section 41 *Privacy Act* application was not filed, nor was it required to elicit the pre-litigation disclosure received in *Abdelrazik*.

Other "Giveaways"

In the project of uprooting dirty data, Gary Marx (1984, 89) used the term "giveaways" to describe examples where "persons do not realize they are revealing dirty data." As described above, the nature of privilege claimed under the rubric of national security may engage overlapping and far-reaching considerations that have more to do with face saving than any serious injury to the security of the nation. This is evident through a comparison of the information released through the initial *Privacy Act* requests in *Abdelrazik* (requests that included important giveaways) with subsequent efforts by the government to suppress the release of information. The dramatic shift by the government occurred during the highly publicized legal campaign to secure Abdelrazik's return to Canada, but giveaways are not obtained exclusively in situations of lesser political sensitivity. Although as a general observation *Abdelrazik* supports the thesis that pre-litigation *Privacy Act* disclosure may see less inertia than widely reported litigation processes, there is nonetheless merit to seeking disclosure through litigation. Opportunities can be produced by engaging multiple and overlapping bureaucratic processes, which by their very nature – particularly when catalyzed by constant media scrutiny – are prone to produce error. Such error may be a manifestation of the reality that many actors cannot efficiently act in tandem to reinforce a unified narrative by suppressing unrelated data from diverse sources. The government's attempts to suppress information through its robust mechanisms of vetting and privilege claims, concomitantly isolate giveaways in a manner such that when small pieces of information are revealed that contradict the dominant government narrative, they cannot be explained away as there is no gray zone against which they can be tempered.

In *Abdelrazik*, some giveaways were produced in the course of the 208 documents that were revealed in the preliminary stage of the section 38 *Canada Evidence Act* process. Similarly, the section 41 *Privacy Act* applications also produced some valuable material for the litigation, albeit none as revealing as in the pre-litigation phase. The complexity of the litigation process and the value of information revealed therein illustrates something other than a linear relationship between information gains and litigation.

Scholars of ATI processes have been silent on the relative merits of different legal applications that may be used to enhance *Privacy Act* requests. To be sure, researchers will encounter a high level of redactions and dead ends; however, the awkward and slow-moving wheels of bureaucracy are ill suited to resist multiple and swift disclosure requests of different government departments, compounded by follow-up litigation within the litigation. Litigation as a data-gathering tool for the social problems researcher provides the researcher with the added benefit of framing a window into the machinations between political decision making, bureaucratic obfuscation, and questionable privilege claims.

Inducing Political Reaction and Information Gathering

The government's abilities to effectively "manage" the disclosure of contentious data are compromised where social problems researchers make simultaneous, overlapping information requests. Yet in the arena of politically sensitive cases, dirty data are not simply information held as an object for discovery by the researcher. They are also generated as a result of political events as they unfold and as they are induced by the process of litigation and underlying social mobilization.

Abdelrazik provides a telling example of this interplay between legal process, mobilization, and political reaction by government agencies. After years of promising him assistance, in December 2008 Passport Canada informed Abdelrazik that he would be provided with an Emergency Passport if only he could produce a confirmed *and paid-for* itinerary from Sudan to Canada (Koring 2009b). This additional condition (requiring a "paid-for itinerary") was made by Canada knowing that, by virtue of Abdelrazik's listing under UN Resolution 1267, it was a federal offence to provide any material or financial assistance to Abdelrazik. At the time, as now, Abdelrazik was impecunious and the Passport Canada condition presented a deliberately untenable requirement.

In response to these conditions, a grassroots social justice campaign was initiated. Motivated by concerns over Abdelrazik's treatment, the campaign was aided by the data gathered by his legal counsel. In an act of civil disobedience, the grassroots coalition known as Project Fly Home[20] decided to purchase Abdelrazik's ticket, thereby risking federal prosecution and a sentence of a fine up to $10,000 or two years in jail.[21] In early March 2009, the group publicly announced its purchase of a ticket for Abdelrazik, departing from Khartoum for Canada on 3 April 2009. While legal counsel for

Abdelrazik attempted to get assurances from DFAIT in the three weeks leading up to the flight, no definitive response was provided. Finally, on the morning of 3 April, shortly after 6:00 AM Eastern Standard Time, just hours before Abdelrazik would have had to report to the airport, legal counsel for Foreign Affairs Minister Lawrence Cannon sent a letter to Abdelrazik's counsel stating that he was now considered to be a threat to the security of Canada or another nation pursuant to section 10.1 of the Canadian Passport Order.[22] Significantly, while Project Fly Home enjoyed popular support (from politicians to famous Canadian celebrities) and published the names of over one hundred contributors to the ticket purchase, the DFAIT has never provided the particulars of how or why it designated Abdelrazik a security threat, this in spite of Abdelrazik's exoneration of any criminal wrongdoing by both the RCMP and CSIS.[23]

The rash response of the Foreign Affairs Minister stood out as a summary conclusion developed in a vacuum of evidence. More telling than the suppressed vaults of dirty data lying beyond the reach of Abdelrazik and the public, the government's own ill-conceived political decision revealed the paltry nature of its case against Abdelrazik. Indeed, it was in large part based on the unsubstantiated, procedurally unfair, and clearly obstructionist measures by Canada that the Federal Court determined that the actions of the government were tantamount to acting in bad faith.[24] And so, while the courts were not immediately willing to impugn the ethical character of the Canadian government, strong aspersions were cast against the conduct of Canadian officials and, by extension, their lawyers.

The Ethics of Information Management

Information discovery as a locus of struggle, we argue, reveals the protectionist attitude of political actors as well as government officials who cooperate in the suppression of dirty data. The most explicit symptoms of these practices are revealed by the vacuous nature of privilege claims asserted in the context of national security cases. In these cases, we have to ask: what do these efforts to obstruct disclosure of information say about the lawyers who advance these claims? The relationship between Crown lawyers and the political interests of government departments represents a special case of the solicitor/client relationship. Should the Crown lawyer act – as do civil litigants – to defend the interests of their clients at all costs, or are there broader interests that militate against this purely adversarial role? It is broadly recognized that government lawyers have certain material and policy encumbrances that make them a different breed. Moreover, since Crown lawyers are paid by public monies, their role, if not directly controlled by the public interest, is one that bears a strong affinity to the welfare and virtue of public concerns (Hutchinson 2008).

Regardless of whether one ascribes a different or higher standard to Crown lawyers, larger ethical issues are raised in cases such as *Abdelrazik* where the suppression of information relates to the complicity of government officials in detaining and torturing a Canadian citizen. The behaviour of Crown lawyers in the case of *Abdelrazik* was completely at odds with the humanitarian urgency of resolving his case as a Canadian citizen in detention and at risk of torture. Instead, it was clearly influenced by the political contingencies of the governing party. Under the guise of national security, the pragmatic consequences of these political interests were reflected in the overbroad privilege claims.

Given the previously described amorphous quality of "national security" privilege, it is open to legal counsel to adopt either circumscribed or more expansive parameters of privilege. There is no necessity to make broad privilege claims when such privilege is discretionary and would require extensive litigation pursuant to section 38 of the *Canada Evidence Act* to be finally resolved. The resulting delay in this sense becomes a political negotiating tool to avoid embarrassment. In another glaring example of ethically questionable conduct, Crown lawyers maintained in Federal Court that DFAIT was doing everything possible to repatriate Abdelrazik back to Canada on a Lufthansa flight in July 2004 (a cornerstone of the government's response), despite information in their possession showing that DFAIT had ordered that he *not* be permitted to board the flight in question.[25] At the very least, it would have been incumbent on the government to have disclosed such relevant information prior to the hearing of Abdelrazik's application. Such information, however, was obtained by Abdelrazik only through a *Privacy Act* request that was disclosed after the application was argued in Federal Court in early May 2009.

Significantly, lawyers for the Department of Justice were able to argue their case by creating a schism between their legal case and the real world. The day before the application was argued (6 May 2009), the coordinator for the monitoring team of UN Resolution 1267 spoke publicly to Canadian media sources saying that the resolution did not pose an obstacle to Abdelrazik's return to Canada (Koring 2009a). In a sidebar, however, Crown lawyers for the Justice Department made it clear that they would strenuously object to any attempt to refer to this fact, which had at the time made national headlines in Canada. In other words, where suppression of information had failed, it appears that government lawyers had instructions to maintain their position and argue it all costs, no matter how absurd it was as a matter of principle and no matter that it conflicted with reason, common sense, and the interests of justice. And so the ethical propriety of information suppression not only by political officials but also by their lawyers must be contextualized within a culture defined by maintaining the narrow self-interest of a government driven by image protection and political self-interest. If the political masters and custodians of dirty data had been interested in squarely addressing controversial social problems in the nature of Abdelrazik's predicament, his repatriation would have been effected years ago, thereby obviating the need to generate troves of information justifying his exile without calling it such. As our investigation reveals, however, the seeds of dirty data are nourished precisely by the dirt of ethically dubious decisions enriched by the legal, political, and bureaucratic manure of government departments.

Conclusions

The cases of *Abdelrazik* and *Monaghan* demonstrate that, despite numerous barriers, social problems researchers can make methodological decisions that can help uncover dirty data. In the field of contentious issues, information gathering is rarely an issue of one-off silver bullets that can be recovered through a single, simple document. Issues that government agencies attempt to conceal often involve layers of complexity and must be pursued through rolling, flexible research manoeuvres. Of course, an example such as the *Abdelrazik* correspondence data proving that his detention and torture in Sudan was initiated "at our request" is an exception to this. Even with examples where seemingly indisputable pieces of data have been obtained, however, these bits of dirty data must be correlated with other information that provides details of context, the names of actors, and other supplementary evidence. In the face of government obfuscation, denial, and the resources to guard secrecy, aggregating large amounts of information that surrounds contentious issues is integral to the abilities of social problems researchers and their allies to mount a public challenge against the dubious actions of government. In a sense, this strategy of rolling, layered research aims to exploit its own form of "mosaic effect."

The mosaic effect occurs because information is released (or acquired) through multiple avenues of access. For researchers to take advantage of mosaic effects, the numerous methods for accessing dirty data must contend with the institutional barriers that limit information disclosure. These include amber lighting, shoddy and unaccountable *ATIA* and *Privacy Act* disclosures, and privilege claims during litigation. We emphasize, however, that the many actors who participate in the concealment of contentious material are prone to error. Mosaic effect strategies can exploit these errors with patient and strategically minded research.

While it is possible for researchers to access information on government malfeasance, these achievements are largely a result of discipline, innovation, and persistence. As Marx notes in the analogy cited at the beginning of this chapter, researchers often follow the path of least resistance, often acquiescing to the suppressive power of government information sources. One could argue that users of *ATIA* are fulfilling Marx's analogy, which laments researchers who behave like the amenable river, which moves according to the will of elites. Although this argument may have some merit, we would suggest that the problems facing access to information in Canada are largely the result of a dysfunctional system and the nature of political power, not the lack of ingenuity or effort by the ethically oriented research community. We might suggest that researchers – many of whom are very well aware – need to develop methods in addition to those most traditionally utilized. Litigation could be an additional resource, but we do have several reservations regarding this. Likewise, we suggest that social problems researchers can benefit from the cultivation of "mosaic effect" strategies, but that these are no substitute for radical transformations in access to information systems.

NOTES

1 See Best 2002 for a discussion of debates concerning the sociology of social problems.

2 See Chapter 2 for an excellent overview of the ATI/FOI ombudsman field and a discussion of the different powers associated with certain jurisdictions.

3 The "sponsorship scandal" involved a series of funds and programs that funnelled money through Liberal Party organs and associates ostensibly to battle the separatist movement in Québec. These activities culminated in a public commission – the Gomery Inquiry – called by Liberal Prime Minister Jean Chrétien. Concluding the inquiry, Justice John Gomery made nineteen recommendations that aimed to improve government transparency, accountability, and access to information. It should be noted that Justice Gomery has been critical of the lack of government action on his recommendations, especially since the Tories adopted much of his report's language and content in their political messaging. He has stated: "The current

government ran for election in 2006 on a platform promising integrity, accountability and transparency. On the transparency issue, its promises have simply not been fulfilled." He added that despite the volume of criticism, the federal government has shown "total inaction" (Casey 2009).

4 In 2006, the Harper Conservatives vowed to "implement the Information Commissioner [John Reid's] recommendations for reform of the *Access to Information Act*," but they abandoned Reid's proposed *Open Government Act* despite their pledge to include Reid's reforms in their *Federal Accountability Act*. In a public speech, Reid speculated: "Somehow, while we were feeling pretty good about the future of accountability through transparency, it all seems to have fallen apart" (Leblanc 2008).

5 We should note that numerous media reports questioned the independence of Marleau, a former Clerk of the House of Commons (Aubry 2007; Auld 2008; Clark 2007). It should also be noted that in May 2007, the Conservatives laid off longtime defender of the *ATIA* Alan Leadbeater. Leadbeater, a fifteen-year veteran bureaucrat in the Office of the Information Commissioner of Canada, was given two weeks' notice and escorted from the building. Officials denied any motives related to Leadbeater's criticisms of the government and insisted that the move was part of reforms to the management structure (Clark 2007).

6 Roberts discusses the use of a software program called *ATIPflow*. As of this writing, however, several federal departments have upgraded to *AccessPro*, a customized program by the same provider, Privasoft, designed to meet specific demands set out by the federal government.

7 For full argument, see *Monaghan v. Canada (Attorney General)*. The RCMP disputes these claims. The proceedings were settled out of court.

8 Predominantly, sections used to omit data were 16(1)(i) and 16(1)(c), pertaining to ongoing investigations.

9 See *Abdelrazik v. Canada (Foreign Affairs)*, 2009 F.C. 580.

10 See, for example, the 3 March 2004 e-mail memo received through a *Privacy Act* request. The memo from consular staff to the Head of Canadian Mission in Sudan indicates that once Abdelrazik was released from detention, he would be provided with "normal consular services available to Canadians released from custody." It is clear, however, that even consular staff were unaware of what "normal consular services" meant in this context.

11 A secret 16 October 2003 memo from R.S. Heatherington, Director of Foreign Intelligence Division, contained within the initial *Privacy Act* disclosure states: "We judge it unlikely that, should Abdelrazik's detention in Sudan become public knowledge, there would be the same sort of outcry that surrounded Maher Arar's arrest and deportation from the USA."

12 The initial *Privacy Act* disclosure contains a secret memo that states in its introduction: "Mr. A. travelled to Sudan in March 2003 in order to visit his family. He was traveling on his Canadian passport. In August 2003, he was arrested and detained by Sudanese authorities [redacted text] Sudanese authorities readily admit that they have no charges pending against him but are holding him at our request [redacted text]."

13 *Abdelrazik v. Canada (Minister of Foreign Affairs),* 2009 F.C. 580 at para. 91.
14 Until 2011, DFAIT was in non-compliance with disclosure requirements under the 2008 *Privacy Act* request. There are still concerns, however, that the ultimate disclosure received is not substantially compliant with DFAIT's obligations under the *Privacy Act.*
15 *Canada Evidence Act,* s. 38.03(3).
16 The mandate and scope of responsibilities of the National Security Group of the Department of Justice is set out at http://www.justice.gc.ca. In practice, the Federal Court does not enforce strict deadlines to pressure the work of the NSG; rather, it offers a parallel form of case management to expedite evidentiary disputes and narrow the breadth of requests.
17 For detailed discussion of the "mosaic effect," see *Henrie v. Canada (Security Intelligence Review Committee); Canada (Attorney General) v. Khawaja;* and *Canada (Attorney General) v. Canada (Commission of Inquiry into the Actions of Canadian Officials in Relation to Maher Arar).*
18 Although documents released were highly redacted, there were certain important revelations that confirmed Abdelrazik's allegations. Importantly, the section 38 *Canada Evidence Act* challenge could not be maintained once the applicant decided that he would proceed to the underlying merits of the case.
19 Section 41 of the *Privacy Act* allows for an application to be made to the Federal Court of Canada within forty-five days following a report issued by the Privacy Commissioner of Canada. The Federal Court has the authority to order disclosure of information where such decision is consistent with the findings of the Privacy Commissioner and appropriate in the circumstances.
20 Project Fly Home is a Montreal-based grassroots organization representing a civil society movement that sought the repatriation of Abdelrazik and now seeks his removal from the UN Resolution 1267 List. See http://www.peoplescommission. org/en/abdelrazik/.
21 See section 3 of the *United Nations Act.*
22 Canadian Passport Order SI/81-86 allows the Minister of Foreign Affairs to refuse to grant a passport to a Canadian citizen on the basis that the person may, in the minister's opinion, constitute a threat to the national security of Canada or another person. Passport Canada's own policies, however, which mesh with common-law principles of procedural fairness, require DFAIT to release a preliminary and final report prior to the ministerial designation, allowing the concerned person to make submissions on each respective report. This procedure was completely ignored for Abdelrazik.
23 Within the 208 documents released by the Attorney General pursuant to a *Canada Evidence Act* application, both CSIS and RCMP in November 2007 concluded that there was "no current and substantive information that indicates Mr. Abdelrazik is involved in criminal activity." See pages 920-21 of the Federal Court application record, File no. T-727-08, in *Abdelrazik v. Canada (Minister of Foreign Affairs).*
24 *Abdelrazik v. Canada (Minister of Foreign Affairs),* 2009 F.C. 580 at para. 153.
25 A 22 July 2004 secret internal memo from the Foreign Intelligence Division of Foreign Affairs to a broad array of interdepartmental actors, including the RCMP,

PCO, Transport Canada, and the Justice Department, confirms the internal position advanced by DFAIT "seeking Canada's agreement not to allow Abdelrazik to board aircraft bound for Canada."

REFERENCES

Aly, Heba. 2008. "Canadian Languishes in Embassy in Sudan." *Globe and Mail*, 1 July, A14.

Aubry, Jack. 2007. "Information Czar Fails Feds on Access." *National Post*, 30 May, A5.

Auld, Alison. 2008. "Getting Information from Feds Taking Ages." *Hamilton Spectator*, 7 January, A10.

Best, Joel. 2002. "Review Essay: Constructing the Sociology of Social Problems: Spector and Kitsuse Twenty-Five Years Later." *Sociological Forum* 17 (4): 699-706.

Bronskill, Jim. 1999. "Response to 'Closing the Window: How Public Sector Restructuring Limits Access to Government Information.'" *Government Information in Canada/Information gouvernementale au Canada* (17).

Campion-Smith, Bruce. 2009. "Info Watchdog Takes Aim at Harper's Stone Wall." *Toronto Star*, 26 June, A1.

Casey, Quentin. 2009. "Jurist Says Feds Fail on Openness; Government Ex-Judge Critical of Harper Tories for Not Fulfilling Pledge." *New Brunswick Telegraph-Journal*, 27 August, A1.

Clark, Campbell. 2007. "Information Office Lays Off Tory Critic." *Globe and Mail*, 29 May, A6.

–. 2008. "Tories in Court to Battle Access Law." *Globe and Mail*, 13 May, A9.

Galloway, Gloria. 2010. "Pattern of Delay: Ottawa's Information Denial." *Globe and Mail*, 3 February, A4.

Greenaway, Norma. 2008. "Government Openness Scrutinized; Complaints Double." *National Post*, 4 February, A4.

Harper, Stephen. 2005. "Cleaning up the Mess in Ottawa: Transparency Is Key to Preventing Scandal." *Montreal Gazette*, 7 June, A21.

Hutchinson, Allan. 2008. "In the Public Interest: The Responsibilities and Rights of Government Lawyers." *Osgoode Hall Law Journal* 46: 105-30.

Kinsman, Gary, Dieter K. Buse, and Mercedes Steedman. 2000. *Canadian State Surveillance and the Creation of Enemies*. Toronto: Between the Lines.

Kirtley, J. 2006. "Transparency and Accountability in a Time of Terror: The Bush Administration's Assault on Freedom of Information." *Communication Law and Policy* 11 (4): 479-509.

Knight, K. 1966. "Administrative Secrecy and Ministerial Responsibility." *Canadian Journal of Economics and Political Science* 32: 77-84.

Koring, Paul. 2009a. "UN: Canada Free to Bring Abdelrazik Home." *Globe and Mail*, 7 May, A1.

–. 2009b. "Return Home Repeatedly Stymied." *Globe and Mail*, 18 June, A4.

Leblanc, Daniel. 2008. "Tories Failing to End Era of Secrecy, Gomery Says." *Globe and Mail*, 14 March, A4.

Marx, Gary. 1984. "Notes on the Discovery, Collection, and Assessment of Hidden and Dirty Data." In *Studies in the Sociology of Social Problems,* ed. by J. Schneider and J. Kitsuse, 78-113. Norwood, NJ: Ablex.

Mashaw, Jerry. 1983. *Bureaucratic Justice.* New Haven, CT: Yale University Press.

McMurdy, Deirdre. 2006. "Information Boss Retiring, but Not Shy." *Ottawa Citizen,* 6 September, A5.

Rees, Ann. 2003. "Red File Alert: Public Access at Risk." *Toronto Star,* 1 November, A32.

–. 2003b. "Transparent Government Needs Obstacles Removed." *Toronto Star,* 6 November, A11.

Roberts, A. 2002a. "Is There a Double Standard on Access to Information?" *Policy Options* (May-June): 49-55.

–. 2002b. "Administrative Discretion and the *Access to Information Act:* An 'Internal Law' on Open Government?" *Canadian Public Administration* 45 (2): 175-94.

–. 2005. "Spin Control and Freedom of Information: Lessons for the United Kingdom from Canada." *Public Administration* 83 (1): 1-23.

Rubin, Ken. 1986a. *Suggested Changes to Canada's 1982* Access to Information Act. Ottawa: Author.

–. 1986b. *Access to Cabinet Confidences: Some Experiences and Proposals to Restrict Cabinet Confidentiality Claims.* Ottawa: Author.

–. 1990. *Using Canadian Freedom of Information Legislation: A Public Interest Researcher's Experience.* Ottawa: Author.

Saskatoon StarPhoenix. 2009. "Broken Promises Slam the Door on ATI Reform." 2 November, A6.

Shapiro, S., and R. Steinzor. 2006. "The People's Agent: Executive Branch Secrecy and Accountability in an Age of Terrorism." *Law and Contemporary Problems* 66: 98-129.

Thompson, Elizabeth. 2006. "PS Brass Get 'Heads Up' over Access Releases." *Ottawa Citizen,* 2 October, A3.

–. 2008. "Mounties Probe Band; Investigate Lyrics, Logo." *Montreal Gazette,* 22 May, A12.

Whittington, Les. 2008. "Information Access System Hobbled." *Toronto Star,* 28 May, A19.

Yeager, M. 2006. "The Freedom of Information Act as a Methodological Tool: Suing the Government for Data." *Canadian Journal of Criminology and Criminal Justice* 48 (4): 499-521.

LEGISLATION CITED

Access to Information Act, R.S.C. 1985, c. A-1.

Canada Evidence Act, R.S.C. 1985, c. C-5.

Canadian Charter of Rights and Freedoms, Part 1 of the *Constitution Act, 1982,* being Schedule B to the *Canada Act 1982* (U.K.), 1982, c. 11, s. 6.

Federal Accountability Act, S.C. 2006, c. 9.

Privacy Act, R.S.C. 1985, c. P-21.

United Nations Act, R.S.C. 1985, c. U-2.

CASES CITED

Abdelrazik v. Canada (Minister of Foreign Affairs), 2009 F.C. 580.

Canada (Attorney General) v. Canada (Commission of Inquiry into the Actions of Canadian Officials in Relation to Maher Arar), 2007 F.C. 766.

Canada (Attorney General) v. Khawaja, [2008] 1 F.C.R. 547.

Henrie v. Canada (Security Intelligence Review Committee), [1989] 2 F.C. 229.

Monaghan v. Canada (Attorney General), 2008 OSC 08-CV-42530SR.

PART 3

ACCESS TO INFORMATION AND CRITICAL RESEARCH STRATEGIES

The *Freedom of Information Act* as a Methodological Tool
Suing the Government for Data

MATTHEW G. YEAGER

The phrase "freedom of information" (FOI) represents a certain kind of public myth. So-called liberal democratic governments keep a lot of information secret, or prevent its disclosure through obfuscation and delay, but use the ideology of access to government information as a means of shoring up the state's legitimacy (Edelman 1971; Scalia 1982; Tudor 1972; Woodbury 1995). If governments were serious about information access, as Woodbury (1995, 51) notes, then information acts would have teeth to them, providing punitive damages, the discipline or dismissal of employees, and access to parliamentary or congressional information as well (information often exempted by legislators). Indeed, this notion of liberal democratic pluralism – that the "public" benefits from the disclosure of government information and thus uses this information to lobby its representatives – is merely false advertising. Because of the complexity of access law, there has arisen a whole cottage industry of access requesters and responders who specialize in the field (thereby limiting entry), not to mention the media, private industry, and political parties, who use the various acts for private or partisan purposes (Kester 1998). Criminological theory suggests that this is a function of ruling elites and class power (Bonger 1916; Chambliss and Seidman 1971; Taylor 1999), which are camouflaged with notions like democracy and access to government information. As Carl Schmitt (1985) observes, the term "citizen" is a facile abstraction that fails to reflect one's gender, race, or class status. It is used liberally to camouflage certain elite interests that have access to information technology, the media, the techniques of information access, and the generally favourable decisions of judicial bodies.

This chapter outlines a method of collecting data rarely used by academic criminologists, one that probably falls within the theoretical gambit of conflict or critical criminology. I will first briefly describe the use of both the American and Canadian access legislation – the *Freedom of Information Act (FOIA)* in the US and the *Access to Information Act (ATIA)* in Canada – by a number of academic researchers[1] and then proceed to highlight two lawsuits in which I was the sole plaintiff. In so doing, I wish to underscore both the potentials of this kind of method – actually suing the government in court – and the tremendous obstacles both from within the university and in general.[2]

Examples from the Literature

Former *Washington Post* managing editor Ben Bagdikian wrote a book on Lewisburg Penitentiary, largely from the point of view of eight federal inmates there, using the *FOIA* to obtain some information from the US Bureau of Prisons (Bagdikian 1976). "The Bureau of Prisons refused information unless I paid for it. It denied access to some records and said that other records had been destroyed" (ix). Bagdikian also observed that the bureau was hostile to his project, censoring mail to and from the penitentiary and punishing inmates who agreed to interviews. With the help of lawsuits and the US *FOIA*, Ward Churchill and Jim Vander Wall (1990a, 1990b) documented the Federal Bureau of Investigation (FBI) counterinsurgency "wars" against the new left in America. This included the Black Panthers, the American Indian Movement, and other progressive organizations that were infiltrated, wiretapped, and subjected to surveillance, to the creation of phoney evidence, and to agents provocateurs.

The journey of *San Francisco Chronicle* journalist Seth Rosenfeld (2002) is very useful for illustrating some of the difficulties academics encounter when using the *FOIA* or even contemplating litigation. In 1981, while a journalism student at the University of California at Berkeley, Rosenfeld filed a *FOIA* request for information pertaining to the Free Speech Movement on campus, as well as to the activities of one hundred luminaries who were prominent during that period. The FBI refused to make disclosures, citing national security concerns among others. Rosenfeld then embarked on a seventeen-year legal battle that eventually reached the US Supreme Court. In the course of this litigation, Rosenfeld obtained legal fees under court order and forced the FBI to disclose its political surveillance of university professors at the Berkeley campus, including efforts to paint former university president Clark Kerr as pro-communist. These machinations ultimately led to Kerr's losing a cabinet position in President Lyndon Johnson's administration and to his subsequent firing by the regents of the University of California in 1967 (see the *Rosenfeld v. Department of Justice* cases).

In the seminal work of Alan A. Block of the Pennsylvania State University, one finds the use of *FOIA* materials from both the FBI and US immigration authorities, but only casually referenced, with the methodology never fully developed. Block (1975, 1980) used FBI files for his dissertation on Jewish gangsters in New York City, and supplemented this information with material that was available from the Central Archives for the History of the Jewish People (Block 1975, 77n55). Not widely known is that he filed a lawsuit against the FBI in 1983 for documents relating to the death of a Puerto Rican political activist (see *Block v. FBI*). Strangely, his early work on historical methods in criminology fails to mention the use of the *FOIA* (Block, Inciardi, and Hallowell 1977).

Professor Athan Theoharis of Marquette University, a historian by training, has spent his career detailing the abuses of intelligence agencies, particularly the FBI, and has published a number of books based in part on records obtained through the *FOIA*. Theoharis's sourcebook on the FBI, co-edited with Tony Poveda, Susan Rosenfeld, and Richard G. Powers (1999), remains a classic in the field and is partly based on his work with the *FOIA*. As early as 1984, Theoharis was writing in the *Public Historian* about the use of the act to research covert government intelligence activities. A chapter in his book *A Culture of Secrecy* deals specifically with the use of the act to investigate FBI activities and outlines its use by numerous historians (Theoharis 1998). Clearly the act has helped many historians in their research, but it also has its limitations: few academics have initiated actual litigation, due to the costs, the commitment of time, and the delays involved. Even the exception tends to prove the rule. In 1967, historian Julius Epstein filed a lawsuit against the Secretary of the Army, asking for documents on the forced repatriation of anti-communist Russian prisoners after the Second World War. Both the trial and appellate courts turned Epstein down, finding that the executive branch had properly classified the documents as secret, national security documents (see *Epstein v. Resor*). After challenging the denial all the way to the US Supreme Court, Epstein concluded that "judicial review is meaningless without judicial examination of the documents in question" (Barker and Fox 1972, 18). This case did lead, however, to the 1974 amendments to the *FOIA* that addressed this very issue, namely, the inability of courts to actually review the challenged documents in camera.

Marc Riedel (2000) has written cogently on the use of the *FOIA* by researchers to obtain data for secondary analysis. His analysis represents a general introduction to the US *FOIA*, but there are no examples of criminologists actually litigating for research data. Further, Riedel (personal communication, 21 July 2002) relied largely on a PhD/lawyer colleague to write about the act and has never litigated or requested documents under the *FOIA*. David Keys and John Galliher (2000) used the *FOIA* in their biography of the late Alfred Lindesmith, who was the subject of a harassment campaign of nearly thirty years by the late Harry Anslinger, the director of the old Federal Bureau of Narcotics (now renamed the Drug Enforcement Administration). Keys (1998), who was Professor Galliher's doctoral student, waited four years for the information to be furnished by the federal government.

Until recently, there have been no lawsuits initiated by academic criminologists in Canada. Access activist and citizen litigator Ken Rubin, who resides in Ottawa, Ontario, has over the last twenty years established himself as a one-man access act litigator. His early research on information legislation (Rubin 1977) helped to initiate passage of the Canadian *ATIA* in 1983. Following the enactment of this legislation, Rubin (1984) was again instrumental in publishing a report on the federal government's abject compliance with the new law. One feature that clearly distinguishes Ken Rubin from others, including researchers in universities, is that he has been the sole plaintiff in at least ten different access lawsuits, spanning the years 1985 to the present, and has often represented himself in these actions before the federal courts (Drapeau and Racicot 2001).

There has been a series of excellent studies on national security and spying by the RCMP and the Canadian Security Intelligence Service (CSIS), the Canadian counterparts to the FBI and the Central Intelligence Agency (CIA). For example, Hewitt (2002) used documents obtained under the *ATIA* to study government spying on university campuses from the First World War up to the present. Hannant (2000) and Badgley (2000) have documented the difficulties that external researchers experience in using the act to research the Canadian national security establishment and its surveillance practices.

One retired academic who was quite active in the field of information rights throughout his career was political scientist Donald C. Rowat (1966, 1979, 1980, 1981, 1983, 1985, 1993). He taught for many years at Carleton

University in Ottawa and was the author of several anthologies on the subject of Canada's public access to information laws, but he never actually used the *ATIA* to obtain information or to litigate.

Yeager v. Drug Enforcement Administration

As for my own two lawsuits, the first one was initiated in the United States. It was filed in 1976, as I was finishing my master's degree in criminal justice at the State University of New York at Albany. Previously, I had finished a paper on the political economy of illicit drugs, which was subsequently published in *Contemporary Drug Problems* (Yeager 1975). This led to my further interest in the class and ethnic composition of those in the drug market and the filing of a *FOIA* request to the Drug Enforcement Administration in Washington, DC, around 1975. In particular, I requested access to the following DEA intelligence data systems:

1 A copy of the record layout outlining the available data stored either electronically or on data cards for NADDIS, KISS, PATHFINDER, and NIMROD. This was analogous to a codebook ("Data Dictionary") and a description of the codes used in all the fields (e.g., [1] = *male*, [2] = *female*, [3] = *unknown*).

2 A description of the computer format in which the data were stored on the computer. This was defined to consist of the code in which the data were written, the record size, the coding technique, the blocking size, the number of bytes per inch, and parity.

3 A cost estimate for obtaining either punch card or magnetic tape copies of data stored in NADDIS, KISS, PATHFINDER, and NIMROD.

4 Magnetic tape or punch card copies of the substantive data in NADDIS, KISS, PATHFINDER, and NIMROD, with personal identifiers deleted.

Strategically, we then filed what is called a *Vaughn v. Rosen* motion, requiring the government to itemize and index the contents of the withheld documents. The trial court granted this motion only with regard to NADDIS (Narcotics and Dangerous Drugs Information System) and completely denied access to the other systems under Exemption 7 of the *FOIA*. This exemption applies to records that might reveal ongoing law enforcement investigations, interfere with enforcement proceedings, disclose the identity of confidential sources, constitute an unwarranted invasion of privacy, or disclose investigative techniques or procedures. Interestingly, in the course of this lawsuit, the DEA destroyed one of the intelligence systems sought (KISS). Subsequently, we filed a motion to preserve all further records.

As to NADDIS, the DEA filed several in camera affidavits and one public affidavit, agreeing to release only those information categories that were not "personal, occupational and/or geographical." Of course, we badly wanted occupational data to explore our research hypothesis. We then argued that the DEA should be ordered to use disclosure-avoidance techniques, including the collapsing or compacting of information on NADDIS into more general categories. We also requested access to the in camera affidavits, requested that counsel be allowed to examine them, and later asked the court to appoint a special master to assist the court in understanding the technical aspects of the case. A master is an external expert appointed by the court to physically inspect the database and report back on the feasibility of disclosure. The DEA filed a motion for summary judgment in its favour, and in October 1980, the District Court granted the DEA's motion for summary judgment and denied our procedural motions regarding access to the sequestered affidavits and the appointment of a master.

We subsequently launched an appeal to the United States Court of Appeals for the District of Columbia, known as the DC Circuit. Here we renewed our argument that the DEA was required to use disclosure-avoidance techniques, much like those the Census Bureau used for its large data sets as a means of segregating non-exempt from exempt records. We also asked the court to review the *Vaughn v. Rosen* motions, our request for counsel to see the in camera affidavits, our motion about the special master, and the denial of access to the other data systems. In response, the DEA filed a cross-appeal and renewed its objection that my request was overly broad and thus "not reasonably described," that the technical information sought was exempt as an "internal agency record," and that Mr. Yeager was not entitled to any records in the form of magnetic tape.

Addressing the main issue in this appeal, the DC Circuit ruled that the DEA was not required to use disclosure-avoidance techniques to address the segregation requirement in the act, because the "FOIA does not contemplate imposing a greater segregation duty upon agencies that choose to store records in computers than upon agencies that employ manual retrieval systems" (*Yeager v. Drug Enforcement Administration* at 322). To quote the decision further:

> The interpretation suggested by Yeager may be desirable in terms of full
> disclosure policy and it may be feasible in terms of computer technology;

these factors notwithstanding, however, we are not persuaded that Congress intended any manipulation or restructuring of the substantive content of a record when it commanded agencies to "delete" exempt information. (at 323)

This, of course, was a major defeat and meant that agencies could frustrate researchers by simply labelling the electronic information potentially "sensitive" and therefore block disclosure. For example, occupational and geographical information in NADDIS would have provided us with some sense of whether elites in North America, Asia, and South America were suspected of financing large-scale drug networks. Some years later, in October 1996, Congress amended the *FOIA* to specifically require agencies to use computer redaction techniques (see the *Electronic Freedom of Information Act Amendments of 1996*).

The Court of Appeals did dispute the DEA's filing of the two in camera affidavits, concluding that they violated the spirit of *Vaughn v. Rosen.* However, because my attorney conceded that if disclosure-avoidance techniques did not apply, then the contested categories in NADDIS were exempt, the Court of Appeal declined to remand the matter to the trial court. Although we lost this case, one of the findings by the Court of Appeals has been cited extensively in subsequent litigation and was later incorporated into law. This is the conclusion that "computer stored records, whether stored in the central processing unit, on magnetic tape, or in some other form, are still 'records' for the purposes of the FOIA" (*Yeager v. Drug Enforcement Administration* at 321). The DEA lost this issue before the District (Trial) Court; it was subsequently affirmed by the Court of Appeals and later incorporated into law by the *Electronic Freedom of Information Act Amendments of 1996.*

Yeager v. Correctional Service of Canada

My second lawsuit began in Canada with some informal requests for research information from the Correctional Service of Canada (CSC), the federal agency responsible for the administration across Canada of penitentiaries and parole supervision for convicts serving at least two years of imprisonment.[3] Initially, I was interested in the question of detention, where convicts serving a fixed determinate sentence were ordered by the National Parole Board to serve every day of their sentence, rather than being released on mandatory supervision at the end of two-thirds of their sentence. From

1994 until a formal request was filed under the *ATIA* in 1997, a series of memos and letters were exchanged with little meaningful result. Unlike Canadian researcher Dawn Moore (2002), who experienced the same wall of silence from the CSC and simply gave up, I made a formal request, asking for the following specific data and software:

> I would like a copy of the Offender Intake Assessment software (current version in operation), which includes the: Custody Rating Scale (CRS), the GSIR, and the Community Risk/Needs Management Scale, among other features. My own computer reads either MS-DOS or WINDOWS, depending upon the software.
>
> Might you be so kind as to forward to me a copy of the following microdata:
>
> (a) the 1992-1993 CSC release cohort currently being used to recalibrate the GSIR. The microdata is in the form of individual cases in a rectangular, fixed format. Personal identifiers should be deleted (such as name of inmate/parolee, FPS number, or full date-of-birth, however year of birth will not violate privacy).
>
> (b) The codebook used to define and identify/locate the variables in each case.

The first request was for a copy of the CSC's Offender Management System (OMS) software so that I could analyze exactly what information was being collected on inmates and for what purposes. The second aspect of this request was to obtain, for the first time, an actual research database that had been compiled with public funds from the CSC's own OMS system, the RCMP, and the National Parole Board. This was the 1992-93 release cohort, which represented a sample of convicts released on parole by the service and followed for a period of several years to ascertain correlates to their success or failure in the community. In order to use this database, I also asked the CSC to prepare a codebook for me that defined and located the data (variables) on the electronic database. Importantly, this was a request for an electronic data file, not the hard copy, to facilitate my own statistical analysis of the raw data.

The Correctional Service denied this request, citing two reasons: (1) that the software could not be unbundled and would not work on a personal computer (PC) in any event; and (2) that the microdata request would require it to create a "new record," which it was not required to do under the act. Immediately, we took the required administrative appeal to the

Information Commissioner of Canada and submitted our own legal opinion for his consideration. This process, from beginning to end, took almost one year, and it was only in March 1998 that we filed our Notice of Originating Complaint in the Federal Court of Canada, Trial Division. Unfortunately, the Information Commissioner also denied our request but misconstrued the issues so badly that we were forced to litigate the issue (see *Yeager v. Information Commissioner of Canada*). In the course of this litigation, we received an affidavit from Lawrence Motiuk, the manager of the CSC's research division, suggesting that this applicant was not really qualified to conduct research (I had allegedly not provided the CSC with my publications list, credentials, or affiliation with an academic organization) and reiterating the government's reasons for denial. Of particular interest was the rationale put forward to deny access to microdata. Here, the CSC alleged that its research databases are created only temporarily from data provided by the National Parole Board, the Royal Canadian Mounted Police, and its own Offender Management System, and are then essentially destroyed. According to Motiuk, there was no need to maintain codebooks or data dictionaries because staff were already familiar with the variable categories. Hence, this particular request for the 1992-93 release cohort study would require the CSC to create or, perhaps more correctly, re-create a record and create a new document (the codebook), which they were not required to do. Motiuk admitted that his agency would create such data for preferred researchers, or if a request fit the agenda of the CSC's research unit, but this was a discretionary decision at the whim of CSC staff.

Strategically, we then elected to depose Motiuk and discovered that this policy was probably a violation of the *National Archives Act* (failing to archive databases for research purposes) and that microdata could be re-created within about two weeks, according to his testimony. We knew, of course, that since the research unit used SAS (Statistical Analysis System) software to analyze its data, creating an export file for outside use would undoubtedly take much less time (McKie 1998). One of the arguments that the government was using was that this process would unduly disrupt the functions of the research unit and that the request could therefore be dismissed under the act's regulations.

In May 2001, after hearing oral arguments, Madam Justice Sandra Simpson issued her judgment in *Yeager v. Correctional Service of Canada*. For the first time, a federal agency was ordered not only to release the sought-after microdata in electronic format but also to create a codebook for a researcher. The government's arguments about processing time were rejected because either the time required was minimal or the arguments were so poorly documented that it was impossible for the judge to make a determination about whether the request was disruptive. With respect to the software, however, Justice Simpson took a new approach by ruling that software was beyond the jurisdiction of the act. In other words, the Canadian Parliament did not intend software to be a permissible record under the act and hence software requests were exempt. Of interest, this was never the government's position throughout this process up to and including oral argument before the trial court. The Crown simply argued that the OMS could not be unbundled and would not work on a personal computer. We replied that it had to have been constructed from different software programs in the first place, and in any event, we had access to mainframe computers at Carleton University.

Since the trial court had largely sided with us, we were content to obtain the microdata and codebook. This was not to be, however. The Correctional Service filed an appeal to the Federal Court of Appeal, and we subsequently filed a cross-appeal on those issues on which we did not prevail (costs, the software, and the issue of political censorship under the *Canadian Charter of Rights and Freedoms*). This matter was argued before three appellate justices in May 2002. On 22 January 2003, Justices Isaac, Stone, and Malone of the Federal Court of Appeal rendered their decision in *Yeager v. Canada (Correctional Service)*. On the question of whether a research database and its codebook were records under the act and could be ordered disclosed, the panel concluded in the affirmative. As noted previously, the CSC had argued that it was not required to produce a codebook (because it didn't exist) or a research database (because it had been destroyed and would have to be re-created). On the question of whether my request constituted an unreasonable burden on the government, however, the appellate court held that Justice Simpson had erred. Citing the Motiuk deposition for the belief that up to forty days might be required to fulfill this request, the appellate court concluded that this burden was too high, and thus denied disclosure.

It must be noted here that the CSC had previously admitted that it purposefully violated the *National Archives Act* by not cataloguing or preserving its research databases and that it did not create appropriate documentation (codebooks) as it was already familiar with the databases. Clearly, therefore, the government's deliberate policies were positively rewarded as a basis for denying an access request. More egregious, however, was the finding that the justices relied upon the wrong evidence to conclude that the burden was excessive. Motiuk's affidavit and deposition largely related to a previous request by this researcher for access to a detention study completed in 1994 and published in 1995 (Motiuk, Belcourt, and Bonta 1995). That study had been destroyed and would have had to be re-created using electronic databases and some manual file coding. But the detention study was not the object of this particular access request. In point of fact, the 1992-93 release cohort was apparently already available and had not been destroyed, and a copy (with apparently some documentation) had been given to Statistics Canada.

Further, on the question of whether all government software was a record under the act, the appeals panel reaffirmed the trial decision that software was simply not a record, giving little new analysis on the issue and failing to respond to our arguments that software is just as much a record as raw data. As to costs, the panel reversed the lower court and awarded this researcher his legal costs in the public interest – a minor victory and hardly one to celebrate with much gusto. Finally, the appeals panel held that we had no standing to make a *Charter* objection that this resulted in unlawful censorship under section 2(b).

In order to exhaust remedies, since the appeals court had effectively eviscerated our access to the 1992-93 release cohort, we filed an Application for Leave to Appeal to the Supreme Court, on 24 March 2003. Here we raised three grounds. First, we argued that software was and should be a "record" under the *ATIA* and that various provincial governments either were silent on the issue or excluded software as well. Second, we put forth the position that software was "under the control" of the Crown, even if it was developed by a private contractor and allegedly licensed to the government. Finally, we disputed the assertion by the Court of Appeal that disclosure would "unreasonably interfere" with the operations of the government. No guidance was provided as to what this limitation meant, and the allegation was factually incorrect in any event.[4] We also tried a Motion for Reconsideration before the Court of Appeal, raising the same issue of evidentiary error in their decision. We argued that the appellate panel didn't read the evidence from the trial court correctly, confused the databases in question, and apparently didn't realize that the 1992-93 release cohort actually existed (it had not been destroyed) and had been given to Statistics Canada with documentation.

The Federal Court of Appeal denied our motion for reconsideration on 26 June 2003, citing technical reasons: we had failed to file our motion within the ten-day rule and our rationale as to why we were late was un-persuasive. On 17 July 2003, the Supreme Court of Canada dismissed our Application for Leave to Appeal, citing no reasons, as is the custom. On the surface, three members of the Supreme Court did not feel that the case raised issues of public importance or new interpretation. One year later, this criminologist contacted all three justices to ask for a research interview to learn more "about how the Court considered this application and the *Access to Information Act* issues which were brought to fore among ... [the] Justices." All three justices, two of whom have since retired, declined, citing the court's rule that it never "discusses its reasons for allowing or dismissing an application for leave." This rule has two effects: it helps the high court manage its workload and gives it flexibility, and it protects members of the state elite from further scrutiny.

Conclusion

Throughout this litigation, we were unable to obtain the outside support of several university-connected, non-profit agencies, and Carleton University's own department of sociology and anthropology was silent about pending litigation by one of its graduate students. Sociologist Maria Mies (1983, 124) has observed that this reaction is not uncommon within the academy. The separation of study from practice is "one of the most important structural prerequisites" within university settings. To quote Kirby and McKenna (1989, 25): "Within the institutions of western education, we are trained as spectators or commentators, to absorb experience, not to act on it. This disdain for the practical, an academic paradigm that is particularly strong within the social sciences, has resulted in a kind of paralysis." Indeed, within the social sciences, there has been a historical debate between a critical, activist form of public sociology and one that emphasizes the distant, expert teacher as sociologist (Burawoy 2003). As Kristin Luker (1999, 9) has noted, "academics often act as if doing research were a process that happens in a vacuum, immune from a larger political process."

One outcome is that a criminologist who persists in suing the government for research data may feel that he has become a pariah within the academy. Part of the explanation for this is clearly related to the fact that most universities depend heavily upon corporate and government funding (Aronowitz 2000; Tudiver 1999). With universities facing defunding and delegitimation, a criminologist who actually sues the government quickly notices his own isolation (Michalowski 2002). Thus, to quote Miliband

(1969, 248): "If anything, the university, including the majority of its teachers, has always tended, particularly in times of great crisis, and precisely when acute moral issues were involved, to take a poor view of its dissenters, staff, and students, and quite often to help the state by acting against them."

In my own case, there was no recognition from my own university or academic department concerning my trial victory, and when we tried to interest several academic-affiliated organizations in filing *amicus* briefs before the federal trial court, not one group responded.[5] In the case of the American *FOIA* lawsuit, I had left the university at that time and was therefore not in a position to ask for official support. Carleton University was not approached because of indications that it was hostile to the project, given the deliberate obstruction by the university's research ethics committee (Yeager 2004). Canadian euthanasia researcher Russel Ogden experienced a similar reluctance by his former university to defend his research from Crown subpoena, although it did ultimately reimburse him for his legal expenses (Lemon 2004). Unfortunately, there is probably no simple solution to the matter of institutional response, given that most universities depend upon the state and corporations for the bulk of their funding.

Total costs absorbed by this researcher now amount to approximately CDN\$21,500, creating a substantial barrier to litigation among most academic researchers – indeed, an almost impregnable wall, considering the amount of time involved. Academic criminologists, and even those with clinical backgrounds, are simply not trained in the rigours of freedom of information law, court pleadings, affidavits, depositions, legal opinions, or legal strategy. These require not only stamina of an intellectual sort but skills outside the usual domain of teaching, publication, and research.

As well, the litigant is at an extreme disadvantage because he or she becomes a de facto attorney general in prosecuting the government, but without all the resources available to the state. For citizens, including researchers, this often translates into a David-versus-Goliath battle, in which the odds are stacked against the citizen (Rubin 1986a, 1986b, 1990). Most citizens simply cannot afford their day in court, so to speak, and these examples are living proof. The cost of litigation against the DEA was absorbed by a public interest lawyer who had just graduated from Georgetown University Law School. In the case against the Correctional Service of Canada, the author sustained costs in excess of CDN\$20,000, of which he recouped a de facto fine of about CDN\$12,000 from the Crown. The additional costs of filing an application to the Supreme Court of Canada and a Motion for Reconsideration before the Court of Appeal were dismissed. This meant that those costs were not reimbursed, and this applicant was ordered to pay the government's court costs. Although the Canadian legislation provides for an award as to costs, this applies only to lawyers, transcripts, and secretarial assistance, not the time put in by private citizens if they attempt to represent themselves (see *Rubin v. Canada [Mortgage & Housing Corp.]*). We were very fortunate to obtain a limited cost order, but we had to litigate it on cross-appeal.

From the point of view of methods, suing the government under the *FOIA* clearly represents an extreme form of applied "conflict" theory. It is extreme because governments oppose access to data and do not want independent researchers rummaging around data banks, historical files, and the like. As well, at least in the present case, elite state interests are supported by the courts, whose members are appointed by those same elite interests. On the other hand, if one accepts the postulates of critical criminology, litigation under the *FOIA* must be incorporated into the methodological arsenal – especially when it is the government that largely controls the data, the funds, and the research agenda.

Still at It: An Epilogue

As is clear after reading the collection in this book, many of the contributors have a long-standing research interest in the *Freedom of Information* and *Access to Information* acts, as they are configured in both the United States and Canada. I have continued my litigation in Canada, and in September 2004 filed another action against the Correctional Service of Canada.

This action stemmed from research I wished to conduct for my dissertation on Dangerous Offenders in Canada. For the most part, Dangerous Offenders in Canada are those who have been convicted of one or more sex offences against women or children, and have been sentenced to an indeterminate (life) term in penitentiary. Very few are on parole (less than 5 percent), and most are housed throughout the Canadian penitentiary system in either maximum or medium security. I became interested in the issue after serving as an expert witness in several Dangerous Offender trials, in which I disputed the risk assessment evidence presented by various prison staff on behalf of the Crown prosecutors.

I had asked the CSC for access to a list of dangerous offenders in the Ontario region, and was getting nowhere. The National Parole Board had responded that they might be willing to send my information packet out to dangerous offenders, but this meant I could not control my sampling frame and it might be tainted, coming as it did from prison authorities. My lawyer and I therefore filed suit in *Yeager v. National Parole Board, et al.* in September 2004.

As we framed the issues, the questions put forth for the Federal Court were as follows: (1) Was there a public interest in allowing a researcher access to the names, penitentiary locations, and prison serial numbers of Dangerous Offenders so that they could be contacted to participate in an interview study? (2) Did the applicant (I) have the right to information in the Decision Registry of the National Parole Board regarding Dangerous Offenders for research purposes?

This became a very lengthy, protracted lawsuit in which the cross-examinations were contentious. At one point, counsel and I amended the application to include a third question: Were the names, penitentiary locations, and prison serial numbers already in the public domain such that we were entitled to this information? The case actually went to case management, where Mr. Justice Harrington tried to extract a settlement between the parties. At the last moment, however, the CSC refused to participate in any further negotiations for access to the Dangerous Offenders in the penitentiary system. It was always my view that the prison industry did not want these convicts interviewed because of what they might say about the actual impact of an indeterminate sentence. This study might have created a "counter" body of evidence that could be used during Dangerous Offender trials to dispute the claims of the Crown prosecutors (Yeager 2008). It certainly did not help matters that I was a well-known prisoner's activist who was critical of the Canadian prison industry.

Unable to secure a settlement, we proceeded to trial before another federal judge. In *Yeager v. Chairman of the National Parole Board, et al.,* Mr. Justice Shore ruled against us and, unfortunately, created some very difficult obstacles for researchers trying to get raw data (here, access to subjects) over the objections of a prison system.

Justice Shore ruled that the information was confidential "personal information" and therefore fell within the prohibitions under both the *Access to Information Act* and the *Privacy Act*. In his view, persons incarcerated – even though publicly convicted in a court of law – have a reasonable right of privacy. As to whether this information was already in the public domain, the court held that the prison industry was under no obligation to determine whether the names of Dangerous Offenders under their jurisdiction were actually in the public domain. The fact that their own research established that at least half of one hundred Dangerous Offenders were found in QuickLaw was irrelevant. Finally, on the all-important question of abuse of discretion under the research provisions of the *Privacy Act* of Canada, Justice Shore simply refused to review the agency's exercise of discretion. Section 8 of the act gives Public Safety Canada the discretion to disclose personal information where "the public interest in disclosure clearly outweighs any invasion of privacy that could result from the disclosure." To quote His Honour: "The Court is not to substitute its view of how the discretion should have been exercised for the manner in which it was exercised by the Minister or delegate" (at 139). The arguments we initially put forward to the Information Commissioner of Canada were ignored. Here, we justified the research on the following public interest grounds: (1) such research fosters PhD dissertations and produces university-trained researchers who will likely go on to teach; (2) it supports critical research about the penal process by those external to the correctional industry; (3) it provides Dangerous Offenders an opportunity to voice their perspectives on the criminal justice system; and (4) it provides the public and Members of Parliament with potentially new information about the workings of the *Criminal Code* and penal administration that may be relevant to future legislative oversight as well as court proceedings.

Costs were awarded to the government "due to the fact that Mr. Yeager rejected a proposal by which the requested information ... would have been available to him without breaching the legislative provisions" of both acts. This final salvo from the Federal Court was likely illegal since section 53 of the *ATIA* allows an applicant who does not prevail to recoup legal costs if a new "principle in relation to this Act" is raised. Unfortunately, at this juncture, having waited four years for a decision and spent thousands of dollars in legal fees, this criminologist was functionally bankrupt and could no longer continue. We did file a *pro forma* appeal with the Federal Court of Appeal, but I instructed counsel that I could not afford this appeal and it was filed to persuade the Crown that they should forfeit legal fees since the court had likely ruled illegally. In exchange for my dropping the *pro forma* appeal, the Attorney General of Canada gave up any legal costs owed over this protracted litigation.

The lesson here is that the federal courts in Canada are reluctant to review the discretion of prison agencies when those state organizations are opposed to certain research that offends their political sensibilities. Agencies will find a way to couch their exercise of discretion in "good faith," and courts are loath to review that discretion. Indeed, the decision gives free rein to prison administrators who find certain outside research proposals threatening to their domain. Finally, a more practical lesson for litigants is to sign a retainer limiting legal costs to what one can afford, or to elect to proceed *in propria persona*.

While the above case was working its way through the courts, I made a new *Access to Information Act* request to then Minister of Public Safety Stockwell Day, in June 2007. The minister had appointed a Correctional Service Review Panel to come up with recommendations related to the federal prison system. Many of us were skeptical of this review panel, as it was stacked with victim's advocates and a former provincial politician who was a known proponent of large, warehouse prisons. I considered this an opening for the Conservative government to generate support for an American-style expansion of federal prison capacity.

My request asked for documents concerning the appointment of the review panel members, the panel's work plan, budget, and submissions from interested parties.[6] Within two weeks, I received a reply that no such documents existed. This was strange, since the appointment of the Correctional Service Review Panel had been announced with great fanfare on television and in print. I had also been in telephone contact with the executive director of the panel, and had sent requests to personally interview the panel members. Immediately, I took an appeal to the Office of the Information Commissioner of Canada. The office would not reply to my appeal for approximately eighteen months (Galloway 2010)! In December 2008, I received a reply affirming the original decision, but with a very strange caveat – namely, that the Minister of Public Safety had likely violated section 8 of the *ATIA,* which requires agencies to forward a request to the appropriate federal agency, or institution within a ministry. Here, the Correctional Service of Canada was an agency under the umbrella of the Ministry of Public Safety.

Almost immediately, I launched an appeal by filing an application in Federal Court titled *Matthew G. Yeager v. Stockwell Day, et al.* I elected to represent myself exclusively in this matter since legal fees are prohibitive. In the course of litigating this matter, we filed two pre-trial motions. The first was for a court order allowing us to cross-examine Minister Day himself since the affiant put in front of us – the access to information (ATI) coordinator for the ministry – was ill-informed, likely had been deceived about available documents, and was not the real decision maker here. The second motion was for Rule 317 disclosure of all ministry documents related to Minister Day's creation and supervision of the review panel. A hearing was held in June 2009, before Deputy Judge Louis Tannenbaum in Toronto. On 11 August, we received an order denying our motions, but subsequently learned that Tannenbaum was over the seventy-five-year-old limit for serving as a federal judge. We then filed a motion to reconsider and vacate his order. Simultaneously, both a constitutional and statutory objection were put before the Chief Judge of the Federal Court of Canada, the Honourable Allan Lutfy. Recently, in *Felipa v. MCI (Ministry of Citizenship and Immigration)*, His Honour denied both claims that a deputy judge has no legal standing, because he or she is above the age limit, to act as a federal judge. Indeed, it appears from the ruling that while appointed superior court judges at the provincial level, designated federal judges, and prothonotaries are bound by the age requirements of the Constitution and the *Federal Courts Act*, a deputy judge appointed by the Chief Judge can sit until he or she is 105 or older! The matter was then appealed by Felipa's lawyer, civil rights specialist Rocco Galati. On 3 October 2011, the Federal Court of Appeal agreed in *Felipa v. Canada (Citizenship and Immigration)* that Deputy Judge Louis Tannenbaum was ineligible to sit as a federal judge. He did not meet either the constitutional or statutory threshold to act under the *Federal Courts Act*. We are now awaiting a ruling on our motion to vacate Deputy Judge Tannenbaum's earlier decision. Hopefully, this will result in a new motions hearing in this long-standing case.

I was also recently involved in a request for historical children's aid documents while researching the history of a Canadian bank robber who had a seventy-year criminal career. With the permission of my subject (who was then eighty-seven years old), we requested access to his Children's Aid Society (CAS) records in Canada, which dated to 1928, and received a two-page letter outlining his legal history in cursory form. Because the *Freedom of Information and Protection of Privacy Act* for Ontario does not apply to children's aid societies across the province, we decided to file an application in Superior Court *(Yeager v. Chatham Kent Children's Services and Her Majesty the Queen)* in 2009.

We presented three arguments to the court. First, there was a public interest by a scholar in these CAS records based on the study of a criminal career, which was clearly a statistical outlier. Second, we asserted the privilege to proceed inasmuch as we had the permission of the subject as well as the permission of his estate (he died in late 2008). Finally, counsel located case law that enabled us to argue that we had a free-standing right to discovery where the object was to do justice. In Canadian law, this free-standing right actually dates to before Confederation and has been recognized by the Ontario Court of Appeal.

After we waited several months to obtain a hearing date on the motion, to which the respondents never filed a single objection, authority, or submission, Mr. Justice Joseph Donohue ruled that I was entitled to both the CAS records and the official family court files. He ruled from the bench (Transcript, 26 January 2010):

> Well, I have had some considerable time to consider this given that I was sitting on an earlier date when these materials were first being put forward by Professor Yeager, and I have had an opportunity to consider the materials prior to today that are now before me.
>
> My impression is that Professor Yeager is engaged in a scholarly inquiry of a historical nature. His expertise is in the area of criminology. It is obviously in the public interest that [a] criminologist have an opportunity to explore background factors which lead to a life of crime.
>
> In my view then the public interest is served by Professor Yeager having this access to historic files. I do not see that a private interest is being offended. These matters are so historic in nature and given that the subject himself and his executor has both been consented to this inquiry.
>
> I have come to the conclusion that the public interest is paramount in allowing this scholarship to go forward and so I [am] going to grant the order as drafted.

Of note, legal counsel for the Children's Aid Society had officially taken no position either in favour of or against the application. When it came time to address His Honour in open court, however, counsel raised objections concerning privacy, standing to make the request as a third party, as well as some concern as to what I might publish about the file. Even in historical cases, agencies of the Crown often engage in a political "litmus test" concerning requesters, preferring their own agency-sanctioned researchers and running *sub rosa* interference on everyone else. In this rare instance, we challenged agency discretion and won a court order for access to the documents. So, it can be done.

As to practical matters, I actually handled the matter myself (filing, motion, service, etc.) until it became obvious that counsel's presence was needed since a pre-trial judge had raised questions of my legal standing to make the application. I was graciously represented by Hassan Law Offices of London, Ontario, who reduced their usual legal fees in this matter.

More recently, I entered a major white-collar criminal case in the United States, by filing a motion as a third party (see *United States of America v. BAE Systems PLC*). This case involves the largest military arms contractor in Europe paying bribes to highly placed individuals in Hungary, Saudi Arabia, and the Czech Republic to facilitate the sale of military aircraft as well as parts. Indeed, the corporation in question pleaded guilty to one count of fraud and was sentenced to three years of probation, monitoring conditions (they basically get to choose their own monitor), and a fine of US$400 million dollars. The whole process from the filing of the Information to sentencing took place in just twenty days – at the request of the defendant and the US government, especially the Justice Department's National Security Division. Our third-party motion asked the court to modify the conditions of probation by extending the supervision period to the maximum allowed (five years), and by ordering BAE Systems to take out newspaper advertisements to describe its guilty plea, apologize to the US public, and describe the sanctions ordered by the court. We also asked the court to order BAE Systems to create a trust fund of $5 million that could be used by non-profit organizations and researchers to study bribery by the military-industrial complex, globally. Our motion asked the judge to unseal his reasons for sentence, to disclose the contents of the pre-sentence report prepared by the US Probation Service, and to examine the discovery in this case, in camera, with a view towards "disclosing relevant documents that might be useful to the public and academic researchers who wish to study state-corporate crime, and specifically the actions of this organizational defendant." Unfortunately, US District Judge John D. Bates, who was appointed by President George W. Bush, denied our motion with the sample notation: "Leave to File Denied." The exigencies of time and finances did not give us the wherewithal to file an appeal to the US Court of Appeals for the District of Columbia. Time will tell regarding the extent to which the Federal District Court will continue to engage in a cover-up of essential details in this case, not to mention a favourable corporate sanction – since not one person has been indicted or even identified in the court record. Nevertheless, there is a basis for intervening in major corporate crime cases as a third party, and we hope that someday a magistrate will grant us third-party status and hear our claims.

I continue to pursue this kind of litigation because of a fascination with state and corporate power, and how the two conspire to keep information away from public intellectuals as well as the public in general. Certainly, the kinds of experiences documented in this book expose the silly notion that the state represents a benevolent consensus of public opinion. On the contrary, the litigation described here provides ample proof that government information is state-filtered and represents elite, often institutional, interests.

ACKNOWLEDGMENTS
This chapter originally appeared in the *Canadian Journal of Criminology and Criminal Justice* in 2006 (48:6) and has been reprinted (with an epilogue) with permission from the University of Toronto Press (www.utpjournals.com). Special thanks are due to Dr. Donald C. Rowat, Professor Emeritus, Department of Political Science, Carleton University; and to Mr. Neil Wilson, Esquire, formerly of Gowling, LaFleur and Henderson, Ottawa, Ontario.

NOTES
1 For the purposes of this chapter, I solicited responses from the membership of the American Society of Criminology by placing a research announcement in the May/June 2002 issue of *The Criminologist* (27 [5]: 5). It read: "I am currently looking at the *Freedom of Information Act* and its use by criminologists in North America. If you have used the Act to facilitate research, advocacy, or even filed a lawsuit for judicial review, I would like to hear from you." It is worth recording that there were only three responses to this announcement: from Prof. John Galliher (University of Missouri), Prof. Mark Hamm (Indiana State University), and graduate student Roger Roots (University of Nevada at Las Vegas).
2 This piece is best described as a discussion of a method or research technique, rather than as the philosophy of methodology or epistemology.
3 The reader may examine the actual court documents, including the affidavits, cross-examinations, and pleadings, in *Yeager v. Correctional Service of Canada* (2001), Ottawa, No. T-549-98 (F.T.D.); and on appeal, (2003), Ottawa, No. A-332-01 (F.C.A.).
4 In the Reasons of the Court of Appeal, several excerpts from the cross-examination of Lawrence Motiuk were reproduced. These pertain to the issue of the burden upon the CSC. In his cross-examination, Motiuk confused the exact nature of the request made by Mr. Yeager. The reference to "at least 40 days full-time of somebody dedicated to that work" probably referred to my earlier request pertaining to the CSC's detention research (Motiuk, Belcourt, and Bonta 1995). Indeed, that is clearly the case, given several comments by Motiuk during his cross-examination (at paras. 260, 311, 344-47, 404-6, 427-28). This confusion resulted in the commitment of an egregious error of fact because this database was not the subject of Mr. Yeager's request under the act. I was interested in the 1992-93 release cohort. In the transcript of oral argument before Madam Justice Simpson, Mr. Rupar (Counsel to the Appellants/Crown) acknowledged this. The alleged reliance on "40 days or two weeks work" was an estimate that was grossly overstated given the CSC's admission and confusion. This is why the Applications Judge found the CSC's reasoning unpersuasive. Her finding of fact was entitled to deference, especially since the Court of Appeal misinterpreted the evidence at trial. Beyond the above, the burden threshold in section 3 of the Regulations raises the significant question of whether the government of Canada can be permitted to manufacture a burden artificially by not archiving electronic research databases and failing to document them properly.
5 These agencies were the Canadian Graduate Council, the Canadian Association of Public Data Users, the Humanities and Social Sciences Federation, the Association

of Universities and Colleges, the Canadian Association of University Teachers, and the Canadian Federation of Students.

6 I also made a request for all memos, e-mails, and Blackberry messages pertaining to the ministry's decision not to consent to panel member interviews by this criminologist.

REFERENCES

Aronowitz, Stanley. 2000. *The Knowledge Factory: Dismantling the Corporate University and Creating True Higher Learning.* Boston: Beacon Press.

Badgley, Kerry. 2000. "Researchers and Canada's Public Archives: Gaining Access to the Security Collections." In *Whose National Security? Canadian State Surveillance and the Creation of Enemies,* ed. by G. Kinsman, D. Buse, and M. Steedman, 223-28. Toronto: Between the Lines.

Bagdikian, Ben H. 1976. *CAGED: Eight Prisoners and Their Keepers.* New York: Harper and Row.

Barker, Carol M., and Matthew H. Fox. 1972. *Classified Files: The Yellowing Pages.* New York: Twentieth Century Fund.

Block, Alan A. 1975. "Lepke, Kid Twist, and the Combination: Organized Crime in New York City, 1930-1944." PhD dissertation, University of California at Los Angeles.

–. 1980. *East Side, West Side: Organizing Crime in New York in 1930-1950.* Cardiff, UK: University of Cardiff Press.

Block, Alan, James Inciardi, and Lyle Hallowell. 1977. *Historical Approaches to Crime: Research Strategies and Issues.* Beverly Hills, CA: Sage Publications.

Bonger, Willem A. 1916. *Criminality and Economic Conditions.* Boston: Little, Brown.

Burawoy, Michael. 2003. "Public Sociologies: Response to Hausknecht." *American Sociological Association Footnotes* 31: 8.

Chambliss, William J., and Robert Seidman. 1971. *Law, Order, and Power.* Reading, MA: Addison-Wesley.

Churchill, Ward, and Jim Vander Wall. 1990a. *Agents of Repression: The FBI's Secret Wars against the Black Panther Party and the American Indian Movement.* Boston: South End Press.

–. 1990b. *The COINTELPRO Papers: Documents from the FBI's Secret War against Domestic Dissent.* Boston: South End Press.

Drapeau, Michel W., and Marc-Aurèle Racicot. 2001. *Federal Access to Information 2002.* Toronto: Carswell.

Edelman, Murray. 1971. *Politics as Symbolic Action.* Chicago: Markham.

Galloway, G. 2010. "Pattern of Delay; Ottawa's Information Denial." *Globe and Mail,* 3 February, A4.

Hannant, Larry. 2000. "What's in My File? Reflections of a 'Security Threat.'" In *Whose National Security? Canadian State Surveillance and the Creation of Enemies,* ed. by G. Kinsman, D. Buse, and M. Steedman, 213-22. Toronto: Between the Lines.

Hewitt, Steve. 2002. *Spying 101: The RCMP's Secret Activities at Canadian Universities, 1917-1997.* Toronto: University of Toronto Press.

Kester, Grant H. 1998. "Access Denied: Information Policy and the Limits of Liberalism." In *Ethics, Information and Technology Readings*, ed. by R. Stichler and R. Hauptman, 207-320. Jefferson, NC: McFarland.

Keys, David Patrick. 1998. "Confronting the Drug Control Establishment: Alfred Lindesmith as Public Intellectual." PhD dissertation, University of Missouri-Columbia.

Keys, David P., and John F. Galliher. 2000. *Confronting the Drug Control Establishment: Alfred Lindesmith as a Public Intellectual.* Albany: State University of New York Press.

Kirby, Sandra, and Kate McKenna. 1989. *Experience Research Social Change: Methods from the Margins.* Toronto: Garamond.

Lemon, Kathe. 2004. "Secret Files, Subpoenas and Suicide." *Peer Review* 2: 18-25.

Luker, Kristin. 1999. "Is Academic Sociology Politically Obsolete?" *Contemporary Sociology* 28: 5-10.

McKie, Craig. 1998. Affidavit of Craig McKie filed on 27 March 1998 in *Yeager v. Correctional Service of Canada.*

Michalowski, Raymond J. 2002. "The Future of Our Workplace: A Challenge to Progressive University Academics." *SSSP Newsletter* 33: 4-6.

Mies, Maria. 1983. "Toward a Methodology for Feminist Research." In *Theories of Women's Studies*, ed. by G. Bowles and R. Klein, 117-39. London: Routledge and Kegan Paul.

Miliband, Ralph. 1969. *The State in Capitalist Society.* New York: Basic Books.

Moore, Dawn. 2002. "'What Exactly Is It You Do?': The Problem of Spanning Jurisdictional Divides in Law and Society Scholarship." *Studies in Law, Politics and Society* 24: 33-48.

Motiuk, Lawrence L., Raymond Belcourt, and James Bonta. 1995. *Managing High-Risk Offenders: A Post-Detention Follow-up.* Ottawa: Research Division, Correctional Service of Canada.

Riedel, Marc. 2000. *Research Strategies for Secondary Data.* Thousand Oaks, CA: Sage Publications.

Rosenfeld, Seth. 2002. "The 17-Year Legal Battle to Get the Campus Files." *San Francisco Chronicle*, 9 June, 1.

Rowat, Donald C. 1966. "The Problem of Administrative Secrecy." *International Review of Administrative Sciences* 32: 99-106.

–, ed. 1979. *Administrative Secrecy in Developed Countries.* New York: Columbia University Press.

–, ed. 1980. *The Right to Know: Essays on Governmental Publicity and Public Access to Information.* Ottawa: Carleton University, Department of Political Science.

–. 1981. "The Right to Government Information in Democracies." *Journal of Media Law and Practice* 2: 314-32.

–, ed. 1983. *Canada's New Access Laws: Public and Personal Access to Governmental Documents.* Ottawa: Carleton University, Department of Political Science.

–, ed. 1985. *The Making of the* Federal Access Act: *A Case Study of Policy-Making in Canada.* Ottawa: Carleton University, Department of Political Science.

–. 1993. "Freedom of Information: The Appeal Bodies under the Access Laws in Canada, Australia, and New Zealand." *Australian Journal of Public Administration* 52: 215-21.

Rubin, Ken. 1977. "The Public's Right to Information Access in the Federal Government." Canadian Committee for the Right to Public Information, Ottawa. Photocopy.

–. 1984. "Testing the Spirit of Canada's Access to Information Legislation," vols. 1 and 2. Ottawa: Author.

–. 1986a. "Suggested Changes to Canada's 1982 *Access to Information Act*." Ottawa: Author.

–. 1986b. "Access to Cabinet Confidences: Some Experiences and Proposals to Restrict Cabinet Confidentiality Claims." Ottawa: Author.

–. 1990. "Using Canadian Freedom of Information Legislation: A Public Interest Researcher's Experiences." Ottawa: Author.

Scalia, A. 1982. "*The Freedom of Information Act* Has No Clothes." *Regulation* 6: 14-19.

Schmitt, Carl. 1985. *The Crisis of Parliamentary Democracy.* Cambridge, MA: MIT Press.

Taylor, Ian. 1999. *Crime in Context: A Critical Criminology of Market Societies.* Boulder, CO: Westview Press.

Theoharis, Athan, ed. 1998. *A Culture of Secrecy: The Government versus the People's Right to Know.* Lawrence: University Press of Kansas.

Theoharis, Athan, with Tony Poveda, Susan Rosenfeld, and Richard G. Powers. 1999. *The FBI: A Comprehensive Reference Guide.* Phoenix: Oryx Press.

Tudiver, Neil. 1999. *Universities for Sale: Resisting Corporate Control over Canadian Higher Education.* Toronto: James Lorimer.

Tudor, Henry. 1972. *Political Myth.* New York: Praeger.

Woodbury, Marsha. 1995. "Clinton, Reno, and Freedom of Information: From Waldheim to Whitewater." *Social Justice* 22: 49-66.

Yeager, Matthew G. 1975. "The Political Economy of Illicit Drugs." *Contemporary Drug Problems* 4: 141-78.

–. 2004. "Getting the Usual Treatment: Censorship and the Marginalization of Convict Criminology." Paper presented at the 56th annual meeting of the American Society of Criminology, Nashville, TN, 18 November.

–. 2008. "Getting the Usual Treatment: Research Censorship and the Dangerous Offender." *Contemporary Justice Review* 11 (4): 413-25.

LEGISLATION CITED

Access to Information Act, R.S.C. 1985, c. A-1.

Canadian Charter of Rights and Freedoms, Part 1 of the *Constitution Act, 1982,* being Schedule B to the *Canada Act 1982* (U.K.), 1982, c. 11, s. 6.

Electronic Freedom of Information Act Amendments of 1996, Pub. L. 104-231 110 STAT. 3048.

Federal Courts Act, R.S.C. 1985, c. F-7.

Freedom of Information Act, 5 U.S.C. s. 552 (1966).

Privacy Act, R.S.C. 1985, c. P-21.

CASES CITED

Block v. FBI, No. 83-0813 (D.D.C., 19 November 1984).

Epstein v. Resor, 296 F. Supp. 214 (N.D. Cal. 1969), aff'd 421 F.2d 930 (9th Cir. 1970), cert. denied, 398 U.S. 965 (1970).

Felipa v. Canada (Citizenship and Immigration), 2011 F.C.A. 272 (3 October 2011).

Felipa v. MCI (Ministry of Citizenship and Immigration), 2010 F.C. 89 (26 January 2010).

Rosenfeld v. Department of Justice, No. C85-2247 (N.D. Cal. 1985).

Rosenfeld v. Department of Justice, 761 F. Supp. 1440 (N.D. Cal. 1991).

Rosenfeld v. Department of Justice, No. C90-3576 (N.D. Cal. 1992).

Rosenfeld v. Department of Justice, 57 F.3d 803 (9th Cir. 1993), cert. denied, 516 U.S. 1103 (1996).

Rosenfeld v. United States, 859 R.2d 717 (9th Cir. 1988).

Rubin v. Canada (Mortgage & Housing Corp.) (13 July 1989), Doc. T-1019-86 (F.C.T.D.).

United States v. BAE Systems PLC, (D.C.D.C., 1:10-cr-00035, filed Feb 4, 2010).

Vaughn v. Rosen, 484 R.2d 820 (D.C. Cir. 1973), cert. denied, 415 U.S. 977 (1974).

Yeager v. Chairman of the National Parole Board, et al. (2008) 322 F.T.R. 113 (F.C.).

Yeager v. Chatham Kent Children's Services and Her Majesty the Queen (2010), No. 4475/09 (Superior Court of Justice, Chatham, Ontario).

Yeager v. Correctional Service of Canada (2001), 204 F.T.R. 297 (T.D. 2001), aff'd and rev'd in *Yeager v. Canada (Correctional Service)* [2003], 3 F.C. 107 (C.A.), Motion for Reconsideration dismissed (2003), 299 N.R. 352, Application for Leave to Appeal refused with costs (2003), 2 S.C.R. xi.

Yeager v. Drug Enforcement Administration, 678 R.2d 315 (D.C. Cir. 1982).

Yeager v. Drug Enforcement Administration et al., Civ. No. 76-0973 (D.D.C. 1976).

Yeager v. Information Commissioner of Canada, 189 F.T.R. 196 (T.D. 2000).

Yeager v. National Parole Board, et al. (2004) No. T-1644-04 (F.C.T.D.).

Yeager v. Stockwell Day, et al. (Federal Court, No. T-91-09, 2009).

"He who controls the present, controls the past"
The Canadian Security State's Imperfect Censorship under the Access to Information Act

STEVE HEWITT

In 1977, it was the turn of the University of New Brunswick in Fredericton to host the annual gathering of Canadian Learned Societies (now the Congress of the Humanities and Social Sciences). Among the delegates was at least one informer for the Security Service of the Royal Canadian Mounted Police (RCMP), there to monitor the Marxist academics involved in the Labour History Group and the Political Economy Network. In a report that he or she wrote afterwards, the source went so far as to warn that the Marxist scholars intended to try to access secret RCMP Security Service records much like the one the informer was writing. "They will claim that it is vital to their research," wrote the learned individual, "but their goal, as stated several times in the company of other Marxists, is to prove that the RCMP is in their terms, 'an agent of state repression' and thus to try to discredit the RCMP." A cryptic handwritten comment by an RCMP member appears. "They've missed the boat," the Mountie wrote, possibly referring to commissions of inquiry, including the Royal Commission of Inquiry into Certain Activities of the RCMP (McDonald Commission), about to investigate the RCMP, or to the destruction of sensitive security documents by the police that had already occurred (see Hewitt 1998).

The irony, of course, is that this informer's account is available because of the *Access to Information Act* enacted in 1983 by the Liberal government of Pierre Elliott Trudeau. Without this crucial legislation, much of the research I and others have done over the last two decades, particularly in relation to the Canadian security state, would not have been possible. It is scholarship created as a result of the *Access to Information Act (ATIA)*, a point not to be forgotten. Because of its usefulness and cost-effectiveness if deployed properly, more and more researchers are using access to information (ATI) for historical research (see, for instance, Kinsman and Gentile 2010). I am not suggesting that the challenges faced by historians who use access to information are more arduous than those faced by researchers who focus on more contemporary topics (see, for example, Chapters 5 and 9). We are all dealing with history, some more recent than others. Some of the challenges faced by historians, however, are unique. The purpose of this chapter is to demonstrate several of the ways in which these differences play out through the research process.

This chapter offers a researcher's perspective on using the *ATIA* in an effort to write about historical aspects of the Canadian security state, while addressing several major issues that have arisen from these twenty years of access requests. I discuss the nature of excisions made to security documents under the ATI process, as well as what these reveal about wider agendas of the security state, including state security agencies, to ensure the dominance of certain discourses. I do this by detailing examples of passages that have either been excised in one place before being released in the same document through a different request under the *ATIA* or inadvertently let out by those doing the censoring. I argue that the human factor makes for imperfect censorship under the *ATIA*, something that benefits researchers. Two other aspects of the administration of the act discussed here raise troubling questions, however. First, the aforementioned human factor allows for the existence of multiple versions of the same document, generating significant methodological issues for researchers. Second, and even more problematic, significantly less security material, even from documents that are over forty years old, is being released now than when I began as a researcher. This suggests the potential for future historical writing about Canada's security state to grind to a halt due to a lack of primary source material as those with a vested interest in the present prevent an interrogation of the past.

Getting a Start with Access to Information

My encounter with the *ATIA* began in 1991 while I was an MA student at the University of Saskatchewan studying the 1935 On-to-Ottawa Trek, in which over a thousand unemployed men attempted to travel to Canada's capital to protest their lack of employment and the absence of proper government support. I discovered that the RCMP had generated hundreds of pages of detailed records about the march, records that were not obtainable through regular RCMP files open and available at the National Archives of Canada. Instead, a censored version of the records could be obtained through a request under the *ATIA* to the National Archives of Canada (now Library and Archives Canada [LAC]) in Record Group 146, the records of the Canadian Security Intelligence Service (CSIS). Even though these are frequently records generated by the RCMP, CSIS controls them after inheriting the RCMP Security Service files in 1984, when CSIS replaced the Security Service (also see Whitaker, Kealey, and Parnaby 2012).

The files contain a treasure trove of material that extends beyond detailed police reports. Of equal or greater value, and this applies to all RCMP Security Service records, are other materials collected by the police in the form of non-police documents such as flyers, minutes of meetings, and other publications generated by a wide variety of organizations. Sometimes undercover police officers would have collected the material; on other occasions, police informers would have been collecting and turning them over to their police masters. These records are an invaluable source for anyone seeking to write a history of a number of organizations, many of them now defunct and lacking detailed archives. For instance, the records collected by the Mounties have proven invaluable in a study of second-wave feminism and the security state (see Hewitt and Sethna 2012).

The MA project eventually became a PhD dissertation on the history of the RCMP in Alberta and Saskatchewan, and then a postdoctoral monograph that explored the history of RCMP spying at Canadian universities (see Hewitt 2002). For this book, *Spying 101*, I made numerous ATI requests covering dozens of Canadian universities and consisting of tens of thousands of pages of documents. In the end, CSIS released only a segment of these documents, many of them heavily censored. In one particular request (96-A-00045), I was told that there were approximately 33,000 pages of documents related to thirty Canadian universities. In the end, I received portions of about 15,000 pages. My experience of *ATIA* continues to the present, as I still make ATI requests for RCMP documents related to new projects (also see Sethna and Hewitt 2009).

Twenty years of dealing with ATI requests and CSIS has led me to a not terribly startling conclusion: on their own, the documents are problematic and offer not "the truth" or even "a truth" but a carefully constructed discourse (also see Kealey 1998). This is not to suggest that the documents are not valuable – of course, they are, as is the legislation that allowed them to be obtained – merely that the researcher needs to be extra-skeptical when using them. This observation is obviously primarily applicable to the portion of the documents that have been vetted by government censors.

Some Notes on Using the *ATIA* for Historical Research

What gets cut under the *Access to Information Act?* Many of the deletions occur under section 19(1), which pertains specifically to personal information about individuals either living or who have been deceased for less than twenty years. The difficulty here is that it can be up to the researcher, particularly in the case of lesser-known individuals, to prove that the individual in the document has been deceased for over twenty years in order to get the name released. Of course, this can require guesswork in the first place, since if the name is censored it is not always easy to determine the person's identity in order to make a case for it to be released.

Then there is section 15(1). This exemption allows the government to remove anything it deems to be "injurious" to the national security of Canada and to "the detection, prevention or suppression of subversive or hostile activities." This rather broad category of censorship might include evidence of the use, lack of use, or sophistication of technical sources, even if occurring as far back as before the Second World War. Such information is deemed sensitive since it could offer an indication to Canada's enemies of the technical capabilities of domestic security, so runs the governing logic, through an extrapolation to the present based on what was available in the distant past. The names of informers are similarly restricted in perpetuity, despite legal attempts to obtain such names in dormant files like that of politician Tommy Douglas, because, as an archivist once told me regarding the Winnipeg General Strike, the informers may be dead but they have descendants and the descendants of the strikers might seek vengeance on the descendants of the informers. In reality, the reluctance to reveal names of long-dead informers has little to do with the safety of their progeny but, as CSIS itself has admitted, is meant to ensure the future recruitment of informers based on their identities being kept secret. People will not inform if they have to worry that their treachery might someday be revealed (also see Hewitt 2010).

Major deletions also occur under section 13(1), information supplied by another government in confidence (see also Gentile 2009; Gilbert 2009). A fundamental rule of any government is not to reveal the secrets of other governments and their agencies, particularly allied ones, lest their own se-crets be revealed in response (BBC News 2000). Hence, governments will wage extensive campaigns to block the accessing of such material, as dem-onstrated in 2009 and 2010 in the United Kingdom regarding the release of counterterrorism information supplied by the Central Intelligence Agency (CIA), and in past years when the US government moved to prevent the release of material within the Federal Bureau of Investigation (FBI) file on John Lennon that had been supplied to it by British intelligence.

Connected to these organized instruments and rules of censorship is the essential human component. As in Orwell's *1984,* numerous censors toil to prepare the documents for release. Their modern equivalent of the Orwellian memory hole are truly "magic markers" and special photocopiers. Any text on a document encircled with the marker appears as a blank space when run through the photocopier. Here is a passage that was inadvertently released, likely because a page stuck to another as it was processed through the spe-cial photocopier. It is from a 1940 report about a communist academic at the University of Toronto named Sam Levine: "You will note in para. 6 of the report [next section was to have been cut] that Sam LEVINE admitted being paid agitator of the C.P. according to Prof. Louden" (LAC 1940). This segment was selected for deletion by CSIS to protect the identity of an in-former among the university academic staff (LAC 1940).

The use of a number of censors also complicates the process. Since the RCMP and other government agencies in the past and present frequently cross-file reports, multiple individuals can prepare multiple versions of the same document for release as the result of an ATI request into the public domain. Indeed, this issue arose in March 2010 in the midst of a scandal over the fate of Afghan detainees in Canadian custody when two versions of the same document were released by the government. A passage about the behaviour of detainees was censored in one document, while the same pas-sage was left in elsewhere (Chase 2010). This human factor invariably lets more information out while revealing what some censors have deemed to be threatening enough to excise.

Having a system in which different individuals censor the same docu-ments can also serve academics with an interest in the past. As mentioned earlier, the use of sources is of central importance to any intelligence agency. Protecting the methods and identities of informers thus becomes one and the same. Witness a lengthy discussion in the 1960s about the push for the RCMP Security Service to gather more intelligence on university campuses, then experiencing growing unrest. It is hardly surprising that informers would have been one method of intelligence gathering at higher educational institutions, particularly since the FBI was using similar methods south of the border. Thus, it is not entirely clear why the following passages contained in a summary of RCMP intelligence gathering on campus were excised by at least one censor. Perhaps it was out of concern about methods being revealed. Had the censor been a historian, he or she would have realized that the use of informers on campuses in Canada in the 1960s was a highly charged political issue because of a failed effort to recruit student informers in 1961; they went to the media instead (Hewitt 2002). It is likely that, in haste, a censor saw the magic word "source" and began to slice out passages (shown in italics below) from an RCMP report to the Department of External Affairs about campus protests:

> In view of the restrictions placed upon us in connection with campus inquiries, we have very little intelligence concerning [deleted: *Trent University*]. As you are no doubt aware, these restrictions resulted from pressure placed upon the Government by the Canadian Association of University Teachers in 1961 [sic] and have seriously restricted our capabilities in this field. Our campus investigations have since been limited to:
>   1 The security screening of individuals requiring access to classified data;
>   2 Personal security briefings for persons travelling to Iron Curtain countries;
>   3 [deleted: *Inquiries through sources in recognized subversive organizations*]. (Hewitt 2000a; DFAIT 1969a, 1969b)

The report added a prescription that was also cut: "It is one thing to know, [deleted: *through 'off-campus,' casual or other source*]s, that a particular subversive organization exists 'on campus'; it is quite another to know what transpires at its meetings." Hence, the need to have informers on campus, a solution that one CSIS censor wanted removed from the following report:

> With the passage of time [deleted: *many of the sources it did have within institutions have disappeared owing to faculty transfers, retirement and graduation. The effect over nine years, of course, has been cumulative and to rebuild an adequate network of sources will take time. Despite vigorous efforts by the Security Service to develop reliable sources outside educational institutions as such, the results have been disappointing. Moreover, casual sources, for a variety of reasons, have often proved to be not very useful.*]

Much of their information is limited to biographical and historical material
and some of it is inaccurate.

4. The inadequacies of the existing situation can best be illustrated by
   mentioning that during the peak of unrest at educational institutions
   in 1968-69 ... [deleted: *the Security Service had one active source in
   the entire radical student movement, and even he was only in the process of development.*] It is understandable, therefore, that while the
   Security Service has gained considerable insight into the nature and
   extent of revolutionary activities at educational institutions, it lacks
   any in-depth knowledge. (LAC 1969)

Ironically, the actual limited number of informers on campus by the late
1960s, which at least one CSIS censor attempted to conceal, renders the
RCMP far less powerful than it otherwise might have appeared. Three different versions of this document have been cleared under the *Access to
Information Act*. All three contain different excisions, including the removal
of the name of Trent University in one of them.

At times, sloppiness seems to have led to censorship. In a July 1970 letter
to a senior civil servant, the head of the RCMP Security Service at the time,
John Starnes, warned the Trudeau government that security needed to be
ascertained from a "continental standpoint." In particular, he added, this required *"an appreciation of the implications for Canada of a breakdown of
law and order in the U.S.A."* (CSIS 1970; LAC 1970). One censor excised
those words, perhaps because of a mistaken belief that the document contained information supplied by the US government instead of what it actually was, an expressed perception by a senior official of the situation at the
time in the US.

There are also passages that appear to have been cut not because of their
potential threat to Canadian security but to reduce embarrassment for the
current federal government in the context of the never-ending Canadian
struggle over national unity. In a failed effort in 2003 to reform the *Access to
Information Act*, then Member of Parliament John Bryden proposed in a
private member's bill that all material older than thirty years be opened to
researchers. He exempted from his proposal, however, any files that could
be "injurious to the constitutional integrity of Canada" (see Canada 2003).
This could have potentially prevented, for instance, the release in 2007 of
the Security Service's file on former Parti Québécois leader and provincial
premier René Lévesque (*Globe and Mail* 2010). The potential for damage to
national unity through the revelation of how extensively the Security Service

was spying on targets in Québec in the 1960s would seem to explain the decision of one censor to remove the following statistics (shown in italics) from a report on the extent of separatist activity in the educational sector in Québec:

2. A recent statistical examination of the Security Service files of persons having Separatist/terrorist sympathies or affiliations is most revealing of the extent to which such persons have gained a strong position within the educational system in Québec. A tabulation of the files according to occupation showed the following results:

    (a) Of the some [deleted: 2600] persons whose files were examined, those known to be in education and related occupations constituted approximately [deleted: 25%].

    (b) Students comprise [deleted: 39%] of this [deleted: 25%].

    (c) Although not conclusive, a correlation analysis of the "no occupation known" group of files indicated that the percentage of persons involved in education could be revised upwards from [deleted: 25%] to [deleted: 30%] of the total files examined.

    (d) Of those from the teaching professions a majority are at secondary and post-secondary level. Some have very senior positions. (LAC 1970)

Beyond these individual examples of censorship is a wider sense, after twenty years of work with *ATIA*-scarred files, that the amount of censorship of security records by CSIS is increasing (also see Wilson 2000). This may seem to be merely a qualitative judgment to be weighed accordingly. My reading has been officially confirmed, however, by an official at the Office of the Information Commissioner of Canada. This was in a series of e-mail exchanges triggered as part of a successful complaint that I had made about some bad cutting-and-pasting that CSIS was doing:

From: [Office of the Information Commissioner]
Sent: 02 August 2007 16:05
To: Steve Hewitt
Subject: ATI requests

Dear Mr. Hewitt:

Thank you for providing me with the file number for LAC's previous response to you. I was able to review both sets of records and compare what information had already been disclosed to you. As a result, CSIS agreed that the information that had been released previously should be disclosed to you in response to your recent request. LAC will provide you with the additional response.

The Canadian Security Intelligence Service has become more stringent in their policies with respect to the disclosure of certain types of information. As a result, even information that could be considered dated or old will be severed or withheld in its entirety if it falls within a certain class of information. To date, the Information Commissioner has accepted the rationale for CSIS' position under subsection 15(1) [the details of this clause are described earlier in this chapter].

Please feel free to provide me with any further representations that you wish to make.

Sincerely,

[Office of the Information Commissioner]

In response, I asked when CSIS had become more restrictive, assuming that it may have been connected to the 11 September 2001 terrorist attacks in New York and Washington. After the attacks, the George W. Bush administration in the United States had removed previously freely available documents from archives, sparking protests from researchers and journalists (see Kaplan 2006; Shane 2006; Shapiro and Steinzor 2006).

> From: [Office of the Information Commissioner]
> Sent: 03 August 2007 15:50
> To: Steve Hewitt
> Subject: RE: ATI requests
>
> Hi Mr. Hewitt,
>
> ... I spoke with CSIS and they advised me that there is not a specific date or time when they became more conservative with the information they release. It has happened over time.
>
> Sincerely,
>
> [Office of the Information Commissioner]

And this prompted me to inquire why CSIS had become more restrictive.

From: [Office of the Information Commissioner]
Sent: 07 August 2007 16:04
To: Steve Hewitt
Subject: RE: ATI requests

Hi Dr. Hewitt,

I would like to explain but I really do not have an answer. Sometimes this occurs in *ATIA* offices with a new coordinator, for example. CSIS changed coordinators about five years ago. I don't know if this is the answer but it is possible. Different analysts as well may have something to do with it. The culture in an *ATIA* office can change as employees change and in many *ATIA* offices there is a high turnover of employees. As long as they are properly applying the Act, the Information Commissioner will not object. In the case of CSIS, they are still applying the Act as the courts (in some cases) have ruled, but more stringently than some of their predecessors.

[Office of the Information Commissioner]

These comments are telling and point to the bureaucratic and arbitrary administration of the *Access to Information Act*. They also demonstrate a troubling unwillingness on the part of the Office of the Information Commissioner of Canada to hold government agencies to account for their restrictive practices (also see Drapeau 2009 and Chapter 12 of this book).

Although this chapter has identified some of the key reasons for censoring documents, there is not necessarily always a deliberate effort to conceal. That multiple versions of the same document are released through the *ATIA* reveals the arbitrariness of the process due to the involvement of human beings. One reason for this is the institutional lack of historical memory in government agencies, including CSIS, which are being asked to vet significant records from the past. An individual familiar with the delivery of *ATIA* at CSIS agreed that this was a problem, not with the recent past within the personal lifetimes of those doing the censoring but with the more distant mists of time. Newer *ATIA* analysts used by CSIS lacked the historical knowledge of the RCMP material they were vetting, and thus were not in a position to judge the true significance of what it was they were being asked to clear. For instance, some of the censors were unaware that a dedicated Communist Party of Canada member in the 1920s named Jack Esselwein was really an RCMP member named John Leopold. We know his real identity because his secret was revealed publicly in 1928. Nevertheless, this information, which had been in the public domain since the 1920s and even previously released through other *ATIA* requests, was removed in a request that I made (Hewitt 2000b). From the perspective of the historically illiterate censor, it is not hard to guess that the default position in such scenarios must be: "When in doubt, cut it out." It is far less trouble for a government agency to withhold material, thereby forcing a researcher to pursue a complaint to the federal Information Commissioner and ultimately legal action, than it is to release the material and risk potential embarrassment for his or her employers. Because the Leopold documents had already been released, I was able to complain to the federal Information Commissioner and have the excised passages released. The case of the Mountie pretending to be a communist in the 1920s was, however, just one of numerous examples of similar inconsistency that I identified in a 1999 official complaint to the Information Commissioner (see Appendix).

The arbitrariness of the application of the *ATIA* is both a boon and a hindrance to researchers. There is the potential for more information to be allowed into the public domain through a number of versions of the same document being prepared by multiple individuals, but this benefit is vastly outweighed by the impact on researchers of multiple versions of the same document, particularly in the case of the RCMP, which cross-filed the same reports, being released by different *ATIA* analysts at different times. This could potentially lead to the circulation of different versions of the same events or more details being available to one researcher through simple luck or because the researcher placed a request years earlier, when the Canadian access system, which a 2008 study now places behind the access laws in place in India, Mexico, and Pakistan (Shochat 2010), was administered in a more open fashion.

Conclusion

Although having no *ATIA* would result in an infinitely worse landscape for researchers, the fact that academics made only 1.3 percent of all ATI requests to the government of Canada between 2009 and 2010 (Treasury Board of Canada Secretariat 2010) only emphasizes the need for reform to a piece of legislation that will soon be thirty years old. Repeated reform efforts to make access to government materials more open have failed, and a shift away from openness appears to be underway (Douglas, Hurtubise-Loranger, and Lithwick 2006). The government, as a result of a lawsuit launched against it by journalist Jim Bronskill over the censoring of the RCMP file of

Tommy Douglas, has now floated the idea of allowing more material out. This could include information of an historical nature, even material supplied by informants as long as it does not reveal the identity of the informers. Although potentially a step forward, this change remains problematic. First, it will only worsen the problem of multiple versions of the same documents being available to researchers. More problematic is that the changes would still allow the government wide leeway to censor files that are decades old, for example, on the grounds of protecting an informer's identity. Instead, there needs to be a fundamental change to the *ATIA* process in which a time limit is imposed on documents, after which they become open unless the government can make a case for keeping them closed. In other words, the onus would shift to the state to justify continued restrictions that prevent the Canadian public from taking control of its own past.

Appendix

Following is the text of my official complaint to the Office of the Information Commissioner of Canada in 1999.

24 June 1999

Information Commissioner
Ottawa, Ontario

Dear Sir/Ms.:

This letter represents an official complaint regarding the handling of my Access to Information request to the National Archives of Canada (98-A-00133).

There are three elements to my complaint.

1. Throughout this request the names of Mounted Policemen and RCMP civilian employees have been deleted under Access. At one time all names were released under Access. Indeed I have a list of several hundred names obtained from previous requests. Then, and I have been told a variety of reasons for the change, the names of those Mounted Policemen making reports began to be deleted. Now in this request not only are the names of those filing reports deleted but so are the names of the officers commanding divisions, etc. For example, on p. 83 the name of the officer filing a memorandum in 1940 is deleted. On p. 161, the name of the officer in charge of Special Section

has been deleted. I believe that in 1949 this was George McClellan, now deceased. On page 306 the name of Insp. D.E. McLaren, the officer i/c of "D" Branch in 1961, is removed even though it was previously released in 98-A-00129.

This is information that is common knowledge and should not be removed. Other names that are routinely removed from requests include John Leopold, Mark McClung, and Ken Green. They are all dead. Leopold, whose career has been well documented, has been dead for nearly forty years.

In general I would like a clarification with respect to the policy governing the deletion of names of Mounted Policemen and civilian employees since its application has, at least in my opinion, been inconsistent. Finally, if it is necessary to remove the names of RCMP members then their rank should be left behind so that it is clear to researchers that the person filing the report or who is mentioned in the body of a report is a member of the RCMP. I see no justification for removing the person's rank from documents released under Access.

2. On pages 87-89 names of suspected Communists at specific universities have been excised under Access. Some of the names should not have been removed. These include Frank Underhill, who has been dead for over twenty years and whose RCMP file has been released under 97-A-0004, Leopold Infeld, another who has been dead for more than twenty years and whose RCMP file has been released under 98-A-00047, George Hunter, again dead for more than twenty years and whose RCMP file has been released under 98-A-00004, and Barker Fairley, a U of T academic who has been the subject of a previous request under the *Access to Information Act* and whose name appears in a 5-6-40 report in 97-A-00044.

3. References to Prof. Watson Kirkconnell have been deleted on pages 160, 161, 171, 173, and 180. Kirkconnell has been dead for more than twenty years, his article from the time period is readily obtainable, and his name has been previously released in a February 12, 1949 document that appears in the University of Alberta material under 96-A-00045.

I find it increasingly distressing that material that should be readily available to researchers, since it has been previously released or the well-known individual has been deceased, is being cut out in subsequent requests. I realize that this is not done intentionally. However, such mistakes will and do have a negative impact on the work of researchers.

Sincerely, Steve Hewitt

REFERENCES

BBC News. 2000. "Judge Releases Lennon letters." BBC News, 19 February. http://news.bbc.co.uk/.

Canada. 2003. Bill C-462, *An Act to amend the Access to Information Act and to make amendments to other Acts*, 2d Sess., 37th Parl., 2002-03 (First Reading, 28 October 2003). http://www2.parl.gc.ca/.

Chase, Steve. 2010. "Gaffe on Detainees File Exposes Role of Politics, Ex-Colonel Says." *Globe and Mail*, 27 March. CSIS (Canadian Security Intelligence Service). 1970. Document no. 95, access request 117-90-123, John Starnes to D.S. Maxwell, Dept. Minister and Dept. Attorney General, 23 July 1970; John Starnes to author, 12 February 1999.

DFAIT (Department of Foreign Affairs and International Trade). 1969a. Access request no. A-1998-0356/mh, file 29-16-2-1-NewLeft, Higgitt to E.T. Galpin, 30 April.

–. 1969b. Access request no. A-1999-0149, file 29-16-1-1-NewLeft, E.R. Rettie, Defence Liaison, to Mr. Williamson, Academic Relations Section, 6 May.

Douglas, Kristen, Élise Hurtubise-Loranger, and Dara Lithwick. 2006. "The *Access to Information Act* and Recent Proposals for Reform." Ottawa: Parliamentary Information and Research Service, Library of Parliament. http://www2.parl.gc.ca/.

Drapeau, Michel. 2009. "A Commentary from Canada: Canada's Access to Information." *Open Government: A Journal of Freedom of Information* 5 (1). http://www.opengovjournal.org/.

Gentile, P. 2009. "Resisted Access? National Security, the *Access to Information Act*, and Queer(ing) Archives." *Archivaria* 68: 141-58.

Gilbert, J. 2009. "Access Denied: The *Access to Information Act* and Its Effect on Public Records Creators." *Archivaria* 49: 84-123.

Globe and Mail. 2010. "RCMP Spies Suspected René Lévesque Was a Communist, Records Reveal." *Globe and Mail*, 17 March.

Hewitt, Steve. 1998. "Intelligence at the Learneds: The RCMP, the Learneds, and the Canadian Historical Association." *Journal of the Canadian Historical Association* 8: 267-86.

–. 2000a. "'Information Believed True': RCMP Security Intelligence Activities on Canadian University Campuses and the Controversy Surrounding Them, 1961-1971." *Canadian Historical Review* 81 (2): 191-228.

–. 2000b. "Royal Canadian Mounted Spy: The Secret Life of John Leopold/Jack Esselwein." *Intelligence and National Security* 15 (1): 144-68.

–. 2002. *Spying 101: The RCMP's Secret Activities at Canadian Universities, 1917-1997*. Toronto: University of Toronto Press.

–. 2010. *Snitch! A History of the Modern Intelligence Informer.* New York: Continuum.

Hewitt, S., and C. Sethna. 2012. "Sex Spying: The RCMP Framing of English-Canadian Women's Liberation Groups during the Cold War." In *Debating Dissent: Canada and the 1960s,* ed. by Dominique Clement, Lara Campbell, and Gregory Kealey. Toronto: University of Toronto Press.

Kaplan, Fred. 2006. "Secret Again: The Absurd Scheme to Reclassify Documents." *Slate,* 23 February. http://www.slate.com/.

Kealey, Greg. 1998. "Filing and Defiling: The Organization of the Canadian State's Security Archives in the Interwar Years." In *On the Case: Explorations in Social History,* ed. by Franca Iacovetta and Wendy Mitchinson, 88-105. Toronto: University of Toronto Press.

Kinsman, G., and P. Gentile. 2010. *The Canadian War on Queers: National Security as Sexual Regulation.* Vancouver: UBC Press.

LAC (Library and Archives Canada). 1940. RG 146, vol. 24, file 93-A-00019, University of Toronto, pt. 4, Supt. Vernon Kemp to Commissioner, 20 February.

–. 1969. RG 146, vol. 30, file 93-A-00069, pt. 1, Higgitt to E.T. Galpin, 30 April.

–. 1970. RG 146, vol. 5008, file 97-A-00076, pt. 7, "Academe and Subversion." June and December 1970.

Sethna, Christabelle, and S. Hewitt. 2009. "Clandestine Operations: The Vancouver Women's Caucus, the Abortion Caravan, and the RCMP." *Canadian Historical Review* 90 (3): 463-95.

Shane, Scott. 2006. "US Reclassifies Many Documents in Secret Review." *New York Times,* 21 February.

Shapiro, S., and R. Steinzor. 2006. "The People's Agent: Executive Branch Secrecy and Accountability in an Age of Terrorism." *Law and Contemporary Problems,* 66: 98-129.

Shochat, Gil. 2010. "The Dark Country." *The Walrus* (January/February). http://walrusmagazine.com/.

Treasury Board of Canada Secretariat. 2010. "Statistical Tables 2009-2010 – Access to Information." In *Info Source Bulletin Number 33B – Statistical Reporting.* http://www.infosource.gc.ca/.

Whitaker, R., G. Kealey, and A. Parnaby. 2012. *Canadian Secret Service.* Toronto: University of Toronto Press.

Wilson, I. 2000. "The Fine Art of Destruction Revisited." *Archivaria* 49: 124-39.

LEGISLATION CITED

Access to Information Act, R.S.C. 1985, c. A-1.

Beyond the Blue Line
Researching the Policing of Aboriginal Activism Using Access to Information

TIA DAFNOS

Perhaps the biggest obstacle in doing research on police lies in gaining access to organizations and employees. For social science researchers, access is largely contingent on the degree to which the research project has potential benefits for the police organization, does not compromise investigations or the safety of employees, and cultivates a positive public image of policing. Access has become increasingly restricted, especially to outsiders, rationalized on the basis of security interests. This chapter discusses the problem of gaining access to information about police organizations and their practices. Underlying this problem is the argument that such access allows for transparency that is necessary to ensure accountability of an organization that holds significant power in society. Here I discuss my experiences using access to information (ATI) as a research method in my current research on the policing of Aboriginal peoples' activism in Ontario.

The research revolves around two specific events: the reclamation at Caledonia that began in February 2006, and the National Day of Action on 29 June 2007. These events occurred in the shadow of a reclamation at Ipperwash Provincial Park in 1995 during which Dudley George, an unarmed protester from the Stony Point First Nation, was shot and killed by an Ontario Provincial Police (OPP) sniper. Criticisms and a public inquiry led the OPP to engage in major reforms of their public-order policing approach, particularly in relation to First Nations communities. This highly politicized context and the historically tenuous relations between Aboriginal peoples and police forces in Canada provide the backdrop for my research examining how reforms have materialized.[1]

The use of ATI is integral to critical social science research in the "muck-raking" tradition advocated by Marx (1972, 1984; see also Yeager 2006). In this approach, the goal of research is to reveal what happens behind closed doors and thereby hold organizations accountable for their actions. This form of "studying up" can reveal practices of power that impact on social relations, which is necessary to engage in "projects of social transformation" (Harding and Norberg 2005, 2011). In my research, I adopt a framework that situates organizations, processes, and practices in the context of Canada's colonial history and the ongoing oppression of Aboriginal peoples. The public police institution is invested with the state's monopoly of legitimate violence, which is both instrument and symbol of nation-state sovereignty. As Razack (2002) argues, the under- and overpolicing of Aboriginal peoples is the most evident practice of ongoing colonization in Canada. The police literally represent a front line in the exercise of colonial power. The policing of Aboriginal peoples' activist struggles entails practices that are directly connected to the Canadian state's interest in protecting its claim of sovereignty and its image as a liberal democratic nation (see Alfred and Lowe 2005; Backhouse 1999). After Ipperwash, the OPP adopted a negotiated management approach to public-order policing, emphasizing respect for and upholding the rights of political dissent. This was consistent with a trend in western nation-states in the 1980s and 1990s to officially shift away from repressive policing to practices that more closely reflect liberal democratic values (see Della Porta and Reiter 1998). The question, however, is how this discourse translates into actual police practices in the context of a concurrent trend of militarization, and what the consequences are for those to whom it is applied. The answers to these questions, *and the process of obtaining them,* have implications that go beyond the specific actors and events of the case studies and speak to the nature of contemporary colonial relations.

While I draw on some of my preliminary findings and their implications, this is simultaneously a reflection on some of ATI's strengths and weaknesses in obtaining information about policing practices. The process of writing this chapter was itself shaped by ATI – or, more accurately, the lack of access to information caused by delays in receiving records. Despite the roadblocks that I have encountered, ATI is a valuable research method, especially for critical researchers engaging in research on law enforcement or security issues. The pursuit and demand for transparency are important in seeking to address social, political, and economic inequalities and move towards decolonization.

I therefore begin by providing an overview of my research as a foundation for discussing why and how I have used ATI as a research method. I then consider some of the strengths and limitations of ATI for doing research on police organizations and practices. In the final part of the chapter, I reflect on my ATI research process by drawing on recent experiences and preliminary research findings gained from them.

Policing Aboriginal Activism after Ipperwash: Caledonia and the National Day of Action

Police forces have historically played a central role in the dispossession and exclusion of Aboriginal peoples in the formation of the Canadian nation-state (Samuelson and Monture 2008; Williams and Murray 2007). In recent history, this has been embodied by the fatal shooting of Dudley George by an OPP sniper during the 1995 Ipperwash Provincial Park reclamation by members of the Stony Point First Nation. These events and the ensuing public inquiry spurred a flurry of structural, organizational, and policy reforms at the OPP reflecting the adoption of negotiated management along with features of militarization.

The OPP after Ipperwash

Although the OPP began reforming its policy and organization soon after Ipperwash, the Ontario government resisted calls for a public inquiry for eight years, until the Liberal party replaced the Conservatives in power. In January 2006, near the conclusion of the inquiry, the OPP introduced revisions to its "Framework for Police Preparedness for Aboriginal Critical Incidents" (OPP 2006a), which outlines changes to organizational structure and practices that reflect a unique approach emphasizing cooperation and negotiation with Aboriginal communities. This policy, in addition to broader changes in the OPP's public-order, intelligence, and emergency response functions, were presented to the inquiry – and thus publicly – as reforms aimed at averting tragedies like George's death. Together, these reforms reflect the integration of negotiated management and militarization. This melding is most evident in the OPP's definition of "critical incident" in the Framework (OPP 2006a, 2; emphasis added):

> *An incident where the source of conflict may stem from assertions associated with Aboriginal or treaty rights*, e.g. colour of right, a demonstration in

support of a land claim, a blockade of a transportation route, an occupation of local government buildings, municipal premises, provincial/federal
premises or First Nations buildings.

With this definition, any "incident" asserting Aboriginal or treaty rights is
designated a "critical incident." The consequence is the automatic activation
of the OPP's integrated response protocol, which is used in "high-risk" situations. This includes the mobilization of paramilitarized units – Emergency
Response Teams (ERT) and the Tactics and Rescue Unit (TRU), which provides heavily armed specialized support for high-risk situations, and includes officers trained as snipers. At the core of the integrated response is a
tri-level command structure adopted from the United Kingdom, with "Gold,"
"Silver," and "Bronze" incident commanders in a clear hierarchical division
of responsibility (OPP 2006b, 2006c).

This militaristic integrated response protocol stands in stark contrast to
the stated purposes of the Framework, which clearly reflect the principles of
a negotiated management model: adopting flexible approaches to resolving
conflict, emphasizing "accommodation and mutual respect of differences,
positions and interests," and using strategies that "minimize the use of force
to the fullest extent possible" (OPP 2006a, 2). It takes a proactive approach
aiming to avoid and prevent the emergence of critical incidents such as reclamations and blockades. Among the initiatives introduced in concert with
the Framework is the Aboriginal Relations Team (ART). The ART is a unit
composed of Aboriginal OPP officers that engages in an ongoing relationship with Aboriginal communities with the goal of building trust between
them and the OPP. Through this open communication and negotiation, the
OPP seeks to avoid "escalation" of potential conflicts (OPP 2006d). In the
event of a critical incident, ART officers act as liaisons to facilitate two-way
communication of the interests and intentions of police and protesters to
each other.[2] Juxtaposed with the ART and the Framework's aims of "flexibility," "respect," and minimization of force is the automatic designation of
"high-risk" evident in the definition of a critical incident, meaning that these
goals are to be operationalized through the militaristic integrated response.
Furthermore, this proactive orientation is to be facilitated by the OPP's
adoption of an intelligence-led policing framework in which operational decisions are guided by intelligence products such as threat assessments (see
OPP 2006e). The events at Caledonia and at Tyendinaga during the National
Day of Action were high-profile opportunities for the OPP to apply its new
approach.

Caledonia

The reclamation action in Caledonia would be the first incident in which the OPP could test its new Framework. The land at the root of the action has been in dispute since 1784, when the Crown granted it to the Six Nations (see Backhouse 1999). Despite an outstanding land claim that was filed in 1985, the Crown sold part of the land in 1992 to Henco Industries, a land developer. On 28 February 2006, a group of protesters reclaimed the site to prevent construction of the planned Douglas Creek Estates housing development. By 17 March, three injunctions had been ordered; they were ignored by protesters, leading to the issuance of arrest warrants. The OPP publicly stated that it would enforce the injunctions and warrants only as a last resort, favouring ongoing negotiations (Harries 2006). In the early morning of 20 April, however, the OPP conducted a raid on the site and arrested twenty-one people. According to the OPP, officers used "the least amount of force that was necessary" in response to an assessment of threat (OPP 2006f). On 22 April, an agreement was reached between Six Nations representatives and the Canadian and Ontario governments to resume negotiations. Protests, rallies, and physical altercations involving non-Aboriginal residents of Caledonia have occurred throughout the reclamation, directed at both the Aboriginal community and the OPP. In June 2006, the Ontario government purchased the disputed land from Henco. As of February 2012, the claim remains unresolved. Throughout the reclamation, the OPP has claimed to be adhering to its Framework.

National Day of Action and Tyendinaga

The National Day of Action (NDA) occurred on 29 June 2007, just over a year after the beginning of the Caledonia reclamation. It was organized by the Assembly of First Nations (AFN) to highlight the situation of Aboriginal peoples across Canada through events and activities. Several other groups organized events that were not endorsed by the AFN, including a blockade of the CN Rail tracks and Highways 401 and 2 near Deseronto, Ontario, and the Tyendinaga Mohawk territory. This action was part of an ongoing struggle by the Tyendinaga Mohawk community to have issues of poverty and the lack of access to safe water addressed, in addition to outstanding land claims. The rail line and highways cross the Culbertson Tract – land that the federal government recognizes as unceded by the Tyendinaga Mohawks. After negotiation with the OPP, the protesters opened up the Highway 401 barriers in the mid-morning of 29 June but maintained the blockade of the rail line and Highway 2 until midnight. As with Caledonia, the OPP claimed its handling of the blockades as a success of its "measured approach" (see Valpy 2007).

The Blue Line: The Problem of Access in Researching the Police

There is a tendency in sociological and criminological work to analyze and compare different models of policing, as sketched out above. One problem with this, however, is that it ignores how historically based forms of domination shape such practices. The presentation of models as objective and rational policies that police decision makers and front-line officers can implement through objective rational choices reflects an abstraction exercise that masks, and therefore reinforces, unequal power relations in society. Models are often developed based solely on the official documents, policies, or statements produced by police and government organizations themselves. An analysis of official rhetoric and discourse has value in providing insights into wider dominant discourses and cultural changes in society. The official adoption of negotiated management, for example, resonates with broader discourses of human rights and liberal democracy (see de Lint and Hall 2009). To stop there, however, and engage in a comparison of this "new" post-Ipperwash model of public-order policing with former practices merely contributes to dominant discourse and sustains existing relations of power. Although important, the main problem is not whether or not the intentions of the actors behind the formal adoption of "new" models are transparent. The actual implementation of policies and models does not always match their intentions. A crucial task for critical researchers, therefore, is to push beyond official rhetoric to examine actual *practices*.

Assessing the degree to which official policy and discourse translates into concrete practice is one of the most important and difficult aspects of doing research on police and policing. Perhaps the biggest obstacle lies in gaining access to police and security organizations and their members. The closed and secretive nature of police organizations is well documented (Chan 1997; Manning 1997). Researchers who are "outside-outsiders" – those who are not affiliated with police forces or government bodies with policing responsibility – experience the greatest difficulties in gaining access to police personnel and organizations (Brown 1996, cited in Reiner 2000).[3] Even if access is granted, outsider researchers tend to be viewed with suspicion, particularly if seen as being "anti-police," which affects their ability to establish rapport with participants (see Ericson 1982). Thus, the problem of access is aggravated for critical researchers.[4]

Access depends on getting approval from gatekeepers – supervisory-level officers, chiefs, or directors. If not denied outright, access usually comes with restrictions set by gatekeepers. Officers are expected to adhere to the party line and one mechanism to ensure against inadvertent slips is to allow the researcher access to designated individuals. For example, when seeking interviews for my MA thesis research (described below), I was not allowed access to front-line officers and all my participants had senior positions. While they provided important insights, for the most part these were management and administrative perspectives articulating the dominant rhetoric of their respective organizations.

Beyond the closed nature of the police institution are additional hurdles and difficulties arising from researchers' identities and the subject matter of the research. A researcher's legitimacy depends largely on establishing his or her neutrality or objectivity, as the positivist paradigm continues to be the dominant framework in mainstream academia and wider society. The identification of a research question or topic that is socially and politically divisive, or that has been the basis for criticism against an institution, may be treated with more suspicion with regard to the intentions of the researcher. While perhaps not as definitively as in the 1960s and 1970s, social science academics tend to be associated with having radical politics and, students in particular, with social activism. To a degree, we can all engage in counter-strategies of dress and grooming to appear more "conservative" to mitigate suspicion, but for some of us the visible markers of our identities automatically flag us to be perceived as being inherently biased. This can compound the problems of gaining access and exacerbate the limitations of research methods such as interviewing.

With obtrusive methods such as interviewing or observation, a key concern is that participants may alter their behaviour or provide responses in order to present the best image of themselves and their organizations. In these situations, the research interaction is shaped by the socially situated identities of both researcher and participant. I experienced this in my MA research when I interviewed several law enforcement and intelligence personnel about the role of ethnic identifiers in the intelligence-led policing of organized crime. Reflecting on my research process afterwards, a concern I had was about how my identity – as a young racialized female graduate student – interacted with the subject matter to shape my interactions with interviewees, all but one of whom were older white men. Horn (1997) describes how female researchers can have difficulties gaining trust in the male-dominated environment of policing, but can also benefit from their gender if they are viewed as being incompetent, harmless, and thus non-threatening. Age and status (e.g., as graduate student) can also contribute to this ascribed identity, particularly if participants are positioned as "experts." While my gender, age, and status could have helped me to gain access to participants and facilitated the sharing of information during interviews, this may have been tempered by my racialized identity, my questions about the use of race and ethnicity in policing practices, and the highly sensitive social/political context of racial profiling.

Navigating the Blue Line: Using Access to Information

ATI requests are an important and valuable research method for obtaining access to closed institutions like the police while avoiding some of the potential difficulties created by socially situated identities in interviewing. Yet ATI itself has significant limitations that are exacerbated in the context of politically sensitive research on policing and security. Gatekeeping and participants' self-censorship have their parallels in ATI-based research. Formally, access is denied or restricted through the use of exemption provisions in ATI legislation to partially or fully withhold certain records from release. Access is further limited through more informal techniques of opacity such as the denial of the existence of records, or practices of stonewalling and delay (see Introduction; Roberts 2002, 2005, 2006).

Like most ATI requesters, I have relied on publicly accessible documents as an important starting point. The increased production and accessibility of official publications in the age of managerial policing can be used to identify specific records that can be requested via ATI.[5] Unfortunately, in light of the barriers to conventional research access described above, researchers may come to rely solely on these official publications produced for a public audience, thus reproducing and legitimizing the discourse of law enforcement organizations (see also Chapter 9). In my research process, an invaluable resource has been the Ipperwash Inquiry website, an archive of the documents produced in the course of the inquiry, such as the OPP's Framework and reports documenting changes to their intelligence, public-order policing, and emergency response sections. Another key resource has been media reports on Caledonia and the NDA that have themselves sometimes drawn on materials obtained using ATI. My experience has been that journalists are more than willing to share ATI records or the request file numbers to facilitate access to these records from the relevant ATI offices. As is evident from the contributions to this book, critical researchers and

journalists share a commitment to freedom of information as an accountability mechanism.

In conducting research on events that occurred some years earlier, I have
been able to take advantage of several already-completed ATI requests directly and indirectly related to Caledonia and the NDA. In most cases, a
formal request is required, citing the file number of the original request.[6]
The benefit of obtaining these materials is that they can usually be processed quickly. In many cases, these records can provide information and
insights to form the basis for future requests. For example, a series of
e-mails released by the Department of National Defence (DND) revealed
that prior to the NDA, an inter-agency subcommittee composed of federal
law enforcement, national security, defence, and other government departments had been formed on Aboriginal issues and met weekly. I was then
able to form a specific request for records of those meetings from Public
Safety Canada (PSC), the ministry in which the subcommittee was convened.[7] One drawback of the existence of previously released records related to the issue of interest is that analysts might try to pressure requesters
to modify their request to consist only of these already-processed records
– dangling the prospect of a timely release as a benefit of not pursuing additional documents.

Timeliness is a major consideration when a significant frustration with
using ATI is the length of time it can take for a request to be processed. Only
my requests for previously released records have been completed within the
prescribed thirty-day framework. All other requests have required extensions, with some offices not even bothering to provide any notice. Even formal deadlines mean little in terms of when one might actually receive
records; several of my requests have ended up as deemed refusals anyway,
having gone far beyond their extension dates. One of the most common
reasons for extensions is the need to consult with other organizations. Law
enforcement and security agencies are increasingly interconnected both
permanently and on an ad hoc basis in response to particular events, making extensions inevitable in policing and security-related research. In the
case of Aboriginal reclamations and protests, multiple police forces, intelligence agencies, and other government departments often play direct roles,
as was evident in both Caledonia and the NDA. While the involvement of
some organizations was publicly known, the extent and the involvement of
others (which I describe in the next section) were more ambiguous and confirmed only through ATI records. This inter-agency collaboration results in
an extended consultation process, as each organization linked to a record

– such as an intelligence report – must be consulted about its release
(Roberts 2006). This increases the amount of time needed to process requests. At the same time, the overlap can provide an opportunity to obtain
records from one agency that may be withheld, left out, or redacted differently by another.

Another barrier to access comes from the statutory provisions in ATI
legislation that allow certain kinds of material to be exempted from release.
The records that I have received have been redacted or withheld based on
many sections of the federal *Access to Information Act*, especially sections
15 (records relating to international affairs and national security), 16 (records relating to law enforcement), and 21 (advice, consultations, positions,
and plans for government), and their equivalents in Ontario's *Freedom of
Information and Protection of Privacy Act (FIPPA)*. Most frustrating is when
the existence of material is neither confirmed nor denied by the department. This occurred with a request I made to the Canadian Security
Intelligence Service (CSIS). Unlike release packages from other departments, pages were not numbered – so I do not know how many relevant
records were found in total – and there is no specific explanation for why
they may have been withheld. In contrast, release packages from the DND
and PSC contained hundreds of completely withheld pages citing the relevant exemption provisions. While frustrating, this at least provided some
indication that these departments do have a significant interest and activity
around the matter of inquiry.[8]

I recount here my attempt to obtain records documenting OPP decision
making at Caledonia. As one of my first major requests, this was a learning
experience not only about limitations and frustrations but also about the
interactional nature of the process. As Lee (2001) suggests, ATI research
can provide insights into organizational decision making and policy development. There is potential for this approach to reveal the everyday activities, tactics, procedures, strategies, and assumptions of organizations,
especially those such as the police that are largely closed to outsiders.
According to reports produced for the Ipperwash Inquiry, the OPP introduced a scribe system to ensure that all decision making and communications of the Gold, Silver, and Bronze incident commanders during critical
incidents are recorded (OPP 2006b, 2006c). This is intended for transparency and accountability. Incident commander notes can potentially reveal
the dynamics between negotiation/communication strategies and militarization by documenting police decision-making processes and the relationship between operations and intelligence practices.

Initially I sought a range of records that I believed would show the decision-making process at Caledonia, including incident commander notes. I filed this request with Ontario's Ministry of Community Safety and Correctional Services (MCSCS), which administers requests for OPP records. The request faced resistance throughout the process. My first attempt, an admittedly broad request in hindsight, was successfully quashed by the analyst. I had requested:

> Copies of the following records and documents produced by the Ontario Provincial Police relating to the occupation of the site of the former Douglas Creek Estates in Caledonia, Ontario between February 1 2006 and August 31 2006: Intelligence reports, analyses, memos or advisories; event documentation (OPP scribe notes); and incident reports.

Immediately, the analyst told me that fees would run into thousands of dollars to pursue the request and that intelligence and incident reports would not be released. He was then unhelpful in assisting me to clarify or even narrow the request. Instead, he asked whether I had tried the Ipperwash Inquiry website and offered to send me the OPP's Framework, which had been available online for at least a couple of years. After I explained that I was interested in obtaining records reflecting the OPP's Framework in operational decision making at Caledonia, the analyst informed me defensively that policing policies are always applied in the same manner in all cases. So whatever the policy says would be how things unfold. I could almost hear the relief in his voice when I said that I would drop the request and do some work on my own to be more specific. After berating myself for letting him push me to completely drop the request, I submitted another one in March 2009, significantly narrowing the scope to "Copies of Ontario Provincial Police scribe notes (and any additional forms of event documentation) from April 13 2006 to April 27 2006 relating to the occupation of the site of the former Douglas Creek Estates in Caledonia, Ontario." This request was assigned to a different analyst, who assisted me in clarifying the request further to obtain the specific documents I was seeking – "incident commander notes," rather than "scribe notes." While the specificity of a request is important to prevent analysts from dismissing them outright, this raises a "black box" problem of being able to know the specific terminology for the records sought (see Lee 2001).

I was notified that an extension to July 2009 was needed, as the request required a search through a large number of records that would interfere with the operations of the OPP. Two weeks after that deadline passed, I was told that the release package was in the approval process, merely awaiting sign-off, and that I should expect to receive it by courier within a week. I hit a brick wall after that. My follow-up calls to the analyst went unanswered until I contacted the main office. I was finally put in touch with a new analyst, who apparently had taken over the file. After that, my request fell into another black hole of unanswered voice mails and e-mails. Almost four weeks later, I reached the analyst, who told me that the package was ready but still waiting for the OPP (as the office of primary interest) to give final approval. She was discernibly frustrated with the delay and offered to describe the records and their contents to me over the phone. I finally received the records on 12 December 2009 – five months after the extension deadline. During all of this, it was hard to keep a conspiracy theory from forming in my mind, or to keep from wondering whether my request had fallen victim to amber-lighting or red-filing processes (Chapter 1; Rees 2003; Roberts 2006). While this could have been a case of an overextended *FIPPA* office or bureaucratic entanglement, the degree of delay in the context of the events of interest suggests deliberate stonewalling to permit communications and image management.[9] In the end, I received just over two hundred pages of significantly redacted notes, reports, and operations plans. Records from the days of the raid on the reclamation site and immediately following were conspicuously withheld.

Getting beyond the Blue Line

Using these OPP records and materials obtained through other ATI requests, I have been able to begin piecing together a backdrop of the state's responses to Caledonia and the NDA – responses that have framed these events as *threats to national security* rather than matters of law enforcement or maintenance of public order. This securitized response is evident in the militarization of police operations concomitant with implementation of the negotiated management approach. The production and use of intelligence is the pivot point for this convergence (see de Lint and Hall 2009). Also consistent with securitization, non-security/law enforcement government departments, particularly Indian and Northern Affairs Canada (INAC), as it was then known, played a central role in intelligence production and pre-emptive measures of "negotiation." These practices reflect an intelligence-led policing approach, guided by intelligence reports and assessments, the fruits of these multi-agency collaborations. The production of intelligence and the discourse they use clearly reflect a national security framing of the events.

This has implications for policing operations as well as the control of information through secrecy. As with stonewalling the release of records, other elements of the ATI process are indicative of the state's security response.

Militarization

Both Caledonia and Tyendinaga were publicly presented as successful examples of the OPP's new emphasis on negotiation. Behind the scenes, however, three aspects of the policing response reflected a convergence of the policing and security functions. First, consistent with the OPP's Framework, the integrated response protocol was activated, meaning that the command-and-control structure and paramilitary units were deployed. The OPP incident commander's notes and operational plans for Caledonia obtained in my ATI request reveal that several ERTs and the Provincial Emergency Response Team (PERT) were deployed at 4:30 in the morning of 20 April 2006 in an operation to "arrest any persons found on site."[10] Before and after the raid, ERT members maintained perimeters. The decision-making structure identified in the operations plan for the raid reflects a hierarchy involving all levels of incident command. The operation commenced after the Gold commander's approval (given on 19 April) was received by the Silver commander, and then was coordinated by the Bronze commander on-site.[11] At Tyendinaga, ERT and TRU teams were on standby.[12]

Second, militarization was evident in the collaborative involvement of a wide range of law enforcement and security agencies in both cases.[13] All parties were coordinated through a centralized command structure. A core task was the development of intelligence, which involved extensive surveillance and the cultivation of informants. According to Royal Canadian Mounted Police (RCMP) employee overtime and expense compensation claim forms, the OPP established a Joint Intelligence Group (JIG) at a Special Operations Centre located in Toronto for the Caledonia reclamation. In terms of methods, this highlights the importance in ATI-based research of thinking outside the box to find ways of getting at the information of interest through records we might not initially think of as relevant. Beyond the OPP's own intelligence bureau, participants in the JIG included representatives of the RCMP, CSIS, and the Canadian Forces National Counter-Intelligence Unit (CFNCIU).[14] The RCMP forms also reveal that some RCMP members took on coordinator positions in the JIG while others acted as incident commanders at the command post in Caledonia. This indicates that the RCMP played a central, rather than supporting, role in decision making and operations. The contingent of RCMP members also included the "O" (Ontario) Division ERT and intelligence officers who participated in the JIG and engaged in surveillance activities.[15] A CFNCIU counter-intelligence information report obtained from the DND indicates that the Canadian Forces were involved in the Caledonia JIG. The 24 April 2006 report refers to information obtained from five sources (informants) in relation to the reclamation and indicates that the information was shared with CSIS "via internal reporting staff members at the JIG."[16] For the NDA, the "Federal Coordination Framework for the AFN National Day of Action" – a strategy document produced by PSC to get all involved federal departments on the same page for the NDA – along with various e-mails obtained from PSC and the DND indicate that coordination and intelligence development occurred at a national level as well as through regional working groups involving the RCMP, CSIS, PSC, the Department of Fisheries and Oceans (DFO), INAC, and regional/local law enforcement.[17]

The active involvement of the Canadian Forces in both cases reflects a third core feature of militarization: the involvement of the armed forces in domestic matters (Kraska 2007). At Caledonia, the involvement of the Canadian Forces via CFNCIU appears to contradict a directive issued by Canada Command on 3 May 2006. The directive stated that Canadian Forces members would "neither visit nor conduct reconnaissance of the sites" and that any assistance – provision of personnel, infrastructure, resources, or equipment – would require approval from the Minister of National Defence. Further, the official public statement would be that the Canadian Forces was not and did not anticipate being involved.[18] Whether this points to a cover-up of Canadian Forces involvement or some kind of exemption for intelligence operations, it raises questions about the nature of armed forces involvement.[19] In the case of the NDA, the DND was directly involved in preparations as a participant in various working groups. As de Lint and Hall (2009, 271) note, militarization (both the presence of military forces and paramilitarized law enforcement) is more likely in cases where "the existential right of the nation-state itself is said to be threatened." With securitization, police become increasingly engaged in "high" or political policing, with increased involvement of government. This erodes the conventional identification of public police as engaging independently in the "low" policing task of crime control by enforcing laws (Brodeur 1983; Murphy 2007). The blurring between "high" and "low" policing has been particularly problematic in relation to Aboriginal peoples (Beare and Murray 2007). The involvement of national security agencies (which have a high policing function) is one part of this. The other part is the direct involvement of government organizations without explicit security or law enforcement mandates.

The Role of Indian and Northern Affairs Canada

As with most instances of blockades and reclamations by Aboriginal peoples, land claims are at the heart of the Six Nations reclamation at Caledonia and the events of the NDA, including the Tyendinaga blockades. First Nations' struggles vis-à-vis the Canadian state have therefore always been an important and inherent political dimension because they are fundamentally questions of sovereignty. INAC is the federal agency responsible for negotiating land claims and more generally for managing the state's relationship with Aboriginal peoples. This raises troubling questions about INAC's significant and active role in both Caledonia and the NDA – one geared towards law enforcement or security strategy rather than a genuine commitment to the resolution of land claims. Records obtained from various departments show that INAC was involved as an active participant in the sharing of information, production of intelligence, and pre-emptive measures leading up to the NDA. In a summary of a federal inter-agency subcommittee meeting, INAC was identified along with RCMP, CSIS, DFO, and Transport Canada as the "top departments with intelligence" relating to the NDA.[20] The "Federal Coordination Framework for the AFN National Day of Action" also indicated that INAC representatives would "enhance [the] analytical capacity" of the Integrated Threat Assessment Centre (ITAC), which produces intelligence reports and threat assessments (see below). This was facilitated by the secondment of representatives from INAC to ITAC. Various e-mail communications obtained from the DND and PSC refer to INAC's provision of information about planning for events in First Nations communities across Canada. This included reporting about First Nations leaders "who are not supportive of the action," which was a significant piece of information with respect to the possible use of divide-and-conquer tactics.[21] A 2007 INAC presentation to the RCMP stated that a key source of such information was INAC's own Hot Spot reporting system – a continuous monitoring of environmental "risks" relating to Aboriginal communities, including protests.[22] According to the Federal Coordination Framework, two indicators of a successful response to "militant incidents" would be to "isolate the splinter group as an anomaly in efforts to improve relations with First Nations" and to "avoid situations developing which cause others to be attracted to the splinter groups (e.g. confrontations which may be provoked for this purpose)."[23]

INAC itself appears to have acted upon this intelligence by engaging in activities aimed at isolating "militants." Bridging its intelligence contribution with an enforcement role, INAC participated in strategic planning and incident management for the NDA, which included taking a central role in pre-emptive efforts.[24] The Federal Coordination Framework released by PSC states: "INAC has proposed to the AFN that events be organized around the theme of *Building Bridges not Blockades.* To this end, they have proposed to the AFN a number of suggested events to build public support and deter militant protests."[25] Revealingly, this statement was fully redacted in the copy of the document released by the DND. The AFN's website for the NDA reflected the adoption of this suggested theme, stating that it did not seek to hold blockades and protests but "to build bridges – not blockades – with Canadians."[26] Interestingly, ITAC uses the same terminology – "build bridges, not blockades" – to describe the position of "some First Nations chiefs" without mentioning the role of INAC in the unclassified reports provided to government departments and other "stakeholders."[27] INAC's activities appear even more surreptitious in attempting to influence the character of the NDA as INAC representatives – including the minister himself – engaged in meetings with First Nations leaders aimed at persuading them to "stand down their plans."[28] In these pre-emptive strategies, INAC drew on its power as land claims arbitrator. Perhaps the most blatant example is evident in an internal DND e-mail marked "secret," stating that "INAC has made a significant offer related to Caledonia and plans to make some broader policy announcements in the coming weeks as preventative measures. *Everything will be timed carefully*"[29] (emphasis added; see Figure 8.1). The offer was a $125 million settlement in four other Six Nations land claims. It was contingent on the protesters' ending the Caledonia reclamation and on some assurance from the Six Nations that members would not engage in further reclamations (Daly 2007).

Intelligence Products

The operations of the various law enforcement, security, and other government agencies such as INAC are informed by, and contribute to, intelligence documents such as situation reports and threat assessments that reflect an obvious blurring of Aboriginal activism with criminality and terrorism. One of the most common types of document that I have received

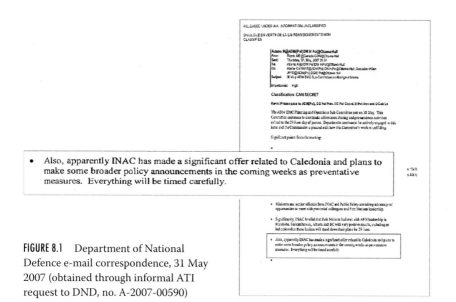

FIGURE 8.1 Department of National Defence e-mail correspondence, 31 May 2007 (obtained through informal ATI request to DND, no. A-2007-00590)

from several organizations in relation to the NDA consists of highly redacted threat assessments produced by the Integrated Threat Assessment Centre (ITAC), housed at CSIS headquarters.[30] ITAC was established in 2004 as part of Canada's National Security Policy to centralize and coordinate the collection and analysis of information and to produce assessments about *terrorist threats* to national security. The first ITAC threat assessment related to "Aboriginal Protests – Summer 2007" was released on 11 May 2007 and was produced on a regular basis until the week of 25 June, at which point they began to be produced daily.[31] Besides law enforcement, versions of these assessments are distributed to government departments and other "stakeholders." The ITAC threat assessments reports were identified in a DND e-mail as being "where the best info is housed."[32] According to the preamble of these reports, "the right of Canadians to engage in peaceful protest is a cornerstone of Canada's democratic society. ITAC is concerned only where there is a threat of politically-motivated violence, or where protests threaten the functioning of critical infrastructure." When political action is tied to a perceived potential for violence or disruption of "critical infrastructure," it becomes classified as a terrorist threat. Both the Caledonia reclamation and the planned Tyendinaga blockades were regularly highlighted items of concern in ITAC reports. Caledonia was also the subject of several LASER threat assessments produced by CSIS.[33] The OPP's definition of Aboriginal protests in its Framework as inherently high-risk "critical incidents" resonates with this threat framing.

The classification of these events as terrorist threats demonstrates the implications of overbreadth in the 2001 *Anti-terrorism Act* in capturing individuals and groups engaging in forms of activism such as blockades and reclamations. As critics argued before passage of the act, these actions could be construed as threats to critical infrastructure (Roach 2001; Schneiderman and Cossman 2001). First Nations representatives expressed concerns that the act would formalize existing tendencies by government, law enforcement, and media to frame Aboriginal activism as terrorism (Orkin 2003). The framing of Aboriginal struggles as problems of national security delegitimizes the underlying issues while simultaneously legitimizing coercive and intrusive intelligence gathering and militaristic enforcement activities, as evidenced at Caledonia and the NDA. The *Anti-terrorism Act* granted all law enforcement agencies enhanced investigative powers, particularly in relation to surveillance, in cases of "terrorism" offences. Aboriginal groups engaging in "disruptive" protest are likely to be subjected to intrusive forms of investigation (Friedland 2001). Significantly, the enhancement of powers comes through decreased external (judicial) oversight. The securitization of policing described above is thus permeated by increased secrecy that extends to the control of information in the ATI process.

The ATI Research Process as Data

Apart from the records obtained, the ATI process itself can illuminate the research topic. Although redactions severely limit access, we can occasionally glean some useful – albeit broad – insights from them. While I expected exemptions of material related to law enforcement (section 16 of the *Access to Information Act*), what is striking about the materials that I have – or rather, have not – received is the high frequency with which section 15 exemptions for information relating to international affairs and national defence are invoked. Taken along with the evident involvement of agencies such as CSIS and the CFCNIU, these redactions emphasize that Aboriginal activism is not treated as just a *policing* issue.[34] This problematization by authorities is important because, as discussed above, it can ease some of the restrictions on police investigative powers while increasing the cloak of secrecy around operations – and limiting the release of information.

The claim of national security can be used to circumvent ATI legislation, and has increased since the attacks on New York and Washington of

11 September 2011 (Earl 2009). There is also concern that security and intelligence personnel may consciously avoid recording certain communications or decisions because of their potential visibility via ATI (Wark 2002; Chapter 4). In response to a request I made to INAC for copies of all their communications with the RCMP, OPP, CSIS, and DND relating to Caledonia, I was informed that they could not provide any such records because "all communications between the agencies mentioned in your request, would have been conducted informally, by telephone or in person and no written records were ever produced" (INAC, personal communication). Although this seems highly improbable in the age of e-mail, there is a concerted effort to eliminate the availability of potentially damaging materials for release. In 2005, the OPP modified its training course for Level 2 incident commanders, adding a component on freedom of information. This component was introduced in recognition "that Incident Commanders need to consider the impact of access and privacy legislation" and "must always be cognizant that communications may be open to public scrutiny." The component aims to train incident commanders to "understand FIPPA as it would relate to the communications before, during and after a major incident" (OPP 2006b, 19). The potential of the scribe system introduced post-Ipperwash to provide greater transparency and accountability may therefore be offset by deliberate practices to filter information or keep it off the record.

Conclusion

The research process – whether based on conventional methods or ATI – is political. Despite obvious differences, the ATI research experience is no less interactional than conducting interviews. The stonewalling, delays, heavy redactions, mass exemptions, failures to confirm the existence of records, and enactment of changes to recordkeeping practices are institutional practices aimed at preserving walls of secrecy and state power. In addition to the records obtained through ATI requests, the process itself can be an important part of the research "data," revealing information about the organization(s) and the exercise of power by the state. It can provide insight into these practices that may be difficult to get at through conventional methods such as interviewing. By engaging in critical research using ATI, we can challenge these barriers and resist the erosion of democratic transparency.

The politicized nature of this process is highlighted by my experience in attempting to gain information about the policing of Aboriginal peoples' activism. The state's problematizing of these struggles as issues of national security allows for the justification of highly coercive practices and decreased transparency. The coercive and intrusive policing practices used, and the secrecy and evasion employed to keep them hidden, are concerns as police forces can navigate limitations on their power through collaboration with national security and military agencies. This is particularly evident as the colonial relations underlying reclamations and blockades by Aboriginal peoples lend themselves to a national security framing. Drawing on Murphy's assertion (2007) that securitization reflects a reassertion rather than a decline of state power, the "securitized" policing of Aboriginal struggles evident in the wide network of institutional actors involved (notably INAC), the reliance on covert surveillance and intelligence production as part of militarized law enforcement responses, and the increased secrecy of information point to the Canadian state's assertion of sovereignty against Aboriginal challenges to its legitimacy. In the context of the Caledonia reclamation and the Tyendinaga blockade during the NDA, the militarized policing evident in institutional practices reveals a much more complex dynamic than a neat and simple post-Ipperwash "shift" to a new negotiation-based approach in the OPP's Framework and ART initiatives. Despite its many limitations, ATI is an important method of getting at this complexity.

Law enforcement and other government agencies are obviously aware that their decisions and operations can be made visible (to varying degrees) through ATI requests, and this appears to be shaping their communication and recordkeeping practices. This has an important implication for academic, media, and public interest researchers using ATI. Making ATI requests is far from being a passive and unobtrusive research method, as we are actually indirectly involved in this changing of institutional practices. The irony is that our demands for accountability and visibility may be leading law enforcement and security agencies to engage in practices to further limit the relevance, utility, or accuracy of records that are produced. We need to be aware of how our use of ATI may be encouraging government organizations to find new ways of evading accountability and transparency, and in turn develop our own means of responding.

NOTES

1 A note on terminology in this chapter: The term "Aboriginal" is used in the Canadian context to include First Nations, Inuit, and Métis peoples, but it is a contested term (see Alfred and Corntassel 2005). I have chosen to use the term "reclamation" rather than the conventional reference to such actions as "occupations." Each of these terms conveys different meanings of belonging: to "reclaim" land implies a prior existence/belonging, whereas to "occupy" implies an encroachment or infringement. I use the

terms "police," "police forces/ institution/organizations" to refer to the public police as a particular manifestation of "policing," in a broader sense understood as practices of control (in a structuralist frame) or governance (in a Foucauldian vein). The "policing" of Aboriginal peoples and activism is therefore understood as practices of (colonial) control or regulation. The public police and other state institutions are a primary source of, and participant in, in this policing. "Public-order policing" refers to activities undertaken by police forces in relation to potentially disruptive gatherings in public spaces, including sporting events and activities such as protests, blockades, or marches.

2 The new approach is referred to as "measured response" by the RCMP in Canada, but I use "negotiated management" because it better reflects the discourse of the OPP Framework and related initiatives that are based on negotiation and cooperation.

3 The other researcher types are inside-insiders (police officers doing research), outside-insiders (former police officers), and inside-outsiders (civilians with positions within police forces or government organizations with policing responsibilities).

4 This is the case, of course, unless covert or deceptive methods are used, which raises ethical issues. For discussions on the ethics for critical researchers studying institutions of power, see Marx 1984 and Lee 1993.

5 Increased managerialism in policing has led to a proliferation in the production of official publications, which are made accessible through forces' websites. These include annual reports, business plans, and even forms of unclassified intelligence based on open sources.

6 The Department of National Defence (DND) will fulfill these requests informally and waive the processing fee. The DND and INAC (among other departments) list recently completed ATI requests on their websites, making these requests easier.

7 DND, e-mail correspondence (15, 24, and 31 May, and 21 June 2007), obtained through informal ATI request to DND, no. A-2007-00590. The PSC file number for these meeting records is A-2009-00070/FA.

8 For example, the DND release no. AI-2009-00443, based on previous ATI request no. 2007-000583 contained records mentioning "Mohawk Warrior Society." Although the bulk of records were withheld, it is evident from the over 750 responsive pages that this is a topic of interest to the DND.

9 In November 2009, a couple that lived on the disputed land in Caledonia sued the province and OPP for failing to protect them during the reclamation. An out-of-court settlement was reached in December 2009 before conclusion of the proceedings. Coincidentally, my request was released soon thereafter.

10 OPP Emergency Response Team Western Region, "Operations Plan: Haldimand Reclamation" (17 April 2006), obtained through ATI request to MCSCS, no. CSCS-2009-0879. PERT was formed after 9/11 as a special response team for terrorist threats.

11 Ibid.

12 Revealed in Tyendinaga Mohawk activist Shawn Brant's preliminary hearing related to his role in the blockades. Transcripts of unauthorized OPP wiretaps of conversations between OPP Chief Julian Fantino and Brant were publicly released after a publication ban was challenged by CBC News and Brant waived his right to the ban.

Transcripts are available on the CBC website, http://cbc.ca/; see "NDP Calls for Fantino 'to Resign or Be Fired' over Brant Wiretaps."

13 The similarities of response should be noted since the Caledonia reclamation is arguably a "local" matter while the Tyendinaga blockades occurred in the context of a national event, the NDA.

14 Canadian Forces National Counter-Intelligence Unit (CFNCIU), Counter-intelligence report (24 April 2006), obtained through informal ATI request to DND, no. AI-2009-00443, based on previous ATI request to DND, no. 2007-000583.

15 RCMP, Compensation, expense, and travel claims, obtained through ATI request to RCMP, no. GA-3951-3-05023/-8, based on previous ATI request by the *Hamilton Spectator.*

16 CFNCIU, Counter-intelligence report (24 April 2006), obtained through informal ATI request to DND, no. AI-2009-00443, based on previous ATI request to DND, no. 2007-000583.

17 PSC, "Federal Coordination Framework for AFN National Day of Action, 29 June 2007" (8 May 2007), obtained through ATI request to PSC, no. 1336-A-2009-0052 (was part of previous release package, no. A-2007-0121).

18 Canada Command, "Commander's Planning Guidance – CF Policy in Support of Law Enforcement Agencies in Caledonia and Other Linked Sympathetic Demonstrations" (3 May 2006), obtained through informal ATI request to DND, previously released file no. A-2006-00447.

19 On the blurring and circumventing of organizational mandates in collaborations between government organizations, see Larsen and Piché 2009.

20 ADM Emergency Management Committee, "Planning and Operations Sub-Committee – Aboriginal Issues, Summary Record" [summary of meeting] (16 May 2007), obtained through ATI request to PSC, no. A-2009-00070/FA.

21 DND, untitled e-mail (7 June 2007), obtained through informal ATI request to DND, no. A-2007-00590.

22 Indian and Northern Affairs Canada, "Aboriginal Hot Spots and Public Safety" [deck presentation] (30 March 2007), obtained through ATI request to RCMP, no. GA-3951-3-00060/11. Examples of the Hot Spot reporting system were obtained through ATI request to INAC, no. A-2010-02632.

23 These points were redacted based on section 16 in the version released by the DND but not in the PSC version. PSC, "Federal Coordination Framework for AFN National Day of Action, 29 June 2007" (8 May 2007), obtained through ATI request to PSC, no. 1336-A-2009-0052 (was part of previous release package, no. A-2007-0121).

24 Ibid.

25 Ibid. at 6.

26 Assembly of First Nations, "National Day of Action Questions and Answers." http://web.archive.org/.

27 Integrated Threat Assessment Centre (ITAC), "ITAC Threat Assessment: Aboriginal Protests Summer 2007" [#07/30] (11 May 2007), obtained through ATI request to CSIS, no. 117-2008-123.

28 DND, e-mail (31 May 2007), obtained through informal ATI request to DND, no. A-2007-00590.

29 Ibid.
30 In June 2011, the Centre was renamed the Integrated Terrorism Assessment Centre.
31 ITAC, "ITAC Threat Assessment: Aboriginal Protests Summer 2007" [#07/46] (21 June 2007), obtained through ATI request to CSIS, no. 117-2008-123.
32 DND, e-mail (26 June 2007), obtained through informal ATI request to DND, no. A-2007-00590.
33 CSIS, "LASER CSIS Threat Assessment [#06/71, 06/91, 06/101, 06/145, 06/202] (3 March, 21 April, 28 April, 13 June, and 21 August 2006), obtained through ATI request to CSIS, no. 117-2008-123.
34 A preliminary comparison with ATI records relating to the activist and protest activities of non-Aboriginal groups suggests that this national security approach is unique to the activism of Aboriginal peoples.

REFERENCES

Alfred, Taiaiake, and Lana Lowe. 2005. "Warrior Societies in Contemporary Indigenous Communities." Ipperwash Inquiry, http://www.attorneygeneral. jus.gov.on.ca/.

Alfred, Taiaiake, and Jeff Corntassel. 2005. "Being Indigenous: Resurgences Against Contemporary Colonialism." *Government and Opposition* 40 (4): 597-614.

Backhouse, Constance. 1999. *Colour-Coded: A Legal History of Racism in Canada 1900-1950.* Toronto: University of Toronto Press.

Beare, Margaret, and Tonita Murray, eds. 2007. *Police and Government Relations: Who's Calling the Shots?* Toronto: University of Toronto Press.

Brodeur, Jean-Paul. 1983. "High Policing and Low Policing: Some Remarks about the Policing of Political Activities." *Social Problems* 30 (5): 507-20.

Chan, Janet. 1997. *Changing Police Culture: Policing in a Multicultural Society.* New York: Cambridge University Press.

Daly, Rita. 2007. "Caledonia Offer: $125 Million: Ottawa Seeks an End to 4 Land Claim Disputes, but Native Chief Calls It a 'Starting Point.'" *Toronto Star,* 31 May.

De Lint, Willem, and Alan Hall. 2009. *Intelligent Control: Policing Labour in Canada.* Toronto: University of Toronto Press.

Della Porta, Donatella, and Herbert Reiter, eds. 1998. *Policing Protests: The Control of Mass Demonstrations in Western Democracies.* Minneapolis: University of Minnesota Press.

Earl, Jennifer. 2009. "Information Access and Protest Policing Post-9/11: Studying the Policing of the 2004 Republican National Convention." *American Behavioral Scientist* 53 (1): 44-60.

Ericson, Richard. 1982. *Reproducing Order: A Study of Police Patrol Work.* Toronto: University of Toronto Press.

Friedland, Martin. 2001. "Police Powers in Bill C-36." In *The Security of Freedom: Essays on Canada's Anti-Terrorism Bill,* ed. by R.J. Daniels, P. Macklem, and K. Roach, 269-86. Toronto: University of Toronto Press.

Harding, Sandra, and Kathryn Norberg. 2005. "New Feminist Approaches to Social Science Methodologies: An Introduction." *Signs* 30 (4): 2009-15.

Harries, Kate. 2006. "Peaceful Solution Best, Native Protesters Say." *Globe and Mail*, 30 March, A11.

Horn, Rebecca. 1997. "Not 'One of the Boys': Women Researching the Police." *Journal of Gender Studies* 6 (3): 297.

Kraska, Peter B. 2007. "Militarization and Policing – Its Relevance to 21st Century Police." *Policing* 14: 501-13.

Larsen, Mike, and Justin Piché. 2009. "Exceptional State, Pragmatic Bureaucracy, and Indefinite Detention: The Case of the Kingston Immigration Holding Centre." *Canadian Journal of Law and Society* 24 (2): 203-29.

Lee, Raymond M. 1993. *Doing Research on Sensitive Topics*. London: Sage.

–. 2001. "Research Uses of the US *Freedom of Information Act.*" *Field Methods* 13 (4): 370-91.

Manning, Peter. 1997. *Police Work: The Social Organization of Policing*. Long Grove, IL: Waveland Press.

Marx, Gary. 1972. *Muckraking Sociology: Research as Social Criticism*. New Brunswick, NJ: Transaction Books.

–. 1984. "Notes on the Discovery, Collection, and Assessment of Hidden and Dirty Data." In *Studies in the Sociology of Social Problems*, ed. by J. Schneider and J. Kitsuse, 78-113. Norwood, NJ: Ablex.

Murphy, Chris. 2007. "'Securitizing' Canadian Policing: A New Policing Paradigm for the Post 9/11 Security State?" *Canadian Journal of Sociology* 32 (4): 451-77.

OPP (Ontario Provincial Police). 2006a. "A Framework for Police Preparedness for Aboriginal Critical Incidents." Ipperwash Inquiry, http://www.attorney general.jus.gov.on.ca/.

–. 2006b. "OPP Emergency Response Services: A Comparison of 1995 to 2006." Ipperwash Inquiry, http://www.attorneygeneral.jus.gov.on.ca/.

–. 2006c. "OPP Public Order Units: A Comparison of 1995 to 2006." Ipperwash Inquiry, http://www.attorneygeneral.jus.gov.on.ca/.

–. 2006d. "Aboriginal Initiatives: Building Respectful Relationships." Ipperwash Inquiry, http://www.attorneygeneral.jus.gov.on.ca/.

–. 2006e. "OPP Intelligence Services: A Comparison of 1995 to 2006." Ipperwash Inquiry, http://www.attorneygeneral.jus.gov.on.ca/.

–. 2006f. "Protesters Removed from Caledonia Housing Development." News release, 20 April.

Orkin, Andrew. 2003. "When the Law Breaks Down: Aboriginal Peoples in Canada and Governmental Defiance of the Rule of Law." *Osgoode Hall Law Journal* 41: 445-63.

Razack, Sherene. 2002. "Gendered Racial Violence and Spatialized Justice: The Murder of Pamela George." In *Race, Space and the Law: Unmapping a White Settler Society*, ed. by S. Razack, 121-56. Toronto: Between the Lines.

Rees, Ann. 2003. "Red File Alert: Public Access at Risk." *Toronto Star*, 1 November, A32.

Reiner, Robert. 2000. "Police Research." In *Doing Research on Crime and Justice*, ed. by R.D. King and E. Wincup, 205-35. New York: Oxford University Press.

Roach, Kent. 2001. "The New Terrorism Offences and the Criminal Law." In *The Security of Freedom: Essays on Canada's Anti-Terrorism Bill,* ed. by R.J. Daniels, P. Macklem, and K. Roach, 151-72. Toronto: University of Toronto Press.

Roberts, Alasdair. 2002. "Administrative Discretion and the *Access to Information Act:* An 'Internal Law' on Open Government?" *Canadian Public Administration* 45 (2): 175-94.

–. 2005. "Spin Control and Freedom of Information: Lessons for the United Kingdom from Canada." *Public Administration* 83 (1): 1-23.

–. 2006. *Blacked Out: Government Secrecy in the Information Age.* Cambridge: Cambridge University Press.

Samuelson, Les, and Patricia Monture. 2008. "Aboriginal People and Social Control: The State, Law, and 'Policing.'" In *Marginality and Condemnation: An Introduction to Criminology,* 2nd ed., ed. by C. Brooks and B. Schissel, 200-19. Blackpoint, NS: Fernwood Publishing.

Schneiderman, David, and Brenda Cossman. 2001. "Political Association and the Anti-Terrorism Bill." In *The Security of Freedom: Essays on Canada's Anti-Terrorism Bill,* ed. by R.J. Daniels, P. Macklem, and K. Roach, 173-94. Toronto: University of Toronto Press.

Valpy, Michael. 2007. "How Police Stared Down Natives: Mindful of History, Officers Shunned Using Force to Keep Peace." *Globe and Mail,* 30 June, A1.

Wark, Wesley. 2002. "Canada's *Access to Information Act* and the Security and Intelligence Community." Canadian Intelligence Resource Centre, http://circ.jmellon.com/.

Williams, Toni, and Kim Murray. 2007. "Commentary: Police-Government Relations in the Context of State-Aboriginal Relations." In *Police and Government Relations: Who's Calling the Shots?* ed. by M. Beare and T. Murray, 172-82. Toronto: University of Toronto Press.

Yeager, Matthew G. 2006. "The Freedom of Information Act as a Methodological Tool: Suing the Government for Data." *Canadian Journal of Criminology and Criminal Justice* 48 (6): 499-521.

LEGISLATION CITED

Access to Information Act, R.S.C. 1985, c. A-1.

Anti-terrorism Act, S.C. 2001, c. 41.

Freedom of Information and Protection of Privacy Act, R.S.O. 1990, c. F.31.

Accessing the State of Imprisonment in Canada
Information Barriers and Negotiation Strategies

JUSTIN PICHÉ

How do we use the law as a vehicle of progressive change, while simultaneously emphasizing the importance of acknowledging the limits of the law?

– Angela Y. Davis, 2005

Access to data is central to scholarly endeavours. For those interested in studying the activities of the state,[1] which "has proved a remarkably elusive object of analysis," access is often difficult to gain as its "agencies instinctively protect information about themselves" (Abrams 1988, 61). Barring access to researchers who may be critical of their activities is one means by which authorities control knowledge about their policies, practices, and decisions.

Prison agencies, among the most opaque of state institutions, have been very resistant to qualitative research conducted by social scientists inside carceral institutions across the world (King and Liebling 2000; Scraton and Moore 2006; Simon 2000; Wacquant 2002). With few exceptions, preferential access has been most often reserved for positivist researchers interested in "risk prediction, accounting, systems engineering, and the like" (Simon 2000, 303). Put differently, it is researchers whose findings generally pose little political risk to prison authorities (Wacquant 2002), with projects that most often seek to buttress, rather than challenge, the use of imprisonment, who typically gain access to spaces of confinement and punishment.

Canadian researchers are not exempt from this trend. For instance, Yeager (2008) was not given permission by the Carleton University Ethics Board to conduct life-history interviews with federal prisoners designated as "Dangerous Offenders" due to his inability to secure permission from prospective host institutions through the Research Branch of the Correctional Service of Canada (CSC). Ultimately, this decision and the denials of his subsequent appeals forced him to change the focus of his doctoral dissertation.

In cases where researchers are given access to prisons and prisoners to conduct their studies, they usually have to make concessions to secure their entry into the prison. For example, Martel (2004) notes that she was able to secure permission from the CSC to conduct qualitative interviews with federally sentenced women regarding their experiences of solitary confinement only by agreeing to incorporate quantitative data – the gold standard of evidence within the prison agency – into her research design. The subsequent findings of her segregation study (Martel 1999), however, based primarily on data obtained through interviews with incarcerated women, were ignored by the CSC, which refused to attend planned meetings to discuss the implications of her conclusions. She also noted that the study received little attention from media outlets that mostly described the interview-based research project as anecdotal and costly (Martel 2004, 173-75). These are but some of the examples of "gatekeeping scrutiny" Martel personally encountered that impaired her ability to conduct and disseminate critical research within the mainstream "correctional" field and wider society (Martel 2004, 162), a phenomenon she describes as the policing of criminological knowledge.

While some are willing to spend the time and resources needed to negotiate entry to prisons or other opaque institutions, most "researchers follow the path of least resistance. Or, perhaps better, like immigrants, we tend to go where, if we are not necessarily welcomed, we are at least tolerated" (Marx 1984, 2). A consequence of such decisions is that most scholars interested in studying the state undertake research that draws primarily on documents that are carefully vetted by officials prior to their publication; thus, they can only capture what the state says about its policies and practices (see also Chapter 5).

One tactic that has been used to move beyond the study of the front stage of the state is to file requests under access to information (ATI) or freedom of information (FOI) protocols enshrined in law at the federal and provincial/ territorial level (Piché and Walby 2010). This approach enables individuals to obtain records regarding "the policies, decisions and operations of their governments" (Vallance-Jones 2008, 6) that otherwise are not made available for public consumption (Marx 1984; Park and Lippert 2008). It should be noted, however, that as the literature on this topic grows, more and more evidence emerges that reveals the existence of processes used by gatekeepers within state governments, some of which are enshrined in ATI/FOI legislation, to regulate and control what can be known about their agencies. When encountering these techniques of opacity, defined by Larsen and Walby in the Introduction to this book as formal and informal processes outside the strict letter of the law that impact the acquisition of information held by state governments, the development of creative approaches to negotiating access to the data sought are required.

This chapter is about the barriers I encountered as a researcher seeking to excavate information on the scope of prison capacity expansion in Canada unfolding at this time.[2] In the following pages, I detail the different stages of this project, involving a search of published online content, informal information requests with the thirteen provincial/territorial and federal government agencies, and submitting requests for unpublished records principally through ATI/FOI protocols. I also review the techniques of opacity deployed by state officials to reduce the scope of information requests, postpone disclosure, and omit or refuse records associated with their recent penal infrastructure initiatives. In particular, I emphasize how these barriers shaped the development of subsequent strategies to generate the data sought. Having documented the use and legitimation of a secretive approach to prison capacity expansion by some governments, I draw on the access to information literature to reflect upon measures that could be taken to undermine the monopoly that state agencies enjoy over the control of information related to their operations.

Negotiating Access

As part of a doctoral dissertation that sought to identify the justifications advanced – both publicly and behind closed doors – by state officials, politicians, and other proponents of incarceration in support of establishing new penal infrastructure (see Piché 2012), there was a need to first identify the scope of prison capacity expansion in Canada. The latter is the focus of this chapter. Below, the four primary phases of data collection used for these purposes are described, with an emphasis on the barriers encountered and actions taken at each stage to obtain information on new prisons and additions to existing facilities.

Phase I: Online Content Search
This study began in February 2009 with an online content search of the fourteen prison agency websites across Canada for relevant web pages, news releases and announcements, and published reports related to prison capacity expansion. It should be noted that the degree of information available appears to be proportional to the amount of input the public has in deciding where these facilities will be constructed. Proactive disclosure by prison authorities regarding the establishment of new penal infrastructure can be evaluated along a continuum, from state authorities that actively provide information to the public for the purposes of receiving input to those that limit disclosure to expedite projects by excluding the public from the process.

On one end of the continuum were agencies like the Yukon Department of Justice (2009), whose ongoing Correctional Redevelopment, which aims to renew the territory's prison system based on the recommendations of the Corrections Consultation, was co-chaired with the Council of Yukon First Nations (CYFN) between November 2004 and March 2006. In the years since implementation began, members of the public have been invited to participate in the process. Many materials related to the initiative, including information on the negotiations between the Yukon Department of Justice and the CYFN regarding the site for the new Whitehorse Correctional Centre, were and continue to be available online.

In the middle range are a few provinces that had provided detailed profiles of new facilities well before their construction. For instance, the government of Ontario posted web pages for the Toronto South Detention Centre and South West Detention Centre in Windsor (Ontario Ministry of Community Safety and Correctional Services 2009a, 2009b). Information on the anticipated economic benefits, location of the facilities, project phases, architectural drawings, and how to give feedback regarding the establishment of the facilities were included.

Agencies such as the CSC sit on the other end of the continuum. Although the federal government did publish the *Roadmap to Strengthening Public Safety: Report of the Correctional Service of Canada Review Panel* (Sampson et al. 2007) that proposed the replacement of aging facilities with multi-level regional complexes for men in each of its five operational regions, information related to this initiative has become increasingly restricted over time.

Following the establishment of a "Transformation Team" to implement the recommendations of the roadmap, a series of articles were included in the CSC's *Let's Talk* staff magazine – a publication buried in the agency's website architecture – outlining related initiatives. One article written by then Senior Deputy Commissioner Don Head (2008, 15) noted that the CSC was undertaking a "comprehensive plan" to modernize its physical infrastructure in light of the review panel's recommendations. As recently as July 2009, one of the CSC's web pages (CSC 2009a) listed "Physical Infrastructure" as a key component of its "Transformation," along with a series of "Quick Wins," including planning priorities. These priorities included the development of a project plan for regional complexes, "looking at opportunities of public/private partnerships for funding and building," and "balancing current construction/infrastructure renewal demands that are critical for current and short-term operations" (CSC 2009a). Having previously been informed that the records I requested pertaining to new federal penitentiary construction "do not exist within the Correctional Service of Canada" (e.g., CSC 2009b), I immediately filed two new requests under the federal *Access to Information Act (ATIA)* when I came across this information on the website. In a conversation with a CSC ATI analyst on 17 September 2009, I was again informed that no records exist within the organization pertaining to new physical infrastructure. I responded that such a decision could not be possible given that the agency's website stated as much. Upon visiting the bookmarked web page where I had previously made note of the CSC's infrastructure plans, I found that the link to CSC 2009a was broken and that the main CSC Transformation web page had been updated that month (CSC 2009c).[3] The content I had cited previously in my July 2009 ATI request had vanished. The only mention of "modernizing physical infrastructure" on the new web page was on a list with other "Transformation Agenda" priorities, without any other details (CSC 2009c).

While the *destruction* of records has been described as "a necessary and legitimate business activity, provided it is conducted rationally and in compliance with law" (Wilson 2000, 127), it can be argued that the foregoing example is an illustration of how this activity can be employed for the purposes of obfuscation. Although not as egregious as the shredding of Health Canada records pertaining to the tainted blood scandal of the 1980s (see Gilbert 2000, 103), the use of this technique of opacity to render invisible published online records signalled either that the agency was pursuing a plan to build new regional complexes and no longer wanted to provide details to the public about it or that this policy proposal was no longer on the table. The gap in knowledge resulting from the adoption of secrecy on this matter kept the CSC's penal infrastructure plans hidden from view until the equivalent of thirty-four new units to be located on the grounds of existing institutions were announced from August 2010 to January 2011 (Piché 2011a). It should also be noted that on 6 December 2010, Public Safety Minister Vic Toews (Parliament of Canada 2010) indicated that the CSC would be presenting its long-term accommodation strategy to cabinet for consideration in March 2011 in response to a question placed on the Order Paper in the House of Commons by then Liberal Public Safety Critic Mark Holland about whether or not the federal government would be building the regional complexes recommended by Sampson and colleagues (2007). By August 2011, no details regarding the submission of this plan had been released to the public.

By the end of my search of all relevant government websites, a number of web pages, press releases, and published reports had been collected. Through an analysis of these texts, eleven new provincial/territorial prisons at various stages of completion were identified,[4] including: (1) a replacement facility for Her Majesty's Prison in St. John's (see Newfoundland and Labrador Department of Justice 2008); (2) new institutions in Montérégie, Roberval, Amos, and Sept-Îles, as well as the reopening of a prison in Percé (see Ministère de la Sécurité publique du Québec 2008); (3) new detention centres in Toronto and Windsor (see Ontario Ministry of Community Safety and Correctional Services 2009a, 2009b); (4) a new women's prison in Headingley (see Government of Manitoba 2006); (5) the newly opened Regina Provincial Correctional Centre (see Saskatchewan Ministry of Corrections, Public Safety and Policing 2008); and (6) a new facility to replace the Whitehorse Correctional Centre (see Yukon Government Cabinet Communications 2009). With this information, I began the next stage of my study.

Phase II: Informal Information Requests

A second method used to obtain information on new prisons was informal information requests via telephone (see Table 9.1). Having worked in various departments of the Canadian government, I encountered many officials who took their jobs as public servants very seriously (see Piché 2006, 146-52). I assumed that those I would contact for information regarding the establishment of penal infrastructure would exhibit openness towards my queries, even in cases where information regarding these facilities was not available online. Based on this preconception, I decided that openness

TABLE 9.1

Informal information requests, 2009

Jurisdiction	Date
Newfoundland and Labrador	February 24
Prince Edward Island	February 25
Nova Scotia	February 24
New Brunswick	February 24
Québec	February 24
Ontario	February 24
Manitoba	February 24
Saskatchewan	February 25
Alberta	February 25
British Columbia	February 24
Nunavut	February 25
Northwest Territories	Phone calls not returned
Yukon	February 26
Canada	February 26

would be the posture I would adopt to negotiate access to the information I was seeking.

With a list of questions in hand (e.g., "Are you currently building or planning to build new prisons?" "What developments led to the decision to construct new facilities?"), I phoned the various prison agencies. Whether I made contact with an official or left a message on their voice mail, I stated my name, that I was a doctoral student from Carleton University conducting research on prison construction across Canada, and that I was hoping to obtain information informally about these projects without having to go through formal channels (such as filing ATI/FOI requests or submitting research proposals).

Of the fourteen agencies I contacted, six provided information regarding the need for constructing new facilities, the planning process, and the groups and organizations consulted. These included: (1) Prince Edward Island's Community and Correctional Services, (2) New Brunswick's Department of Public Safety, (3) Ontario's Ministry of Community Safety and Correctional Services, (4) Manitoba's Corrections Division, (5) British Columbia's Ministry of Public Safety and Solicitor General, and (6) Yukon's Community and Correctional Services. A seventh agency, Newfoundland and Labrador's

Department of Transportation and Works, also provided similar information after I was referred to it by the Department of Justice in that province. Of the remaining jurisdictions contacted, five departments – Nova Scotia's Correctional Services Division, Québec's Ministère de la Sécurité publique, Saskatchewan's Ministry of Corrections, Public Safety and Policing, Alberta's Correctional Services, and Nunavut's Department of Justice – limited their disclosure to the number of projects planned and their locations.

In my conversations with officials from the CSC, I was unable to obtain any information on new penitentiary construction initiatives. The respondent legitimated this *denial* of information by noting that any proposal to build facilities, should they exist, would be subject to cabinet confidence. With this established from the outset, the official provided me with a list of criteria the agency would consider if it were to establish new penitentiaries, demonstrating at least some willingness to impart how the facility planning process works at the federal level.

While most agencies I contacted exhibited varying degrees of openness in response to this initial round of informal information requests, the Northwest Territories Department of Justice never returned any of my four phone calls over the period of a month, employing a technique of opacity that can be described simply as *non-acknowledgment.* I encountered this tactic less frequently than others who have conducted cross-jurisdictional studies using only ATI/FOI requests (see Vallance-Jones 2008, 4).

As noted previously, eleven new prisons at various stages of completion in Canadian provinces and territories were identified through an online content search. While no new information was obtained regarding prospective CSC facilities, information on another nine prospective provincial/territorial facilities in the process of being established was obtained through informal requests over the phone. These included: (1) potentially another facility to replace Her Majesty's Prison in St. John's, Newfoundland, in addition to the one institution previously discussed publicly; (2) a new prison to replace the Prince County Correctional Centre in Prince Edward Island; (3) a new prison in Antigonish County and another in Cumberland County, Nova Scotia; (4) a new remand centre near Moncton and a new prison in Dalhousie, New Brunswick; (5) a new Edmonton Remand Centre in Alberta; (6) a new remand centre in Burnaby, British Columbia; and (7) a new prison for women in Iqaluit, Nunavut. After completion of this stage in the study, all relevant data were compiled and included in targeted formal information requests with Canadian prison authorities.

Phase III: Formal Information Requests

Whereas one's ability to obtain information on the activities of state agencies using informal requests relies principally on the willingness of officials to divulge their knowledge, formal information requests – including those filed using ATI/FOI protocols – involve an on-the-record application for information that necessitates an on-the-record response from public bodies. In the case of ATI/FOI requests, individual applicants are resorting to law to coerce information from state governments regarding issues such as the construction of new penal infrastructure – records that "should be public in the first place" (Vallance-Jones 2008, 6).

In an attempt to maximize record disclosure, I partitioned each of the formal requests at this stage of the study into three parts. To mitigate the possibility that respondents would claim that no records existed pertaining to my requests because no new prisons were in the process of being built, the first paragraph would provide an overview of new facility construction in the jurisdiction in question where applicable. In the second and third paragraphs, details concerning the records I deemed essential to my study, such as the justifications legitimating their construction, were provided. Anticipating that many authorities would claim my requests were overly broad, which would result in time delays and high processing cost estimates, the fourth paragraph included requests for details pertaining to projected prison construction over the next five years that could be discarded, if necessary, to preserve the other aspects of the requests.

For purposes of comparison, ATI/FOI requests were filed with all of the thirteen provincial/territorial prison agencies, excluding the Ontario Ministry of Community Safety and Correctional Services, with whom five formal requests were filed by e-mail (see Table 9.2). Five similar ATI requests were filed with the CSC. Of these twenty-two formal requests, sixteen were fully processed by prison agencies. Three other such agencies each partially processed a request and forwarded portions of my file to infrastructure departments at no extra cost, concluding that they did not possess all the records relevant to my requests.[5] Another three agencies each partially processed a request and recommended that I file additional requests to other departments that held the remainder of the records sought.[6] While request transfers are described by Gilbert (2000) as a way for authorities to avoid the disclosure of records, based on the additional records I obtained I would make the case that such actions and recommendations on behalf of state officials can yield benefits in some instances, particularly in the case of government infrastructure projects involving

TABLE 9.2

Formal information requests, 2009

Jurisdiction	Department	File number(s)
Newfoundland and Labrador	Department of Justice	JUS/10/2009
Prince Edward Island	Office of the Attorney General	AG-09-04
Prince Edward Island	Department of Transportation and Public Works	TPW 003/09
Nova Scotia	Department of Justice	JUS-2009-19
Nova Scotia	Department of Transportation and Infrastructure Renewal	TIR-09-24
New Brunswick	Department of Public Safety and Solicitor General	No file number
New Brunswick	Department of Supply and Services	No file number
Québec	Ministère de la Sécurité publique	70843
Ontario	Ministry of Community Safety and Correctional Services	CU09-00740 CU09-00741 CU09-00742 CU09-00743 AC09-00513
Ontario	Ontario Realty Corporation	No file number
Manitoba	Department of Justice	2009-39
Saskatchewan	Ministry of Corrections, Public Safety and Policing	CPSP0909G
Saskatchewan	Ministry of Government Services	GS01/09G
Alberta	Solicitor General and Public Security	2009-G-0057
British Columbia	Ministry of Attorney General/Ministry of Public Safety and Solicitor General	292-30/PSS-2009-00615
Nunavut	Department of Justice	1029-20-JUS0206
Nunavut	Department of Community and Government Services	1029-20-CGS0613
Northwest Territories	Department of Justice	No file number
Yukon	Department of Highways and Public Works	A-2626
Canada	Correctional Service of Canada	A-2008-00338 A-2008-00339 A-2008-00340 A-2008-00341 A-2008-00342 A-2009-00049 A-2009-00143

departments other than agencies responsible for public works. As new information became available on the CSC website, two additional ATI requests regarding new regional complexes were filed (see Phase I). By the end of this phase of my study, a total of thirty formal requests had been filed, twenty-nine of which have been processed.[7]

Based on previously unpublished records obtained from these requests that included internal reports, ministerial briefing notes, memoranda, and other documents, information on an additional four facilities was obtained, including: (1) a new pre-trial detention centre for youth, women, and individuals with mental illnesses at an unspecified location in Labrador (see Kennedy 2008); (2) a replacement remand centre in Saskatoon, Saskatchewan (see Saskatchewan Ministry of Corrections, Public Safety and Policing 2007); (3) a new prison for men in Rankin Inlet, Nunavut (see Nunavut Department of Community and Government Services 2008); and (4) a replacement prison for women in Fort Smith, Northwest Territories (see Northwest Territories Department of Justice 2009). At this stage in the study, twenty-three new provincial/territorial prisons had been identified.

As data on new prisons using formal requests were obtained, I became aware that state authorities were omitting key information from previously published documents concerning these infrastructure projects destined for public consumption. What makes the use of omission as a technique of opacity problematic is that it does not involve the explicit denial of information, but rather denies disclosure without even acknowledging the existence of records. Evidence of this practice can be drawn from the presence of information pertaining to the planning of new prisons in ATI/FOI records that were not posted on the websites of the governments of Prince Edward Island, Nova Scotia, New Brunswick, British Columbia, Nunavut, and the Northwest Territories at the time I filed my requests. The failure of officials to mention, in phone conversations, plans to construct new provincial/territorial facilities in Labrador, Saskatoon, and Rankin Inlet that were outlined in documents obtained by ATI/FOI is also an example of omission in practice.

The ATI/FOI process is one where designated state officials – who may or may not have knowledge of the subject of the request – are tasked with obtaining information from other state officials who hold the records sought by the applicant. The actions of those responsible for the management of requests are also shaped by their compliance and case clearance objectives. As a result, ATI/FOI coordinators do, on occasion, seek to reduce the scope of information searches where the disclosure process may be viewed as overly cumbersome, by requesting that applicants rephrase or narrow their queries for the purpose of clarification. Of the twenty-nine formal requests that were processed as part of this study, officials from three public bodies asked that I clarify certain passages to ensure that they were searching for the records sought.[8] Two other public bodies sought a reduction in the scope of my requests, which I refused as I was not given any indication of the types of records that the organizations possessed that would point to how the applications could be revised.[9] Most agencies did not seek clarification regarding my formal information requests, however.[10]

A technique of opacity I encountered frequently during this stage of my study was *postponement*, where state officials would process requests with delays beyond the statutory limits outlined in legislation and other guidelines (see Badgley, Dixon, and Dozois 2003; Gilbert 2000; Shapiro and Steinzor 2006). For instance, in four cases, ATI/FOI requests were processed with delays of thirty days or under with notification.[11] Six other ATI/FOI requests were processed with delays in excess of thirty days without notification,[12] a practice not permitted by law. The first four of five formal requests filed via e-mail to Ontario's Ministry of Community Safety and Correctional Services, although not processed under the auspices of the province's FOI laws, were completed with a delay of over ninety days. The most egregious example of postponement in action pertains to a request for records filed with the Ontario Realty Corporation, the branch of the Ontario government responsible for the acquisition of properties, who had not responded to my July 2009 FOI request as of February 2012.

Those who file ATI/FOI requests are also likely to encounter "high fee estimates and high public interest thresholds to waive fees" (Snell and Sebina 2007, 60). Gentile (2009) argues that cost estimates for searching, photocopying, and reviewing records pertaining to such requests often act, whether intended or not, as a *deterrent* mechanism that forces individuals to modify or abandon their efforts (see also Chapter 13; Yeager 2006). During this study, the Prince Edward Island Office of the Attorney General sent a fee notice of $5,607.50 to process my FOI request, which prompted me to drastically revise the scope of the query when an appeal to obtain a fee waiver was rejected. As a result, there was a radical disjuncture between the records initially sought and those received, although at a reduced cost of $275. To avoid paying the initial $625 processing estimate, I also reduced the scope of my request to Nunavut's Department of Justice by removing the passage that sought information pertaining to the construction of new prisons in the territory over the next five years. In another case, I filed a fee waiver in response to a request processing cost estimate of $270 from the

British Columbia Ministry of Attorney General and Ministry of Public Safety and Solicitor General, which was rejected. I decided, however, that the cost was reasonable and kept the request unchanged. In the end, these records were obtained without cost, as the officials responsible for processing the request had determined that the file had taken an unreasonable amount of time to process. Although the tactic of deterrence, whether by intent or outcome, through high cost estimates was used by some government officials, it should be noted that the total cost of processing the ATI/FOI requests for this portion of my study was $638.50, a reasonable price considering the number of records disclosed.

In this phase of the study, I encountered many instances where records on new prisons in Canada were denied, not only through the withholding of information by state agencies but also through redactions to released records. In principle, ATI/FOI legislation across Canadian jurisdictions mandates that records can be deemed partially or fully refused only if agencies can demonstrate that the injury resulting from their disclosure would unreasonably harm the operations of state governments or would violate the privacy interests of an individual named in the records (Gilbert 2000).

It should be noted that only seven of the twenty-nine formal requests processed as part of my study were returned without the denial of records.[13] The remaining twenty-two requests processed included a variety of exemption clauses covering seven broad categories: (1) policy or legal advice and recommendations from a public body to Cabinet/Executive Council ($n = 9$);[14] (2) disclosure of information would be harmful to law enforcement or the security of an institution ($n = 7$);[15] (3) disclosure of information would unreasonably reveal personal information of, or invade the privacy of, a third party ($n = 6$);[16] (4) deliberations of Cabinet/Executive Council ($n = 4$);[17] (5) disclosure of deliberations of a public body would be harmful to intergovernmental relations (i.e., negotiations with another department or government) ($n = 4$);[18] (6) disclosure of records would be harmful to the financial and economic interests of a public body ($n = 3$);[19] and (7) records produced by members of legislative assemblies ($n = 1$).[20]

One major consequence of the techniques of opacity encountered and the inadequate channels of recourse available to challenge state secrecy was that I did not obtain substantial information regarding the long-term penal infrastructure plans of Canadian prison authorities. Thus, the findings at this juncture of the study were limited to the punishment plans unfolding in the short term, with no idea of what would be coming down the road.

Despite having some information withheld through the exemption clauses listed above, I was not inclined to file complaints with the independent bodies responsible for overseeing ATI/FOI in the provinces and territories, as I was generally satisfied with the records obtained. I did, however, file complaints with the Office of the Information Commissioner of Canada (OIC) with regard to the claims made by CSC officials that no records existed regarding the construction of new federal penitentiaries, since there was contradictory evidence that did not support such claims (e.g., Head 2008). In those complaints, I also asked the OIC to investigate the processing delays for these requests. Although the portion of my complaints concerning delays was partially successful, resulting in friendly reminders being sent to the CSC stating that they had obligations to process requests within the prescribed time periods, as in the case of Yeager (2006) my grievances did not result in the production of additional information. While the OIC considers the complaints to be resolved, I consider their resolution to be toothless and seriously doubt that the CSC has significantly altered its practices as a result of a few checks in the "you've been very bad" column (see Piché 2010a).

Phase IV: Further Informal Information Requests
Earlier in this chapter, I reviewed the approaches to negotiating access to information on prison capacity expansion, including being open about my research objectives when requesting information from state officials informally over the phone and using formal channels, such as ATI/FOI, to coerce the release of additional information and unpublished documents. Some of the data were analyzed months after they were originally obtained, as records from several jurisdictions were obtained later than others. It was then necessary to confirm the accuracy of the information generated. Since the intent was to eventually disseminate related findings to inform ongoing debates in penal policy, it was necessary to find a way to obtain or verify data regarding the number of prisoner beds that were being added to prison systems across the country, and the fiscal costs associated with their construction, including additions to existing facilities.

At this stage in the study, I anticipated that it would be difficult to obtain the information for two reasons. First, since most jurisdictions in Canada were faced with significant budgetary deficits, I expected that they would resist disclosing the costs of new prison spaces. Second, many of the redactions in the documents I had obtained using ATI/FOI pertained to the internal properties of new facilities such as cells. To negotiate the disclosure of

TABLE 9.3

Informal information requests, 2010

Jurisdiction	Date
Newfoundland and Labrador	February 12
Prince Edward Island	February 11
Nova Scotia	January 28
New Brunswick	January 28
Québec	February 1
Ontario	January 28
Manitoba	January 28
	February 18
Saskatchewan	January 28
Alberta	February 3
British Columbia	January 28
Nunavut	February 3
	February 11
Northwest Territories	February 5
Yukon	February 5
Canada	January 28

the information sought, I concluded that a measure of coercion and bluffing would be required.

In order to coerce the disclosure of information not obtainable by more conventional means, I organized a public forum entitled *Prorogation as Opportunity: Proposing New Directions for Criminal Justice Policy in Canada*, where I would present preliminary findings. Having enlisted four other participants for a panel during January 2010,[21] I contacted all the prison agencies by phone or e-mail to inform them that I would be presenting my findings on the establishment of new penal infrastructure at a public forum in Ottawa (see Table 9.3). As noted elsewhere (Piché 2011b), I stated that I was going public with my findings – both from agencies that had previously disclosed information related to the costs of building new facilities and the number of additional prisoners they could house and from those that had not – and that I wanted to ensure I had the most up-to-date information. In cases where I did not have the above information, I was, of course, bluffing.

With the exception of the CSC, which continued to practice the technique of denial, all prison authorities responded positively to this round of informal queries, either confirming figures and information previously obtained or by providing new information without necessarily being aware because I never fully disclosed my preliminary findings to them at this juncture. One key piece of information that emerged was the decision by the recently elected New Democratic Party government in Nova Scotia to cancel the prison projects in Antigonish and Cumberland counties in favour of building one facility. I also discovered that a pre-trial detention centre, which the government of British Columbia originally planned to build in Burnaby, was being moved to Surrey because of community resistance. I also confirmed details related to ten additions to existing provincial/territorial prisons. A similar approach to data collection was repeated on three other occasions: I provided officials with the figures I had compiled and asked them to update the information as I prepared reports for the bi-annual meeting of the Provincial-Territorial Heads of Corrections in May 2010 (Piché 2010b), a March 2011 hearing of the House of Commons Standing Committee on Public Safety and National Security (Piché 2011a), and an October 2011 hearing of the House of Commons Standing Committee on Justice and Human Rights (see Table 9.4).

Using this approach to data collection proved to be significant in that I could point to the most up-to-date information on new penal infrastructure in Canada when publicizing findings on the scope and cost of prison capacity expansion. Furthermore, this tactic enabled me to insulate myself from criticism should the information I disseminated be deemed inaccurate, as responsibility for errors could be attributed to the lack of transparency and the dishonesty exhibited by state officials during the research process.

Democracy, Secrecy, and Access as a Negative Reform

Over a quarter-century ago, advances in information management technology, freedom of information legislation, and an emerging body of literature dedicated to its study led Marx (1984) to express hope for the future of scholarship on the state. Although it is difficult to quantify whether the landscape for such research has improved or deteriorated, my experience leads me to conclude, like Abrams (1988), that it remains difficult to access the backstage of the state.

One of the primary lessons of this cross-jurisdictional study is that no single method of inquiry is equipped to generate comprehensive knowledge regarding specific developments in state confinement and punishment. The tendency of scholars to exclusively use published government documents when studying the state reveals as much as it obscures (see O'Malley, Weir, and Shearing 1997; Chapter 10). Had I relied on such material only, I would

TABLE 9.4

Scope of ongoing prison capacity expansion in Canada

Date	Provincial/territorial	Federal
17 February 2010	• 22 new prisons • 10 additions • 5,788 additional prisoner beds • $2.724 billion for construction-related costs	No plans disclosed
31 May 2010	• 22 new prisons • 16 additions • 6,514 additional prisoner beds • $2.829 billion for construction-related costs	No plans disclosed
3 March 2011	• 23 new prisons • 16 additions • 7,348 additional prisoner beds • $3.049 billion for construction-related costs	• 34 additions • 2,552 additional prisoner beds • $601 million for construction-related costs
2 October 2011	• 22 new prisons[a] • 17 additions[b] • 6,312 additional prisoner beds[c] • $3.375 billion for construction-related costs[d]	• 34 additions • 2,552 additional prisoner beds • $601 million for construction-related costs

a A prison was removed from the list when the government of Newfoundland and Labrador cancelled plans to build a new remand centre in Labrador in June 2011 in a stated effort to divert funding towards programming for prisoners. It should be noted that no funding had been allocated towards the project and estimates about the number of new prisoner beds in this facility were never disclosed, and thus did not impact the other figures I had compiled.

b Adjustments to the number of additions, new prisoner beds, and construction-related costs were made when I became aware of the 30 March 2011 announcement of a 32-cell addition to Pine Grove Correctional Centre in Saskatchewan that is estimated to cost $12 million (Saskatchewan Ministry of Corrections, Public Safety and Policing 2011).

c Further adjustments to this figure were made following the receipt of a 26 September 2011 e-mail from a British Columbia prison official who revised the estimated number of prisoner beds being built at the new remand centre in Surrey from 432 to 324 beds, and at the new prison in the Okanagan from 720 to 540 beds. Prisoner bed figures were also modified for a second addition to the Alouette Correctional Centre for Women from 208 to 156 beds, and for an addition to the Prince George Correctional Centre from 24 to 30 beds. A prison official from Alberta also noted in a 2 October 2011 e-mail that a recent decision had been made to close the 734-bed Edmonton Remand Centre once the 1,952-bed New Edmonton Remand Centre came online. It should be noted, however, that if it is deemed that additional remand spaces are required, the new facility will be able to expand by three pods totalling another 864 beds, which would bring the institution to 2,816 prisoner beds.

d The total for construction-related costs associated with the establishment of new penal infrastructure was also modified when the government of Ontario announced the costs to build, finance, and maintain the $336 million South West Detention Centre in Windsor in April 2011 (see Infrastructure Ontario 2011). This figure was also adjusted when prison officials with whom I had been in contact lowered the estimated budgets for constructing the new remand centre in Surrey and the new prison in the Yukon by $17.5 million and $4 million, respectively, via e-mail on 26 September 2011.

have concluded that there were at least eleven provincial/territorial prisons at various stages of completion across Canada. As a result, eleven other penal infrastructure projects identified through informal information requests by phone and formal information requests using primarily ATI/FOI would have not been considered at this juncture of the study. Many other details pertaining to the justifications given for these prison capacity expansion initiatives but not found in published documents would not have been brought to light for further research.

Conversely, had the informal information request portion of the study been jettisoned, it is likely that fewer records would have been obtained using ATI/FOI, as the absence of such information would have resulted in a lack of specificity in the composition of the latter requests. Outdated information, such as the establishment of two prisons in Nova Scotia that were consolidated into one facility (see Nova Scotia Department of Justice 2009) and the selection of Surrey as the location for a new detention centre in British Columbia (see British Columbia Ministry of Public Safety and Solicitor General 2010), would have not been identified if informal information requests had not been undertaken following the ATI/FOI requests. The foregoing observations suggest that ATI/FOI research on its own cannot generate the information sought, necessitating the use of a number of methodological tools to generate data and exercise our "responsibility to act on it" (Roberts 2006, 238).

Reflecting upon the amount of work needed to identify which jurisdictions had recently built or were currently constructing new penal infrastructure in Canada, it is alarming that most of the information obtained was not readily available for use in deliberations upon the justifications, benefits, and costs of these large-scale initiatives at a time when such deliberations could have led to a different conclusion. Badgley and colleagues (2003) argue that there are plenty of incentives for government employees to generate records, including the existence of regulations they are meant to follow to ensure that their practices and recommendations are documented. However, the fact that much about the policies and practices of the state, including the construction of new prison spaces, is hidden from the public suggests that there is not enough incentive for disclosure.

As noted by Gilbert (2000, 91), Information Commissioners in Canada have repeatedly criticized the "bureaucratic resistance" to the federal access to information legislation. Staff ignorance of their obligations to release records to the public (Badgley, Dixon, and Dozois 2003, 17), "ingrained conservatism" when managing records in order to preserve the status quo of operations, and a sentiment that disclosure would lead to unjustified challenges of their decision making given their expertise (Gilbert 2000, 90) are all factors that may influence the availability of information on the Canadian government's activities, as well as those of other public bodies across the country and elsewhere.

A consequence of the techniques of opacity employed by governments to limit access to their activities is the maintenance of information asymmetries where "those who have been mandated to govern have greater access to information on policies, programs and services that are meant to satisfy the needs of the public, while the public themselves have limited access to this information" (Snell and Sebina 2007, 64-65). This issue needs to be addressed because it signals that debates necessary for the development of informed and representative policy in democratic societies are being jettisoned in favour of political expediency that comes with secrecy in a manner that permits the activities of bureaucracies and political representatives to go unchecked. As a result, citizens are left to endure the financial costs and other consequences of policies that they know little or nothing about until their implications become visible well after implementation. This is the case for those living in communities across Canada who now find a new prison in their backyards, often with little to no debate about the merits and pitfalls of these initiatives.

Shapiro and Steinzor (2006, 101) argue that individuals "have a right to know about the business transacted in their name." If we accept this argument, the question then becomes how to ensure that state agencies respect this right, and what mechanisms can be put in place to enable individuals to exercise it. In recent decades, the response among jurisdictions in Canada has been to create and periodically revise ATI/FOI laws. If the black boxes in which information regarding state policies and practices disappear from view are to be reduced, however, more than laws are needed. Writing on advances in FOI in Australia, Snell and Sebina (2007) argue that the development of technology is enhancing government information sharing with non-state actors there. While additional technologies ought to be developed and implemented in Canada, if such advances do not coincide with the development of a culture of open government among state officials and a citizenry that demands that its right to information be respected (68), information asymmetries will continue to exist, diminishing the possibility for debate about state projects, including whether or not to develop new prison spaces.

In my view, reforms in this area of public policy must not bolster the state monopoly over the (non-)disclosure of information. If the limits of ATI/FOI legislation are to be acknowledged, negative reforms are required to chip away at the information firewalls of government that shut citizens out from acquiring and making use of information that may reveal problematic aspects of proposed and enacted state policies. Kazmierski (2009) has made a case that access to information should be enshrined as a right under the *Canadian Charter of Rights and Freedoms,* which would further limit the ability of state governments to withhold information from citizens. It is argued that such a measure would allow individuals to exercise their fundamental freedoms under section 2(b) – "freedom of thought, belief, opinion and expression, including freedom of the press and other media of communication" – as their arguments would benefit from timely knowledge of the activities of state governments rather than hearsay. Kazmierski also makes the case that greater access to information ought to be protected under section 3, which affords every Canadian the right to vote, arguing that the non-disclosure of information restricts the ability of voters to deliberate on the record of, and promises made by, those in power. In addition to Kazmierski's proposition, there is a need to dismantle clauses in ATI/FOI legislation that prevent the disclosure of much of the information that is kept secret under the guise of cabinet confidence and similar provisions. This would enrich debates on policy options and decisions, including matters appropriated by the penal system and its appendages. Such a visibility-enhancing measure would make officials and politicians more accountable to the individuals they claim to represent and serve, thereby bolstering democratic governance.

Conclusion

I have documented the tactics I used to access information held by prison agencies regarding their penal infrastructure initiatives during the primary data collection phase of my doctoral research. In light of the resistance I encountered from gatekeepers who used a number of techniques of opacity to police the criminological knowledge I sought to make visible, my research highlights the importance of using mixed methods to conduct research on this aspect of imprisonment. It needs to be reiterated that had my mapping of prison capacity expansion in Canada relied exclusively on an online search for published records, many of the projects noted here would have remained unknown until they were formally announced. What, then, is the larger lesson that can be drawn from this experiment in information gathering?

Dostoevsky (1860) remarked that "the standard of a nation's civilization can be judged by opening the doors of its prisons." Similarly, Winston Churchill (1910) stated that "the mood and temper of the public in regard to the treatment of crime and criminals is one of the most unfailing tests of the civilization of any country." The empirical materials amassed during this component of my study are not well suited to commenting on these important declarations, but another decree regarding the state of the Canadian state is in order.

I submit that a measure of democracy in any society can be found in the way its governments decide and implement their policies, such as their penal infrastructure initiatives. Individuals have a right to know about the activities of the elected and non-elected representatives who are supposed to act in their best interests. Without "access to reliable, high quality and timely information," the public are not in a position to know, let alone make decisions, about issues affecting their lives (Snell and Sebina 2007, 56). My encounters as a researcher with a number of state agencies reveal how information regarding the establishment of new prison spaces is often systematically concealed. While jurisdictions release some of their records under the banners of "access to information," "freedom of information," and "proactive disclosure," much work is needed if the federal government and its provincial/territorial partners are to measure up to the claim that Canada is a world leader in democratic governance. Whether citizens would use such information if governments meet their obligations is another question, but in a democratic society they should at least be given the choice.

NOTES

1 Not to be understood as "a unified, unitary, coherent ensemble or agency," the state "is always specific sets of politicians and state officials located in specific parts of the state system. It is they who activate specific powers and state capacities inscribed in particular institutions and agencies" (Jessop 1990, 366-67).

2 Here I am referring to penal institutions built to warehouse criminalized adults.

3 In response to an ATI request with the CSC (file number A-2010-00164) for records concerning the removal of this Transformation web page, an agency official claimed that the web page still existed, pointing me to an article published in *Let's Talk* magazine written by then Senior Deputy Commissioner Don Head (2008) that discussed the modernization of physical infrastructure.

4 The establishment of a prison is a complex and long-term process involving an assessment to determine whether or not to build a new facility; selection of a preliminary site for its construction; environmental and geotechnical assessments of a site if it has not already been designated for such a use to determine whether the land is suitable for the construction of such an installation; facility and design procurement; facility construction and eventual operation.

5 These ATI/FOI requests include: (1) Prince Edward Island Department of Transportation and Public Works; (2) Nova Scotia Department of Transportation and Infrastructure Renewal; and (3) Nunavut Department of Community and Government Services.

6 These ATI/FOI requests include: (1) New Brunswick Department of Supply and Services; (2) Saskatchewan Ministry of Government Services; and (3) Ontario Realty Corporation.

7 As of February 2012, I have yet to receive a response from the Ontario Realty Corporation regarding my FOI request pertaining to the new Toronto South Detention Centre or the proposed South West Detention Centre in Windsor, mailed in July 2009.

8 These ATI/FOI requests include: (1) Nova Scotia Department of Justice; (2) British Columbia Ministry of Attorney General and Ministry of Public Safety and Solicitor General; and (3) Correctional Service of Canada.

9 These ATI/FOI requests include: (1) Alberta Solicitor General and Public Security; and (2) Northwest Territories Department of Justice.

10 These formal information requests include: (1) Prince Edward Island Department of Transportation and Public Works; (2) Nova Scotia Department of Transportation and Infrastructure Renewal; (3) New Brunswick Department of Public Safety; (4) New Brunswick Department of Supply and Services; (5) Ministère de la Sécurité publique du Québec; (6) Ontario Ministry of Community Safety and Correctional Services; (7) Manitoba Department of Justice; (8) Saskatchewan Ministry of Corrections, Public Safety and Policing; (9) Saskatchewan Ministry of Government Services; (10) Nunavut Department of Community and Government Services; (11) Yukon Department of Highways and Public Works; and (12) Correctional Service of Canada (*n* = 2).

11 These ATI/FOI requests include: (1) Newfoundland and Labrador Department of Justice; (2) Nova Scotia Department of Justice; (3) Ministère de la Sécurité publique du Québec; and (4) Northwest Territories Department of Justice.

12 These formal information requests include: (1) Ontario Ministry of Community Safety and Correctional Services; (2) Alberta Solicitor General and Public Security; (3) British Columbia Ministry of Attorney General and Ministry of Public Safety and Solicitor General; and (4) Correctional Service of Canada ($n = 3$).

13 These ATI/FOI requests include: (1) Nova Scotia Department of Transportation and Infrastructure Renewal; (2) Ontario Ministry of Community Safety and Correctional Services ($n = 5$); and (3) Yukon Department of Highways and Public Works.

14 This type of information exemption clause was used in processing the following ATI/FOI requests: (1) Newfoundland and Labrador Department of Justice; (2) Nova Scotia Department of Justice; (3) New Brunswick Department of Supply and Services; (4) Ministère de la Sécurité publique du Québec; (5) Saskatchewan Ministry of Corrections, Public Safety and Policing; (6) Saskatchewan Ministry of Government Services; (7) Alberta Solicitor General and Public Security; (8) British Columbia Ministry of Attorney General and Ministry of Public Safety and Solicitor General; and (9) Northwest Territories Department of Justice.

15 This type of information exemption clause was used in processing the following ATI/FOI requests: (1) Newfoundland and Labrador Department of Justice; (2) Prince Edward Island Office of the Attorney General; (3) Nova Scotia Department of Justice; (4) Ministère de la Sécurité publique du Québec; (5) British Columbia Ministry of Attorney General and Ministry of Public Safety and Solicitor General; (6) Nunavut Department of Justice; and (7) Nunavut Department of Community and Government Services.

16 This type of information exemption clause was used in processing the following ATI/FOI requests: (1) Prince Edward Island Department of Transportation and Public Works; (2) Nova Scotia Department of Justice; (3) New Brunswick Department of Public Safety; (4) New Brunswick Department of Supply and Services; (5) Nunavut Department of Justice; and (6) Nunavut Department of Community and Government Services.

17 This type of information exemption clause was used in processing the following ATI/FOI requests: (1) Nova Scotia Department of Justice; (2) Ministère de la Sécurité publique du Québec; (3) Manitoba Department of Justice; and (4) Saskatchewan Ministry of Corrections, Public Safety and Policing.

18 This type of information exemption clause was used in processing the following ATI/FOI requests: (1) Newfoundland and Labrador Department of Justice; (2) Prince Edward Island Department of Transportation and Public Works; (3) Ministère de la Sécurité publique du Québec; and (4) Alberta Solicitor General and Public Security.

19 This type of information exemption clause was used in processing the following ATI/FOI requests: (1) Newfoundland and Labrador Department of Justice; (2) Ministère de la Sécurité publique du Québec; and (3) British Columbia Ministry of Attorney General and Ministry of Public Safety and Solicitor General.

20 This type of information exemption clause was used by the Ministère de la Sécurité publique du Québec.

21 Eugene Oscapella (co-founder, Canadian Foundation for Drug Policy) was the chair of this panel. Panellists included Craig Jones (then executive director of the John Howard Society of Canada), Kim Pate (executive director of the Canadian Association

of Elizabeth Fry Societies), and Tara Lyons (then executive director of the Canadian Students for Sensible Drug Policy).

REFERENCES

Abrams, Philip. 1988 [1977]. "Notes on the Difficulty of Studying the State." *Journal of Historical Sociology* 1 (1): 58-89.

Badgley, Kerry, Margaret J. Dixon, and Paulette Dozois. 2003. "In Search of the Chill: Access to Information and Record-Keeping in the Government of Canada." *Archivaria* 55: 1-19.

British Columbia Ministry of Public Safety and Solicitor General. 2010. "Consultation Begins on New Jail Site." Information bulletin, 6 December. http://www2.news. gov.bc.ca/.

Churchill, Winston. 1910. Speech to the House of Commons. Hansard, 20 July, col. 1354.

CSC (Correctional Service of Canada). 2009a. "Physical Infrastructure." http://www. csc-scc.gc.ca/.

–. 2009b. Request pursuant to the *Access to Information Act,* federal ATI request A-2008-00341.

–. 2009c. "Transforming Corrections." http://www.csc-scc.gc.ca/.

Davis, Angela Y., and Eduardo Mendieta. 2005. *Abolition Democracy: Beyond Empire, Prisons, and Torture – Interviews with Angela Y. Davis.* New York: Seven Stories Press.

Dostoevsky, Fyodor M. 1961 [1860]. *The House of the Dead.* London: Heinemann.

Gentile, Patrizia. 2009. "Resisted Access? National Security, the *Access to Information Act,* and Queer(ing) Archives." *Archivaria* 68: 141-58.

Gilbert, Jay. 2000. "Access Denied: The *Access to Information Act* and Its Effect on Public Records Creators." *Archivaria* 49: 84-123.

Government of Manitoba. 2006. "Province Accepts Recommendations to Reform Women's Corrections: Independent Committee Calls for Relocation of 113-Year-Old Women's Facility; Development of Healing Lodge, Culturally Appropriate Programming." News release, 3 April. http://www.gov.mb.ca/.

Head, Don. 2008. "Modernization of Physical Infrastructure." *Let's Talk* 33 (1): 13-15. http://www.csc-scc.gc.ca/.

Infrastructure Ontario. 2011. "Contract Awarded for South West Correctional Centre." Media release, Toronto, 11 April. http://infrastructureontario.org/.

Jessop, Bob. 1990. *State Theory.* Cambridge: Polity.

Kazmierski, Vincent. 2009. "Something to Talk About: Is There a Charter Right to Access to Government Information?" *Dalhousie Law Journal* 31 (2): 351-99.

Kennedy, Jerome P. 2008. Letter to Mr. Todd Russell, MP, prepared by the Minister of Justice and Attorney General, Government of Newfoundland and Labrador, 11 September. Obtained through provincial request JUS/10/2009 with the Department of Justice, Government of Newfoundland and Labrador.

King, Roy D., and Alison Liebling. 2000. "Doing Research in Prisons." In *Doing Research on Crime and Justice,* ed. by Roy D. King and Emma Wincup, 431-54. Oxford: Oxford University Press.

Martel, Joane. 1999. *Solitude and Cold Storage: Women's Journeys of Endurance in Segregation.* Edmonton: ACI Communication.

–. 2004. "Policing Criminological Knowledge: The Hazards of Qualitative Research on Women in Prison." *Theoretical Criminology* 8 (2): 157-89.

Marx, Gary. 1984. "Notes on the Discovery, Collection, and Assessment of Hidden and Dirty Data." In *Studies in the Sociology of Social Problems,* ed. by J. Schneider and J. Kitsuse, 78-113. Norwood, NJ: Ablex.

Ministère de la Sécurité publique du Québec. 2008. "Annexe: Investissements dans les infrastructures carcérales, Québec." http://www.securitepublique.gouv.qc.ca/.

Newfoundland and Labrador Department of Justice. 2008. "Minister Meets with Federal Minister Regarding New Penitentiary." News release, 3 April. http://www.releases.gov.nl.ca/.

Northwest Territories Department of Justice. 2009. "Minister's Briefing/Justice: Territorial Women's Correctional Centre Building." Yellowknife, 2 May. Obtained through territorial ATI request (no file number), processed by the Department of Justice.

Nova Scotia Department of Justice. 2009. "Province Moves Forward with New Correctional Facility." News release, 1 December. http://www.gov.ns.ca/.

Nunavut Department of Community and Government Services. 2008. "Building Project Brief: Men's Correctional Healing Facility – Rankin Inlet, Iqaluit (NU): Department of Community and Government Services." Obtained through territorial ATI request 1029-20-CGS0613, processed by the Department of Community and Government Services.

O'Malley, Pat, Lorna Weir, and Clifford Shearing. 1997. "Governmentality, Criticism, Politics." *Economy and Society* 26: 501-17.

Ontario Ministry of Community Safety and Correctional Services. 2009a. "Proposed Toronto South Detention Centre." http://www.ontario.ca/tsdc.

–. 2009b. "South West Detention Centre." http://www.ontario.ca/swdc.

Park, Grace, and Randy Lippert. 2008. "Legal Aid's Logics." *Studies in Law, Politics, and Society* 48: 177-201.

Piché, Justin. 2006. "Restorative Prisons?" MA thesis, University of Ottawa.

–. 2010a. "Now You [Don't] Know and Knowing Is Half the Battle." *Tracking the Politics of 'Crime' and Punishment in Canada,* 14 April. http://tpcp-canada.blogspot.com/.

–. 2010b. "An Overview of New Prisons in Canada." Report submitted to the Federal-Provincial-Territorial Heads of Corrections, May.

–. 2011a. "Canada at a Crossroads: A Brief on Prison Expansion." Report submitted to the House of Commons Standing Committee on Public Safety and National Security, 3 March.

–. 2011b. "'Going Public': Accessing Data, Contesting Information Blockades." *Canadian Journal of Law and Society* 26 (3): 635-43.

–. 2012. "The Prison Idea (Un)interrupted: Penal Infrastructure Expansion, Research and Action in Canada." PhD dissertation, Carleton University.

Piché, Justin, and Kevin Walby. 2010. "Problematizing Carceral Tours." *British Journal of Criminology* 50: 570-81.

Roberts, Alasdair. 2006. *Blacked Out: Government Secrecy in the Information Age.* New York: Cambridge University Press.

Sampson, Rob, Serge Gascon, Ian Glen, Chief Louie Clarence, and Sharon Rosenfeldt. 2007. *A Roadmap to Strengthening Public Safety: Report of the Correctional Service of Canada Review Panel.* Ottawa: Minister of Public Works and Government Services Canada.

Saskatchewan Ministry of Corrections, Public Safety and Policing. 2007. "Saskatoon Correctional Centre – Site Review" [cover letter]. In *Saskatoon Correctional Centre Site Review,* by P3 Architecture, O'Neill O'Neill Procinsky Architects, and AODBT Architecture and Interior Design. Obtained through provincial FOI request GS01/09G, processed by the Ministry of Government Services.

–. 2008. "New Regina Correctional Centre Officially Opened." News release, 6 August. http://www.gov.sk.ca/.

–. 2011. "New Building to Address Overcrowding at Pine Grove." News release, 30 March. http://www.gov.sk.ca/.

Scraton, Phil, and Linda Moore. 2006. "Degradation, Harm and Survival in a Women's Prison." *Social Policy and Society* 5 (1): 67-78.

Shapiro, Sidney A., and Rena I. Steinzor. 2006. "The People's Agent: Executive Branch Secrecy and Accountability in an Age of Terrorism." *Law and Contemporary Problems* 66: 98-129.

Simon, Jonathan. 2000. "The 'Society of Captives' in the Era of Hyper-Incarceration." *Theoretical Criminology* 4 (3): 285-308.

Snell, Rick, and Peter Sebina. 2007. "Information Flows: The Real Art of Information Management and Freedom of Information." *Archives and Management* 35 (1): 54-81.

Parliament of Canada. 2010. Question No. 471, 40th Parliament, 3rd Session, Edited Hansard No. 111, 6 December.

Vallance-Jones, Fred. 2008. *National Freedom of Information Audit – 2008.* Toronto: Canadian Newspaper Association.

Wacquant, Loïc. 2002. "The Curious Eclipse of Prison Ethnography in the Age of Mass Incarceration." *Ethnography* 3 (4): 371-97.

Wilson, Ian E. 2000. "The Fine Art of Destruction Revisited." *Archivaria* 49: 124-39.

Yeager, Matthew. 2006. "The *Freedom of Information Act* as a Methodological Tool: Suing the Government for Data." *Canadian Journal of Criminology and Criminal Justice* 48 (4): 499-521.

–. 2008. "Getting the Usual Treatment: Censorship and the Marginalization of Convict Criminology." *Contemporary Justice Review* 11 (4): 413-25.

Yukon Department of Justice. 2009. "Moving Forward Together: Implementation of Correctional Redevelopment." http://www.correctionsconsultation.yk.ca.

Yukon Government Cabinet Communications. 2009. "New Correctional Facility Highlights Treatment and Women's Living Unit." News release, 17 March. http://www.gov.yk.ca/.

LEGISLATION CITED

Access to Information Act, R.S.C. 1985, c. A-1.

Canadian Charter of Rights and Freedoms, Part 1 of the *Constitution Act, 1982,* being Schedule B to the *Canada Act 1982* (U.K.), 1982, c. 11, s. 6.

Accessing Information on Streetscape Video Surveillance in Canada

SEAN P. HIER

The aim of this chapter is to complement the literature on access to information (ATI) and freedom of information (FOI) legislation and policy design by examining information access through the lens of criminological research on streetscape video surveillance in Canada.[1] Since 1981, community members in a growing number of Canadian cities have installed video surveillance cameras to monitor city streets. Criminologists were slow to examine the rise of monitoring programs across the country, and the main data sources used in the first phase of research were newspaper stories and promotional and administrative documents accessible on the Internet. The initial set of research findings contributed to an understanding of some of the ways in which monitoring programs are designed and administered. Yet the near-total reliance on easily obtainable documents – research materials, moreover, that were initially screened or selected by information gatekeepers and monitoring advocates – resulted in limited understandings of how systems are developed and applied, and it encouraged a set of concomitant deductive theoretical claims about inequitable power dynamics and social control processes.

The same broad investigation that produced the first set of findings on streetscape video surveillance also led to a comprehensive comparative analysis of the policy dynamics involved in establishing monitoring programs between 1981 and 2005 (Hier 2010). The latter analysis supplemented data sources used in the first phase of research with a larger set of documents and reports acquired through information requests directed at municipal, community, provincial, and federal agencies and organizations. The materials acquired through informal data requests and formal FOI submissions – that is, requests granted without much conflict or organizational resistance – did not simply lead to a deeper understanding of the ways in which the privacy policy sector conceptualizes and addresses monitoring programs in Canada.[2] Accessing these data also revealed how the privacy policy sector's policy orientation, which is intended to reduce idiosyncratic variation in the ways that monitoring systems are designed, simultaneously reinforces progressive and regressive trends in design and administrative processes across the country.[3]

These data shed light on the relationship between academic researchers and information handlers. ATI researchers commonly conceptualize formal information requests to government officials in conflictual terms (e.g., Roberts 2005; Yeager 2006). Understood in this way, academic researchers make formal requests to access information, and the requests are met with varying degrees of hostility by institutional representatives who hold competing interests and goals. Not only has our formal information gathering (e.g., FOI requests) been straightforward and productive but we have also garnered considerable information through informal means. By building rapport and dealing directly with information handlers (often in interview settings), we have acquired a large amount of data informally through simple verbal requests. Hence, in some ways the information-gathering strategies we use resemble the source-cultivation approach favoured by many journalists.

This chapter has three sections. The first provides a brief overview of the main theoretical and methodological assumptions that guide criminological research on streetscape video surveillance. The next section examines some of the ways in which gaining access to a wide range of information influences interpretations of and explanations for monitoring programs in Canada. Three empirical examples are presented to illustrate how accessing information that is not readily available enables a deeper understanding of system design beyond existing explanations in the Canadian literature. The examples provide a more sophisticated understanding of the privacy policy sector's role in influencing and legitimizing systems is achieved. The final section briefly considers how criminological methods have broader implications for understanding the relationship between academic criminology and public policy on streetscape video surveillance.

Criminological Methods and Streetscape Video Surveillance

Three primary data-gathering techniques, each informed by a set of theoretical assumptions about crime control, are used to study streetscape video surveillance. The first, quantitative technique is intended to measure the effects of camera monitoring practices on crime rates and the displacement of crime (e.g., Gill 2003; Gill and Spriggs 2005; Waples and Gill 2006; Welsh and Farrington 2003, 2004a, 2004b, 2005, 2009). By manipulating statistical data on the prevalence of crime, researchers strive to assess how video surveillance systems contribute to reducing crime, fear of crime, nuisance, and public mischief. Researchers interested in the effects of camera monitoring share the implicit theoretical assumption that effectiveness can be measured or inferred after monitoring occurs.

The second, discursive approach examines the material, ideological, and emotional dimensions involved in establishing systems prior to the onset of monitoring activities (e.g., Coleman 2003a, 2003b, 2005, 2006; Coleman and Sim 2000; Hier 2004, 2010; Hier, Greenberg, and Walby 2006; Hier et al. 2007). The argument is that video surveillance becomes invested with meaning and significance through the many ways in which social problems are constructed, understood, and contested. Researchers share the belief that support for monitoring surveillance is based on neither the effects of cameras nor actual crime rates (although claims to effectiveness and high crime rates are common in promotional efforts). Rather, these researchers maintain that support for systems is consolidated through the activities of people with different interests and goals who lay claim to social problems and preferred surveillance solutions.

The third approach is situated between research on establishing systems and measuring their effects: investigations into the specific applications or daily uses of camera systems. The underlying assumption of research on the applications of monitoring programs is that once systems are established, it is necessary to understand how the effects of camera monitoring are produced prior to being measured. Ethnographic studies investigate how systems are applied in practice and the ways they are shaped by existing social and political relations (Goold 2004; Norris and Armstrong 1999).

Policy and Governance

A small body of research has begun to investigate the policy environment that informs how monitoring systems are designed and applied, and thereby the results they allegedly produce. According to Webster (1996, 2004, 2009), for example, although monitoring programs in the United Kingdom were initially developed in the absence of formal government regulations and controls, standard approaches to self-regulation of operations and governance steadily developed through policy networks composed of service providers, police, and politicians. Ranging from the stated intentions of monitoring systems to the formation of codes of conduct/practice, an agreed-upon set of standards emerged over the 1990s to progressively shape the administrative structure of monitoring systems. An informal administrative structure developed organically from networks of service providers based on voluntary self-regulation protocols. Co-regulatory measures involving service providers and policy makers also subsequently emerged from the non-governmental policy environment.

The rise of Canadian streetscape monitoring programs and their attendant regulatory/policy structures share certain similarities with monitoring programs in the UK. Monitoring programs in Canada, especially English Canada, were developed in a short period of time, primarily between 1997 and 2005. Although certain cities experienced greater success in launching systems by the early 2000s (see Walby 2006), a partial learning process occurred among networks of service providers, police, and politicians that progressively informed systems design in the mid- to late 1990s (e.g., data-handling rules, codes of practice, oversight committees, auditing committees). This suggests not that the learning process was thorough, uniform, or comprehensive but rather that certain forms of diffusion took hold by the late 1990s and influenced how specific monitoring programs were designed.

Despite certain similarities with the UK, however, there are also core differences. The most salient difference between the rise and diffusion of streetscape monitoring programs in Canada and the UK (beyond the sheer number of systems) is that British systems were encouraged by the central government's closed-circuit television (CCTV) promotional policies and funding programs from the outset. Government sponsorship/funding protocols provided an important sense of legitimacy to monitoring initiatives, and they facilitated standardization of the design process by encouraging the formation of community safety partnerships.

In the absence of formal government policy, governance structures in Canada have been forged largely based on a small number of available written documents and the promotional efforts of certain key regional proponents. Consequently, greater inconsistency in the diffusion of streetscape programs across Canada entailed a process of policy reinvention that lacked a comprehensive or consistently cumulative character – even after the privacy policy sector began encouraging adherence to fair information principles and, eventually, privacy protection guidelines in the late 1990s and early 2000s. From 1997 to 2005, progressive trends towards voluntary compliance and standardized self-regulation outside formal policy advocacy characterized some Canadian monitoring programs. Formal privacy protection guidelines contributed to patterns of self-regulation,[4] yet they also simultaneously enabled variation in the reasons why monitoring programs are developed and in the ways that privacy protection principles (laid out in guideline protocols) are addressed (Hier 2010; Hier and Walby 2011). The latter paradoxically reinforced regressive trends in system design.

Streetscape Video Surveillance in Canada

In this section, I provide three empirical examples to illustrate how accessing information through informal data requests and formal FOI submissions advances understanding of streetscape video surveillance in Canada. Prior to acquiring a large set of information, the focus of research was on how monitoring systems are designed to act on certain population groups for purposes of social control. Newspaper reporting and easily obtainable promotional materials were examined to glean insights into how key regional and international events focus attention on certain social problems and preferred surveillance solutions.

Accessing a variety of data that are not readily available serves a dual purpose. First, it shifts analytical focus from social control processes to governance structures at the regional/city/community level. Second, in doing so it provides insights into how the privacy policy sector simultaneously reinforces progressive and regressive trends in system design at the provincial and federal level by encouraging compliance with fair information principles. Each example illustrates how accessing information provides deeper insights into the policy dynamics informing system design and application.

The data also shed light on "warm" and "cold" information requests. In the course of our research, several dozen requests for information were made. Many of our requests – be they informal or formal – were "warm," having been finessed by building rapport with information handlers prior to soliciting information (e.g., through telephone conversations, face-to-face interviews, written communications/statement of purpose, informal consultation on policy and planning). While all of the information presented in this chapter was garnered from warm requests, we also issued several cold requests. Cold information requests netted a remarkably smaller amount of data; in a few cases, requests were simply ignored.

Beyond KPMG

In 2005, a comprehensive investigation was launched by our research team into the ways that Canadian monitoring programs are promoted and designed. By the time data gathering was completed in 2008, members of the research team had made a few contributions to the video surveillance literature, but the regional, provincial, and federal policy parameters were not well understood.

We began the investigation by arranging interviews and a site visit in the city of Sudbury, Ontario (where English Canada's first streetscape system was introduced). The primary aim of the interviews was to better understand the reasons why the monitoring program was introduced and some of the ways the system was promoted and designed. At the time of the interviews, Walby (2005, 2006) had drawn primarily on an independent audit of the system (the KPMG report) (Polani 2000) and on newspaper reporting to argue that Sudbury was the initial point of system diffusion in Canada. Walby argued that programs developed after 1997 were inspired by Sudbury's monitoring system to contain social anxieties, and that the KPMG report was the primary document that enabled system diffusion after 2000. Neither Walby nor members of the research team were in a position to fully understand exactly how Sudbury's system design mattered to the policy diffusion/reinvention process.

Our initial fieldwork (April 2006) entailed interviews with representatives of the Sudbury Police Service and the Metro Centre, the two main founding organizations of the monitoring program. During the interviews, we discussed the origins of the system and some of the organizational details. In key interviews with the deputy chief of police and the director of the Metro Centre, we also requested organizational documents pertaining to operations and governance. Our information request concerned an unspecified number of documents. The deputy police chief assigned a summer student to compile relevant information, and a large box of information arrived late in 2006. The director of the Metro Centre also provided a large number of meeting minutes and planning documents that dated to 1996. Both ATI requests were made outside the formal FOI process (and free of charge); we surmised that the requests were honoured based on rapport building and the perception that we were serious about understanding how the monitoring system was designed and administered.

The information was important for understanding the policy dynamics of streetscape video surveillance in and beyond Sudbury. When the program was formally established in 1997, neither the federal nor provincial information and privacy commissioners published guidelines on the use of video surveillance cameras in public places.[5] Sudbury's system was designed in the absence of an explicit provincial video surveillance privacy protection policy framework, yet a promotional and administrative design structure emerged that influenced other cities where monitoring programs were being promoted.

Still, few cities have been willing or able to emulate the administrative design of Sudbury's system. One main consequence of the lack of cumulative administrative diffusion from Sudbury is that subsequent programs have not always built progressively on Sudbury's system. The development of Sudbury's program entailed a community partnership model, complete with an oversight committee, evaluation protocols, public relations strategies, and responsibility-sharing arrangements. However, the Ontario privacy commissioner's recommendation to commission an independent evaluation of the system (intended to strengthen accountability) actually shifted attention away from progressive trends in the diffusion process based on Sudbury's governance structure and towards negative trends in the design process by emphasizing the perceived benefits of streetscape systems.

The Lions Eye in the Sky

The administrative design of the system can be traced to November 1996, when an ad hoc Downtown CCTV Committee (consisting of police officers and businesspeople) met to finalize plans for a pilot project (Sudbury Metro Centre 1996). When the committee expanded the system in 1997, its first task was to establish terms of reference for developing a long-term monitoring system. Among other things, this involved changing the composition of the advisory committee to better reflect the community. The committee created the Video Monitoring Advisory Committee (VMAC) to manage and steer the monitoring program and to report to the Police Services Board on matters pertaining to applications, effectiveness, funding, and expansion of the system.

In 1997, the VMAC began planning the expansion of the monitoring system. To generate funds to purchase equipment and maintain and upgrade the system, it approached the Lions Club of Sudbury (the club subsequently donated $48,000 for two more cameras and equipment). Once the system became operational, the committee – renamed the Lions Video Monitoring Advisory Committee (LVMAC) to commemorate the Lions Club donation – began developing a public relations strategy. Its goal was to promote a positive public image of the system as a cost-effective way to reduce crime and increase public safety, and to generate money through donations and local fundraising to cover the costs of maintaining and upgrading the system (e.g., fibre optic rental fees, upgrades).

To achieve these goals, the LVMAC formed a public relations subcommittee. The subcommittee held a series of press conferences, collected police crime statistics and anecdotal incident reports (communicated through monthly press releases to publicly demonstrate the tangible benefits of the cameras), and eventually distributed "Lions Eye in the Sky" stickers to downtown businesses (Video Monitoring Advisory Committee 1997). To generate money for maintaining and expanding the program, the committee held an annual "hot dog day" fundraiser for the camera system (designated as Video Monitoring Day). It also developed a more complete information package that included a five-minute promotional video; the package was initially distributed to financial institutions, service clubs, small businesses, and some police forces around the country. Fundraising efforts included a Christmas gift-wrapping fundraiser, and in 2001 the committee even explored the possibility of outsourcing the monitoring facilities to surrounding organizations and communities.

The sustained promotional activities not only generated operational capital and public awareness but also helped project a positive image of the system within and beyond Sudbury. The *Sudbury Star* published regular updates on the varied uses of the cameras. Other news outlets, such as the *Thunder Bay Chronicle* and *Toronto Star,* also focused on the system. The image fostered by the public relations committee was so positive that police representatives from several other Ontario cities contacted city representatives in Sudbury to gather information about streetscape monitoring. Towards the end of 1998, the Lions Eye in the Sky was emerging as the primary reference point for streetscape monitoring programs in English Canada.

Legitimizing the Lions Eye in the Sky

In 1998, the Office of the Information and Privacy Commissioner of Ontario (OIPC) received a complaint about the downtown cameras. The office reviewed the monitoring program and encouraged the police to commission an independent audit. By this time, the monitoring program was attracting attention from other Canadian municipalities. Members of the LVMAC repeatedly claimed that the surveillance cameras produced positive results pertaining to crime rates, fear of crime, and economic revitalization, and their claims were being repeated outside Sudbury. Members of the LVMAC were under pressure to validate their claims that the program was effective at reducing crime and enhancing public safety.

In 1999, the Sudbury Police Services Board commissioned the accounting and consultancy firm KPMG to audit the program. The final KPMG report (Polani 2000) evaluated several aspects of the Lions Eye in the Sky (e.g., benefits, impact on crime, displacement, the costs and benefits of camera monitoring, community acceptance) based on interviews and statistical analyses informed by data provided by the Sudbury Police Service. Its main conclusions were that in the three-year period following the introduction of the monitoring system, detectable criminal activity in the downtown area decreased dramatically. KPMG reported that between 1996 and 1999, assaults and robberies decreased by 38 percent and property crimes by 44 percent. It also reported that Sudbury's crime levels had declined at greater rates without evidence of displacement to other areas.

Besides claims about the impact of camera monitoring on the crime rate, the audit also concluded that the monitoring system was beneficial to safety and perceptions of safety on the part of law enforcement officers and members of the public. For instance, 79 percent of downtown-resident survey respondents (a total of fifty-eight participants) and 98 percent of business respondents approved of the system; 65 percent of residents and 98 percent of business respondents reported that CCTV did not invade privacy. In terms of the possible benefits of CCTV in increasing business revenues, KPMG concluded that 9 percent of residents increased their shopping habits since the cameras were installed; 6 percent of business respondents reported that CCTV had improved business. The LVMAC was particularly keen to promote claims presented in the report that 300 to 500 criminal offences were deterred by the cameras, that no displacement effect had occurred, and that downtown Sudbury had saved $600,000 to $800,000 (Lions Club 2002).

Although some members of the LVMAC were skeptical about the validity of the findings presented in the KPMG report, the document was posted on the Sudbury Police Service's website to address the OIPC's request for an independent assessment and to further promote the system. Once the report was posted on the Internet, it became a primary reference document in promotional efforts in other Canadian cities (Hier 2010; Walby 2006).

Advocates of streetscape monitoring systems in other cities were no more convinced of the KPMG findings than LVMAC members but the report served as a convenient reference to justify pilot programs around the country. Indeed, responses to the OIPC's privacy protection recommendation number 4b (2001), that use of video surveillance cameras should be justified based on verifiable evidence attesting to public safety concerns, overwhelmingly relied on the claims in the KPMG report.

One of the problems with relying on the LVMAC's claims about the effectiveness of video surveillance is that most other cities have not been able to emulate either the LVMAC's administrative design or public relations strategies. Prior to the KPMG report, when city representatives outside Sudbury consulted the LVMAC, they received information about governance and operations. With the publication of the KPMG report, however, claims regarding camera effectiveness increasingly displaced the earlier emphasis on administrative design (terms of reference, auditing and oversight, public awareness, signage, fundraising, information packages, etc.). This is not to suggest that there was a clear cumulative administrative diffusion prior to the KPMG report, but simply that an emphasis on governance and design was increasingly displaced by one on effectiveness.

In retrospect, instead of passively encouraging an independent external evaluation, the OIPC could have worked more closely with the LVMAC to facilitate a cumulative process of building greater accountability and sharing of responsibility into the design of monitoring systems outside Sudbury (Ontario guidelines had yet to be published when the KPMG report was completed). The Lions Eye in the Sky by no means exemplified a perfect administrative structure, but there were several progressive components to the system design that could have been encouraged by the OIPC based on a detailed understanding of the program. That is, the OIPC could have reached beyond KPMG by drawing on a broader range of information and documentation to encourage stronger governance in other cities (as well as in Sudbury). Alternatively, the OIPC's passive approach to streetscape video surveillance encouraged the consolidation of regressive trends in the design and implementation process, with the result that "needs assessment" in other cities repeatedly invoked the dubious claims about camera effectiveness presented in the KPMG report.

Beyond FASE

In April 2006, we also visited the city of London, Ontario. Some of the communications and promotional dynamics that contributed to the formation of the Downtown Camera Project have been examined elsewhere (Hier, Green-berg, and Walby 2006; Hier et al. 2007). Based on newspaper reporting and documents available on the Internet, the primary aim of earlier analyses was to better understand the promotional and fundraising efforts that gained momentum when a citizens' group (Friends Against Senseless Endings, or FASE) was formed in the immediate aftermath of the murder of a young person in London's downtown bar district. It is improbable that the monitor-ing system would have been launched in the absence of the sympathy evoked by FASE. Until we gained access to a large set of council minutes, planning documents, and city memoranda, however, neither researchers nor the OIPC and representatives in other cities that were planning monitoring systems realized the extent of the Downtown Camera Project's operational design.

The data-gathering strategies used in London were similar to those used in Sudbury: we conducted a set of interviews and requested relevant docu-ments from key informants. Based on the rapport we built with the London Police Service's (LPS) point man on the project, as well as with business-people and city councillors, we received a useful set of documents directly from interviewees. To facilitate data gathering, interviewees also encour-aged us to speak with London's city manager. Our meeting with the city manager was not planned; we visited his office, explained our purpose and intentions, and left a business card. Several months later, a large set of docu-ments, council minutes, planning documents, and memoranda arrived (free of charge). The information shifted our attention from the power of promo-tional claims-making activities to the importance of responsibility sharing and operational accountability in system design.

The Downtown Camera Project

In early 1999, the London Police Service began investigating the use of video surveillance in public places. The investigation entailed examining Sudbury's monitoring program, as well as monitoring programs in Glasgow, Scotland, and Ipswich, England. While this was taking place, twenty-year-old Michael Goldie-Ryder was stabbed to death after a fight broke out in downtown London.

Following the stabbing, a public meeting was organized to talk about vio-lence in the downtown area. After the meeting, the Coordinating Committee for Community Safety (CCCS) was formed to develop crime reduction strategies. The committee was co-chaired by David Tennant from the London business community and Amanda Alvaro. Alvaro represented the newly created Friends Against Senseless Endings, which was organized by friends of Michael Goldie-Ryder to develop strategies to resist community violence through education and awareness, as well as to pressure the federal government for legislative changes pertaining to criminal assaults involving knives. The CCCS made several recommendations to amend the *Criminal Code of Canada* regarding weapons offences, to communicate the recommended deterrents to young people in and around the London area, and to reduce crime (Coordinating Committee for Community Safety 1999a, 1999b, and 1999c). Among the recommendations was a call for monitored video surveillance cameras in the downtown core.

The CCCS reported initially to London's Police Services Board and estimated start-up costs at approximately $200,000. Concomitantly, the LPS produced a feasibility study outlining a plan to establish a monitoring site in downtown London that would be governed by a community-based agency and maintained by London Hydro. The feasibility study (London Police Service 1999) was based on the premise, borrowed from Sudbury's administrative design, that any monitoring initiative must be community-based rather than police-based, to avoid the charge of "Big Brother" surveillance. The feasibility study recommended that the LPS enter into a partnership with existing organizations, such as Neighbourhood Watch or the Block Parent Program. A major component of the community-based approach had to do with fundraising for the acquisition of initial hardware, as well as a public relations campaign to articulate the utility of surveillance cameras.

After the feasibility study was completed, the Police Services Board added the estimated costs of the first year of operations to the police budget projections for 2000 ($200,000 to cover half of the projected first-year budget in the feasibility study; the total amount was estimated at $397,219.52). The projected operational expense was earmarked for release to the Environmental Services Department (which would take control of budget management) pending approval from Municipal Council. Until this point, the proposal outlined the perceived utility of streetscape surveillance, technological and hardware requirements, desired camera locations, and start-up and operational costs. It did not address liability facing the city, privacy protection, or operational protocol. Municipal Council approved the proposal subject to the development of a governance structure, a data management policy, and an assessment of the implications of the program under the *Municipal Freedom of Information and Protection of Privacy Act (MFIPPA)*.

The CCCS subsequently reported on the roles and responsibilities of stakeholders in the proposed monitoring program. The major stakeholder identified in the report was Neighbourhood Watch, whose board of directors agreed to govern the monitoring program in consultation with the police. The city's Civic Administration reported on liability and privacy protection. Based on the CCCS's proposal and clarification of roles and responsibilities, the city's Legal Department concluded that with proper safeguards (e.g., confidential data handling and storage) in place, the city's liability would be minimal. The Legal Department cautioned, however, that the city could incur costs if an individual sued the city on the basis that the cameras failed to deter a crime.

The city's Freedom of Information (FOI) Coordinator reported on the implications of the proposed system under the *MFIPPA*. Based on the privacy principles stipulated in the *MFIPPA*, the FOI Coordinator concluded that because the Neighbourhood Watch board was not appointed by Municipal Council, it was not considered part of the municipal corporation of the City of London. The FOI Coordinator also concluded that videotapes generated from surveillance activities would not constitute records of a municipal institution under the *MFIPPA*, as long as the information collected was not under the control and custody of the London Police Service. The FOI Coordinator warned that the police could take control and custody of records if videotapes were used for law enforcement purposes. Nevertheless, the FOI Coordinator explained: "From the available IPC jurisprudence (Orders, Investigations and Judicial Reviews), this appears to be 'unchartered territory' at present."[6]

Based on the reported information, $200,000 was approved for the annual operating expenses of the monitoring program. In response to the significantly lower annual operating budget than the requested $350,000, Police Chief Albert Gramolini argued that the reduced budget required a reduction in the number of cameras and monitoring staff. The reductions, he maintained, posed liability issues for the police based on the system's reduced effectiveness in monitoring high-crime areas. Gramolini pointed to the community-based consultation process that had led to the proposed system, and he outlined how neither Neighbourhood Watch nor London Hydro could maintain the system on a reduced budget.[7] He also publicly declared that the project would not be viable on a reduced operating budget and threatened to terminate the proposal process.

A special meeting of the city's Community and Protective Services Committee was convened to propose a revision to the initial proposal. It was decided that, provided the CCCS generated $200,000 in start-up funds, the city would release $200,000 to the Police Services Board on an annual basis. To address the police chief's concerns about scaling back the monitoring system, the committee proposed that the monitoring site be located in City Hall, where the streetscape system could be integrated into the existing security system run by the city's Environmental Services Department and staffed by the Core of Commissionaires (City of London 2000).

The amendments had implications for the design of the monitoring program, for the city's accountability to the OIPC, and for the potential influence of London's system on to-be-developed systems in the country. The decision to locate the monitoring control centre in City Hall meant, first, that London Hydro would no longer have control of the system and, necessarily, of surveillance records. When the city (a municipal institution under the *MFIPPA*) assumed ownership of the program, it also assumed responsibility for managing surveillance records, thereby becoming accountable to the OIPC. This provided the OIPC with access to the organizational structure of the system that could have served as a model for other programs in the province.

Rather than developing a detailed understanding of London's program to disseminate to other cities, however, the OIPC consulted with the city on its code of practice and some of the requirements it faced under the *MFIPPA*. The OIPC also encouraged London to advertise the system on its website. Although this recommendation was accepted, the information provided pertained only to the general purpose of the system. No information was provided on governance and operations, and there is no evidence that the OIPC used London as a model for other cities, such as Windsor and Hamilton. When the OIPC's guidelines were published in 2001, the city was asked to address some of the stipulations. The OIPC never fleshed out the importance of London's governance structure, and when the Privacy Commissioner of Canada initiated a constitutional challenge to public video surveillance in Canada, attention was drawn away from the gains made in London's responsibility-sharing and ownership design.

Beyond Radwanski: The Federal Privacy Agenda

The information acquired through informal information requests in Sudbury and London effectively shifted our analytical focus from social control processes (intended effects) to governance structures (design). It was becoming clear that a necessary and hitherto neglected focus of research concerns the design and administrative structure of existing systems, as well as the privacy policy sector's approach to dealing with governance and administration.

As the focus of research began to shift, we received information from a formal FOI request submitted to federal agencies the previous year. Shortly after we launched the investigation of monitoring systems in Canada, federal Transportation Minister Jean Lapierre announced a security review of Canadian transportation systems in the aftermath of the 7 July 2005 bombings in London (in August 2005). We submitted an FOI request to Transport Canada and other agencies that were connected with it on this matter, such as the RCMP, Department of Justice, and the Office of the Privacy Commissioner of Canada (OPC). Most of the information came from the OPC following consultations. The information enabled us to understand the broader policy dynamics concerning public-area video surveillance in Canada and the implications federal developments had on regional systems.

A considerable amount of material received through our FOI requests concerned Privacy Commissioner of Canada George Radwanski's efforts to stop public video surveillance in the city of Kelowna, British Columbia.[8] In 2001, Radwanski launched an investigation into the legality of public video surveillance conducted by the RCMP in that city. He concluded that the RCMP was not justified in recording general public activity twenty-four hours a day, seven days a week.[9] After the ruling, RCMP Commissioner Giuliano Zaccardelli ordered the Kelowna RCMP to stop recording continual images to comply with the *Privacy Act,* but the RCMP continued to use the camera to survey public space (Royal Canadian Mounted Police 2003).

Following a set of public relations activities centring on the argument that the spirit of the privacy protection law concerned the presence of the camera rather than whether or not images were recorded (Radwanski 2002a, 2002b, 2002c, 2002d), Radwanski filed a Statement of Claim against the Solicitor General of BC, the Attorney General of BC, and the Commissioner of the RCMP with the Supreme Court of British Columbia. Reacting to the Statement of Claim, the RCMP and the Department of the Solicitor General initiated strategic action to defend against the challenge (Blondin 2002).

Immediately following the Statement of Claim, representatives of the Department of the Solicitor General of Canada began meeting with representatives of the RCMP to discuss the use of public-area video surveillance cameras by federal law enforcement agencies. Representatives of each agency agreed to work together to develop an overarching national public policy position on the use of "Public Safety Cameras" (Blondin 2002). They decided to base the national framework on the principles laid out in the provincial policy frameworks adopted in Alberta, Ontario, and British Columbia, but with stronger language in order to "effectively communicate that the Department and the RCMP are committed to enhancing public safety and crime prevention through the Public Safety Camera initiative while at the same time giving full consideration and respect to the privacy rights of Canadians" (Blondin 2002, 2).

Beyond concerns pertaining to the use of video surveillance by federal law enforcement agencies, however, Radwanski's actions touched a nerve among government agencies concerning the perceived growing assertiveness of parliamentary commissioners:

> Parliamentary Commissioners such as the Privacy Commissioner and the Information Commissioner have shown increased interest in expanding their role beyond their statutory mandates as ombudsmen who are ultimately responsible to Parliament. This is confirmed in the pleadings of the Privacy Commissioner in this case when he states that he has the powers beyond those provided for in the *Privacy Act.* The Privacy Commissioner openly claims to be the protector of privacy interests of Canadians and asserts that it is his responsibility to bring to the courts issues which threaten the privacy of Canadians.
>
> The Privacy Commissioner's view of his role in bringing forward this court challenge is incompatible with the role assigned by Parliament. It threatens a shift from Parliamentary accountability to judicial accountability and could lead to future court challenges to government actions or programs and even legislation. For example the Privacy Commissioner could initiate a Charter challenge to the CCRA database or to the proposed lawful access scheme ...
>
> In addition, if the Privacy Commissioner's authority to bring this case is not challenged it will set a precedent that will be difficult to overcome both legally and in the public environment. This case, if it proceeds, is likely to make it to the Supreme Court of Canada. If that happens, it will be very difficult to argue in subsequent cases that the Commissioner does not have the authority to initiate an action of this kind. What is more, this precedent will not be limited to the Privacy Commissioner but would extend to other Parliamentary Commissioners (e.g., the Information Commissioner, the Human Rights Commissioner, the Auditor General, etc.) and possibly to other statutory office holders. (Department of Justice n.d.)

Radwanski's challenge to public-area video surveillance tapped into existing concerns among government agencies regarding the perceived shift in the role of parliamentary commissions from advocates for parliamentary accountability to regulators pursuing judicial accountability. The challenge, however, was subsequently rejected; the court ruled that the Privacy Commissioner of Canada did not have the legal authority to challenge the RCMP's use of video surveillance under the *Charter*. Radwanski planned to continue his fight against public-area monitoring practices, but resigned on 23 June 2003 after a committee of Members of Parliament claimed that he had falsified financial documents and violated standards of office and human management. He was cleared of charges on 13 February 2009, and maintained that he was discredited for his strong opposition to post-9/11 government surveillance initiatives in general and CCTV surveillance in particular.

Radwanski's termination had three implications for public video surveillance in Canada: (1) the substantive constitutional issues of public video surveillance were never debated in a Canadian court; (2) the *Charter* challenge became associated with a discredited Privacy Commissioner; and (3) a pragmatic, reactive, complaints-based approach to addressing public video surveillance was reinforced among Canadian Privacy Commissioners in the period 2003-06. When Radwanski initiated the challenge, cities across the country halted efforts to develop systems (Thunder Bay and Hamilton, Ontario, and Vancouver, British Columbia) or to expand them (Sudbury, Ontario, and Sherbrooke, Québec). Few proponents of public monitoring systems were willing to forge ahead in the climate of uncertainty. The OPC's subsequent withdrawal of the challenge gave a green light for implementation and expansion efforts.

In the aftermath of the abandoned challenge, the OPC abandoned Radwanski's aggressive approach for a conciliatory one and began working with the RCMP (Office of the Privacy Commissioner of Canada 2003). An OPC-RCMP task force sought to strike a balance between RCMP policing duties and the OPC's commitment to minimizing privacy intrusions. The OPC took the lead in developing national guidelines for the use of public-area video surveillance cameras by consolidating existing knowledge in-house and trying to educate Canadians about public video surveillance. Tellingly, members of the OPC recognized from the outset that they were limited in what they could say about public video surveillance because they did not even know the extent of public-area monitoring systems in Canada (Office of the Privacy Commissioner of Canada 2004).

The OPC's draft guidelines were sent to the Community, Contract, and Aboriginal Policing Services (CCAPS) of the RCMP for comments.[10] The CCAPS concluded that, if adhered to, the guidelines proposed by the OPC would entail significant expenditure of resources by the RCMP and the wider Canadian policing community, and would lead to significant delays in the implementation of video surveillance systems. Identified as especially problematic were principles pertaining to privacy impact assessments, restricting the use of video surveillance to serious exceptional circumstances, and responding to information access requests for segments of video recording that excludes other individuals. The analysis also warned of the potential danger that the guidelines – designed to apply to "community cameras" – might be extended to other forms of video surveillance (such as cell blocks).

By late 2005, the OPC had not received RCMP endorsement for the guidelines and proceeded to publish *OPC Guidelines for the Use of Video Surveillance of Public Places by Police and Law Enforcement Authorities* in March 2006. The preamble explains that the guidelines were developed in the context of a discussion group of stakeholders established jointly by the OPC and the RCMP. By the time the federal guidelines were published in 2006, the provinces of Alberta, British Columbia, Ontario, Nova Scotia, Saskatchewan, New Brunswick, Newfoundland and Labrador, and Québec has put measures in place. In effect, the publication of the OPC guidelines marked the institutionalization of the pragmatic policy framework on public-area video surveillance already developed across the provinces that sought to educate and encourage compliance.

Essentially, the regulatory approach that Commissioner Radwanski adopted to address public video surveillance threatened to shift the emerging policy framework in Canada from a passive, complaints-based educational approach to a more active, regulatory one. Beyond his efforts to call into question the expanding number of public video surveillance programs, the challenge tapped into existing concerns pertaining to appointed parliamentary commissioners. With his challenge terminated, a pragmatic CCTV surveillance policy initiative was institutionalized that reinforced the policy framework that inadvertently permits a diversity of responses to monitoring initiatives in communities across Canada. If nothing else, Radwanski's efforts could have focused more attention on the ethics of public-area video surveillance. Instead, the effort to challenge its constitutional nature actually reinforced existing patterns in the promotion and design of monitoring systems across the country.

Academic Criminology and Public Policy on Streetscape Video Surveillance

The data presented here illustrate how the admittedly protracted process of identifying, pursuing, and accessing information on streetscape monitoring

programs has wider implications for understanding the relationship between academic criminology and the production of publicly useful criminological knowledge. To be sure, during the investigation certain police and
city representatives blocked, diverted, and, in rare cases, simply ignored information requests. Yet resistance to data requests (in the form of charging
high fees, denying the existence of documents, or unnecessary delays) was
the exception rather than the norm, and requested data were often granted
outside formal FOI processes. Rather than encountering pervasive patterns
of institutional defiance that restricted knowledge acquisition and understanding through the preservation of inequitable power divisions and information control, we found that the initial barriers to information access
stemmed from academic criminologists' lack of methodological appreciation for the value of accessing information in its many forms.

In addition to exposing methodological problems with existing research
on streetscape video surveillance systems, the data also illustrate how accessing information that was not readily available changed interpretations of
and explanations for how streetscape video surveillance programs are administered and designed. Before we gained access to a broad range of policy
and planning documents, streetscape video surveillance was explained primarily in conceptual and theoretical terms as a means of reinforcing differential power and social control processes. The primary targets for criticism,
consequently, consisted of claims makers, advocates, moral entrepreneurs,
and a set of cultural prejudices. Even when the complexity of relations involved in establishing monitoring systems was recognized (see Hier et al.
2007), only a weak understanding of the policy dynamics informing ongoing
design and administrative structures was developed. Analyzing a set of hard-
to-access documentation not only complicated previous theoretical argumentation but also shifted the focus of investigation away from social control
to policy governance and from promotional claims-making activities to the
privacy policy sector's strategies for addressing monitoring initiatives.

Beyond methodological and explanatory problems, the findings have a
third set of broader implications for the relationship between academic
criminology and public policy on streetscape video surveillance. There is
currently considerable discussion about the professional status and public
influence of criminological research. The growing consensus is that academic criminologists exercise an insufficient degree of influence on public
policy debates about crime and social disorder generally.

Part of the reason for the decline of publicly influential academic criminology concerns the difficulties that criminologists experience in disseminating

their research findings to policy makers, police, politicians, and the public (see also Haggerty 2004 and Mathews 2009). Another reason is a perceived ideological bias in criminological research. According to this argument, a large number of criminologists have narrowed their specializations and oriented their arguments towards other, like-minded criminologists. The consequence has been a growing tendency among academic criminologists to maintain the intellectual boundaries of criminology at the expense of producing politically influential research (Hier 2010).

One place to begin addressing these problems is method, a final issue requiring consideration. Accessing diverse information from a variety of agencies and organizations has not figured prominently in criminological research on streetscape video surveillance, and especially the policy relevance that underscores or informs the structure and application of monitoring systems. Indeed, beyond recognizing the importance of gaining access to research sites and key informants, criminologists generally are not trained to think about information access as a methodological component essential to sound information gathering. From the existing literature on access to information, criminologists are led to believe that information access (when pursued) is an antagonistic process that pits researchers against gatekeepers. What I explain in this chapter, however, is that gaining access to relevant information on streetscape video surveillance can be facilitated by greater attention to well-established methodological issues of rapport building and matters of entry, what I have called "warm" information requests.

The extent to which our experiences in gathering information on streetscape video surveillance can be generalized to other criminological research domains is not clear. Admittedly, we dealt mostly with local governments and organizations in the absence of formal provincial and federal policy on video surveillance practices. The data we gathered were not, for the most part, deemed sensitive by information gatekeepers. Nor was there great concern among those gatekeepers that the information would be used to subvert their efforts to monitor city streets. Still, we faced ongoing challenges in gaining entry to research sites (e.g., securing interviews) and building rapport. The latter was necessary before information gatekeepers agreed to devote large amounts of their time to searching for documents and reports. Rapport was built through dozens of hours of telephone conversations, e-mail exchanges, and in-person visits. Accessing information involved much more than simply asking for documents and reports. It required convincing information handlers that we were serious about understanding video surveillance practices and that we valued their time and opinions. Hence, rather than seeing gatekeepers pitted against researchers in antagonistic encounters over access to information, our experience suggests that information handlers are willing to cooperate with researchers in a "warm" environment characterized by mutual respect, trust, and professional integrity – age-old requirements for site entry and data collection.

NOTES

1 Streetscapes encompass the entire area between buildings located on opposite sides of city streets. Elements of the streetscape include sidewalks, landscapes, utilities, roads, businesses, residential properties, rest areas, bus stops, vehicles, vendors, pedestrians, and cyclists.

2 The privacy policy sector consists of a range of agencies devoted to encouraging best practices in information-gathering and data-handling procedures. The federal and provincial privacy commissioners' offices are the main organizations responsible for encouraging best practices concerning video surveillance.

3 The pragmatic orientation tries to balance the needs and desires of law enforcement with privacy protection ideals. In practice, pragmatism takes the form of advocacy and education rather than regulation and oversight.

4 The Office of the Privacy Commissioner of Canada and the provincial Offices of the Information and Privacy Commissioner offer a basic set of standardized quasi-legal guidelines for the use of public-area video surveillance. The guidelines consist of principles or key issues to assist federal, provincial, and municipal institutions and law enforcement agencies in deciding whether the collection of personal information by means of video surveillance is justified and, if so, how to build privacy protection into monitoring programs.

5 In 1998, David Flaherty, Information and Privacy Commissioner of British Columbia, published "Video Surveillance by Public Bodies: A Discussion" (British Columbia Information and Privacy Commissioner 1998). That same year, Ann Cavoukian, Information and Privacy Commissioner of Ontario, published "Video Surveillance: The Privacy Implications" (Ontario Information and Privacy Commissioner 1998). Both documents sketched out general privacy protection principles for public video surveillance.

6 "Downtown Surveillance Camera System," memorandum to Chairs and Members, Community and Protective Services Committee, from Jeff Malpass, Deputy City Manager (27 March 2000). Document released by Manager of Records and Information Services, City of London.

7 Letter from Police Chief Gramolini to Councillor Ab Chahbar, Chair of the CPSC (30 March 2000). Document released by Manager of Records and Information Services, City of London.

8 Hundreds of pages of memoranda, e-mail correspondence, briefing documents, and assessment reports pertaining to the OPC, the RCMP, the Department of Justice, and Emergency Preparedness were released.

9 "Privacy Commissioner's Findings on Video Surveillance by RCMP in Kelowna," letter from Commissioner Radwanski to Commissioner Loukidelis (4 October 2001).
   Document released by the Office of the Privacy Commissioner of Canada.
10 The analyst charged with reviewing the proposed guidelines was given a single business day to report on issues/concerns to the RCMP, as well as to identify differences
   between the federal guidelines and those guidelines listed on a provincial comparison chart provided by the OPC. In the analysis, the analyst notes the inappropriate-
   ness of the CCAPS's making recommendations to the RCMP, and the inadequate
   time allocation for performing the task.

REFERENCES

Blondin, Stephanie. 2002. "National Framework: Policy Considerations." Ottawa:
    Office of the Privacy Commissioner of Canada. Document released by the
    Office of the Privacy Commissioner of Canada.
British Columbia Information and Privacy Commissioner. 1998. "Video Surveillance
    by Public Bodies: A Discussion" (Investigation P98-012). http://www.oipc.
    bc.ca/.
City of London. 2000. "Chairs and Members, Community and Protective Services
    Committee: Downtown Camera Surveillance System." Meeting Minutes, 3
    April. London, ON: City of London. Document released by Manager of Records
    and Information Services, City of London.
Coleman, R. 2003a. "Images from a Neoliberal City: The State, Surveillance and
    Social Control." *Critical Criminology* 12: 21-42.
–. 2003b. "Researching the Emergent City States: Articulating the Proper Objects of
    Power and CCTV." In *Researching the Crimes of the Powerful: Scrutinising
    States and Corporations*, ed. by S. Tombs and D. Whyte, 88-104. New York:
    Peter Lang.
–. 2005. "Surveillance in the City: Primary Definition and Urban Spatial Order."
    Crime, Media, and Culture 1 (2): 131-48.
–. 2006. "Confronting the Hegemony of Vision: State, Space, and Urban Crime
    Prevention." In *Expanding the Criminological Imagination: Critical Readings
    in Criminology*, ed. by A. Barton, C. Corteen, D. Scott, and D. Whyte, 38-64.
    Cullompton, UK: Willan Publishing.
Coleman, R., and J. Sim. 2000. "'You'll Never Walk Alone': CCTV Surveillance,
    Order and Neo-Liberal Rule in Liverpool City Centre." *British Journal of Soci-
    ology* 51 (4): 623-39.
Coordinating Committee for Community Safety. 1999a. "Educational Recommen-
    dations," 14 June. London, ON: City of London.
–. 1999b. "Legislative Recommendations," 25 March. London, ON: City of London.
–. 1999c. "Police/Public Interaction Subcommittee: Report and Recommendations,"
    29 April. London, ON: City of London.
Department of Justice. n.d. "Memorandum for the Minister." Department of Justice,
    MLU2002-004643. Document released by Office of the Privacy Commissioner
    of Canada.

Gill, Martin. 2003. *CCTV.* Leicester, UK: Perpetuity.

Gill, M., and A. Spriggs. 2005. *Assessing the Impact of CCTV.* Home Office Research Study Number 292. London: Home Office.

Goold, B. 2004. *CCTV and Policing.* Oxford: Oxford University Press.

Haggerty, Kevin. 2004. "Displaced Expertise: Three Constraints on the Policy Relevance of Criminological Thought." *Theoretical Criminology* 8 (2): 211-31.

Hier, Sean P. 2004. "Risky Spaces and Dangerous Faces: Surveillance, Social Disorder, and CCTV." *Social and Legal Studies* 13 (4): 541-54.

–. 2010. *Panoptic Dreams: Streetscape Video Surveillance in Canada.* Vancouver: UBC Press.

Hier, Sean P., Joshua Greenberg, and Kevin Walby. 2006. "Supplementing the Panoptic Paradigm: Surveillance, Moral Governance, and CCTV." In *Theorizing Surveillance: The Panopticon and Beyond,* ed. by David Lyon, 230-44. Cullompton, UK: Willan Publishing.

Hier, Sean P., Joshua Greenberg, Kevin Walby, and Dan Lett. 2007. "Beyond Responsibilization and Social Ordering: Media, Communication, and the Establishment of Public Video Surveillance Programs." *Media, Culture, and Society* 29 (5): 727-51.

Hier, Sean P., and Kevin Walby. 2011. "Privacy Pragmatism and Streetscape Video Surveillance in Canada." *International Sociology* 26(4): 844-61.

Lions Club. 2002. "Fact Sheet." Document released by Greater Sudbury Police Force and Sudbury Metro Centre.

London Police Service. 1999. "Downtown Crime Study, 30 April." London, ON: Crime Analysis Unit.

Ontario Information and Privacy Commissioner. 1998. "Video Surveillance: The Privacy Implications." *IPC Practices* no. 10. http://www.ipc.on.ca/.

Mathews, Roger. 2009. "Beyond 'So What?' Criminology: Rediscovering Realism." *Theoretical Criminology* 13 (3): 341-62.

Norris, C., and G. Armstrong. 1999. *The Maximum Surveillance Society: The Rise of CCTV.* Oxford and New York: Berg.

Office of the Privacy Commissioner of Canada. 2003. "MEMORANDUM: Terms of Reference: Task Force on Video Surveillance." From Raymond D'Aoust, 12 December. Document released by the Office of the Privacy Commissioner of Canada.

–. 2004. "Proposed Project on Video Surveillance." From Brian K. Stewart, 22 March. Document released by the Office of the Privacy Commissioner of Canada.

–. 2006. *OPC Guidelines for the Use of Video Surveillance of Public Places by Police and Law Enforcement Authorities.* http://www.priv.gc.ca/.

Polani, Oscar. 2000. "Evaluation of the Lions Eye in the Sky Video Monitoring Project." http://www.police.sudbury.on.ca/.

Radwanski, George. 2002a. Speech to Kelowna Chamber of Commerce, Kelowna, BC, 6 February. Ottawa: Office of the Privacy Commissioner of Canada.

–. 2002b. "Video Surveillance in Public Places." Speech delivered to Ontario Bar Association, Toronto, 27 May. Ottawa: Office of the Privacy Commissioner of Canada.

–. 2002c. "Watching You: Privacy Rights and Video Surveillance." Speech delivered to BC Branch of the Canadian Bar Association, Vancouver, BC, 7 February. Ottawa: Office of the Privacy Commissioner of Canada.

–. 2002d. "Watching You: Privacy Rights and Video Surveillance." Speech delivered at McMaster University, Hamilton, ON, 13 February. Ottawa: Office of the Privacy Commissioner of Canada.

Roberts, Alasdair. 2005. "Spin Control and Freedom of Information: Lessons for the United Kingdom from Canada." *Public Administration* 83 (1): 1-23.

Royal Canadian Mounted Police. 2003. "ASSESSMENT." RCMP Memorandum, 17 September. Document released by the Office of the Privacy Commissioner of Canada.

Sudbury Metro Centre. 1996. "Downtown CCTV Committee Minutes," 13 November. Sudbury, ON: Sudbury Metro Centre.

Video Monitoring Advisory Committee. 1997. "Committee Minutes," 26 August. Sudbury, ON: Sudbury Metro Centre.

Walby, Kevin. 2005. "Open-Street Camera Surveillance and Governance in Canada." *Canadian Journal of Criminology and Criminal Justice* 47 (4): 655-83.

–. 2006. "Little England? The Rise of Open-Street Closed Circuit Television Surveillance in Canada." *Surveillance and Society* 4 (1): 29-51.

Waples, Sam, and Martin Gill. 2006. "Effectiveness of Redeployable CCTV." *Crime Prevention and Community Safety* 8 (1): 1-16.

Webster, William R. 1996. "Closed Circuit Television and Governance: The Eve of a Surveillance Age." *Information Infrastructure and Policy* 5 (4): 253-63.

–. 2004. "The Diffusion, Regulation, and Governance of Closed-Circuit Television in the UK." *Surveillance and Society* 2 (2/3): 230-50.

–. 2009. "CCTV Policy in the UK: Reconsidering the Evidence Base." *Surveillance and Society* 6 (1): 10-22.

Welsh, Brandon C., and David P. Farrington. 2003. "Effects of Closed-Circuit Television on Crime." *Annals of the American Academy of Political and Social Science* 587 (1): 110-35.

–. 2004a. "Evidence-Based Crime Prevention: The Effectiveness of CCTV." *Crime Prevention and Community Safety* 6 (2): 21-33.

–. 2004b. "Surveillance for Crime Prevention in Public Space: Results and Policy Choices in Britain and America." *Criminology and Public Policy* 3 (3): 497-525.

–. 2005. "Evidence-Based Crime Prevention: Conclusions and Directions for a Safer Society." *Canadian Journal of Criminology and Criminal Justice* 47 (2): 337-54.

–. 2009. *Making Public Places Safer*. Oxford: Oxford University Press.

Yeager, Matthew G. 2006. "The *Freedom of Information Act* as a Methodological Tool: Suing the Government for Data." *Canadian Journal of Criminology and Criminal Justice* 48 (4): 499-521.

LEGISLATION CITED

Access to Information Act, R.S.C. 1985, c. A-1.

Municipal Freedom of Information and Protection of Privacy Act, R.S.O. 1990, c. M.56.

Privacy Act, R.S.C. 1985, c. P-21.

DISPATCHES FROM THE FOURTH ESTATE – ACCESS TO INFORMATION AND INVESTIGATIVE JOURNALISM

11

Access, Administration, and Democratic Intent

FRED VALLANCE-JONES

Access laws are the embodiment of one of our most important democratic rights, the right to know what public officials are doing with our money and our trust. But that right, which has been characterized as quasi-constitutional, can be difficult to exercise. Exemptions allow information to be blacked out before documents are released, and in some jurisdictions process has come to rival or surpass the formal exemptions as a barrier to access. The latter problem is the focus of this chapter. Provisions of the acts that were meant to regulate their day-to-day operations have become what I call "quasi exemptions" that themselves delay or block the release of information to the public. This chapter delves deeply into the biggest of the quasi exemptions: widespread failure, particularly at the federal level, to meet the thirty-day response requirement that is standard in most of the acts. It will also examine the effects of high fees, most notably in Ontario.

Below I explore the roots of the ongoing struggle between power and openness, consider understaffing of access to information branches, and suggest that without tougher, legislated requirements, expecting anything near full compliance is simply unrealistic. You'll also hear from users and others involved with the system, such as Harvey Cashore. "Most of my access requests don't get fulfilled quickly," said the longtime investigative producer with CBC News and author of a book on the Airbus scandal. "They are subject to long delays, they cost too much, and when you get them, you almost have to start over again; you have to appeal and complain, complain about blacked out information, so by the time you finish that process, you can literally be two or three years or four years down the road. Well, who has that kind of attention span?" (Cashore interview, Toronto, 10 December 2009). Indeed, the poor compliance record of many federal agencies with regard to the most basic requirements in the *Access to Information Act (ATIA)* has put the access regime under severe strain.

Quasi Exemptions

Parliament passed the *Access to Information Act* in 1982 and it became law on 1 July 1983. Ottawa insiders have called it "Trudeau's gift to Mulroney" because while it was proclaimed in the final months of Pierre Trudeau's Liberal government, it was Brian Mulroney's Progressive Conservative regime that had to deal with its effects (Savoie 2003, 49). Over the next few years, stories followed on diverse topics such as the "Tunagate" scandal, expensive renovations at the opposition leader's residence of Stornoway, and cabinet ministers' travel (Attallah and Pyman 2002, Appendix D). The act quickly became known for something else, however: delay.

As do the other Canadian freedom of information (FOI) laws, the *ATIA* contains provisions dealing with how to apply for records, the time limit for responding, whether that limit can be extended, and how much requesters can be charged for finding and preparing records, computer programming, and photocopies. Key among these provisions is the thirty-day response period. During that time, public servants have to obtain the records from the branch that holds them, review them for any exemptions that might apply, remove exempt information if necessary, and, often, obtain sign-offs from superiors before notifying the requester of the access decision. The effort required depends on the volume and complexity of the work, but there seems to be a consensus among legislators that this is a reasonable standard. The thirty days, or the equivalent in business days, is nearly uniform across the country, and beyond Canada as well, with the United States *Freedom of Information Act* allowing twenty business days and the United Kingdom's act twenty working days (Glover et al. 2006, 14). Official statistics show that it is a standard that many Canadian government organizations have struggled to meet, however. Time has become the most significant of the quasi exemptions, because of the use of administrative provisions that effectively deny access to records for long periods, which very often attenuates the information value of the records. These quasi exemptions, which also include large fees, rival the formal exemptions in the act in importance, and perhaps are even more potent in that they result in no information at all being disclosed for long periods of time.

A History of Delay

Chronic delay has been documented often, but a short history is instructive. The *Access to Information Act* contained a provision requiring a review within three years of proclamation, and the House of Commons Standing Committee on Justice and the Solicitor General issued its final report, *Open and Shut*, in 1987. The committee was one of the first to make the connection between long delays and the loss of value of the information itself:

> For some users, information delayed is information denied ... problems of inadequate record keeping and inexperienced personnel can no longer justify lengthy delays. Very often it appears that the difficulties arise not with Access Coordinators but with senior officials in particular government institutions. The extent of the delay problem is perhaps best captured by Treasury Board statistics: approximately one in five complaints to the Information Commissioner involved delay. (Standing Committee on Justice and the Solicitor General 1987, 66)

For many requesters, particularly journalists or opposition staffers researching developing issues, delayed information becomes "yesterday's news." Other users, such as investigative journalists or academic researchers, may be able to wait out the extensions and delays because their research unfolds over longer periods, but the delays still make the system far more difficult and frustrating to use.

Three years after the parliamentary committee report, Federal Court Justice Francis Muldoon rendered judgment in *Canada (Information Commissioner) v. Canada (Minister of External Affairs)*. For months, the department had delayed releasing records related to the free trade negotiations with the United States. It claimed a 120-day time extension but released the records after the commissioner went to court. A federal lawyer argued that the release made the point moot, but Muldoon disagreed, declaring that the department "acted unreasonably in processing the access requests with only the extended deadlines in mind." He continued (at 10):

> The Court is quite conscious that responding to such requests is truly "extra work" of government departments and other information-holding

organizations of government. But when as in the *Access to Information Act,* Parliament lays down these pertinent additional responsibilities, then one must comply ... It cannot be doubted that one principal purpose of the Act is to force a change of public servants' habitual, ingrained reluctance to give out the government's information.

But little changed, and for the next two decades delay would be an issue in almost every report of the Information Commissioners of Canada. A sample:

- In his 1990-91 report, John Grace noted that "delays in responding to requests for information have been particularly frustrating, much too frequent and much too long." He continued: "An unjustifiable delay is a refusal to give information, a denial of a right, a breach of the law and that is simply unacceptable" (Information Commissioner of Canada 1991, 5).
- In the 1990s, cuts in department budgets, including the offices that process requests, became an issue. With the Liberals having replaced the Conservatives in government, Grace's successor, former MP John Reid, said in his report for 1995-96: "Many public officials appear to have decided, in days of dwindling resources, to amend the law to a 'do-your-best' deadline" (Information Commissioner of Canada 1996, 13).
- In 1998-99, Reid began issuing "report cards" on the performance of individual departments. That year, he complained that "the paternalistic belief by many public officials that they know best, what and when to disclose to citizens, remains strong," while two years later he wrote of "the ignominious 18-year record of disrespect for the requirement that responses to access requests be timely" (Information Commissioner of Canada 1999, 5; 2001, 18).
- Jump ahead eight years to 2007 and Reid's short-lived successor, Robert Marleau. In his first report for 2006-07, he noted that delay complaints were being found to have merit more often than complaints about the formal exemptions. "It would appear that the most serious compliance problem in the system is one of process" (Information Commissioner of Canada 2007, 30).
- Finally, in a special report to Parliament in 2010, *Out of Time,* then Interim Information Commissioner Suzanne Legault warned that the right to timely access to information "is at risk of being totally obliterated because delays threaten to render the entire access regime irrelevant in

our current information economy" (Information Commissioner of Canada 2010, 2).

It adds up to nearly thirty years of failure to meet legislated timelines, all captured in the official statistics from the Treasury Board of Canada Secretariat, the central agency that oversees administration of the *ATIA*. From proclamation in 1983 to the end of the 2009-10 fiscal year, about four in ten requests took longer than thirty days to process. Nearly a quarter took longer than two months (Treasury Board of Canada Secretariat 2010a). The Treasury Board publishes slightly more detailed statistics for the most recent years. In 2008-09, 12.5 percent of requests took longer than four months to process, while in 2009-10 the figure was 11.1 percent (Treasury Board of Canada Secretariat 2009a, 2009b, 2010a).

"You Can Have That ... a Year from Now"

Under pressure from Reid, many departments reduced the number of requests that ended up in "deemed refusal," that is, when a request passes its legal deadline without a response. Even as these diminished in number, however, journalists and other users found officials making greater use of the time-extension provisions in the *ATIA*, which does not contain the checks on extensions found in most of the other acts across Canada. Organizations are permitted to claim extensions of almost any length for requests with a large volume of records or that require consultations with other departments. The only proviso is that extensions be reasonable. Treasury Board statistics show that extensions have grown in both number and length (Table 11.1), although there was a modest improvement in 2009-10.

TABLE 11.1

Extensions under the *Access to Information Act*, by fiscal year

Reason and length	2004 -05	2005 -06	2006 -07	2007 -08	2008 -09	2009 -10
Volume – 30 days or fewer	955	973	1,499	1,209	1,128	1,418
Volume – 31 days or more	1,481	1,461	1,831	1,864	2,674	2,251
Consultations – 30 days or fewer	1,935	1,599	1,350	921	711	879
Consultations – 31 days or more	1,472	1,330	2,320	2,889	3,064	2,807
Total extensions	5,843	5,363	7,000	6,883	7,577	7,355

Sources: Treasury Board Secretariat 2005, 2007, 2008, 2009a, 2010a.

In 2007-08, additional organizations were brought under the access to information regime as a result of the *Federal Accountability Act*. Most requests, however, are still received by the ten largest federal departments and agencies (Treasury Board of Canada Secretariat 2009a, 2009b). In his annual report for 2004-05, Reid noted that the number of deemed refusals was declining, that there had been a doubling in complaints to his office regarding extensions, and "widespread failure to meet the extended response times" once extensions had been applied (Information Commissioner of Canada 2005). The dramatic increase in the longest consultations in 2006-07 is paralleled by increases in the number of complaints about extensions received by the commissioner. From almost no complaints in 2005-06 – save for more than three hundred against the Canada Revenue Agency by one requester – the number of complaints about extensions against some of the largest federal departments and agencies mushroomed (Table 11.2).

TABLE 11.2

Number of extension complaints filed with the Information Commissioner of Canada, by agency, 2005-06 and 2008-09

Institution	2005-06	2008-09
Department of National Defence	15	138
Privy Council Office	3	108
Canada Revenue Agency	3[a]	96
Department of Foreign Affairs and International Trade	3	39
Industry Canada	2	31
Public Works and Government Services Canada	9	26
Royal Canadian Mounted Police	0	21
Environment Canada	2	18
Transport Canada	3	17
Canada Border Services Agency	3	16
Fisheries and Oceans Canada	3	11
Health Canada	4	11
Public Safety Canada	0	11
Citizenship and Immigration Canada	2	10
Canada Post Corporation[b]	n/a	9
Canadian Heritage	1	9
Department of Justice Canada	3	9

a Excluding 351 complaints against Canada Revenue Agency by one individual.
b Canada Post was not subject to the *Access to Information Act* until 2006-07.
Source: Office of the Information Commissioner of Canada, unpublished data.

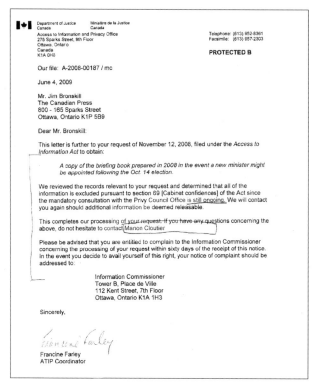

FIGURE 11.1   Letter to reporter Jim Bronskill from Department of Justice Canada, 4 June 2009

Jim Bronskill, an award-winning reporter with the Canadian Press in Ottawa who has written extensively about national security issues, finds that his requests are taking longer. "It is a large black hole mystery what happens and I try to find out in some cases" (Jim Bronskill interview, by telephone, December 2009). He gives one example of a request he submitted to the Justice Department in November 2008 asking for a copy of the briefing book prepared by the department in case a new minister was appointed. "They asked for a 175-day extension on December 4 2008 and then on June 4 2009 I got this letter. 'We reviewed the records and determined that all of the information is excluded pursuant to section 69 of the Act since the mandatory consultation with PCO [Privy Council Office] is still ongoing" (see Figure 11.1). The Privy Council Office was taking so long that Justice decided to just close the file, a decision Bronskill describes as arbitrary.

As with Jim Bronskill's request, many extensions are sought in order to allow consultations with the Privy Council Office. According to the Treasury

Board, however, only if departmental legal counsel determine "that the content may be or may contain Cabinet confidences then it must be sent to the Office of Counsel of the Privy Council Office for further consultation" (Treasury Board of Canada Secretariat 2010b). Required or not, however, many departments feel that consultations with the PCO are increasingly necessary. Said Bronskill's colleague at the Canadian Press, Dean Beeby: "All of the ATI shops tell me, 'I am really sorry Mr. Beeby but I am going to have to invoke a 180-day extension because we have to send it to PCO and they are very backlogged over there' ... I honestly believe that PCO believes it has to stiffen the spines of the ATIP shops and make sure they are using the exemptions to the fullest extent" (Dean Beeby interview, Ottawa, 5 December 2009).

Extensions are applied to what appear to be relatively innocuous requests. During the 2009 Canadian Newspaper Association Freedom of Information Audit, the Privy Council Office applied a 190-day extension to a request for "media lines," pre-prepared responses to questions anticipated from the media. The Defence Department asked New Democratic Party researcher Scott Harris for a 350-day extension when he asked for documents related to a press release the department had put out (Scott Harris interview, Ottawa, 8 December 2009). And a request made in the course of research for this chapter, for any business cases submitted by the Access to Information and Privacy branch in the Department of Foreign Affairs and International Trade for additional resources, was extended for 210 days to allow for consultations with the Privy Council Office. The twenty-six pages of documents were released in September 2010, just short of nine months after the request was received.

Of course, many interpretations can be placed on the number of extensions, and the reasons for them and for delays in general. The problem is surely rooted in a combination of bureaucratic inertia and resistance, overly complicated processes for handling requests deemed to be sensitive, under-resourcing of ATIP offices, less-than-ideal recordkeeping practices, political interference with files, and, at times, increasingly complex requests that simply take longer to process. In a working paper on access prepared for the World Bank, University of Manitoba professor Paul Thomas (2010, 23) notes: "The number of open-ended 'fishing expeditions' for 'incriminating' documents being conducted by opposition parliamentarians, the media, and advocacy groups in society seems to be increasing." We turn now to some of these cases.

Bureaucratic Inertia and Resistance

> *There is nothing in it for a deputy or an ADM to do a*
> *particularly good job on ATIP ... because normally what it*
> *does is get them into trouble with their political master.*
>
> – Ross Hodgins, former ATIP coordinator,
> Health Canada

Although bodies such as the Treasury Board Secretariat don't measure it, and don't acknowledge its existence publicly at all, there can be little doubt that one of the reasons requests have consistently been subject to long delays is that officials sometimes like to keep secrets. As Rick Snell and Peter Sebina point out, given the ability to determine what will be disclosed, "government will release only the information depicting it in a good light while the rest will be withheld" (Snell and Sebina 2007, 66). Access laws are a way of counteracting that instinct. Shapiro and Steinzor (2006) see politicians and bureaucrats as agents of the broader public who sometimes act in their own interests rather than solely on behalf of the principal [the public], creating what is called an "agency cost" (102-3). Access legislation is one means by which the public can reduce agency costs by monitoring the behaviour of the agents, the elected politicians, and the bureaucrats, allowing for the diminishment of "information asymmetries" where the agents have information that the public does not (Shapiro and Steinzor 2006, 112).

It has always been a struggle, however. Resistance to openness was evident from the time the US *Freedom of Information Act* was signed into law by President Lyndon Johnson in 1966, over the objection of every agency and department of the US government and only a day before it would have died via a pocket veto[1] (Kirtley 2006, 481; Relyea 2009, 314). A generation and a half later, speaking to the US National Press Club in 1994, President Bill Clinton's attorney general, Janet Reno, characterized the challenge of persuading bureaucrats to be more open as "much like the one faced by a captain who must bring an aircraft carrier about." She went on, "You touch the controls. You hear a lot of noise and grinding and gnashing of gears, but you don't see much movement" (Reno 1994).

In his book *Blacked Out: Government Secrecy in the Information Age*, Alasdair Roberts placed the phenomenon within Sidney Blumenthal's theory that once elected to government, politicians run a "permanent campaign":

Precisely because they must maintain broad popular support, governments are usually susceptible to populist demands for reforms that check or disperse the power of the executive ... [including] ... more powerful disclosure laws. These reforms, if taken seriously, weaken the capacity of executives to wage a permanent campaign ... Governments maintain a law on the statute books but develop less obvious techniques – exclusion of certain institutions, increases to fees, internal procedures for sensitive requests – for restricting its actual impact. (Roberts 2006, 103)

Access to information is perhaps a greater challenge to Canada's Westminster system than it was to the American system, the latter operating on the principle that power flows from the people. In *Breaking the Bargain: Public Servants, Ministers, and Parliament,* Donald Savoie points out that the primary imperative of public servants is to protect the minister, and that in the traditional way of governance in Canada, "career officials know full well that they must not only work away from the media, but must take great care not to create embarrassment for their ministers or the government" (Savoie 2003, 49). And again, "the shroud of secrecy that embraces cabinet deliberations applies to the public service as a whole. Since the minister is responsible for departmental policies and actions, this secrecy enables him or her to control the facts of the situation and all public comment" (Savoie 2003, 42). Access to information turns this idea on its head. It has a fundamental premise, that all is public unless specifically exempted, that seems fundamentally at odds with the traditional idea that all is secret unless specifically made public.

Former Information Commissioner of Canada John Reid, appearing before the deputy ministers' advisory meeting of the ATI task force in February 2001, called secrecy "deeply entrenched – primarily at the senior levels of the bureaucracy." He went on: "The access law – with a positive right of access by anyone present in Canada to most records held by government, coupled with a deadline for response – constitutes a frontal attack on ... perceived virtues of secrecy. Consequently, there is every incentive for officials to resist, if not impede, the operation of the law" (Reid 2001). Colonel Michel Drapeau, a former ATI coordinator with National Defence, experienced this first hand. "I would have bureaucrats raid my office with files with documents in answer to a request and I would have to listen to them as to why we shouldn't release documents and if we wanted to we could ... delay release" (Michel Drapeau interview, Ottawa, 4 December 2009). After leaving the military, Drapeau became a lawyer and the co-author of a comprehensive guidebook to the *ATIA*. He has filed thousands of requests. He said that the administrative hurdles that are the focus of this chapter "are manifestations of an unwritten policy ... It comes from the bottom up this reflex of bureaucrats, 'how dare you, whose business is it to ask for this?' It colours almost everything that gets done ... nothing will happen to them if they just slow down, put the brakes on, invent reasons to exempt and exclude. If you do the job you are considered zealous and perhaps disloyal and will no longer enjoy the company of others when they go to the cafeteria" (Michel Drapeau interview, Ottawa, 4 December 2009).

Ross Hodgins, the former Health Canada ATI coordinator, said that although there are many deputies who try to make the system work, in the case of some deputy and assistant deputy ministers, if they move to a new department "you can pretty well predict there is going to be an issue in that institution sooner or later" (Ross Hodgins interview, Ottawa, 8 December 2009).

One means by which senior managers in the public service are supposed to be held accountable for their stewardship of the access system is the Management Accountability Framework (MAF), but it seems to have had minimal impact. Overseen by the Treasury Board Secretariat, it is intended to "ensure government is well managed and to promote management excellence" (Treasury Board of Canada Secretariat 2011). Performance on access to information was added for the 2005-06 round of the MAF, but it doesn't deal with contentious issues such as response times, application of exemptions, or "the overall culture of openness in various departments." Instead, the concern is mostly with meeting internal policies and statutory reporting requirements (Thomas 2010, 52). According to Thomas's World Bank working paper (2010, 6), "including an access component has made a marginal difference in terms of obliging deputy heads and their organizations to pay more attention to the reporting requirements of the *ATIA* and related administrative policies."

Being Sensitive

A significant reason for delays that has been documented repeatedly is the fact that systems have been designed to manage the release of information considered sensitive or contentious. Both British Columbia and Ontario have developed such protocols (Roberts 2006, 97), as have a number of federal departments, as we shall document shortly. In British Columbia, a legislative committee recommended in 2004 that only the complexity of the request, and not the requester's identity, should be taken into consideration in flagging a request as sensitive (Special Committee to Review the Freedom of Information and Protection of Privacy Act 2004, 37), but it would take several more years before the system there would be abolished. Protocols for handling sensitive requests can add weeks to a request's processing time because of the need for additional layers of approvals, often to the highest levels of the bureaucracy or to ministers' offices.

Critics have often charged that the sensitivity system is concerned as much with the type of requester as it is with the content of requests. The Canadian Newspaper Association (CNA), for example, complained to the federal Information Commissioner in 2005 about what it charged were "secret rules" applied to media requests. The truth is probably a little more complex, with both the request content and the requester considered in any decision on whether a file deserves closer scrutiny. That said, a survey of access coordinators in thirteen large federal departments, conducted for the Access to Information Task Force in 2001, revealed that "additional attention is often given to requests that originate from the media, political parties or other high profile categories of requesters ... The complexity of these requests are heightened as institutions attempt to prepare for any possible questions or potential for any public scrutiny which may arise as a result of the release of records" (Yvon Gauthier Inc., 2002). A report for the same task force by David Flaherty, former Information and Privacy Commissioner in BC, noted:

> Disclosure of records to the media is almost always politically sensitive, so the communications specialists in government departments will often be involved with preparing media lines and answers but also at times may try to manage release by various stratagems (disclose the records to everyone with a press release; disclose the records at a time when it will be hard to use them effectively; delay responding to reduce the utility of the records ... ATI requests are only bad news and potential sources of trouble for risk-averse public servants. (Flaherty 2001)

Submissions by federal departments as part of the commissioner's investigation of the CNA complaint showed that a variety of criteria were being used to identify some requests for sensitive handling. Some, such as Indian Affairs, stated that they did take the source of the request, "such as Media, political, researcher," into account. Environment Canada classified requests as sensitive or very sensitive if they were likely to result in "possible media attention" or "significant media attention," while Industry Canada indicated that requests involving "hot topics or subjects that may be of interest to the Minister's Office" were likely to be tagged as sensitive. Citizenship and Immigration, on the other hand, defined sensitive files as those that were more complex and involved internal or external consultations, while Justice said a request was sensitive if the subject matter was considered sensitive (Erin Research 2007).

The investigation became complex, with the Treasury Board of Canada hiring two research companies who argued that there was no evidence of special treatment of media requests, while the CNA relied on the expertise of FOI researchers Ann Rees and Alasdair Roberts, as well as this author, who argued the opposite. In the end, the Office of the Information Commissioner concluded that sensitivity systems do slow down requests unacceptably, but said that there was no evidence of special rules just for media requests (Information Commissioner of Canada 2008, 11). According to Information Commissioner Legault, "the obligation is to disclose within 30 days or within legitimate time extensions. However they get about doing that is their business, but there is no excuse for additional delays that are occasioned because of additional approvals" (Suzanne Legault interview, Ottawa, 8 December 2009).

Interestingly, Information Commissioner Marleau's report concluded that there was nothing inherently wrong with sensitive-handling protocols. This put him at odds with many others who have criticized the practice, including the former BC Information and Privacy Commissioner David Loukidelis (British Columbia Information and Privacy Commissioner 2009b, 7). The BC government says it has since eliminated its sensitivity rating system (British Columbia Information and Privacy Commissioner 2009a). Ontario's "contentious issues management" system remains in place, although that province's commissioner takes the position that while it is acceptable to give a "heads-up" to senior managers about potentially controversial releases, such a system must not interfere with the appropriate handling of requests or with statutory timelines (Ontario Information and Privacy Commissioner 2011).

Sensitivity systems provide a means by which more difficult requests can be selected for special approval processes, but there are times when delays are caused by more blatant political involvement. When Dean Beeby was denied access to large parts of a report on the government's portfolio of real estate – after months of delay – he filed a new request for records documenting the handling of his request. From that emerged what journalists call "smoking gun" evidence. The memo (see Figure 11.2) showed that

From: Sébastien Togneri
To: Sylvie Lepage
Sent: Mon Jul 27 16:13:09 2009
Subject: RE: A-2009-00125 / lb

Well unrelease it and only release Section 11!!!!

What's the point of asking for my opinion if you're just going to release it!

Call it back from PCO.

Sébastien Togneri
Director of Parliamentary Affairs | Directeur des Affaires Parlementaires
The Hon. Christian Paradis, Minister of PWGSC | L'hon. Christian Paradis, Ministre des TPSGC
819-956-5681 Off | Bur
:ell
sebastien.togneri@pwgsc.gc.ca   s. 19(1)

FIGURE 11.2   Memo from Sébastien Togneri calling on ATIP manager to "unrelease" records, 27 July 2009

Sébastien Togneri, the director of parliamentary affairs for the Minister of Public Works, had ordered an access to information manager to "unrelease" most of the report just as it was being mailed out to Beeby. Togneri later resigned after it was revealed he had intervened in at least four access requests (Canadian Press 2010). In March 2011, Information Commissioner Suzanne Legault determined that there had indeed been political interference in the processing of Beeby's request. Public Works promised changes in what it called its "purple file" process to ensure that political staff no longer had any say over access requests. "Real or perceived political interference in the administration of the *Access to Information Act* has been a long standing issue," Legault wrote in her investigation report. "When it occurs, it often creates an adversarial environment between political and bureaucratic personnel within institutions. In its more egregious manifestations, it has directly contributed to the erosion of individuals' rights to government information" (Information Commissioner of Canada 2011).

The *ATIA* gives the ultimate authority to release, or not release records, to the minister in the case of departments or to the chief executive officer or other top executive in agencies and Crown corporations. Provincial legislation by and large does the same.

Ross Hodgins, now with the Office of the Information Commissioner, said that much can be divined about how open a department is likely to be by examining the formal order by the minister delegating authority to make decisions under the act. "If it is delegated to a lot of deputies or the ADM or communications, it means a lot of that information is never going to get out of the institution" (Ross Hodgins interview, Ottawa, 8 December 2009).

The challenge faced by access coordinators was noted by Assistant Information Commissioner Bruce Mann in a 1986 article for the journal *Canadian Public Administration.* Mann described coordinators, and it is undoubtedly equally true today, as the "meat in the sandwich," caught between bureaucrats who prefer non-disclosure and requesters. Mann pointed out that coordinators occupy an unusual position in the bureaucratic power structure, with multiple working relationships with subordinates, those at a similar level in government, and much higher-level officials such as assistant deputy ministers. "Like the meat in the sandwich, the coordinator does not know where the next bite is going to come from" (Mann 1986, 580-81). Hodgins said that when he was ATIP coordinator at Health Canada, he insisted that full authority be delegated to him but there were still tensions. "If they didn't like what you were sending out, they would say, 'we gave it to you, we can take it away.' That is very common."

Under-Resourcing

Answering access requests is demanding, meticulous work and there is a shortage of skilled staff. "Often institutions will claim longer time extensions than before for the same thing and very often it is because of their resources in the ATIP office," said Sandra George, director of the intake and early resolution unit at the Office of the Information Commissioner (Sandra George interview, Ottawa, 8 December 2009). The issue goes back many years and became acute during the Jean Chrétien years because of cuts to government budgets under Finance Minister Paul Martin (Rankin 2008, 325). The problem continued into the new millennium and was exacerbated by the Harper government's *Federal Accountability Act.* It added more agencies to those covered by the legislation, creating intense competition for staff trained to deal with demanding ATIP duties. "Any of us could have gone to Canada Post," said Ross Hodgins. "They headhunted like crazy" (Ross Hodgins interview, Ottawa, 8 December 2009).

Several internal documents obtained through access requests show how the staff shortages have affected ATIP offices. An internal review of the organization and structure of the Information Privacy Rights Administration Office in Industry Canada complains of challenges related to recruitment, retention, and absenteeism resulting from chronic understaffing and overwork:

There is an unacceptably high level of turnover in the IPRA office. This is due largely to "poaching" by other departments promising higher classification levels [rates of pay] and less complex work. In the past year, one department directly recruited no less than 3 employees from IPRA ...

As a result of high levels of stress, fatigue and resulting burnout, there are currently several cases of excessive absenteeism. (Industry Canada n.d., 4-5)

Another document showed frustration building in the Department of Foreign Affairs and International Trade as the access coordinator, Monique McCulloch, grappled with a 3 percent across-the-board budget cut in the spring of 2009 that threatened to roll back progress in eliminating a backlog of access requests:

I really have a hard time believing that all our efforts over the past year and in previous fiscals will be wasted ... The [Office of the Information Commissioner] will definitely see a significant regression in our ability to meet legislative obligations, which will no doubt cause ongoing friction in our relationship which may even escalate to senior levels ... the [other government departments] who had started to see better turnaround times in our consultation responses will no doubt see an even worse service in 09/10 and this has a huge negative impact on the ATIP community and my entire team gets labeled as incompetent!! (Department of Foreign Affairs and International Trade, e-mail, 8 May 2009, 2)

A 2007 summary prepared in the Privy Council Office underlined the problem. "ATIP offices throughout the government are in the same position of having increased workload ... There is [sic] not enough fully trained officers within the government to meet the current demands. Many institutions, including PCO, are resorting to hiring contractors to fulfill their staffing needs" (Privy Council Office n.d., 3). In a discussion paper prepared for the Information Commissioner of Canada, lawyer Murray Rankin, a noted expert on the Canadian law, argued that "adequate resourcing of all the components of the system (ATI units, programs, central agencies providing support, and the Office of the Information Commissioner) is critical. Access to information needs to be resourced in the same way as any program delivered by the government of Canada" (Rankin 2008, 349). In 2009, the government hired a consulting firm to conduct a "capacity and resource review" related to the processing of access and privacy requests in parts of the government. The review was not complete when this chapter was written (Treasury Board of Canada Secretariat 2010b).

The Federal Experience in the Broader Canadian Context

Requesters under the *ATIA* are not alone in facing the quasi exemptions created by administrative hurdles. The information commissioner in British Columbia, who resigned in January 2010 to take a deputy minister's position, hammered home on the issue of delays for the decade that he held the post. In his last year, his office produced what was to be the first in a series of detailed evaluations of timeliness that noted "an unacceptable pattern of government-wide failure to respond to access requests in as timely a fashion as it should. In fact, this report shows that in a significant number of cases – almost one third – government is in breach of its legal obligations to respond in the times set under the Freedom of Information and Protection of Privacy Act" (British Columbia Information and Privacy Commissioner 2009b).

The BC government's own statistics show that only 53 percent of requests were completed during the statutory period of thirty business days in 2008-09 (British Columbia Citizens' Services 2009), but there are signs of modest improvement since the government reorganized its access establishment. At the start of 2009, the government centralized its processing of requests in the Ministry of Labour, Citizens' Services and Open Government. "The focus of this new approach is to facilitate more efficient request processing by standardizing government-wide practices and streamlining business processes," the ministry said in its 2010/11–2012/13 service plan (British Columbia Citizens' Services 2010a, 13). In the first year of centralization, the government improved its thirty-business-day compliance to 67 percent while processing a larger number of requests. (British Columbia Citizens' Services 2010b).

Statistics are also available in Manitoba, which had 57 percent of requests completed during the thirty-day period in 2008 (Robinson 2009), and in Nova Scotia, which recorded 75 percent (Clarke 2009, 2). Ontario's Information and Privacy Commissioner reports a much higher compliance rate with deadlines, but Ontario requesters often face another quasi exemption, a higher cost of processing requests.

The only national data comparing open records regimes from coast to coast come from the Canadian Newspaper Association's annual freedom of information study. The CNA team, led by this author, sends a small set of identical requests to all of the provinces, another set to municipalities across the country, and another to federal departments, agencies, and Crown corporations. The CNA report for 2008, the first to use the current methods, found that the best performance meeting the standard thirty-day deadline for the test requests was on the Prairies, while New Brunswick, Québec, Newfoundland, and Nova Scotia processed barely half, or fewer, of the requests in that time (Canadian Newspaper Association 2009, 14). Fifty-eight percent of federal requests were completed within thirty days. Jurisdictions also differed widely in their charging of fees, with no fees assessed in Alberta, Saskatchewan, Newfoundland, Prince Edward Island, Yukon, and New Brunswick, and 40 and 33 percent of requests attracting fees in Ontario and Manitoba, respectively. Only 4 percent of federal requests were subjected to fees, reflecting requesters' experience that the federal system is not expensive to use.

Ontario's information commissioner, Ann Cavoukian, expressed concern in her 2008 report that the high compliance rate of provincial agencies with the thirty-day timeline might not tell the whole story. In Ontario, appeals about delay are handled with an expedited process and an order can be issued requiring a decision by a certain date (Ontario Information and Privacy Commissioner 2004, 8). "Prompt replies to access requests do not necessarily mean that information that should be routinely available is always disclosed. Further, unreasonably high fees and a number of other reasons can also hinder an FOI request" (Ontario Information and Privacy Commissioner 2009, 21). And, indeed, Ontario is an unusual case when it comes to fees. With time less of an issue, these have become the predominant quasi exemption in Canada's largest province. Just as the federal legislation is nearly unique in allowing open-ended extensions in time, the Ontario law is the only one that provides no grace from fees, either free hours of search and processing time, or a set amount below which fees are not payable (as in Alberta). Ontario once had two free hours, but this was removed under the government of Premier Mike Harris in the 1990s through the *Savings and Restructuring Act, 1996*. A $5 application fee and $25 fee to file an appeal were introduced at the same time.

From the start, Ontario's acts have operated on what the provincial Information and Privacy Commissioner's Office has described as a "user-pay" principle" (Ontario Information and Privacy Commissioner 1989). "The user-pay system is founded on the premise that requesters should be expected to carry at least a portion of the cost of processing a request unless it is fair and equitable that they do not do so," as a 2007 order puts it (Ontario Information and Privacy Commissioner 2007). And users do pay more.

TABLE 11.3

Access to information requests received and fees collected by the federal government and the provinces, where available

Jurisdiction	Year	Requests	Fees collected ($)	Cost per request ($)
Ontario[a]	2008	9,850	420,989.00	42.74
Federal	2008-09	34,041	305,683.90	8.98
Alberta[b]	2007-08	1,768	72,900.00	26.37
Manitoba[c]	2008	1,270	10,475.00	8.25

Note: The data above do not include requests under legislation applying to municipal authorities.

a General records requests to provincial agencies. Total fees for Ontario were calculated by multiplying the average per general record request given in the report by the number of requests reported.

b Fees and fee per request in Alberta include requests for personal records and requests for general records. "Requests" reflects requests for general records only. Alberta charges $25 to file a request. Most other jurisdictions charge $5 or have no fee.

c Manitoba does not separate general records and personal information requests in its statistical reporting.

Sources: Treasury Board of Canada Secretariat 2010a; Ontario Information and Privacy Commissioner 2009, 2010; Alberta government FOIP statistics; Manitoba *Freedom of Information and Protection of Privacy Act Annual Report 2008.*

Official statistics show that Ontario actually collects more in fees than the much larger federal government (Table 11.3). There was a large drop in the average cost per request for general records requests in 2008, although the figure is still far higher than in other jurisdictions that report fee information. Table 11.4 shows the average cost per request, under the two Ontario acts (the *Freedom of Information and Protection of Privacy Act* and the *Municipal Freedom of Information and Protection of Privacy Act*), from 2003 to 2008.

It is difficult to gauge the effect that higher fees have on requesters, partly because little research has been done on the question. In an early study, FOI researcher Alasdair Roberts found that the number of requests filed dropped after the fees went up. He found that the effect was greatest on requests for personal information, which have not been the focus of this chapter. He also found that with increased fees, far more of the personal information requests were abandoned (Roberts 1999, 429). Since Roberts's study, the overall number of general-records requests received in Ontario has risen to levels higher than in 1995, although agencies have been added over that time and others have been reconfigured.

TABLE 11.4

Average fees for requests for personal information and general records under the Ontario provincial and municipal acts

Year	Provincial act		Municipal act	
	Personal ($)	General ($)	Personal ($)	General ($)
2008	11.26	42.74	8.82	23.54
2007	10.54	50.54	9.67	23.49
2006	11.55	51.11	8.64	21.04
2005	11.28	48.89	7.88	18.95
2004	7.20	43.97	8.65	17.93
2003	8.89	41.82	7.67	19.52

Note: Provincial act: *Freedom of Information and Protection of Privacy Act;* municipal act: *Municipal Freedom of Information and Protection of Privacy Act.*
Source: Ontario Information and Privacy Commissioner, unpublished data.

Some journalists suggest that fees can be a significant barrier. "We get hammered," said Jim Rankin, a reporter with the *Toronto Star* who has specialized in analyzing large and complex databases. "Before, there was some embarrassment; if there was a long delay on the part of the institution, they would waive fees. What is happening, just anecdotally, [is] institutions on controversial files, if you follow all the way through, they are going to want to charge you for every cent they can." Rankin has more reason than most to feel this way. In late 2009, his newspaper paid over $12,000 to the Toronto Police Service for a disk containing information on arrests and times when police questioned people on the street. The newspaper appealed the fee (Jim Rankin interview, Toronto, 10 December 2009).

Harvey Cashore of the Canadian Broadcasting Corporation's *the fifth estate* has also had to pay large fees under the Ontario legislation. In 2006, he was working on a story about insider wins by lottery retailers and was assessed large fees. "In one case we paid half the fees before they would do anything. I think they thought we weren't going to pay the fees because they were so expensive." As the *Star* did in the case of the police data, Cashore appealed the fees. But he says a lot of requesters wouldn't be able to do that. "When they give us the big fees, we say 'fine,' we pay the half, and we immediately file an appeal. We know they are going to come down, so we pay half anyway, and then we proceed with the request. But if you don't have the resources to be able to do that, then you are stuck" (Harvey Cashore interview, Toronto, 10 December 2009).

In the CNA study for 2008, twenty-six requests were subjected to fee estimates (an initial notice of the projected fee, provided by the ATI office). Twelve, or almost half, of those estimates came from agencies in Ontario (Canadian Newspaper Association 2009, 34). Robert Cribb, another investigative reporter with the *Toronto Star*, files sixty or more requests under the provincial acts every year. He says fees are a way of life in Ontario. "For a small request it can be forty bucks up to $300, depending on the exemptions and the amount of private information and the amount that has to be expunged from the records." The largest fee estimate Cribb ever got was $148,000 for restaurant inspection data from the city of Toronto. He eventually got it for $300. "It was a $120,000 miscalculation" (Robert Cribb interview, Toronto, 10 December 2009). Interestingly, in recent years, the number of appeals with fees as the main issue has never been large (Ontario Information and Privacy Commissioner 2010, 16). A fairly steady proportion of requests is abandoned, however, although the statistics do not indicate why (Ontario Information and Privacy Commissioner 2010, 1).

Solutions and Conclusion

Almost thirty years from the passage of the *ATIA*, and over thirty years since the passage of the first Canadian access law in Nova Scotia in 1977, quasi exemptions have become a way of life. As Jim Bronskill of the Canadian Press says, "The trains don't run on time. There is no incentive for the trains to run on time aside from the complaining passengers. There are no repercussions for public servants or politicians and no incentive to make the system better" (Jim Bronskill interview, by telephone, December 2009).

So what is to be done? Many of these issues have been studied and dissected so many times that most of the proposed solutions are almost as old as the act and any attempt to provide a prescription will almost certainly suggest many of the same remedies suggested before. Undoubtedly, agencies need to provide more resources to the offices that process ATIP requests. Some of these shops are so badly resourced that officials take time extensions because they, not the rest of the department, become overwhelmed by requests. The act cannot function as it was intended to if officials aren't given enough people and money to do the job.

Governments should find ways to make the access system work more efficiently. British Columbia has taken steps in this direction through its centralization of request processing, and Yukon also processes requests through a single department. Other efficiencies could include allowing requests to be filed electronically via the World Wide Web, as BC already does, to eliminate the time lag associated with mail going back and forth between requesters and public organizations, and allowing electronic payment rather than requiring applicants to use cheques to pay for application and processing fees.

Another suggestion that has been made many times is to impose penalties for not living up to the deadlines in the act. Former Information Commissioner of Canada John Reid suggested in 2005 – as part of a larger package of proposed reforms – that agencies be barred from collecting fees for late requests. Others, such as the CBC's Cashore, suggest that there should be consequences for public servants. "If they really want to be transparent, why aren't there proper punitive measures in place to make bureaucrats comply? ... I have always thought that no law works if there is no punitive measure to them, and serious punitive measures" (Harvey Cashore interview, Toronto, 10 December 2009).

Limiting time extensions seems another obvious reform. The 1987 report of the Standing Committee on Justice and the Solicitor General recommended shortening the response period to twenty days with a maximum extension of forty days unless the Information Commissioner agreed to a longer extension (Standing Committee on Justice and the Solicitor General 1987, 67). Aside from the shorter initial period, this would have brought the federal act in line with most of the provincial laws, which usually limit extensions to thirty days unless the oversight body gives permission for a longer extension. Former BC Information and Privacy Commissioner David Loukidelis told a House of Commons committee meeting in March 2009 that such limits were a disincentive to taking long extensions (House of Commons Standing Committee on Access to Information, Privacy and Ethics 2009, 11). Colonel Michel Drapeau suggests that the time limit could be increased to sixty days, but that this deadline should be firm (Michel Drapeau interview, Ottawa, 4 December 2009). Whatever the formula, a limit on extensions is badly needed, as is a limit on the length of investigations by the Information Commissioner of Canada. Right now, reporters say it can take months for a complaint to be even acknowledged. Officials in the commissioner's office say they are trying to create more efficient processes, but limits would ensure that the right to access was not squelched by backlogs in the complaint process.

A measure that could go hand in hand with stricter time limits would be the introduction of processes to expedite urgent requests, such as those from the media and parliamentarians. Such processes could counteract the tendency for these requests to take longer than others. Tied to this, and long overdue, would be the elimination of special processes for handling "sensitive" requests. BC says it has been able to do so. Ottawa and Ontario should do the same.

The government should provide full decision-making delegation to the heads of the offices that process requests. Decision making should not be delegated to deputy ministers and others who may have a greater interest in seeing some records withheld than released. Access professionals should have the final say, subject only to a veto by the minister that would have to be indicated publicly to ensure accountability. Equally important, there should be a reintroduction of at least some free search and processing time to the Ontario *Freedom of Information and Protection of Privacy Act*. Ontario is curiously alone in allowing no free time for a request. "The clock starts running the second they open the envelope," Cribb of the *Toronto Star* said. "Some sort of initial research allowance, whether it be five hours or three or even one, would go a long way toward easing the fee burden" (Robert Cribb interview, Toronto, 10 December 2009).

Finally, governments should expand the amount of information they make available without waiting for access requests; this is often called "proactive disclosure." The federal government has been posting information online about the travel and hospitality expenses of senior officials, contracts valued at greater than $10,000, and grants and contributions for the better part of a decade, and Ontario began posting travel and hospitality information for its senior officials in 2010. Other information routinely released online in various jurisdictions includes restaurant inspection results, public sector salaries, and various downloadable datasets such as Health Canada's adverse drug reaction database and Transport Canada's CADORS (Civil Aviation Daily Occurrence Reporting System) data. "Open data" websites established by Ottawa and several municipalities are also slowly expanding the amount of electronic information easily available to Canadians. Collectively, these are a good beginning and provide an excellent example of what truly open government might look like.

It is easy to suggest improvements, but quite another matter to see them to fruition. Power and openness have an uneasy relationship, and although the latter is a goal everyone in the system subscribes to in public, airing all one's dirty laundry is nobody's first instinct. Measures put in place to control information, including heavy-handed involvement by central agencies such as the Privy Council Office, will not give way easily. And if they are to do so, there will need to be strong support from the top of the power pyramid on down. In the United States, President Obama's first act in office was to indicate that openness would be the presumption in government. But a point made repeatedly by people interviewed for this chapter is that this has never happened at the federal level in Canada – no prime minister has ever, while in office, personally sent the message down the food chain that access, not secrecy, should be the presumption. Even with such a message, there will need to be a sea change in attitudes among many in the apparatus of government, and a real acceptance that transparent government equals better government. As Paul Thomas notes (2010, 6): "The support of cabinet ministers and senior public servants is more important than management process in making access principles central to the practice of good government and to the promotion of a public service culture that favours openness over secrecy."

As long as public servants and their masters believe that erring on the side of non-disclosure is the most prudent course, the one least likely to result in adverse career consequences, it is difficult to envisage real change, no matter how much noise is made by information commissioners, journalists, or academics. The bureaucracy has had nearly thirty years to get this right, and the fact that it has struggled so much is a measure of the difficulty of the task at hand. The current Conservative government has rejected making further changes to the *Access to Information Act,* preferring that any changes should be administrative in nature. Despite seemingly bleak prospects, however, this is a task worth taking up for as long as it takes to produce results that will ensure that access legislation can facilitate democracy, as the Supreme Court said it was designed to do.

NOTE

1 The term "pocket veto" refers to an instance where a bill passed by the Senate and House of Representatives is left unsigned by the President on an occasion when Congress has adjourned, thereby effectively killing the measure.

REFERENCES

Attallah, Paul, and Heather Pyman. 2002. *How Journalists Use the Federal* Access to Information Act. Report 8 – Access to Information Review Task Force. http://www.atirtf-geai.gc.ca/.

British Columbia Citizens' Services. 2009. "Processing Times by Applicant and Disposition Types: 30, 60, More than 60 Days (1 Year 'Fiscal' Trend) 2008-2009." http://www.gov.bc.ca/citz/.

–. 2010a. *2010/11–2012/13 Service Plan.* http://www.bcbudget.gov.bc.ca/.

−. 2010b. "Processing Times: 30, 60, More than 60 Days (1 Year 'Fiscal' Trend) April 01, 2009 to March 31, 2010 − All Government." http://www.gov.bc.ca/citz/.

British Columbia Information and Privacy Commissioner. 2009a. *Annual Report 2008-2009*. Victoria: Office of the Information and Privacy Commissioner.

−. 2009b. *Timeliness of Government's Access to Information Responses − Report for Calendar Year 2008*. Victoria: Office of the Information and Privacy Commissioner.

Canadian Newspaper Association. 2009. *National Freedom of Information Audit 2008*. Toronto: Canadian Newspaper Association.

Canadian Press. 2010. "Paradis Aide Resigns over Info Meddling." http://www.cbc.ca/.

Clarke, Cecil P. 2009. *Nova Scotia* Freedom of Information and Protection of Privacy Act *Annual Report 2008*. Halifax: Nova Scotia Department of Justice.

Erin Research. 2007. "Analysis by Erin Research Inc. of Alasdair Roberts and Ann Rees Paper." Unpublished report prepared for Treasury Board of Canada Secretariat.

Flaherty, David H. 2001. *Managing Response Times under Canadian Access to Information Legislation*. Report 25 − Access to Information Review Task Force. http://www.atirtf-geai.gc.ca/.

Glover, Mark, Sarah Holsen, Craig MacDonald, Mehrangez Rahman, and Duncan Simpson. 2006. *Freedom of Information: History, Experience and Records and Information Management Implications in the USA, Canada and the United Kingdom*. Pittsburgh: ARMA International Education Foundation.

House of Commons Standing Committee on Access to Information, Privacy and Ethics. 2009. "Evidence, Wednesday, March 11, 2009" (print version). http://www.parl.gc.ca/.

Information Commissioner of Canada. 1991. *Annual Report Information Commissioner 1990-1991*. Ottawa: Minister of Supply and Services. http://www.oic-ci.gc.ca/.

−. 1996. *Annual Report Information Commissioner 1995-1996*. Ottawa: Minister of Public Works and Government Services Canada. http://www.oic-ci.gc.ca/.

−. 1999. *Annual Report Information Commissioner 1998-1999*. Ottawa: Minister of Public Works and Government Services Canada. http://www.oic-ci.gc.ca/.

−. 2001. *Annual Report Information Commissioner 2000-2001*. Ottawa: Minister of Public Works and Government Services Canada. http://www.oic-ci.gc.ca/.

−. 2005. *Annual Report Information Commissioner 2004-2005*. Ottawa: Minister of Public Works and Government Services Canada. http://www.oic-ci.gc.ca/.

−. 2007. *Annual Report Information Commissioner 2006-2007*. Ottawa: Minister of Public Works and Government Services Canada. http://www.oic-ci.gc.ca/.

−. 2008. "Appendix 'A' Canadian Newspaper Association Complaint." Unpublished.

−. 2010. *Out of Time: A Special Report to Parliament by Suzanne Legault, Interim Information Commissioner of Canada*. Ottawa: Minister of Public Works and Government Services Canada. http://www.oic-ci.gc.ca/.

−. 2011. *Interference with Access to Information − Part 1: A Special Report to Parliament by Suzanne Legault, Information Commissioner of Canada*. Ottawa:

Minister of Public Works and Government Services Canada. http://www.oic -ci.gc.ca/.

Kirtley, Jane E. 2006. "Transparency and Accountability in a Time of Terror: The Bush Administration's Assault on Freedom of Information." *Communication Law and Policy* 11 (4): 479-509.

Mann, Bruce. 1986. "The Federal Information Coordinator as Meat in the Sandwich." *Canadian Public Administration* 29 (4): 579-82.

Ontario Information and Privacy Commissioner. 1989. *Order P-111: Appeal 890029, Human Resources Secretariat*. Toronto: Information and Privacy Commissioner/Ontario.

–. 2004. *Code of Procedure for Appeals under the* Freedom of Information and Protection of Privacy Act *and the* Municipal Freedom of Information and Protection of Privacy Act. Toronto: Information and Privacy Commissioner/ Ontario. http://www.ipc.on.ca/.

–. 2007. *Order MO-2163: Appeal MA-050457-1, City of Hamilton*. Toronto: Information and Privacy Commissioner/Ontario. http://www.ipc.on.ca/.

–. 2009. *Access and Privacy: The Challenges and Opportunities. 2008 Annual Report.* Toronto: Information and Privacy Commissioner/Ontario. http://www.ipc. on.ca/.

–. 2010. *A More Detailed Look at Compliance Rates and Other 2009 Access and Privacy Statistics: 2009 Annual Report*. Toronto: Information and Privacy Commissioner of Ontario. http://www.ipc.on.ca/.

–. 2011. *Report into Contentious Issues Management in the Ministry of Finance*. Toronto: Information and Privacy Commissioner/Ontario. http://www.ipc. on.ca/.

Rankin, Murray. 2008. "The *Access to Information Act* 25 Years Later: Toward a New Generation of Access Rights in Canada." *Canadian Journal of Administrative Law and Practice* 21: 323-59.

Reid, John. 2001. "Information Commissioner's Notes for Speech to the ADM Advisory Committee, Ottawa, Ontario – February 23, 2001." Ottawa: Access to Information Review Task Force. http://www.atirtf-geai.gc.ca/.

Relyea, Harold C. 2009. "Federal Freedom of Information Policy: Highlights of Recent Developments." *Government Information Quarterly* 26: 314-20.

Reno, Janet. 1994. Speech to National Press Club, Federal News Service, as retrieved from LEXIS/NEXIS.

Roberts, Alasdair. 1999. "Retrenchment and Freedom of Information: Recent Experience under Federal, Ontario and British Columbia Law." *Canadian Public Administration* 42 (4): 422-51.

–. 2006. *Blacked Out: Government Secrecy in the Information Age*. Cambridge: Cambridge University Press.

Robinson, Eric. 2009. Freedom of Information and Protection of Privacy Act *Annual Report 2008*. Winnipeg: Government of Manitoba.

Savoie, Donald J. 2003. *Breaking the Bargain: Public Servants, Ministers, and Parliament*. Toronto: University of Toronto Press.

Shapiro, Sidney A., and Rena I. Steinzor. 2006. "The People's Agent: Executive Branch Secrecy and Accountability in an Age of Terrorism." *Law and Contemporary Problems* 68: 99-129.

Snell, Rick, and Peter Sebina. 2007. "Information Flows: The Real Art of Information Management and Freedom of Information." *Archives and Manuscripts* 35 (1): 54-81.

Special Committee to Review the *Freedom of Information and Protection of Privacy Act*. 2004. *Enhancing the Province's Public Sector Access and Privacy Law*. Victoria: Legislative Assembly of British Columbia.

Standing Committee on Justice and the Solicitor General. 1987. *Open and Shut: Enhancing the Right to Know and the Right to Privacy*. Ottawa: Queen's Printer for Canada.

Thomas, Paul. 2010. "Advancing Access to Information Principles through Performance Management Mechanisms: The Case of Canada." World Bank Working Paper. Washington, DC: World Bank.

Treasury Board of Canada Secretariat. 2005. *Info Source Bulletin Number 28*. http://infosource.gc.ca/.

–. 2007. *Info Source Bulletin Number 29*. http://infosource.gc.ca/.

–. 2008. *Info Source Bulletin Number 30*. http://infosource.gc.ca/.

–. 2009a. *Info Source Bulletin Number 31B – Statistical Reporting*. http://infosource.gc.ca/.

–. 2009b. *Info Source Bulletin Number 32B – Statistical Reporting*. http://infosource.gc.ca/.

–. 2010a. *Info Source Bulletin Number 33B – Statistical Reporting*. http://infosource.gc.ca/.

–. 2010b. "Access to Information Briefing: Media Call, Follow Up." Unpublished document prepared in response to questions from Fred Vallance-Jones, 19 February 2010.

–. 2011. "Management Accountability Framework." http://www.tbs-sct.gc.ca/.

Yvon Gauthier Inc. 2002. *Access to Information Review Survey of ATI Units*. Report 22 – Access to Information Review Task Force. http://www.atirtf-geai.gc.ca/.

LEGISLATION CITED

Access to Information Act, R.S.C. 1985, c. A-1.

Federal Accountability Act, S.C. 2006, c. 9.

Freedom of Information Act, 5 U.S.C. s. 552 (1966).

Freedom of Information and Protection of Privacy Act, R.S.O. 1990, c. F.31.

Municipal Freedom of Information and Protection of Privacy Act, R.S.O. 1990, c. M.56.

Savings and Restructuring Act, 1996, S.O. 1996, c. 1.

CASE CITED

Canada (Information Commissioner) v. Canada (Minister of External Affairs), [1990] 3 F.C. 514.

12

Access to Information
The Frustrations — and the Hope

DAVID McKIE

Narratives concerning Canada's *Access to Information Act (ATIA)* follow what has become a disturbingly familiar pattern, punctuated with words including "broken," "dysfunctional," and "useless." What is more, this characterization comes from the very people who should be champions of greater and more efficient use: journalists. Many intrepid members of the fourth estate are among the most infrequent users compared with other categories of individuals who employ the act, such as business. Journalists account for a mere 10.5 percent of the total number of requests for the federal government's 2009-10 fiscal year (Treasury Board of Canada Secretariat 2010, 3). This figure represents an almost a 4 percent decrease compared with the federal government's previous fiscal year. The narrative that paints this bleak picture is infectious, and could dissuade a new generation of journalists from employing an act that, despite its weaknesses, is still worth using. The trick lies in adopting practices that ensure success, which in the speed-driven, twenty-four-hour news cycle demands a skill set that needs to be improved significantly.

This chapter opens with a discussion of the 2009-10 report of the Office of the Information Commissioner of Canada, and a description of several endemic or structural issues within the Canadian federal access to information (ATI) regime. A central reason for these structural problems, I argue, is an absence of political will and strong leadership. Having set the stage, we proceed to a case study of ATI research in the context of the listeriosis crisis in Ontario in 2008, in order to highlight the ways in which endemic problems can hamper journalists' ability to access information in a timely fashion during an unfolding story. More importantly, however, I will argue that the listeriosis crisis provides not a disincentive but rather an important example of what is at stake if we give up on the act, which, despite its serious shortcomings, represents an indispensable tool for journalists. I discuss a number of instances in which ATI research has enabled journalists to break important stories that have led to important changes in public policy, including checks and balances to ensure more judicious spending, and the improved monitoring of adverse drug reactions. Strategies for success, such as the mining of available information for clues that will inform ATI request construction and the use of databases such as Coordination of Access to Information Requests System (CAIRS), are discussed. Besides being a valuable resource for the ATI community, CAIRS is itself an important case study in the politics of access, and I discuss its discontinuation by the Harper government and the efforts of ATI researchers to keep it operational as a public resource. Although the CAIRS database goes no later than October 2008, there is a small but increasing number of departments, agencies, and Crown corporations proactively disclosing the requests that their officials have processed. We discuss some of the ways in which journalists can utilize this useful inventory, which by no means provides an alternative to CAIRS. The chapter closes with a brief discussion of best practices, arguing that the public interest benefits of the *ATIA* ultimately outweigh the frustrations that stem from its endemic problems.

The Scope of the Problem

To understand just how much of a problem the *Access to Information Act* has become for practitioners, one need look no further than the morning of 30 March 2010, when the Interim Information Commissioner of Canada, Suzanne Legault, released her report card (Information Commissioner of Canada 2010). Among the journalists familiar with her office and her tendencies as the top information watchdog in the nation's capital, Legault, who began her permanent, seven-year appointment on 30 June 2010, was seen as more cautious and conciliatory than predecessors such as John Grace or John Reid. She was not given to strident criticism, and had stayed clear of the kind of heated rhetoric that had characterized the tenure of previous commissioners.

Still, the years leading up to the publication of her annual report had arguably been the worst ever for access to information. The irony of this situation was not lost on anyone, especially Legault. Journalists who attended the "lock-up" (a closed and formal press briefing) were aware that these report cards issued by a succession of information commissioners inevitably contained bad news for governments of all political stripes. But this was different, given the circumstances that initially brought Stephen Harper's Conservative party to power in January 2006. The Conservatives used appeals to the need for increased accountability and widespread public anger towards the governing Liberal party in the wake of the sponsorship scandal to propel their rise to power (see also Chapter 3).

Enter a new era of accountability expressed in a law appropriately named the *Federal Accountability Act.* Based on its name, the law's intent was welcome news to those of us who had endured years of Liberal government secrecy and lack of political will to provide true access to information. Although Harper's new law had little to say about the *Access to Information Act,* there was some good news: the number of agencies covered by the law was expanded to include Crown corporations such as Canada Post and my employer, the Canadian Broadcasting Corporation (CBC). Access officials also had a "duty to assist" requesters, which also meant helping individuals obtain information informally, instead of always enduring the more time-consuming process of submitting a formal request and then dealing with the inevitable delays. Perhaps what was more important for journalists like me was the hope that a new spirit of openness and transparency would make it easier to obtain a range of records I had been demanding for several years. Unfortunately, increased openness was not to be, as the Prime Minister developed a well-established and well-documented penchant for withholding information. Certain political staffers were accused of interference; cabinet ministers avoided journalists unless they had specific policies to peddle. And e-mail became the preferred method of responding to requests for basic information.

So it was with resignation that I and several other journalists attended the lock-up and subsequent news conference, and reviewed the information commissioner's report card. Although it contained none of the fire and brimstone of her predecessors, the news was bad, coming as it did during a week when the Harper government was being accused of political interference in the release of documents to media outlets and being slammed for its refusal to hand over documents involving Afghan detainees. Departments such as National Defence and the Canadian Food Inspection Agency received poor grades because they took too long to provide journalists and other requesters with the information they demanded. For its part, the Department of Foreign Affairs and International Trade was so bad that it failed to earn any grade at all. Instead, it received a red alert.

The reasons for the poor marks became disturbingly familiar, but it all seemed to come down to a well-worn and clichéd complaint: the lack of political will. Legault's language was gentler. She didn't accuse the Harper government of anything malicious. Rather, she contrasted its penchant for secrecy with US President Barack Obama's declaration that his government was open for business. "Do we have a government right now that is instilling a culture of transparency?" she asked rhetorically during her news conference. "I haven't seen evidence of that yet." This complaint was being levelled against a government that came to power promising to be more open, transparent, and accountable.

This lack of political will has manifested itself in many ways. While the volume of requests is increasing, the number of staff to handle those requests remains stagnant. From a personal point of view, this is most disturbing because during my appearance before a committee of Members of Parliament studying the Harper government's *Federal Accountability Act*, then known as Bill C-2, I made this plea:

> I would ... urge you to argue for more funding so that departments can adequately staff their [Access to Information] offices. Too frequently, I deal with harried bureaucrats who are crumbling under the weight of requests, resulting in lengthy delays. You can implement all the reforms you want, but if ATIP offices are understaffed, then that information that needs to get out, becomes stuck in a proverbial bottleneck. Information delayed is information denied. (Legislative Committee on Bill C-2 2006)

It was with some distress that I read that the lack of staff was one of five weaknesses Suzanne Legault considered "systemic."

> Evidence shows that insufficient resources – funds, staff and tools – undermine the effectiveness of access to information. This deficiency also creates excessive risks, including the erosion of requesters' right to information. Sustained compliance can only be achieved with permanent, qualified staff and proper tools. An integrated human resources action plan is urgently required to address the shortage. (Information Commissioner of Canada 2010)

Sadly, the criticisms about staffing continued. Legault lamented the lack of training and the high turnover. Indeed, it is not unusual for junior analysts to accept justifications for withholding records that more experienced staff would have questioned. More training in areas such as what constitutes data or what can be classified as a true cabinet confidence could potentially lead to the disclosure of more records.

In part, systemic problems can be accounted for by bureaucratic practices and resistance to transparency on the part of the civil service (Roberts 2006; Rowat 1966, 1982). What underscores many of these structural weaknesses, however, is a lack of political will or leadership. Unlike President Barack Obama in the United States, who publicly claimed that his government would be open for business, operating under a framework of presumptive disclosure, the Harper government in Canada has failed to champion access to information in its rhetoric.

What is unfortunate about the absence of political will is that it delivers a severe body blow to any hope of reform. The proclamation of increased accountability through an act of the same name means little without the commitment to reform. Examples of departments facing questions about their lack of openness abound. One case that hits close to home stands as an example of what is at stake if Canadians are left in the dark about the evolution of public policy.

The Canadian Food Inspection Agency and the Listeriosis Crisis

In the summer of 2008, news began to trickle out of Canadians falling ill and dying from listeriosis, a food-borne illness that few people knew anything about. The bacterium *Listeria monocytogenes* was the deadliest of the six strains found in products, in this case ready-to-eat meat produced by Maple Leaf Foods, which was headed by Michael McCain, whose family had achieved near-mythic status in the food business. The outbreak, which would eventually be linked to the deaths of at least twenty-three people, many of them elderly residents living in nursing homes, was traced to a food-processing plant at the north end of Toronto. The deadly strain of *Listeria* had become lodged in the food-cutting machine.

A casually clad and telegenic McCain promptly shouldered the blame, issued a heartfelt apology on YouTube, and settled lawsuits before any of them got to court (Maple Leaf Foods 2008). Maple Leaf Foods also shut down the facility until the Canadian Food Inspection Agency (CFIA) was satisfied that the machines were properly cleaned and the company had implemented proper protocols to prevent a similar tragedy. The CFIA announced new rules that force companies to clean their processing plants more vigorously. Agriculture Minister Gerry Ritz, who was responsible for the CFIA, took credit for cleaning up the system, deftly handled questions during two reviews of the crisis, and promised that all the players involved would do better next time.

During the year that began with the tainted meat and ended with the government's response to recommendations from special investigator Sheila Weatherill and the Parliamentary Food Safety Committee, I published and aired many stories. A common thread in the reports was a food safety system that lacked a sufficient number of inspectors and specific rules to ensure that food remained free of contamination. From September 2008 to June 2009, I teamed up with Robert Cribb, an investigative reporter with the *Toronto Star,* to dig for answers and write stories about what we had found.

We uncovered a 2005 audit that cited many of the same weaknesses identified at the time of the listeriosis crisis. We learned the extent of the contamination in nursing homes. We used sources to obtain newsletters that Michael McCain wrote to his staff, in which he criticized the very lawyers with whom he would eventually settle out of court months later, and in which he doubted the legitimacy ("tummy ache stuff") of some of the people making claims in those lawsuits (CBC News 2008).

What we were unable to report was how well the various federal players handled what became the largest food recall in Canadian history. The crucial months were between August 2008, when officials first learned that people were dying, and a month later, at the end of September, when government officials and Maple Leaf Foods finally had the situation under control. Granted, there were several players at the federal, provincial, and municipal levels. The complexity of the situation and the number of agencies involved made using the *Access to Information Act* challenging because before releasing records, each of those agencies would have to check with all the officials they consulted in other departments for permission to release the information. History has demonstrated that these extensive consultations rarely lead to permission to release the information, in large part due the need to protect negotiations between different departments or levels of government. Federal/provincial relations (section 14 in the *ATIA*) is an exemption, the rationale goes, because if officials knew their deliberations would eventually end up on the CBC airwaves or in the *Toronto Star,* they would refrain from negotiating freely.

Still, it was worth filing requests. Canadians had a right to know how their officials handled the crisis. We needed a discussion that went beyond the platitudes expressed in so-called Lessons Learned documents that were posted on the websites of the three federal agencies responsible for food safety: the Canadian Food Inspection Agency, the Public Health Agency of Canada, and Health Canada. Federal departments and agencies routinely produce these documents after major events as a way to find out what went wrong and to ensure that the same mistakes are not repeated. Sometimes the documents are available only through access to information. In this case, all three departments posted electronic versions of their findings on-line. Given the sensitive nature of the requests regarding the recall crisis, and the reality that journalists and other categories of requesters would be making similar demands, we expected delays. On 12 September 2008, I made the following request: "I would like access to the records generated between the Office of Food Safety and Recall and the rest of CFIA. The time frame in question is from July 1, 2008 to Sept. 12, 2008. The records should include, but not be limited to management action plans, e-mail corres-pondence and reports." After acknowledging my request six days later, the CFIA followed up with a response that would become a pattern: the need for more time to process the request – the dreaded time extension. The re-sponse read in part:

> Your request is for a large number of records and/or necessitates a search through a large number of records, and meeting the original time limit would unreasonably interfere with the operations of the Agency. We are therefore taking a time extension of 550 days, as defined in paragraphs 9(1) (a), (b) and (c) of the Act, to complete the processing of your request. The revised due date is May 25, 2010.

Needless to say, I complained about the delay in this request and others that Robert Cribb and I received during our investigation. Frustrated by the lack of progress with our access-to-information requests, we decided to do a story about the roadblocks we encountered. But first we sought comment from the agency officials, who were more candid than we expected. They admitted that the time delays were unacceptable, and said that they were due in part to staff shortages. When writing the story, we decided to empha-size the harm that would be done if Canadians were deprived of access to the information in the documents that were generated during the crucial months after the recall.

The agency's 2008-09 annual report blamed part of the delay problems on staff shortages. That told only part of the story, however, because 56 requests from the previous year had to be carried over, meaning that the agency began 2008 already behind schedule. Of the 327 requests it handled in 2008-09, 31 percent took longer than 120 days to process. In its response to the information commissioner, the agency promised to hire consultants to help pick up the slack, but stopped short of promising to hire significantly more permanent staff (Information Commissioner of Canada 2009, 7). Delays, though, were only part of the problem. When the agency did release information, it used provisions in the law, often citing cabinet confidences, to withhold information.

After Sheila Weatherill delivered her report in July 2009, the government, to its credit, quickly made the report public. Agriculture Minister Ritz promised that his department would adopt the recommendations, as well as study the recommendations made by the food safety committee, which had released its report the previous month. But what did Ritz mean by "adopt"? Which recommendations would take precedence? How soon would the government respond? Answers to these and many questions would finally help shed light on the crisis, which had fallen away from the headlines, presumably much to Ritz's relief. Figuring that it might be easier to obtain information in this phase of the investigation, I filed requests hoping for better results. No luck.

The Canadian Food Inspection Agency asked for a delay of 150 days. I complained to the Office of the Information Commissioner of Canada. To my surprise, the department released records sooner than I expected, but too much information was missing. The agency cited sections of the *ATIA* that allowed the inspection agency to withhold information. It used section 21, which is "advice or recommendations developed by or for a government institution or a minister of the Crown" (see Drapeau and Racicot 2004, 1102). This section is what is called a "class exemption," excluding advice, recommendations, consultations, and deliberations for twenty years, that is, sensitive information subject to cabinet discussions. Unlike section 69, however, which is information the cabinet actually discusses and therefore is classified as a mandatory "exclusion," section 21 exemptions are discretionary, meaning they can be challenged. I recall the advice I received from a sympathetic and equally frustrated ATI officer, who said that whenever I saw a section 21 exemption, I should complain because chances were the so-called office of primary interest, in this case the Privy Council Office (PCO), was using the section as an excuse to hide information that was embarrassing rather than sensitive. Taking that advice, I complained on 9 November 2009:

> Dear Ms. Legault, This is a follow-up complaint to the one I made in September regarding the 150-day extension for my request A-2009-00062. To my surprise, the department has complied and provided records. Unfortunately, the PCO, as usual, has gutted the request of any meaningful content. The result is that beyond general promises to "develop a plan of action to respond to the issues raised in these reports," we still lack specifics on how the government has responded to the worst food crisis in Canadian history.

Three months later, on 16 March, I filed yet another complaint after receiving more censored documents related to the government's deliberations over the food safety investigations:

> Dear Ms. Legault, I'd like to complain about the exemptions the department used to withhold information in request no. A-2009-00100. While the department is willing to tell me what messages it planned for journalists, it was unwilling to provide any indication of what was discussed. As such, we are no closer to learning how effective the department has been in dealing with one of the worst recalls in Canadian history.

Sadly, as of 11 March 2012, we are no closer to knowing how the government handled the crisis, and as a result are unable to hold it to account. The CFIA continued to release heavily censored records. I persisted with complaints and intend to pursue the story, even as the listeriosis crisis fades further into the background. The families of those who died and individuals who got sick finally received their settlement money from Maple Leaf Foods. The law firm managing the settlement mailed the cheques on Friday, 3 February 2012. Although it was a relief to receive the money, there was residual anger, pain, and continued suffering (McKie 2012).

As you can see from my persistence, however, now is not the time to give up because of the importance of food safety. Once more records are released, there will be ample opportunity to publish and air stories that will advance the discussion of this issue, and hopefully generate the kind of discussion that can help policy makers, consumers, and the food industry avert another major crisis. Thus, it is important to continually complain, write stories about the delays, look for nuggets of information in the records you do receive, and find better ways to word requests to ensure success.

The Benefits of the *ATIA*

Despite lack of success on the food safety file thus far, I remain convinced of the importance of the *ATIA*. If we are to make the government more accountable for the safety of food or any other consumer product, we must continue to use the act and seek new and innovative ways to succeed. Before discussing some of the strategies, however, it is important to explain why the *ATIA* matters. In the mid-nineties, the country was gripped by the Somalia scandal, which involved the Canadian military's involvement in the killing of a Somali teen (CBC News 2010d). Although Prime Minister Jean Chrétien shut down the inquiry, he was unable to stop people from talking about it. Journalists became wise to some of the ways in which officials hide information, such as writing information on Post-it Notes, which would then be removed when the request was going out the door (see Kelly 2006). Journalists also learned about meetings where participants neglected to take minutes. Such revelations put pressure on the military to become more forthcoming, which did happen for a while. For example, the Department of National Defence began handling requests more quickly and proactively posted previously processed requests on its website to enable requesters to determine what queries had already been made.

Towards the end of Jean Chrétien's tenure, he had to contend with a scandal that broke thanks to a *Globe and Mail* ATI request for an audit for work that turned out to be bogus. In March 2002, Daniel LeBlanc and Campbell Clark reported that the Chrétien government paid $550,000 for a report by the Liberal-friendly Groupaction Marketing "of which no trace can be found. Documents also show, in a separate $575,000 contract signed with the government, Groupaction agreed to undertake two specific tasks, but the company only delivered on one. Groupaction said it did a partial job after reaching an agreement with the bureaucrat in charge of the program," the story reported. "It will now prove difficult for the government to defend the $1.1-million in contracts to a generous Liberal donor, with little to show for its payment but 122 pages for the second report" (Cribb et al. 2006, 150).

Of course, that story with allegations of corruption and secrecy led to the Liberal government's eventual downfall. Without access to information, the initial discovery would have been impossible. Around the same time, I was researching adverse drug reactions, and wanted to know what kinds of drugs were problematic. My battle with Health Canada for this information began a few years before the sponsorship scandal broke, but that fight was prolonged because of the department's refusal to hand over its database that keeps track of the unexpected side effects that prescription drugs can cause.

The battleground became the information commissioner's office. Health Canada refused to release the information, citing, among other things, the need to protect the identity of the people reporting the adverse drug reactions. It did not seem to matter that there were a number of reasons why such identification would be virtually impossible, especially because our negotiating team agreed to set aside some of the contentious fields, or columns of information, in the adverse drug reaction databases that would have made it slightly easier – but still virtually impossible – to pinpoint individuals. This development also speaks to the discussion Mann (1986) raises about the role of information coordinators in facilitating disclosure, or what Larsen and Walby (see Introduction) call brokering access.

In the summer of 2003, Health Canada finally chose to negotiate. That fall, the CBC had about forty years' worth of data in several tables exported into the database manager *Microsoft Access* (Vallance-Jones and McKie 2009, 255). That data enabled us to do two years' worth of stories about Health Canada's inability to warn Canadians about dangerous drugs, especially those destined for children and seniors. As well, the CBC posted a version of the database online so that Canadians could search for themselves if they had concerns about certain drugs. Both the CBC and the *Globe and Mail* were nominated for the Michener Award that year, with the *Globe* taking the top prize for its coverage of the sponsorship scandal. The other winners were Canadians, who, thanks to the *ATIA*, learned important details about how their government spent money and kept track of potentially dangerous drugs. The Harper government would pass the *Federal Accountability Act* as its first order of business after assuming power in 2006. And Health Canada now hosts a searchable online database – the Canada Vigilance Adverse Reaction Online Database – that enables Canadians to obtain information about drugs they're taking. These are two of many examples that provide ample and compelling evidence that the law can work, especially for those who are creative, persistent, and knowledgeable – three traits that are important for journalists and others who want to use the act successfully.

What to Do When Patience and Persistence Fail to Pay Off in the Short Term

The battles to obtain sponsorship program documents and Health Canada's adverse drug reaction database also contain lessons that extend beyond persistence. The long struggles to obtain information from a recalcitrant government department or agency usually set important precedents. Now audits like the ones that assessed the sponsorship program are routinely disclosed on government websites. An increasing number of federal, provincial, and municipal institutions, including Health Canada, Transport Canada, the Ontario Ministry of Health and Long-Term Care, and the city of Vancouver, are posting more databases online. Non-governmental organizations such as the Canadian Council for Refugees are also posting data and other kinds of records that they obtain through access to information (Rehaag 2010). In an age when the Internet has emboldened a range of academics, activists, and journalists to become self-publishers, records that were once hidden are finding their way into the public arena.

This is all good news for journalists and others who can use this information for more immediate purposes while they might be waging longer-term battles to obtain records through more formal means, such as access to information. Again, the beneficiaries are Canadians. For instance, every time a vehicle manufacturer recalls a car, Transport Canada publishes that information online. So on 7 October 2010, when Toyota launched what would become a series of recalls related to sliding floor mats jamming gas pedals in a number of models, I used the vehicle recall database to produce breaking stories. On 23 March, I wrote a story about a similar Toyota recall that took place in 2003. The problem was eerily similar: sliding floor mats interfering with the pedals in the Celica model. The recall warning read in part: "On certain Panasonic Edition vehicles, the driver's floor mat may slide along the interior floor carpet when pressure is applied to the mat by getting in or out of the vehicle. As a result the floor mat may come in contact and interfere with the accelerator pedal" (CBC News 2010a). So prevalent was the problem with mats and accelerator pedals that Transport Canada issued an advisory in 2007, warning drivers that "the floor mat can then move under the driver's feet and become lodged either between the pedals, on top of the pedals or under the pedals" (Transport Canada 2007).

Those stories were possible because of the easy access to data that an increasing number of public agencies are making publicly available. In their report entitled *Unlocking Government: How Data Transforms Democracy*, Macmillan and colleagues (2010) delve into this trend of increased access to data that has been unfolding for some time but received a boost when US President Barack Obama declared that his government was open for business on his first full day on the job. He issued an executive memorandum that outlined the US commitment to providing what on the surface appears to be an unprecedented level of openness, and to establishing a system of transparency, public participation, and collaboration. "Openness will strengthen our democracy and promote efficiency and effectiveness in government," said Obama (Macmillan, Eggers, and Dovey 2010, 5). While the authors see this increased access through the lens of an enhanced citizen engagement, the opportunities for journalists are obvious, as we saw in the Toyota example. It is important for journalists to use innovative research techniques to hunt for data and documents online. I came across Transport Canada's vehicle recall database when preparing a session on a research technique that uses tools such as *Microsoft Excel* to analyze publicly available data. After copying and pasting the recall data into *Excel* and using the program's sort and filter functions, I was able to see patterns emerge that became the subject of my Toyota stories. For those unfamiliar with *Excel*, these databases can also be searched online using keywords similar to the ones you would plug into a search engine like Google.

Those keyword searches on websites can also turn up documents that government departments are obliged to produce, such as performance reports and audits. Although often written in opaque and overly bureaucratic language, they can be excellent tipsheets for story ideas, follow-up questions, or even extremely targeted and narrowly focused ATI requests. For instance, a search on the Canadian Food Inspection Agency's site turned up a document called *Report on Plans and Priorities: 2010-2011 Estimates*. On page 15, there is a reference to the listeriosis crisis and a vague promise to do a better job:

> To mitigate these risks, the agency will focus its efforts in 2010-11 on the delivery of activities identified under the following five priorities:
>
> - Design and deliver risk-based inspection and surveillance services.
> - Improve compliance through compliance management activities.
> - Modernize the Agency's regulatory components and tools.
> - Increase transparency and strengthen strategic partnerships and communications with key partners and stake holders.
> - Develop a workforce and workplace such that the Agency is innovative, more effective and well-managed. (Canadian Food Inspection Agency 2009, 15)

As vague as these references may be, they signal that something is happening at the agency that officials may not want to make public, at least not until they've figured out the best way to explain or "spin" the idea to journalists. But why wait for the agency to explain itself? Journalists and researchers can use these references as guides in asking probing questions. They can also use the information to craft more strategically worded requests, such as this one that I found on page 30 of a CFIA summary of access to information requests processed from 1 January to 25 December 2009. Using the explanation in the priorities document as a guide, the journalist asked for:

> Final copies of reviews and procedures in relation to the outbreak of Listeria in ready-to-eat meats in the summer of 2008. This is referenced on page 15 (hard copy) of the CFIA's 2009-10 estimates (Part 3 – Report on Plans and Priorities). Limit the scope to only those records held by National Headquarters.

This request is instructive for two key reasons: (1) its precision in referring to a particular document; and (2) its narrowing of the search for records to a particular office, in this case the CFIA's headquarters in Ottawa.

The CAIRS Website

The Canadian Food Inspection Agency document that tracks requests the agency has processed, such as the one cited above, was once a matter of public record that I posted on a website. There was a time when the federal government centralized access requests from many of its departments through a program called CAIRS, an acronym for Coordination of Access to Information Requests System. The Treasury Board of Canada Secretariat, a central federal agency, used to collect monthly reports from many government departments that listed all the requests they processed for a given time period. The text file for all the departments' requests for a given month contained information, including the date, request number, a generic description of the source of the request (media, business, public, political party, etc.), and a summary of the request, minus details that would identify individuals. The Treasury Board compiled these reports in an internal CAIRS database.

Alasdair Roberts, a professor who taught at Queen's University in Kingston, Ontario, had a standing request each month for a large text file that contained the requests for all the departments that reported to the Treasury Board. Roberts would then upload that information to his searchable online database. He took a service that was initially designed as a tool to be used only within government to manage the flow of access to information requests and turned it into a public resource, enabling anyone – including journalists such as myself, academics, and federal politicians, as it turned out – to use it as an indispensable research tool. I was able to monitor the kinds of requests that departments such as Health Canada were processing. If there was a request that interested me, I would simply contact the access coordinator for Health Canada and ask whether the record had been released to the original requester. If the answer was yes, then by law, I also had access to it. Access coordinators could give a short grace period of a few days during which the original requester has exclusive access to the record(s). When the grace period was over, the record was fair game. Since most requesters are not journalists (as noted earlier, in the 2009-10 fiscal year, journalists comprised only 10.5 percent of the total number of requesters), the chances were good that the information could be used for an exclusive story (Treasury Board of Canada Secretariat 2010, 3).

When Roberts decided that he lacked the time to maintain the database, he asked me to take over. I agreed and continued his work.[1] Not only could journalists and other users piggyback on requests, but they could get good ideas of the kinds of requests they could craft. Unfortunately, in the spring of 2008 the Harper government opted to kill CAIRS, arguing that it was no longer useful and too expensive to manage. This move, which effectively removed a valuable tool for journalists and ATI users, is not without recent precedent. Several authors have commented on concurrent actions by the Bush administration to curtail and circumvent freedom of information law in the United States (Shapiro and Steinzor 2006; Snell and Sebina 2007). In the House of Commons and in the Senate, Conservatives argued that there was another reason CAIRS was on life support: it had been a tool of the previous Liberal government to centralize control of access to information requests for the purpose of information management. The leader of the government in the Senate and Secretary of State for Seniors, Marjory LeBreton, stuck to her party's talking points when questioned about CAIRS:

> The fact is that the Coordination of Access to Information Requests System, better known as CAIRS, was set up by the previous government in order to control and manage access to information requests. It was set up in such a way as to bring all access of the press to the desk of the Prime Minister, rather than let the access to information system work properly. (Debates of the Senate 2008)

What she neglected to mention was that many Canadians had come to use CAIRS as a tool, the kind of source that supporters of open government like President Obama would applaud. And it was also interesting to note that the government also pondered allowing public access to CAIRS as far back as 2001. The revelation was contained in a document from the Treasury Board Secretariat that I received through access to information (CBC News 2010c). Although I was still able to obtain the monthly requests for my website, CAIRS ceased to become a living document but a historical one that contained access to information requests from 1993 to October 2008. I still maintain the database online for my journalism students at Carleton University.

About a year after the Conservatives cut off the material I used to update the site, I received the following e-mail from Michael Geist, a law professor at the University of Ottawa:

> I thought you might be interested in this site that I just launched today. You obviously recall how the Conservatives cancelled the CAIRS database last spring, effectively cutting off access to information on access to information requests and leading to a House of Commons committee resolution to reinstate the database.
>
> I have been working with some students on an interim solution. Today I launched CAIRS.Info, a new site that provides access to searchable PDF copies of the same information that was contained in the CAIRS database. Requests are sent to most government departments each quarter for a list of the most recent access to information requests. The resulting documents are uploaded and can be searched by government department, date of the request, or keywords within the requests. All request documents can be viewed online or downloaded as a PDF file. The files include the wording of the original access-to-information request, date, department, file number and general information about whether the requester was with the media, business, academic or other.[2]

"The idea was to identify 20 to 25 departments that were the biggest targets for these sorts of things," explained Geist. "So at least it would capture the bulk of the requests out there" (interview with Michael Geist, Ottawa, 25 April 2010). Information Commissioner of Canada Suzanne Legault has also taken up the fight to revive CAIRS, and released a report that, while

lamenting the passing of CAIRS as a living document, heralded a new development that she hoped would be a trend: a small but increasing number
of federal departments, including her office, that had decided to begin proactively posting their previously processed requests online. The departments were given a deadline of 31 January 2012 to begin posting summaries
of ATI requests in which records had been released. As expected, most departments missed the deadline, but began slowly posting the summaries
once it had passed. Although the format is inconsistent (for instance, some
departments post summaries going back several months, whereas others
post summaries beginning only in 2012), it fills part of the gap left by the
passing of CAIRS.[3]

Better Use of the *ATIA*

To promote the smarter use of public records such as databases, audits,
planning reports, and previously processed requests that are proactively
released is not to diminish the importance of access to information. There
are times when it is necessary to file requests, even with the knowledge that
the material will be delayed. Some matters of public policy are too important to leave unattended. Food safety will always be important to Canadians.
Thus, it is imperative that journalists continue to officially complain to the
information commissioner's office when they are faced with unreasonable delays and exemptions. Unfortunately, complaining can also be plagued
with delays, as it can take the information commissioner's office months to
simply acknowledge that you want it to intervene. As Commissioner Legault
admitted during her news conference to discuss her report card, "We are
part of the problem." She has hired more staff and says they are attempting
to process complaints more quickly, something that is happening.

Delays and complaints notwithstanding, it is important to develop good
habits that help ensure success. It is much easier to ask for an exact piece
of information than records, including, but not limited to, briefing notes,
e-mail correspondence, and reports. This is one reason I and a handful of
other Canadian journalists and academics have been able to negotiate for
databases that track everything from long-gun registration to the registration of federal lobbyists to medical devices. Once you have negotiated with
the department or agency for specific fields, or columns of information, in
the database, the release of the information can occur within thirty days, the
initial time allotted to fulfill a request.

It helps to make regular requests for specific kinds of information. For
instance, cabinet ministers and their deputies are regularly briefed on a

range of issues that may not seem topical at the time you receive the records but could turn out to be gold if a particular issue becomes news. Briefing notes, then, should become part of your routine requests. I ask for lists of briefing notes but make sure to specify that I only want a list that excludes material that could be a matter of cabinet confidence. This is important because these records are sent to the Privy Council Office, which usually has the effect of delaying the entire request. Excluding material considered to be a cabinet confidence is not something I would routinely recommend, but such a request for a list of briefing notes allows me to cherry-pick material that looks interesting. And because the record is not considered a cabinet confidence, there's a greater likelihood that when I make a new request for that record, I will receive something either within the initial thirty-day time limit or shortly afterwards.

Here's an example of a request for such a list that I sent to the Department of Finance on 3 December 2010:

> I would like access to a list from the department's computerized document tracking system of Briefing Notes, Deck Presentations, and Memorandums submitted to the Minister from January 1, 2010 to Dec. 5, 2010. The list should include, but not be limited to, the following fields from the tracking system database where applicable; Document Type; Author Type or Author; Issue; and Synopsis. The list should also include the record's document reference number. If there's material that is deemed cabinet confidence, I ask that the information that does not fall under the category be subject to a partial release.

It's also wise to think about the timing of your request. Given that bureaucracies spend much of their time fighting metaphorical fires, that is, responding to a particular crisis at hand, there is always lots of e-mail traffic around a particular issue. If a topic makes news in a particular week, wait a few days and then file a request for all the records that were generated by that controversy. Such was the case with the e-mail correspondence between Toyota and Transport Canada, days before the first floor mat recall on 7 October 2009. On 2 October, the head of the department's recalls forwarded two complaints regarding a model called the Venza to Toyota and asked that it become part of the initial recall. Toyota failed to heed that "immediate" request for action, which necessitated another e-mail a month later, asking for action once again. Toyota eventually issued a recall notice the following month (CBC News 2010b).

Conclusion

As a journalist who has been using access to information, teaching it, and writing about it, I remain a believer and an advocate. The *ATIA* has enabled me to tell important and award-winning stories that have forced Health Canada, the RCMP, and others to change policies, which I would suggest has saved lives. The stakes are too high to throw up our hands and declare that the obstacles are too high and too numerous to overcome. Although we live with the frustration of a system that has become increasingly difficult to navigate, we do so at a time when there is increased pressure on governments to be more open. Citizens will begin making demands for more access to databases and documents, and there is ample evidence that governments are beginning to oblige, even if reluctantly. For instance, because of the excellent work of the *Hamilton Spectator* and the *Toronto Star,* Transport Canada was forced to make its Civil Aviation Daily Occurrence Reporting System (CADORS) available (Vallance-Jones 2010) in the form of an online, searchable database. Besides using the *ATIA,* journalists must also demand speedier access, write stories when officials impose unreasonable delays, and make it harder to withhold information by formulating requests that are clear and precise. Extracting information from governments has never been easy, and many journalists have the battle scars to prove it. Whether it be fighting publication bans, fighting for greater access to courts, or waging campaigns to protect sources, journalists have always dug in their heels when the stakes are high. Access to information is worth the fight.

NOTES

1 The Canadian Access to Information Requests System – CAIRS can now be found at http://http-server.carleton.ca/~dmckie/CAIRS/CAIRS.htm.
2 CAIRS.Info can be found at http://cairs.michaelgeist.ca/.
3 The summaries of completed access to information requests can be found at http://open.gc.ca/open-ouvert/ati-aai-eng.asp.

REFERENCES

Canadian Food Inspection Agency. 2009. *Report on Plans and Priorities: 2010-2011 Estimates.* http://www.tbs-sct.gc.ca/.
CBC News. 2008. "Maple Leaf CEO's Memos to Workers Give Glimpse of Struggles with *Listeria:* Special Investigation by CBC News/Toronto Star." 8 November. http://www.cbc.ca/.
–. 2010a. "Toyota Floor-Mat Problems Arose in 2003." 23 March. http://www.cbc.ca/.

–. 2010b. "Toyota Problems Seen Months before Recall." 29 April. http://www. cbc.ca/.

–. 2010c. "Hold the Applause: Some Government Departments Are Posting Access to Information Requests Online." 3 December. http://www.cbc.ca/.

–. 2010d. "Think WikiLeaks Will Cause More Government Secrecy? Think Back to the Somalia Inquiry." 23 December. http://www.cbc.ca/.

Cribb, R., D. Jobb, D. McKie, and F. Vallance-Jones. 2006. *Digging Deeper: A Canadian Reporter's Research Guide.* London: Oxford University Press.

Debates of the Senate (Hansard). 2008. "2nd Session, 39th Parliament, Volume 144, Issue 56, Tuesday, May 6, 2008." http://www.parl.gc.ca/.

Drapeau, M., and M. Racicot. 2004. *Federal Access to Information and Privacy Legislation Annotated.* Toronto: Thomson Carswell.

Information Commissioner of Canada. 2009. *Maximizing Compliance for Greater Transparency: 2008-2009 Annual Report on the* Access to Information Act. http://www.infocom.gc.ca/.

–. 2010. *Out of Time: A Special Report to Parliament by Suzanne Legault, Interim Information Commissioner of Canada.* Ottawa: Minister of Public Works and Government Services Canada. http://www.oic-ci.gc.ca/.

Kelly, Paul. 2006. "Information Is Power." *Open Government: A Journal of Freedom of Information* 2 (1). http://www.opengovjournal.org/.

Legislative Committee on Bill C-2. 2006. "Evidence, Tuesday, May 30, 2006." 39th Parliament, 1st Session. http://www2.parl.gc.ca/.

Macmillan, Paul, William D. Eggers, and Tiffany Dovey. 2010. *Unlocking Government: How Data Transforms Democracy.* http://www.deloitte.com/.

Mann, B. 1986. "The Federal Information Coordinator as Meat in the Sandwich." *Canadian Public Administration* 29 (4): 579-82.

Maple Leaf Foods. 2008. "A Message from Maple Leaf Foods Regarding *Listeria* Recall." http://www.youtube.com/.

McKie, David. 2012. "Listeriosis victims receive reduced compensation." CBC News, http://www.cbc.ca/.

Rehaag, S. 2010. "2009 Refugee Claim Data & IRB Member Grant Rates." Canadian Council for Refugees. http://www.ccrweb.ca/.

Roberts, Alasdair. 2006. *Blacked Out: Government Secrecy in the Information Age.* New York: Cambridge University Press.

Rowat, D. 1966. "Administrative Secrecy and Ministerial Responsibility: A Response." *Canadian Journal of Economics and Political Science* 32: 84-87.

–. 1982. "The Right of Public Access to Official Documents." In *The Administrative State in Canada,* ed. by O. Divivedi. Toronto: University of Toronto Press.

Shapiro, S., and R. Steinzor. 2006. "The People's Agent: Executive Branch Secrecy and Accountability in an Age of Terrorism." *Law and Contemporary Problems* 66: 98-129.

Snell, R., and P. Sebina. 2007. "Information Flows: The Real Art of Information Management and Freedom of Information." *Archives and Management* 35 (1): 54-81.

Transport Canada. 2007. "Vehicle Floor Mats – Interference with Accelerator (Gas) and Brake Pedals: TP 14665E Vehicle Safety Advisory V 2007-01 E." http://www.tc.gc.ca/.

Treasury Board of Canada Secretariat. 2010. *Info Source Bulletin Number 33B – Statistical Reporting.* http://infosource.gc.ca/.

Vallance-Jones, Fred. 2010. "Collision Course: Winners of the CAJ's Top Award for Investigative Journalism in Canada, the Don McGillivray Award for Investigative Journalism, and the CCNMatthews/CAJ Computer-Assisted Reporting (CAR) Award." Canadian Association of Journalists. http://caj.ca/.

Vallance-Jones, F., and David McKie. 2009. *Computer Assisted Reporting: A Comprehensive Primer.* Toronto: Oxford University Press.

LEGISLATION CITED

Access to Information Act, R.S.C. 1985, c. A-1.
Federal Accountability Act, S.C. 2006, c. 9.

The Quest for Electronic Data
Where Alice Meets Monty Python
Meets Colonel Jessep

JIM RANKIN

From a government perspective, releasing paper documents is about as painless and routine as going through an airport metal detector. Forking over raw electronic data to a journalist? Well, that's a full body X-ray, strip search, and a finger up you know where. It's indeed the full monty of freedom of information (FOI) requests, and things tend to get weird, fast. Also – as will be highlighted in this chapter in a few personal war stories and those of fellow Canadian journalists – data requests can be lengthy, surreal, absurd, obstructionist, secretive, patronizing, hilarious, infuriating, and costly. By the time some of these requests result in disclosure, the Stanley Cup may have been decided five times, the federal government may have changed three times and been prorogued twice, there may be a new mayor, new premier, and new chief of police, and there are several changes in top newsroom management. No wonder, then, that so few journalists use our access and freedom of information laws to go after government-held data.

There are, I estimate, fewer than a dozen Canadian media organizations that embrace what is known as computer-assisted reporting and employ journalists who regularly use access laws to get at government data – and know how to analyze it. It is a small club. We are masochists. We commiserate, yes, but we also cheer each other on whenever another's access or FOI odyssey – which begins with a letter and, depending on the jurisdiction, a $5 cheque, but can take a lot more money and varying numbers of lawyers and years to complete – results in a blockbuster story or groundbreaking freedom of information decision that makes it easier for us all.

As flawed as the laws are, access requests for data do yield results and lead to institutional openness. The Canadian Broadcasting Corporation's David McKie fought and won access to a federal database used to track adverse drug reactions, and the CBC's investigative team questioned whether enough was being done to protect the health of Canadians (Moore 2004). Not long afterwards, Health Canada made the data available to the public on its website. In a joint project, former *Hamilton Spectator* reporters Fred Vallance-Jones and Tamsin McMahon and the *Toronto Star*'s Robert Cribb waged a successful battle for a federal aviation database that tracks close calls, and that data set, too, is now publicly available (Vallance-Jones 2010). The *Vancouver Sun*'s Chad Skelton got his hands on Vancouver's parking ticket data and made all of it available online in 2009 in an interactive project (see *Vancouver Sun* 2009a) that, at time of writing, had generated more than two million hits. Another article of his on public sector salaries (see *Vancouver Sun* 2009b) has hit the two-million mark.

As for me, I've worked with some terrific *Star* colleagues on projects that began with requests I made for data. We've used inmate address data to illustrate where we are spending the most money to incarcerate citizens, and to question penal policy that will put more people from already socially disadvantaged groups behind bars for longer periods and for more crimes (*Toronto Star* 2008). We also obtained Toronto police data that showed how people were treated after arrest and who were more likely to be stopped for certain traffic offences (Rankin et al. 2002). That group effort led to a human rights inquiry into the impacts of racial profiling in Ontario (see Ontario Human Rights Commission 2003) and sparked a sea change in how Canadian police view biased policing. Many police services are taking steps to deal with it.

In an age when governments are turning more and more to e-records and databases, and using hard data to make more and more policy decisions, such as anti-poverty strategies, police deployment choices, and budget cuts that affect small and large segments of the general population, unfettered public access to e-records is of utmost importance. Similarly, agencies may be ignoring or missing out on stories buried within their own databases. To deny access to e-records is to shut down the ability of citizens to scrutinize government decisions.

This chapter is about flawed, wacky systems, but ones that *can* be worked to expose broken systems, identify corruption and bias, broaden understanding of how our society works, hold governments accountable, and generate positive social policy changes. On the pages that follow, I will, along with some of the best data-based investigative journalists in the country, flag problems and share lessons and practical advice on how to navigate the system. For information keepers, this chapter will provide a sense of what it is like on the requesting end, and what can be done to improve the process for both the requester and the organization. I will also provide a toolkit for requesters, which, due to the constraints of this chapter, is far from complete. The process may seem intimidating to the uninitiated, but it begins with a simple question. I encourage those who have no experience with requests to seek help from the journalists you will read about in the coming pages. They are a solid and sharing lot. The chapter also looks at the perils, particularly for academics, of suing the government for raw electronic information. It concludes with a brief look at the future of data access requests and investigative journalism.

The Truth: Why Data Requests Are Difficult

"You can't handle the truth," Colonel Jessep, Jack Nicholson's character in the dramatic thriller *A Few Good Men,* shouted at the young naval attorney, played by Tom Cruise. He wanted the truth, but may as well have been asking for raw electronic data from government – the reaction often seems the same. Most organizations are naturally suspicious of access requests, and enormously more so when it involves raw data. Like Colonel Jessep, they *really* don't trust you, at least not initially.

Skillful negotiation and brokering for access can be fruitful in some cases, but the relationship between journalists and access coordinators can be adversarial from the get-go. "I think there's a great deal of concern within government about allowing internally maintained data [to be] placed in the hands of outsiders who can use it to draw specific conclusions according to their own analysis or even pair data with a different data set to find links," says Robert Cribb, an investigative journalist at the *Toronto Star* who has won many freedom of information battles for data and is a past president of the Canadian Association of Journalists. "It represents a loss of control far more profound than the simple release of documents, which are static and whose conclusions are plainly evident and easy to prepare for should they reach public attention. All of this is, of course, a natural reaction by government."[1]

In Canada, the advent in 1982 of the *Access to Information Act (ATIA)* and a spirit of openness soon spawned efforts to hide or omit information and "message discipline," as explored by Alasdair Roberts (2006) in *Blacked Out*. Requests became more probing and the handling of them more political, which in turn caused more probing by requesters. What exactly were ministers and departments doing to manage the message? Through the 1990s, the Liberal government used litigation to try to block access to records held in the offices of cabinet ministers and in the Prime Minister's Office (PMO). The government also attempted to hide information by shifting responsibilities to quasi-governmental bodies not bound by the act.

Sensitive requests were also being flagged, or "amber lighted," as journalist Ann Rees discovered in an access request that led to the release of documents relating to how the government reacts internally. Requests from journalists and opposition parties received special and immediate attention, with the ministers' offices receiving notice of such requests within a day of receipt. Certain requests resulted in the pre-emptive creation of "media lines" and "house cards" that could be called upon by department spokespersons and ministers should the requests lift the lid on something the government would like to massage, such as stories about mismanagement.

These measures, noted Roberts (2006), resulted in delay in the processing of sensitive requests, which provides an advantage to government. The government is "on-message" when the you-know-what hits the fan. This, for journalists, is to be expected. The subsequent filing of an access request concerning how a government department behaved behind the scenes in response to your request is not always newsworthy but well worth the $5, if for nothing more than the entertainment value. To go back to the airport security analogy, it's the fear. What might a third party find out about you that you might not know yourself? Or maybe you're hiding something, like love handles or exploding underwear.[2] Either way, scary – or potentially embarrassing, possibly game changing.

TIP: You may not want an agency to know why you want data but, whenever possible, be transparent. While this is not required, you may ease some of the suspicion by letting an agency know what you intend to do with the data.

Another hurdle is the relative newness of data requests. It is worth noting here that, in my experience, despite differences in the language describing the various acts and laws – "access to information" (ATI) and "freedom of information" – data requests are, by default, less about openness and more about control. Also, many organizations still don't know how to handle them. They simply begin by saying no.

So, how to get to the data? Data requests, as Cribb points out, are more "surgical" than document requests, "largely because the bureaucratic default position is even more firmly switched to the 'denial' position." While documents, says Cribb, have been the historical "currency" of access disclosure, data release is still seen by many ministries as foreign, discretionary, or beyond the scope of the act, and thus is met with resistance. "This likely has much to do with the ability of data to be manipulated according to the wishes of the requester," says Cribb. "This brings with it a loss of control that many within government appear to find threatening. In any case, there's no question that a large data request is an exercise in patience and persistence." It is almost always a two-step request process rather than a single request, which is typical for documents. In seeking data, begin by seeking a record layout, sometimes informally, but often through a formal request, that tells you what is in the database and allows you to filter out sensitive data, such as personal information.

> TIP: Access and freedom of information laws are complicated. School yourself on the act that applies to your request. Search privacy orders and decisions that apply to, and support, your arguments for the release of the data. Cite them in your requests. Always appeal a bad decision. Hold agencies to mandated deadlines. Typically, an agency is required to respond to a request within a month. Count the days. Some journalists use a spreadsheet to track their requests.

Organizations sometimes feel that the data they collect is not meant to be analyzed or released in electronic format. "I think a lot of officials thought databases were internal resources and that only summaries from the data should be released externally," says former *Spectator* reporter Fred Vallance-Jones, now a journalism professor at the University of King's College in Halifax. "Right away there was a reluctance. This held across the board – from municipalities right up to federal departments." Case in point: In 2008, an annual audit of freedom of information laws (which Vallance-Jones is involved with) saw journalists from across the country file similar requests. The audit found that organizations at all levels would release paper records only, even when electronic records had been expressly requested (Vallance-Jones 2009).

Chad Skelton, a reporter with the *Vancouver Sun*, began making requests for raw electronic data only recently, but he quickly had a number of successful hits. Not all were accomplished without either a fight or institutional holdback on electronic release. A request for British Columbia government salaries in electronic format was met with refusals by agencies that insisted instead on sending paper printouts from what were clearly *Microsoft Excel* spreadsheets. The government itself fought the electronic release, despite a privacy ruling in favour of the *Sun* that said agencies should release data electronically. "The argument I've gotten from some agencies is that they have a policy not to release records in a 'modifiable format,'" says Skelton. "In other words, if they give me a printed list of salaries, it's harder for me to fiddle with the numbers than an *Excel* spreadsheet. I frankly think this argument makes no sense."

TIP: Once you have the data, do not assume anything. Question the data, probe it for weaknesses, and bulletproof your analysis. If you lack expertise in this area, visit your information technology (IT) department. Chances are, there is someone there who will be interested in the task at hand and who can and will want to help. Librarians are also quite often well versed in spreadsheet and database software. Keep an open line with the agency and ask follow-up questions.

It's unfortunate that these fights continue to play out despite decisions by many privacy czars and courts across the country that say organizations must provide records in electronic format when requested. Like Bill Murray's TV weatherman character in the movie *Groundhog Day* – trapped in a loop where he wakes every day to the same day and must cover the emergence of Punxsutawney Phil from a hole in the ground – journalists are forced to make the same arguments over and over again.

The result? Accessing electronically held government data in a timely manner typically becomes impossible. In a news culture consumed with feeding the maw of a 24/7 news cycle, your request for data will not be ready for the evening news. Try instead years from now. Governments gain time, as Roberts (2006) points out, to get their message straight and prepare for potential negative fallout. Some requesters simply abandon their efforts. Others carefully word their requests to make it clear they want the most up-to-date data at time of release, whenever that may be (this is not possible in all jurisdictions). "I think the cultural resistance within most government departments is the single largest obstacle to accessing data," says Cribb. "Despite numerous rulings reaffirming the public's right to government data, departments again and again issue denials that force lengthy appeals that inevitably come to the same conclusion." In the meantime, says Cribb, months or years are lost with no public access to sometimes "vitally important information." A recent two-year fight of Cribbs to access private career college inspection data was denied based on "tired, old arguments that have been roundly dismissed by the Ontario information commissioner in numerous other appeal cases, many of which I had fought myself. Those lengthy, hard-fought battles appear to have little impact beyond the specific release they trigger. We are left to re-invent the wheel each time in the face of bureaucratic intransigence."

It shouldn't be this way. In the case of the electronic release of data, any resistance should have melted away following an Ontario court ruling in 2002 that ended a five-year fight by *Toronto Star* reporter Phinjo Gombu for electronic city of Toronto campaign contribution data. Gombu wanted to analyze the contributions for possible contribution breaches. Although the contributions were public records that document names and amounts contributed, and could be viewed by any member of the public in paper format, the city refused Gombu the electronic version, saying it had already been published in paper format. Ontario's Information and Privacy Commissioner found that this argument rang hollow but denied Gombu access because the data contained "personal information," such as phone numbers, even though they could be viewed on the paper documents by anyone (Ontario Information and Privacy Commissioner 2000). Gombu took the case to divisional court, and Mr. Justice J. David McCombs, writing for a three-judge panel, set things straight, finding that it would be in the public interest to disclose the electronic data.

McCombs accepted the *Star*'s position, saying "that the only way that [Gombu] can meaningfully scrutinize the information about campaign contributions is through the electronic database." Public interest in disclosure, wrote the judge, outweighed other considerations, including the telephone number information, which the judge noted was already required to be public anyway *(Phinjo Gombu v. Tom Mitchinson, Assistant Commissioner et al.).* The judge ordered the city to hand over the data. Gombu recalls that

> TIP: Negotiate with the agency. An open dialogue goes a long way, provided, that is, the agency is willing to talk.

the Ontario Information and Privacy Commissioner was set to appeal but suddenly dropped the case. He believes the commissioner was looking for an easier fight on the personal information angle.

Journalists familiar with data requests have learned to make sure of a few things in their initial requests to help speed things along. Although Gombu received personal information, the information came from publicly available records. In almost every other instance, names, addresses, and other personal information are non-starters, as are free-form text entry fields that could contain names and other personal information. If you do not want this information, make it clear from the beginning that you do not want it.

In the following example, government data keepers sought to end a request by releasing a watered-down version of the aviation safety data that the journalists were seeking.

Case Study: "Collision Course"

"Collision Course." June 2006. *Hamilton Spectator, Kitchener-Waterloo Record,* and *Toronto Star.* Robert Cribb, Fred Vallance-Jones, and Tamsin McMahon.
Act: Federal *Access to Information Act*
Start to finish: About five years

Transport Canada tracks aviation close calls in a massive database called the Civil Aviation Daily Occurrence Reporting System, or CADORS. In 2001, Fred Vallance-Jones, then with the *Hamilton Spectator,* decided he wanted all of it. He made a formal request that set in motion an Alice-in-Wonderland journey that he learned more about in a follow-up request for internal correspondence that dealt with his initial request. Federal bureaucrats had routinely released paper reports on incidents, most often to aviation industry insiders and the odd journalist. They were initially perplexed by the thought of releasing the whole thing electronically. The document trail uncovered by Vallance-Jones in the subsequent request provides a glimpse of life inside the information and privacy rabbit hole.

His request resulted in a slew of internal e-mails, set off a series of meetings, led to the production of a *Microsoft PowerPoint* presentation, a review of who did receive occurrence reports and whether anyone should get them, period, and sparked debate over whether third-party information, such as names of major airlines, would be released. It was thought that the data could be "injurious to third parties," such as WestJet and Air Canada, due to a large number of incidents. The data included aircraft make, locations, registration numbers, airline names, narratives of the incident, pilot information. Was this private information or commercially sensitive? The debate went on and on internally. It is also clear the department was misinterpreting the request, and at one point would not release "software." Vallance-Jones had never asked for that, just the data. They also claimed he had amended his request, which he hadn't. "I thought the issue of the database was resolved. Does the requester still want the database?" reads one internal document.[3]

"I don't know whether this wasn't some tactic they were using to slow it down, buy themselves more time," says Vallance-Jones. "That was weird. I never got an explanation for that." Another party involved in the internal debate suggested that the data was intellectual property and perhaps could be bought "through proper channels," since the system cost $250,000 to create.

A year after the request, in 2001, a meeting was held. It included access to information and privacy (ATIP) people and database specialists. The seemingly stunned department determined that the data were not transfer-able electronically and just decided to say no. Vallance-Jones appealed to the Office of the Information Commissioner of Canada complaining that the information requested was being shared with stakeholders, so why not with the public as well? An investigator unfamiliar with database requests was assigned to look into the roadblock but he and the Information Commissioner's office went to school and hired a computer expert to help. This moved things along, but internally the department was still thinking paper. A draft estimate shows they were considering an electronic release but were also going to ask for $18,000 to cover the cost of manually severing information they didn't intend to share.

"I actually laugh more now when I look back at it, but it was initially very frustrating," says Vallance-Jones. At one point the department released a stripped-down electronic version, which was useless. Vallance-Jones felt they were now simply stonewalling, so the Information Commissioner went to Federal Court. In mid-2005, in the midst of the court challenge, Transport Canada suddenly forked over the commercial data but withheld private aircraft data.

Vallance-Jones and Cribb had previously talked about doing a joint airline project, and the pair eventually teamed up with McMahon from the *Kitchener-Waterloo Record*. The reporters went to work. To make more sense of the data, Vallance-Jones, Cribb, and McMahon pored over the narratives in the data, and classified the incidents to check for patterns of pilot and air traffic controller error. They interviewed officials, insiders, pilots, accident victims, and others. Pilot fatigue, among other problems, was flagged as an issue.

The resulting series won the Canadian Association of Journalists' top award for investigative journalism in Canada – the Don McGillivray Award for Investigative Journalism – and the CCNMatthews/CAJ Computer-Assisted Reporting (CAR) award. It earned Vallance-Jones and McMahon Journalist of the Year honours at the Ontario Newspaper Awards and received a citation of merit in the Michener Awards for public service journalism.

In 2006, Vallance-Jones received the private aircraft data and the five-year battle was over. "This wasn't my worst experience. But it was a horrible sort of long grinding process." The internal ATIP documents illustrate how the department shifted its thinking on the release of electronic data; most satisfying for Vallance-Jones, the data are available online today. The safety issues raised by the journalists continue to reverberate through the aviation community.

Curiouser and Curiouser: You Do Have Some Cheese Here?

Just when you think you've stumbled across an agency that understands requests for raw data – and there are some out there – things turn absurd. Fee estimates for programming can be comically astronomical, well-meaning coordinators dig in, common sense takes a vacation, and the spirit of disclosure intended in access and freedom of information acts is all but exorcised.

TIP: Speak "geek to geek." Connect as soon as possible with an agency's database analyst. FOI coordinators are notoriously ill versed in databases, the software required to extract data, and the process of electronically redacting personal information. A good coordinator will connect you with an analyst who can explain the data and how they work. This speeds the process and helps tailor the request to get what you want. If you don't speak "geek," find someone – a librarian, one of us journalists, or an IT guru – to help you.

On fees, my personal favourite is a request I made in May 2003 for a copy of the database used to document Canada's criminals. It's part of the Canadian Police Information Centre database maintained by the Royal Canadian Mounted Police. They quickly connected me with their "geek" who knew how the database worked and what was in it. This hardly ever happens, and if it happens at all, it is late in the process. Getting to the analyst is like finding cheese in the famous Monty Python cheese shop skit, where an obstructionist cheese shop owner frustrates a customer looking for cheese. We spoke geek to geek, and in short order it was agreed that the data could be cleansed of personal information that potentially might enable me to identify individuals. Fantastic. I modified my request to eliminate problematic fields.

Then came the official decision from the Mounties' access coordinator. Yes, this was doable. I got a receipt for my $5 cheque and a request for a deposit on estimated programming fees that would need to be paid to cover the cost of extracting the data. I flipped to page 2 of the decision and read: "A total cost of $1,599,840.00 has been assessed for the processing of this request ... If you wish to proceed with the processing of your request, forward a deposit" in that amount.[4]

The letter went on to assure me that this was just an estimate and that the final total might not be as high, and also that "should you continue your request, please note that there are no guarantees that any part of the information will be released, bearing in mind that the material may qualify for exemption under the Act." They wanted $1.6 million for the cheese, but there was no assurance there would even be cheese. As Alice in Wonderland remarked, things were getting "curiouser and curiouser."

The fee estimate was based on antiquated regulations that mention costs associated with duplicating "microfilm" and "magnetic tape-to-tape duplication," which I suspected and pointed out in my complaint letter. I also cited a 2002 report to Parliament by the Information Commissioner of Canada, in which the office had flagged these outdated fees (Reid 2002). The Mounties said it would take two hundred days of "central processor" time to complete the request. That came to $16.50 per minute, or at least it did when they had machines like that.

I complained to the Information Commissioner. At the time, he was reviewing these old regulations, partly as a result of requests by other journalists for other federal databases. In December 2005, a letter and a CD arrived. For the most part it was what I'd asked for: electronic summaries of 2.9 million criminal records. The letter suggests that it took less than five hours of an analyst's time to extract the data, and stated that "we have waived all processing and reproduction fees."[5] From $1.6 million to free. Cheese, after all.

The database, along with two other inmate data sets I obtained through additional requests, served as the foundation for "Crime & Punishment," an eight-part series that examined the wisdom of Canadian penal policy and the financial and societal costs of jailing people for problems that would be cheaper to deal with at an earlier stage (*Toronto Star* 2008).

> TIP: Challenge programming and other fees. Often, the initial estimates are grossly more than what it will actually cost to extract and release the data. If you feel that the dissemination of the data is in the public interest, request a fee waiver or fee reduction. Be prepared to argue why. Don't know how? Get help.

Often the tone of how a data request will proceed is set by the co-ordinator handling the request, and there are good ones and not-so-good ones. Some are well schooled on the act and seek to use it fairly. Others see this as war and are prepared to use every weapon available to thwart a request. Yet another group is motivated, I think, by fear of reprisals from higher-ups, and this is understandable and justified.

To be fair, we journalists, as Bruce Mann (1986), former Assistant Information Commissioner of Canada put it, do indeed like to poke sticks at the federal information coordinator, and the same is true of their counterparts at the provincial and municipal levels. Just three years into the fledgling existence of the *ATIA*, Mann likened the federal coordinator to the meat in the sandwich, which gets worse when you don't know who will take the next bite.

Coordinators are seen as obstructionist and the face of government by journalists, a "thorn in the side" by department colleagues who must take time to discuss matters of disclosure, a threat to third parties with corporate interests (such as airlines in the case of Vallance-Jones's request), and a "consummate slave-driver" to support staff for trying to adhere to deadlines and the letter of the law. As for the Information Commissioner, any investigation could result in an overruling of the coordinator. And what of the boss? What if the release of information causes embarrassment or scandal to government?

Tough job, and one that varies in its demands according to the department and number of requests. The *Star's* Robert Cribb, who began making data requests in 1997, says he can tell five minutes into a telephone call with a coordinator which camp they fall into. "Good FOI coordinators do exist; they are fair, open and feel vested in playing an advocacy role for the public in mediating between requesters and departments," says Cribb. "The good ones ask questions, listen intently and respond in a timely way, not simply with blanket denials or excuses, but also suggestions and alternatives that move the process forward. In other words, they mediate, problem-solve and seek a solution that ultimately serves the spirit of the legislation under which they work." More typically, says Cribb, access coordinators are "firmly entrenched defenders of their department, seemingly anxious to thwart any efforts that could bring them – or their bosses – any headaches in the press."

TIP: Coordinators unschooled in databases often cite the size of a database in what feels like an effort to persuade you to tighten the scope of a request or suggest that it would be a burden to respond to it. Size, however, matters little. It takes a programmer the same amount of time and effort to write queries to extract data from a database containing 100 records as it does from a database containing 2 million. Don't buy the volume argument. It's a red herring.

There is, of course, a balance that must be struck between disclosure and protection of privacy, and even we journalists understand this. Sometimes, however, particularly in data requests, well-intentioned coordinators become hypervigilant about the possibility of determining who people are, and in some instances hamper the ability to meaningfully interpret and study government-held data. Imagine a data set that has had names replaced with unique, randomly generated numbers, exact dates replaced with month and year, or year only, and exact addresses removed. This data set on its own does not allow one to determine individual identities. But connect it to another database and theoretically it may be possible to determine who some of the individuals are – damn hard, and costly to do so, but theoretically, in some cases, possible. Known as the "mosaic" or "matrix" effect, some agencies are using the argument that the release of their data set may enable one to connect dots that are in other domains and beyond their control, and determine who people are.

I've run up against this a number of times, most notably with Ontario's Ministry of Community Safety and Correctional Services in a quest to obtain the full home postal codes of inmates who have been sentenced to a term of less than two years. I asked for a one-day snapshot of who was sitting in prison, and for only two pieces of information about each inmate: the length of their sentence in days and the full postal code of the last address they had before entering prison. I asked that the snapshot come from any day of the ministry's choice in 2007. I did not ask for the day. I did not ask for the crime for which the inmate was sentenced. I did not ask for age, gender, or any other pieces of information. We intended to use the postal code and sentence lengths to calculate and map high-incarceration pockets of Toronto. With full postal code, we could then look at underlying demographic and socio-economic factors at play in these areas, and also calculate what we spend in these areas to jail people. The ministry denied full postal code, saying it was personal information that could be used to identify inmates. Instead, we got the first three characters. I appealed and won access to the full postal code data. We produced the map we wanted, and it revealed a clearer pattern of costly jail areas and underlying social conditions (*Toronto Star* 2009).

> TIP: More and more agencies are allowing the public to access data online through one-off search queries, but do not make the entire data set available for download. Rather than making a formal request for the data, it may be possible to create an automated script that lifts — or "scrapes" — the entire data set from the agency's website. Don't know how? Find a geek.

Skelton sees the "mosaic" effect as a real threat to future data releases. In his words, it drives him "bonkers. I've had it applied in some pretty ridiculous cases. For example, a while back I asked for disciplinary records from a bunch of professional associations. I knew I wouldn't get the disciplined members' names, so I asked for the details on their offence and punishment with the names redacted. A few of the associations balked. They argued that their membership was so small that even releasing something generic like 'Massage therapist B sexually assaulted his patient' could be an invasion of privacy." Their reasoning, says Skelton, is that even without other identifying information – such as where the person worked, or even what city the person was in – if the patient or someone familiar with the case read the story they'd probably be able to identify whom the case referred to.

Programming fees are another area of concern. Although the access and freedom of information acts are being modernized to reflect the modern-day ability to extract and modify data with off-the-shelf software and a laptop, costs do add up and fee estimates remain out of reach for most private citizens; they are also becoming an issue for news organizations as budgets shrink. Requesters can claim financial hardship and public interest overrides, but these arguments are routinely dismissed. The existing laws, says Cribb, are "entirely ill-equipped" and open to the "whims of the bureaucracy in conjuring up extortionate fees and expansive timelines can become authoritative policies, beyond questioning."

Kevin Donovan, a *Toronto Star* journalist and the paper's investigations editor, has overseen several successful fee appeals and waivers, but has grown frustrated by the "Groundhog Day" phenomena to the point that he avoids formal requests altogether. "On a recent story I convinced a government official to give me data. It took a lot of work, but ultimately much easier than getting it [through the Act]. I also try and find data that I can prove is releasable without an FOI or ATIP request. Charity is a good example. The tax returns of all 83,000 charities are in electronic form and each year I get a CD with all the data."

Andrew Bailey, the *Star*'s database specialist, feels the same way, and has taken to web scraping as a way to bypass the formalities. "Rather than try to dance my way to the whole," he says, "I grab each record one at a time and rebuild them into a whole for analysis."

Case Study: "Race and Crime"

"Race and Crime." October 2002. *Toronto Star*. Jim Rankin, Scott Simmie, Michelle Shephard, John Duncanson, and Jennifer Quinn.
Act: Ontario's *Municipal Freedom of Information and Protection of Privacy Act*
Start to finish: initial request, 2.25 years; follow-up request, 7 years

The genesis of this investigative series on race, policing, and crime in Toronto was a routine police blotter item in 1999, about a routine crime and an unusual description of a suspect's skin colour: yellow. As it turned out, yellow was code for Asian, pulled, embarrassingly for Toronto police, from an internal database that tracks people who had been booked and fingerprinted for previous crimes. That got me thinking about what police document in terms of race and ethnicity. A 1989 policy forbids Toronto police to analyze race-based data out of fear it might be used to stigmatize communities, but that didn't mean that they didn't collect it, and it didn't mean we couldn't have a look at it.

After informal attempts to obtain police data failed, we made a formal request in March 2000, asking for record layouts for two internal police databases and the data themselves. Police denied both requests. In the case of one of the databases, which tracked police contacts with the public, we appealed the denials and focused our efforts on one of the two data sets that detailed arrests and charges and certain non-criminal offences, such as traffic tickets.

In 2001, another ruling in our favour by the Ontario Information and Privacy Commissioner led to mediation, which proved most productive. Working together, the police FOI coordinator, the police analyst in charge of the database, a mediator from the Office of the Information and Privacy Commissioner, and I found solutions to privacy concerns. In June 2002, police handed over the data on a single CD, and asked $800 for programming, an amount they said they had reduced because of the length of time the request had taken. They would never be that charitable with me again. It's also worth noting that we did not need legal help in this request.

We spent several months "interviewing" the data. Almost immediately, we saw patterns in terms of arrest outcomes for black people facing certain drug and other offences. We also looked at people ticketed for a driving offence that we had coded as "non-moving." These were offences that an officer would discover after a traffic stop, such as not carrying a licence or having no insurance. We isolated those facing only one such offence in a single incident, and found that black motorists were ticketed at a rate three times higher than the proportion of blacks in Toronto's population. We looked deep into the data to see whether other factors were at play, and they were indeed. A previous record, for example, affected whether you were released at the scene or held for bail. Nothing in the data could make the race factor go away, however. Prior to publication, we had a statistical expert from York University go through our work and replicate the analysis. A team of five reporters spent a month reporting and writing, and brought the numbers to life.

Over two weekends in October 2002, we published the series on paper and online. Reaction was huge, mixed, and heated. Toronto's black communities embraced the series as affirmation of what they had been complaining of anecdotally for decades. They also acknowledged another part of our analysis showing that blacks were being disproportionately charged for violent crimes, and renewed calls for social policy changes that would help youth in at-risk neighbourhoods. Police denied there was a problem, however. The Toronto Police Association first called for a boycott of the _Star_, and followed this up with a class-action libel suit, alleging that the series had branded every member of the service as racist. They sought $2.7 billion in damages (the action was dismissed by two levels of court, and died in 2004 when the Supreme Court of Canada refused to hear the case,

thus affirming the lower court decisions). There were calls for a race relations summit and the Ontario Human Rights Commissioner announced an
inquiry into the impact of racial profiling across all of society (see Ontario
Human Rights Commission 2003). Meanwhile, the police hired an academic
and a lawyer to analyze our analysis, and a sideshow of duelling statisticians
began. The police experts called the *Star* analysis "bogus" and "junk science"
(see Gold and Harvey 2003; Harvey and Liu 2003). A later academic study of
the police experts' analysis of our analysis found fundamental flaws in that
one (Wortley and Tanner 2003).

The series was lauded by many, and in 2003 won a National Newspaper Award for investigation, the Canadian Association of Journalists'
CCNMatthews/CAJ Computer-Assisted Reporting award, and the Gover-
nor General's Michener Award for public service journalism, the highest
honour in Canadian journalism. Attitudes have changed dramatically since
then. Police across the country acknowledge that racial bias is a problem, as
it is in any aspect of society. Toronto police partnered with the Ontario
Human Rights Commission to find ways to improve hiring, promotion, and
retention of minority officers, and ways to improve how they police.

I made a follow-up request in 2003 for updated arrest and offence data,
and renewed the request for the database that tracks whom police stop and
choose to document in mostly non-criminal encounters. In early 2010,
nearly seven years and many appeals and two court challenges later (both
the Canadian Civil Liberties Association and Ontario Information and
Privacy Commissioner were interveners at the latter Court of Appeal stage),
Toronto police handed over the data sets.

We needed legal help this time. The final Court of Appeal decision
(*Toronto [City] Police Services Board v. Ontario [Information and Privacy
Commissioner]*) was a win for journalists and others who wish to obtain
electronic data. It clarified what an agency must do to extract electronic
data and corrected a lower court decision that would have hamstrung future data requests. Police were ordered to pay our legal costs, which was
perhaps why they were not cutting any deals on programming fees this
time. They billed us $12,000. The *Star* paid the fee, obtained the data, and
appealed the cost.

We published "Race Matters," the follow-up series, in February 2010. The
lead piece, based on our analysis of police stops in mostly non-criminal situations, showed that black people in Toronto were 2.5 times more likely than

whites to be stopped, questioned, and documented by officers (Rankin et al. 2010).

On appeal, the programming cost was cut in half. In a subsequent request for updated data, police in 2011 released the data at no cost, presumably because the program to extract the data had already been written. "Known to Police," the latest chapter in this decade-long look at race, policing, and crime, was published in March 2012. This time, we used the data to ask a provocative question: was it possible that police in certain areas of Toronto had documented every young man of colour? (Rankin and Winsa 2012).

We've now heard of some victories, and the possible application of data analysis is obvious for researchers who might be refused informal requests for raw data. Many of these victories by journalists well versed in the access and freedom of information laws came, however, following expensive legal manoeuvrings prohibitive to most, academics included.

To Sue or Not to Sue? *"Send lawyers, guns and money"*

The late singer-songwriter Warren Zevon wrote of a guy in deep trouble following gambling problems in Havana, and unspecified girl trouble involving Russians, who, as a result, was in hiding in Honduras – in need of lawyers, guns, and money. Unhappy with an information and privacy ruling, you can go to court. If, however, you are unprepared to represent yourself and argue in court about the intricacies of access laws, you will need both lawyers and money.

In the access request arsenal, there is the option of going to court. In federal, provincial, and municipal acts, a requester – or government department – can take a complaint about a decision to either deny or release information to a "higher" level. This has mixed results and will lead to victories and defeats. All of this can cost a lot of money, as Matthew Yeager, an academic, illustrates in his study of two cases he was intimately involved in, one in the United States and one in Canada (Chapter 6). As a researcher, he waged a seventeen-year battle for raw Drug Enforcement Administration data, which ultimately did not result in disclosure and left behind a horrible precedent – agencies were not required to use electronic redaction techniques, such as eliminating fields that were deemed "sensitive" or that contained personal information – in responding to a request for government data. This is similar to the Ontario Divisional Court decision in *Toronto (City) Police Services Board v. Ontario (Information and Privacy*

Commissioner) that I was involved in during the *Star*'s successful bid to get police arrest and stop-and-search data. In my case, a higher court overturned the lower court decision. In Yeager's fight, he lost. Years later, however, the US *Freedom of Information Act* was amended and electronic redaction was normalized.

In Yeager's Canadian request, he lost a bid for Correctional Services of Canada inmate and parole data that went as high as the Federal Court of Appeal, and was left personally holding the bag for a $21,000 legal bill. Perhaps most troubling for Yeager, who was then a graduate student at Carleton University – and for academics toying with the idea of suing for data – Yeager wasn't able to get financial help from "university-connected, non-profit agencies," nor did Carleton offer help. Although the university was "silent" on the issue, Yeager wrote that he learned that the agency was "hostile to the project." Taking on the government, a source of university funding, can make one a "pariah within the academy." Suing the hand that feeds is frowned upon.

As Yeager concludes in Chapter 6, suing the government for information "clearly represents an extreme form of applied 'conflict' theory." Governments oppose the release of data and don't want outside researchers "rummaging" through raw data and "elite state interests are supported by the courts, whose members are appointed by those same elite interests." Yeager contends, however, that as a methodological tool suing for data is a must, since it is the government that "largely controls the data, the funds, and the research agenda."

As highlighted by the experiences of Yeager and Canadian journalists, taking matters to court often requires money and expertise, and even then the courts can get it absolutely wrong. The government, on the other hand, has plenty of money and expertise.

There is also a fear in academe that access requests and other social research tools such as surveys and interviews as employed by journalists may result in "ethics creep," where researchers become more "journalist" than academic, as highlighted by Kevin Haggerty (2004), a professor of criminology and sociology at the University of Alberta. Journalists may pursue similar information, but the means and goals may differ, and the work of journalists is not scrutinized to the same degree as that of academics. Academics tend to draw broader conclusions than journalists, writes Haggerty, and "employ more sophisticated statistical tools," yet use similar methodologies. "There is a heightened concern in the academy about the

ethical implications of forms of knowledge production that, when performed by journalists, raise few, if any, ethical concerns. Ultimately, this
raises the provocative question of whether university ethical protocols are
making it easier to produce certain forms of knowledge as a journalist rather
than as a university-affiliated researcher."

Haggerty argues for a reform of academic research standards and protocols that would allow researchers to dig deeper, and he calls for a reconsideration of whose interests are being served by the current protocols and
of what is "being lost as a result." "However, my suspicion is that the systematic creep of the ethical structure will continue its expansionist dynamic and
the bureaucracy will become larger, more formal, and more rigid," he writes.
"The more ethical roadblocks [that] are installed for innovative and critical
research, the more we risk homogenizing inquiry and narrowing vision, as
scholars start to follow what they perceive to be the path of least institutional
resistance."

Journalists are indeed not bound by the same standards. We are not academics, but are increasingly employing similar social science tools. With
the exception of publicly funded news operations, we work for employers
looking to turn a profit. We do things differently. We may go undercover. We
do stakeouts on unwilling subjects. Our rules of engagement, as Haggerty
points out, are different from those of an academic doing social research.
Nonetheless, investigative journalism is about telling stories that will be
consumed by the general public and, due to space and time constraints, the
stories must get to the point. The stories themselves – and how journalists
go about collecting them – are subject to libel and defamation laws. We do
adhere to ethics codes. We also tend to go hard after organizations, and part
of that is through seeking raw government data. Typically we don't care if
the process or the end result annoys the government or embarrasses it into
fixing something that is broken. That is the point of it all.

Conclusion

Although the frustration level and costs can be high – and the access and
freedom of information acts are wanting when it comes to requests for raw
electronic data – journalists have successfully used the tools of ATI to pinpoint and expose flaws and precipitate change. The examples in this chapter
prove that the laws can be successfully navigated. But what does the future
hold in store for such requests by media? Advertisers are abandoning traditional media. Newsroom budgets continue to shrink. Desks sit empty.

Computer-assisted reporting is viewed by some journalists and bosses as an expensive "time suck." What this means for the future of data requests and investigative journalism in general is unclear.

In a January 2009 lecture at Carleton University on the future of newspapers, John Honderich, publisher of the *Toronto Star* in 2002, when the series on "Race and Crime" was published, and now chairman of the parent company, Torstar, lamented the impact the World Wide Web has had on newspapers, and questioned whether serious journalism, which requires money and resources, would survive. But he also pointed to other models worth watching, among them foundation-funded projects and not-for-profit journalism. On the "Race and Crime" series, he had this to say: "It took fortitude, patience and hundreds of thousands of dollars. Was it worth it? You bet. We nudged the world a little bit" (Reid 2009).

Other traditional news media outlets engaged in serious journalism are facing the same uncertain future. Yet, with more and more people turning to the Web and digital devices for news and information, digital applications for data are proving to be a reason for optimism. The *Vancouver Sun's* Skelton points to two recent projects as proof. The online hits are in the millions and continue to accumulate on the parking ticket and salary disclosure data projects he was involved in. Another important thing to note is that once you have won the data, requests can be made for updated data with a fraction of the hassle and cost. In other words, the shelf life of these database projects is infinitely longer than a series published in print over several days. "If done right – database journalism projects can drive much more traffic to news organizations' websites than a typical series of stories," says Skelton. "I don't think we've ever had a story on our website – even if it's about Jon & Kate – that got 2 million hits. So these projects hold out the possibility of a big bang for your buck." The dynamite question, of course, is whether hits can be translated into profit that will support journalism on the Web or on other content-delivery media, such as smart phones and tablet computers.

Cribb, too, sees a future for data-based journalism, albeit a limited one. "It's obviously tough times with shrinking resources and less patience for long-term projects, all of which might suggest the future for computer-assisted reporting is dim. That said, the commoditization of news has made investigative, contextualized reporting a method of differentiation for big-picture news organizations looking to distinguish themselves from the competition. Exclusive stories based on hard-fought data and analytical skills has the power to set the public agenda, change public policies and laws and bring distinction to a news organization with unmatched force. It's harder to do this work in tough times. But tough times likely represent the best opportunity."

Data requests represent an opportunity, and more sectors could and should be using them. It is, as illustrated in this chapter, often a struggle to free raw electronic data. While there are indeed elements of Alice, Kafka, and Monty Python, it is, above all else, a war – but data requests are a tool that should be utilized to secure something otherwise unattainable.

Brokering access is indeed is a vital element in requests for raw data. Unlike requests for paper documents, a great battle is also to be expected. On a positive note, data requests under the acts, flawed as they are, have led to more proactive disclosure on the part of organizations, which has brought greater transparency and enhanced accountability to the public realm. Outside of journalism, the use of access and freedom of information acts to obtain and analyze raw electronic data presents nearly unlimited areas of study for graduate students, human rights groups, lawyers, and criminologists and other academics – provided, that is, that they have a masochistic bent.

NOTES

1 Unless noted otherwise, all quotes are from interviews by the author or from e-mail responses to the author's questions.
2 A reference to the December 2009 arrest of Nigerian Umar Farouk Abdulmutallab, the so-called "underpants" bomber charged with trying to detonate explosives in his underwear aboard a US-bound airline flight.
3 Internal correspondence provided to the author by Fred Vallance-Jones. This includes copies of e-mail, handwritten notes, and letters.
4 RCMP correspondence to Jim Rankin regarding programming fee estimate, Ottawa (8 July 2003), obtained through request to RCMP no. 03-ATIP-21960.
5 RCMP correspondence to Jim Rankin regarding release of criminal record data, Ottawa (1 December 2005), obtained through request to RCMP no. 03-ATIP-21960.

REFERENCES

Gold, A.D., and E.B. Harvey. 2003. "Executive Summary of Presentation on Behalf of the Toronto Police Service." http://www.torontopolice.on.ca/.
Haggerty, Kevin. 2004. "Ethics Creep: Governing Social Science Research in the Name of Ethics." *Qualitative Sociology* 27 (4): 391-414.
Harvey, E., and R. Liu. 2003. "An Independent Review of the Toronto Star Analysis of Criminal Information Processing System (CIPS) Data Provided by the Toronto Police Service (TPS)." http://www.torontopolice.on.ca/.

Mann, Bruce. 1986. "The Federal Information Coordinator as Meat in the Sandwich." *Canadian Public Administration* 29 (4): 579-82.

Moore, Paddy. 2004. "From Coloured Tabs to Computerized Signals: How Canada Tracks Dangerous Drugs." CBC News. http://www.cbc.ca/.

Ontario Human Rights Commission. 2003. "Paying the Price: The Human Cost of Racial Profiling. Inquiry Report." http://ohrc.on.ca/.

Ontario Information and Privacy Commissioner. 2000. *Order MO-1366: Appeal MA-990197-1, City of Toronto.* Toronto: Information and Privacy Commissioner/Ontario. http://www.ipc.on.ca/.

Rankin, Jim, A. Bailey, D. Bruser, M. Welsh, B. Popplewell, M. Henry, and D. Brazao. 2010. "Race Matters." *Toronto Star,* 6, 7, and 8 February, A1.

Rankin, Jim, Scott Simmie, Michelle Shephard, John Duncanson, and Jennifer Quinn. 2002. "Race and Crime." *Toronto Star,* 19 and 20 October, A1; 26 and 27 October, A1.

Rankin, Jim, and Patty Winsa. 2012. "Known to Police: Toronto Police Stop and Document Black and Brown People Far More than Whites." *Toronto Star,* 9 March. http://www.thestar.com/.

Reid, Daniel. 2009. "Print Journalism's Days Numbered: Former *Toronto Star* Publisher." *Carleton Now,* 8 February. http://www.now.carleton.ca/.

Reid, John. 2002. *Response to the Report of the Access to Information Review Task Force: A Special Report to Parliament by the Honourable John M. Reid, P.C., Information Commissioner of Canada.* Ottawa: Minister of Public Works and Government Services Canada.

Roberts, Alasdair. 2006. *Blacked Out: Government Secrecy in the Information Age.* Cambridge: Cambridge University Press.

Toronto Star. 2008. "Crime and Punishment." 19-27 July. http://www.thestar.com/.

–. 2009. "Toronto's Provincial Inmates." 18 July. http://www.thestar.com/.

Vallance-Jones, F. 2009. *National Freedom of Information Audit – 2008.* Prepared for the Canadian Newspaper Association. http://www.newspaperscanada.ca/.

–. 2010. "Collision Course: Winners of the CAJ's Top Award for Investigative Journalism in Canada, the Don McGillivray Award for Investigative Journalism, and the CCNMatthews/CAJ Computer-Assisted Reporting (CAR) Award." Canadian Association of Journalists. http://caj.ca/.

Vancouver Sun. 2009a. "Parking Secrets." 14 December. http://www.vancouversun.com/.

–. 2009b. "Public Sector Salaries." 19 December. http://www.vancouversun.com/.

Wortley, S., and J. Tanner. 2003. "Data, Denials, and Confusion: The Racial Profiling Debate in Toronto." *Canadian Journal of Criminology and Criminal Justice* 45 (3): 367-90.

LEGISLATION CITED

Access to Information Act, R.S.C. 1985, c. A-1.

Freedom of Information Act, 5 U.S.C. s. 552 (1966).

Municipal Freedom of Information and Protection of Privacy Act, R.S.O. 1990, c. M.56.

CASES CITED

Phinjo Gombu v. Tom Mitchinson, Assistant Commissioner et al., [2002], 214 D.L.R. (4th) 163; 59 O.R. (3d) 773 (Div. Ct.), leave to appeal granted, [2002] O.J. No. 3309.

Toronto (City) Police Services Board v. Ontario (Information and Privacy Commissioner), [2009] O.J. No. 90 (Ont. C.A.); reversing [2007] O.J. No. 2442 (Ont. Div. Ct.).

Postscript

SUZANNE LEGAULT, Information Commissioner of Canada

After reading this book, one might think that the access to information regime in Canada is beyond repair and will continue to be plagued by problems that will go unsolved. Indeed, one gets the same impression of doom from reading the multitude of reports containing recommendations to reform the *Access to Information Act (ATIA)* or the many recommendations contained in previous Information Commissioners' reports, since practically all have remained unresolved after thirty years. I suggest, however, that access to information is currently going through a profound transformation due to the expectations of citizens and parliamentarians, as well as increasing national and international pressure. I believe that these forces will lead to the necessary improvements.

When it passed the *Access to Information Act* thirty years ago, Canada was among the first five countries to empower its citizens by giving them a right of access to government information. The operating environment then was rather simple by today's standards. There were few personal computers, no search engine tools, no World Wide Web, and no Blackberry devices. Information was primarily paper-based; valuable statistical data were stored on giant reels that made retrieval of any specific information highly time-consuming.

In the 1990s, the Web 1.0 digital revolution enhanced access to information and service delivery by providing a more efficient dissemination platform. Over the following decade, further developments in information and communications technologies (ICTs) accelerated government/citizen transactions while increasing the number of delivery channels. The arrival of Web 2.0 democratized the creation process itself through its collection of web-based applications that foster interactivity, modular interoperability, and collaboration. Today's technology enables everyone to be a content creator, publisher, and sharer of information. There is now a massive accumulation of information that constantly flows across vast distances and at Twittering speed.[1] These realities have obvious ramifications for the administration of access to information regimes. The public expects faster access to wider sources of government information, at little or no charge, in a variety of formats that enable reuse and redistribution.

The digital revolution has brought about an important shift in the balance of power between government and citizens. Members of the public not only expect faster and greater access to government information but also demand direct accountability and immediate response. Citizens increasingly expect that government organizations will solicit and take their views and knowledge into account in public decision making. Empowered by new technologies, individuals can now join forces in creative, collaborative communities and quickly mobilize across wide distances in support of or against specific policy issues or decisions.

These new expectations are precisely the driving forces behind the recent "open government" movements. In the United States, Australia, and the United Kingdom in particular, groundbreaking initiatives are occurring to foster information sharing and collaboration among public servants and between public servants and citizens. These initiatives represent a paradigm shift in the use and dissemination of public sector information.

In Canada, open government initiatives of varying scopes are occurring at different levels of government but without the benefits of central coordination and guidance. At the federal level, there have been only very modest attempts at proactive disclosure. Almost ten years ago, the government issued a policy requiring all officials above a certain level to post, online, the specific details of their travel and hospitality claims. A few years later, with the development of more sophisticated systems and programs, the posting of this information, along with other information, including provisions in contracts and grants and contributions, is now done reasonably well by government organizations. There are further signs of progress. For instance, Natural Resources Canada offers free access to databases that once entailed substantial user charges. Its GeoConnections Discovery Portal is a metadata catalogue that enables users and data suppliers to access, evaluate, visualize, and publish Canadian geospatial and geoscience data products and Web services. Unfortunately, in the fast-moving information world of 2012, these attempts to open up government information do not represent the wave of the present, much less the wave of the future.

As I stated before the House of Commons Committee on Access to Information, Privacy and Ethics on 29 April 2010, to lead the paradigm shift from reactive to proactive disclosure, and ultimately to open government, there must be a made-in-Canada strategy. The strategy must reflect the unique characteristics and informational needs of our society. I offered five overarching principles:

> First, there must be commitment at the top to lead a cultural change conducive to open government. At a minimum, this involves issuing a declaration on open government with clear objectives. The commitment also entails assigning responsibility and accountability for coordination, guidance and deliverables. It requires prescribing specific timeframes.
>
> Second, there should be ongoing and broad public consultations. Citizens should be encouraged to participate using electronic means. It is critical to determine what government information the public wants and how they want to receive it.
>
> Third, information should be made accessible in open standard formats and rendered re-usable. Information should be derived from various sources and integrated to reduce the silos inherent in bureaucratic structures.
>
> Fourth, privacy, confidentiality, security, Crown copyright and official languages issues need to be addressed and resolved.
>
> Finally, open government principles should be anchored in statutory and policy instruments.

A well-functioning access to information legislation is a key component to an open government strategy. Citizens of today are demanding an effective regime that responds to their growing expectations in terms of timeliness and completeness of access to public sector information.

The text of the current federal law should be conducive to timely and complete responses to access requests, but the data clearly show that it is not. The *ATIA* provides for a thirty-day response time, which can be extended in a number of limited circumstances. Further, the recently added section 4(2.1) of the act states:

The head of a government institution shall, without regard to the identity of a person making a request for access to a record under the control of the institution, make every reasonable effort to assist the person in connection with the request, respond to the request accurately and completely and, subject to the regulations, *provide timely access* to the record in the format requested [emphasis added].

Yet, the statistics collected by the government paint a picture of increasing delays and a steady decrease in the number of requests where all information is disclosed. Whereas 69 percent of requests were responded to within the thirty-day limit in 2002-03, only 56 percent were within that time frame in 2009-10. Further, section 2(1) of the act states:

The purpose of this Act is to extend the present laws of Canada to provide a right of access to information in records under the control of a government institution in accordance with the principles that government information should be available to the public, *that necessary exceptions to the right of access should be limited and specific* [emphasis added].

Notwithstanding this legislative framework, Treasury Board of Canada statistics indicate a significant and steady decline in the number of requests where all information was disclosed. In 1999-2000, all information was disclosed in 40 percent of the requests. In 2009-10, that number stood at 16 percent (Treasury Board of Canada Secretariat 2010). These data support the view among stakeholders that less information is being disclosed year after year when one would expect that, with a mature system, the trend would be towards more disclosure of public sector information.

The reform of the *Access to Information Act* in 2006 failed to address much-needed reforms that have been proposed and repeated many times since the first review of the legislation in 1987 (Standing Committee on Justice and the Solicitor General 1987). Yet experts agree that the federal legislation is falling behind its national and international counterparts (see Tromp 2008). At the national and international level, many legislative reforms have either occurred recently or are currently developing. The federal access to information legislation will need to move towards convergence with the most progressive regimes, both national and international, if it is to remain faithful to its original intent, but most importantly, if it is to address citizens' expectations.

Success may well come about only as citizens and other stakeholders, including the government, develop a more constructive dialogue to genuinely advance the fundamental purpose of access to information laws, based on sound research and data, and collaborate to find pragmatic solutions that take into account the fine balance between the need for transparency and the need, in some circumstances, to protect certain information against disclosure. As the Supreme Court of Canada put it recently:

> Access to information in the hands of public institutions can increase transparency in government, contribute to an informed public, and enhance an open democratic society. Some information in the hands of those institutions is, however, entitled to protection in order to prevent the impairment of those very principles and promote good governance. [*Ontario (Public Safety and Security) v. Criminal Lawyers' Association*]

NOTE

1 The recent disclosure of massive amounts of information outside of official government channels on WikiLeaks is a case in point.

REFERENCES

Standing Committee on Justice and the Solicitor General. 1987. *Open and Shut: Enhancing the Right to Know and the Right to Privacy.* Ottawa: Queen's Printer for Canada.

Treasury Board of Canada Secretariat. 2010. "Statistical Tables 2009-2010 – Access to Information." In *Info Source Bulletin Number 33B – Statistical Reporting.* http://www.infosource.gc.ca/.

Tromp, Stanley L. 2008. "Fallen Behind: Canada's *Access to Information Act* in the World Context." http://www3.telus.net/index100/report.

LEGISLATION CITED

Access to Information Act, R.S.C. 1985, c. A-1.

CASE CITED

Ontario (Public Safety and Security) v. Criminal Lawyers' Association, 2010 SCC 23.

Contributors

Reem Bahdi is an associate professor at the University of Windsor Faculty of Law. Her current research focuses on two areas. The first concentrates on the human rights dimensions of national security laws and policies in Canada. The second focuses on access to justice in the Palestinian context. Professor Bahdi is co-director of KARAMAH, the Project on Judicial Independence and Human Dignity, which supports access to justice in Palestine through research, continuing judicial education, and directed civil society engagement. She is the editor-in-chief of the *Windsor Yearbook of Access to Justice* and a board member of the BC Civil Liberties Association. She has taught courses in access to justice, torture and national security, torts, and legal theory.

Jim Bronskill is a reporter in the Ottawa bureau of the Canadian Press (CP) news agency, specializing in security and intelligence, policing, and justice-related issues, including civil liberties and human rights. He has considerable experience using information laws to uncover stories. Jim holds a master's degree in journalism from Carleton University, where he has been a sessional lecturer since 2003. A frequent speaker on access to information issues, he was a co-founder and steering committee member of Open Government Canada, a national coalition formed to guard against undue government secrecy. In 2008, he was part of a team that won the Michener Award for its coverage of taser use by the Royal Canadian Mounted Police.

Dr. Ann Cavoukian, Information and Privacy Commissioner of Ontario, is recognized as one of the leading privacy experts in the world. Noted for her seminal work on Privacy Enhancing Technologies (PETs) in 1995, she developed the concept of Privacy by Design, which seeks to proactively embed privacy into the design specifications of information technology and accountable business practices, and for which, along with her work on privacy protection in modern international environments, she has been honoured with the prestigious Kristian Beckman Award. Her office has developed a number of tools and procedures to ensure that privacy is strongly protected, not only in Canada but around the world. She has been involved in numerous international committees focusing on privacy, security, technology, and business, as well as on strengthening consumer confidence and trust in emerging technology applications. Dr. Cavoukian also serves as the chair of the Identity, Privacy and Security Institute at the University of Toronto. She is also a member of several boards, including the European Biometrics Forum, Future of Privacy Forum, and RIM Council, and is a Distinguished Fellow of the Ponemon Institute. She was named by *Intelligent Utility Magazine* as one of the "Top 11 Movers and Shakers for the Global Smart Grid industry for 2011."

Tia Dafnos is a PhD candidate in sociology at York University in Toronto. She has co-edited, with Alan Bourke and Markus Kip, the book *Lumpencity: Discourses of Marginality | Marginalizing Discourses* (Red Quill Books, 2011). Her MA thesis examined the use of racial and ethnic identifiers in the production of criminal intelligence and law enforcement discourse on organized crime in Canada. She has since been interested in exploring methodologies for studying state agencies. The current focus of her research is the criminalization and policing of indigenous peoples' activism in Canada in the context of neoliberal discourses of democracy and human rights. She has been involved in a collaborative ATI-based research group on police and government decision making in relation to the Toronto G20 Summit protests of June 2010.

Willem de Lint was trained at the Centre of Criminology at the University of Toronto, where he obtained his MA and PhD in Criminology. He has taught at the University of Windsor, Canada, and at Victoria University of Wellington, New Zealand, and is now professor in Criminal Justice at the Flinders Law School, Flinders University, Australia. His research over the years has concentrated on policing and security, and his latest books are

Security and Everyday Life (co-edited), *Intelligent Control: Developments in Public Order Policing in Canada* (co-authored), and *Crime and Justice: A Guide to Criminology* (4th edition) (co-edited). Currently, he is studying the relationship between intelligence and common knowledge about insecurities, particularly in the interaction between counterterrorism and national security issues. He is also researching and writing on military subjectivity in crime policy, self-medication by victims of crime, and eco-terrorism.

Gary Dickson, QC, is Saskatchewan's Information and Privacy Commissioner. He was first appointed by the Legislative Assembly of Saskatchewan in November 2003, and then reappointed to a further five-year term in 2009. He practised law in Calgary for twenty-three years, was elected MLA for Calgary Buffalo in a 1992 by-election, and was re-elected in 1993 and 1997. He was directly involved in the development of Alberta's access and privacy laws, including the *Freedom of Information and Protection of Privacy Act* (1995) and the *Health Information Act* (2001), and he co-chaired a Canadian Bar Association panel advising the Alberta government in the development of the *Personal Information Protection Act* (2003). He has written and spoken extensively on access to information, privacy, and health information issues. He is a member of the Saskatchewan and Alberta Law Societies.

Steve Hewitt is Senior Lecturer in American and Canadian Studies at the University of Birmingham in the United Kingdom. He is the author of several books, including *Spying 101: The RCMP's Secret Activities at Canadian Universities, 1917-1997* (University of Toronto Press, 2002), *The British War on Terror: Terrorism and Counter-Terrorism on the Home Front since 9/11* (Continuum, 2008), and *Snitch: A History of the Modern Intelligence Informer* (Continuum, 2010). He has also written a number of articles and book chapters related to security and intelligence in the past and present. In April 2011, he became president of the British Association for Canadian Studies.

Sean P. Hier is associate professor of sociology at the University of Victoria. Dr. Hier has published in such journals as *Media, Culture, and Society, Surveillance and Society, Social and Legal Studies, Critical Sociology, British Journal of Sociology, Race and Class, Ethnic and Racial Studies, Women's History Review, Research in Race and Ethnic Relations, Journalism Studies, Canadian Journal of Sociology, Canadian Ethnic Studies, International Sociology, Socialist Studies, Theoretical Criminology,* and *New Media and Society.* He has edited a number of books, including *Contemporary Social*

Thought: Themes and Theories (Canadian Scholars' Press, 2005), *Race and Racism in 21st-Century Canada: Continuity, Complexity, and Change* (with B. Singh Bolaria, Broadview Press, 2007), *Identity and Belonging: Rethinking Race and Ethnicity in Canadian Society* (with B. Singh Bolaria, Canadian Scholars' Press, 2006), *The Surveillance Studies Reader* (with Joshua Greenberg, Open University Press, 2007), *Surveillance: Power, Problems, and Politics* (with Joshua Greenberg, UBC Press, 2009), and *Racism and Justice: Critical Dialogue on the Politics of Identity, Inequality and Change* (with Dan Lett and B. Singh Bolaria, Fernwood Press, 2009).

Mike Larsen is an instructor in the Department of Criminology at Kwantlen Polytechnic University, British Columbia, a PhD candidate in Sociology at York University in Toronto, and a researcher at the York Centre for International and Security Studies. He has a master's degree in Criminology from the University of Ottawa. Since 2008, he has served as the co-managing editor of the *Journal of Prisoners on Prisons.* His research deals with Canadian national security practices, particularly as they involve the deprivation of liberty and contestations around government secrecy, public accountability, and the right to know. His current work focuses on the Canadian security certificate regime, with an emphasis on practices of detention and surveillance, and makes extensive use of access to information requests. Mike has published in the academic and popular press, including the *Canadian Journal of Law and Society, Contemporary Justice Review,* the edited volume *Surveillance: Power, Problems, and Politics* (UBC Press, 2009), and *Embassy Foreign Policy Newsweekly.* He is a regular contributor to *Prism: The Security Practices Monitor.*

Suzanne Legault was appointed as Information Commissioner of Canada on 30 June 2010. She was the Interim Information Commissioner for the previous year. From 18 June 2007 until 30 June 2009, Ms. Legault was Assistant Commissioner for the Office of the Information Commissioner of Canada, responsible for the Policy, Communications and Operations Branch. In 2006, she participated in the Federal Public Servant in Residence Program and worked with Dr. David Zussman, Jarislowsky Chair in Public Sector Management at the University of Ottawa. Ms. Legault began her career in the Public Service in 1996 at the Competition Bureau, where she held increasingly senior positions, including Special Advisor to the Commissioner of Competition. She then served as Legal Counsel with the Department of Justice, before returning to the Competition Bureau, where she was Assistant

Deputy Commissioner, Legislative Affairs, then Deputy Commissioner, Legislative and Parliamentary Affairs. Prior to joining the Public Service, Ms. Legault practised law as a criminal defence lawyer from 1991 to 1996, and as a Crown prosecutor from 1994 to 1996. She holds a Bachelor of Civil Law and a Bachelor of Common Law from McGill Law School, which she obtained in 1988.

David McKie is an award-winning journalist with CBC News who depends on access to information and computer-assisted reporting for his stories that appear online and on radio and television. His past stories include investigations into drug, food, and workplace safety, the Toyota vehicle recall, and marriages of convenience among recent immigrants. In 2008, he was part of a team that won the Michener Award for its coverage of taser use by the Royal Canadian Mounted Police. Working out of the Parliamentary bureau in Ottawa, David is now part of the network's political coverage. He also teaches journalism part-time at Carleton University and Algonquin College, and is an adjunct professor at University of King's College in Halifax. David has also co-authored two journalism textbooks.

Jeffrey Monaghan is a PhD candidate in the Department of Sociology at Queen's University. With Kevin Walby, he has co-authored articles in *Current Sociology, Canadian Journal of Criminology and Criminal Justice, Alternatives, Upping the Anti, Social Movement Studies,* and *Policing and Society.* His research focuses on policing and surveillance, particularly police responses to the tactics of radical social movements. He is a member of Books2prisoners Ottawa, as well as the Ontario Public Interest Research Group at Carleton University.

Justin Piché is assistant professor of sociology at Memorial University of Newfoundland and co-managing editor of the *Journal of Prisoners on Prisons* (http://www.jpp.org). Recent publications include articles in the *Howard Journal of Criminal Justice* (2012, with Kevin Walby), the *Canadian Journal of Law and Society* (2011), *Punishment and Society* (2011, with Kevin Walby), the *British Journal of Criminology* (2010, with Kevin Walby), and *Contemporary Justice Review* (2010, with Mike Larsen). Research interests include the sociology of punishment with a focus on Canadian penality, public criminology, and prison writing. Commentary related to his doctoral dissertation findings can be found on his blog "Tracking the Politics of 'Crime' and Punishment in Canada" (http://www.tpcpcanada.blogspot.com).

Jim Rankin is a *Toronto Star* reporter-photographer. He has covered the murder trials of Paul Bernardo and Karla Homolka, the ice storm in Eastern Ontario and Québec, floods in the Saguenay, crime in the Caribbean, and a couple of futile Toronto Maple Leafs playoff runs. He has investigated international adoption practices, high-cost payday lenders, unscrupulous immigration consultants, the costs of impaired driving, and the wisdom of mandatory jail sentences for more crimes. In 2002, Rankin was part of a team of reporters, editors, and researchers involved in the Michener Award–winning investigative series into race, policing, and crime in Toronto. He specializes in data-based stories, many of which involve lengthy and novel freedom of information requests. His work has been nominated for seven National Newspaper Awards.

Ann Rees teaches journalism at Kwantlen Polytechnic University in Surrey, British Columbia, and is also a PhD candidate in the School of Communication at Simon Fraser University. She was a reporter with *The Province* newspaper for twenty-one years, working for the last decade of her journalism career as an award-winning investigative reporter who made extensive use of federal access to information (ATI) and provincial freedom of information (FOI) laws to obtain government records. As the 2002 winner of the Atkinson Fellowship in Public Policy Journalism, Ann spent a year researching ATI and FOI in Canada for a newspaper series that ran in the *Toronto Star* in 2003. Her PhD research concerns secrecy and transparency in Canada's federal government, and also considers public access to government information as a communication right of citizens in a democracy.

Fred Vallance-Jones is associate professor of journalism at the University of King's College in Halifax. He spent twenty-five years as a working journalist before joining King's in 2007, and now teaches introductory reporting, investigative reporting, and database journalism at the undergraduate and graduate levels. He has a special research interest in access issues and is an experienced user of access legislation at the federal, provincial, and municipal levels. On behalf of Newspapers Canada, he conducts an annual comparative study of access responses by governments across Canada.

Kevin Walby is Assistant Professor of Sociology at the University of Victoria, Canada. He is co-editor of *Emotions Matter: A Relational Approach to Emotions* with Alan Hunt and Dale Spencer (University of Toronto Press, 2012). He is the Prisoners' Struggles editor for the *Journal of Prisoners on*

Prisons. He has published articles in *Social and Legal Studies, British Journal of Criminology* (with Justin Piché), *Punishment and Society* (with Justin Piché), *Crime, Law and Social Change* (with Randy Lippert), *Policing and Society* (with Jeffrey Monaghan), *Current Sociology* (with Jeffrey Monaghan), *Criminology and Criminal Justice* (with Nicolas Carrier), *Antipode* (with Randy Lippert), *International Sociology* (with Sean Hier) and *Social Movement Studies* (with Jeffrey Monaghan). He is author of *Touching Encounters: Sex, Work, and Male-for-Male Internet Escorting* (University of Chicago Press, 2012). He is currently co-editing an international volume called *Policing Cities: Urban Securitization and Regulation in the 21st Century* (Routledge, forthcoming) with Randy Lippert.

Matthew G. Yeager obtained his bachelor's degree in criminology from the School of Criminology, University of California at Berkeley, in 1972. He has a master's degree in criminal justice from the State University of New York at Albany (1975), and a PhD in sociology from Carleton University in Ottawa (2006). He has published over thirty articles and studies in theoretical and applied criminology, in addition to being a clinical criminologist with expertise in sentencing alternatives and parole release. He still carries a caseload of Lifers and Dangerous Offenders in the Canadian federal penal system, whom he assists with parole representation. Dr. Yeager is currently an associate professor in the Department of Sociology at King's University College at the University of Western Ontario. He specializes in dangerous offenders, convict criminology, critical criminology, crimes of the powerful, and political economy.

Index

Abdelrazik, Abousfian, 24, 143, 152-60, 162-64, 166
Aboriginal activism, 25, 209-31
Aboriginal Relations Team (Ontario Provincial Police), 212-13, 226, 230
access to information: community, 2, 27, 84, 88, 161, 302, 315; and freedom of information, xii, xv, 1, 3, 8, 10, 12, 14-15, 27-28, 40, 46, 47, 51, 54, 60, 63, 68-77, 79, 81-92, 109, 146, 169-89, 217-18, 227, 249, 254, 261, 273, 288, 294, 295, 298, 303, 305, 306, 309, 328, 335-39, 344, 347, 349, 351, 352, 353, 355; and political leadership, 69, 73, 74, 91, 125, 314, 318
Access to Information Act (Canada), xiv, 1, 8, 9, 27, 35, 38, 54, 55, 69, 81, 97, 100, 106, 108, 115, 137, 142, 162, 170, 180, 182, 183, 185, 194, 195, 197, 200, 203, 206, 218, 226, 238, 288-92, 300, 310, 314-16, 319, 337, 342, 358, 361, 362
access to information and privacy co-ordinators, 4, 5, 18, 19, 68, 76, 77, 91, 203, 244, 289, 298, 301, 324, 328, 337, 344-46
accountability, xvii, 3, 6, 7, 9, 16, 25, 27, 38, 39, 48, 49-56, 62-65, 74, 76, 83, 87-90, 103, 104, 110, 111, 115, 120, 123-25, 127-29, 132, 136, 144, 146, 147, 152, 161, 162, 209, 217-18, 227-28, 267, 270-71, 274, 276, 277, 292, 297, 301, 309, 316-18, 324, 355, 359-60, 368
Afghanistan, detainee treatment, 110, 125, 127, 130
Alberta, 12, 71-83, 87, 90, 92, 196, 206, 240, 241, 243, 248, 250, 255, 256, 275, 278, 304, 305, 352, 367
amber-light process, 20, 22, 57, 58, 148, 152, 161, 220, 338
Arar, Maher, xv, 44, 117, 119, 121, 122, 124, 126, 131, 153, 154, 162, 163
archives, 171, 177, 178, 196, 202, 205
Assembly of First Nations, 213, 230
aviation security, 24, 98-111, 309, 332, 336, 341-43

backlogs, 16, 86, 294, 302, 308

barriers to access, 16, 25, 26, 85, 143-51, 160, 161, 216, 227, 234-56, 287-310
Beeby, Dean, 3, 19, 294, 299, 300
British Columbia, 12, 35, 60, 71-83, 85, 87, 90, 92, 240-50, 251, 255, 256, 275, 276, 278, 281, 297, 299, 303, 307, 339, 368, 370
brokering access, 2, 3, 5, 17-19, 25-26, 121, 128, 136, 324, 337, 355
Bronskill, Jim, 24, 100, 101, 105, 108, 109, 146, 204, 293, 294, 307
bureaucracy, 8, 17, 18, 44, 59, 61, 64, 107, 119, 133, 146, 147-57, 296, 298, 310, 348, 353

cabinet confidence, 8, 17, 23, 28, 38-43, 45, 60, 62, 70, 106, 108, 137, 146, 241, 253, 294, 318, 321, 331
Caledonia, 25, 209, 211-13, 216-30
Canada Evidence Act, 153, 156, 159, 163
Canadian Air Transport Security Authority, 101
Canadian Food Inspection Agency, 316, 318, 320, 321, 326, 327
Canadian Forces National Counter-Intelligence Unit, 221, 230
Canadian Newspaper Association, 89, 147, 294, 298, 303, 304, 307
Canadian Security Intelligence Service, 20, 97, 119, 130, 153, 172, 196, 202, 218
Cavoukian, Ann, 73, 74, 281, 304
Central Intelligence Agency (US), 136, 172, 198
Charkaoui, Adil, 127, 129, 130, 131
Citizenship and Immigration Canada, 120, 292
Civil Aviation Daily Occurrence Reporting System (Transport Canada), 309, 332, 342
civil society, 88, 91, 163
closed-circuit television, 261-82
Colvin, Richard, 126, 127, 132
Commission for Public Complaints Against the RCMP, 124-25

Community, Contract, and Aboriginal Policing Services (RCMP), 277
computer-assisted reporting, 335, 343, 350, 354, 369
Coordinating Committee for Community Safety (London, ON), 271-72
Coordination of Access to Information Request System (Canada), 315, 327-32
Correctional Service of Canada, 175, 177, 181, 182, 185, 189, 235, 237, 248, 253, 255
Council of Yukon First Nations, 237
courts, xiv, 3, 8, 39, 41-44, 46, 56, 62, 69, 70-72, 80-82, 86, 103, 115, 124-27, 129, 133-34, 137, 144, 147, 151-62, 163, 170-89, 203, 229, 273, 276, 277, 289, 310, 318, 319, 332, 340, 341, 343, 349, 350, 351, 352, 362

deemed refusal, 18, 85, 217, 291, 292
delay, 2, 3, 8, 16, 17, 18, 20, 21, 26, 28, 36, 37, 38, 57, 59, 71, 85, 86, 99, 102, 104, 109, 143, 147, 148, 150, 151, 154, 159, 169, 171, 210, 216, 220, 227, 242, 245, 247, 278, 279, 287-306, 316, 317, 320, 321, 323, 330-32, 338, 361
democracy, xv, 23, 40, 47-49, 52, 54, 56, 57, 64, 89, 109, 123, 128, 146, 169, 214, 249, 254, 310, 325, 326
Department of Fisheries and Oceans, 222
Department of Foreign Affairs and International Trade (Canada), 120, 141, 143, 152, 153, 158, 162, 163, 292, 294, 302, 317
Department of National Defence (Canada), 20, 59, 217, 225, 229, 292, 323
Dickson, Gary, 23
dirty data, 6, 23, 24, 142-49, 151, 152, 156, 157, 158, 160
Drapeau, Michel, 21, 22, 172, 203, 296, 297, 307, 321

Drug Enforcement Administration
(US), 172-75, 351

electronic data, 176, 179, 335-55
Emergency Response Team (Ontario
Provincial Police), 212, 216, 221,
229
exemption clauses, 16, 18, 19, 20, 23, 25,
26, 28, 38, 40, 44, 45, 60, 62, 70,
71, 100, 106, 115, 137, 184, 185,
197, 202, 205, 218, 226, 230, 246,
253, 256, 319, 321, 360-61

Federal Accountability Act (Canada),
27, 144, 146, 147, 162, 292, 301,
316, 317, 324
Federal Bureau of Investigation (US),
178, 198
fees, 11-13, 26, 87-88, 219, 245, 279,
287-88, 296, 304-8, 344-50
freedom of information, xii, xv, 1, 3, 8,
10, 12, 14-15, 27-28, 40, 46, 47, 51,
54, 60, 63, 68-77, 79, 81-92, 109,
146, 169-89, 217-18, 227, 249, 254,
261, 273, 288, 294, 295, 298, 303,
305, 306, 309, 328, 335-39, 344,
347, 349, 351, 352, 353, 355
Freedom of Information Act (US), 14,
40, 46, 47, 109, 170, 189, 288, 295,
352
*Freedom of Information and Protec-
tion of Privacy Act* (Canadian
provinces/territories), 12, 28, 32,
60, 71, 73, 79, 85, 87, 90, 92, 186,
218, 272, 298, 303, 305, 306, 309,
348, 367

governmentality, 118, 128, 133-35
Grace, John, 59-60, 290, 315

Indian and Northern Affairs Canada,
223
informal information requests, 229,
236, 239, 240-43, 247, 248, 251,
252, 264, 265, 274, 316

information and communications technology, 6, 90, 359
information brokering, 5, 25
Information Commissioner of Canada,
18, 78, 89, 109, 146, 162, 177, 184,
201, 203, 205, 247, 290, 291-92,
296, 299, 300, 302, 308, 314, 315,
317, 321, 329, 344, 356, 346, 368
Integrated Border Enforcement Team
(RCMP), 124
Integrated National Security Enforcement Team (RCMP), 122, 150
Integrated Threat Assessment Centre
(Canada), 223, 225
intelligence, 15, 20, 62, 72, 97-110, 117-
37, 153, 162, 171-73, 196-98, 202,
211, 212, 215, 216-30
investigative journalism, 2, 3, 7, 22, 26,
110, 148, 289, 337, 343, 353, 354;
and data-based journalism, 27, 354
Ipperwash (ON), 28, 209, 211, 214, 216,
218, 227, 228

Legault, Suzanne, 37, 109, 110, 290,
299, 300, 315-19, 322, 329-30
Library and Archives Canada, 196
Lions Video Monitoring Advisory Committee (Sudbury, ON), 268-70
litigation, 24-26, 115, 143-63, 170, 190,
338
live archive, 4, 5, 16, 20, 21, 22, 23
London Police Service, 271-73

Management Accountability
Framework (Canada), 297
Manitoba, 11, 71, 101-6, 303, 305
Mann, Bruce, 18, 301, 324, 345
Marleau, Robert, 21, 59, 108, 147, 299
Marx, Gary 6, 23-4 142-45, 210, 235, 249
McKie, David, 27, 336, 161, 163
Member of the Legislative Assembly,
74, 87
Ministry of Community Safety and
Correctional Services (Ontario),
219, 237, 239, 244-45, 279-80

mosaic effect, 144, 154, 346-47
Municipal Freedom of Information and Protection of Privacy Act (Ontario), 11, 90, 272, 305-6, 348

Narcotics and Dangerous Drugs Information System (US Drug Enforcement Administration), 173
National Security Criminal Investigations (RCMP), 122, 148
National Security Group (Department of Justice Canada), 154, 163
neoliberalism, 118, 134-36
New Brunswick, 10, 77-83, 240, 243
Newfoundland, 10, 78, 79, 83, 304
non-governmental organizations, 81, 264
Northwest Territories, 13, 71, 75, 77, 78, 91, 241, 243, 244
Nova Scotia, 11, 68, 71, 75, 78-79, 82, 86, 89, 90, 241, 243, 244, 248-49, 251, 303-4, 307
Nunavut, 13, 71, 77-78, 91, 240-41, 243, 244, 245, 248

Offender Management System (Correctional Service of Canada), 176-77
office of primary interest, 20, 220, 321
Office of the Information and Privacy Commissioner (Ontario), xiv, 11, 71-74, 78, 79, 82, 267, 268, 299, 303-4, 307, 340-41, 349, 350
Office of the Information Commissioner of Canada, 8, 10, 17-18, 21, 40-42, 59-62, 78, 89, 99, 106-10, 146-47, 177, 184-85, 201-5, 247, 276, 289-92, 296, 298-302, 314-16, 321, 324, 329, 330, 342-45, 368
Office of the Privacy Commissioner of Canada, 78, 85, 155, 274-77
official discourse, 23, 116-17, 128, 195, 210, 214, 216
Ontario, xiv, 11, 27, 70-72, 74-79, 81-82, 90, 133, 182, 156, 187, 287, 297, 299, 303-9, 336, 340-41; and

Aboriginal activism, 209-11, 213, 219; prison expansion in, 237, 239, 245, 248; streetscape surveillance in, 266, 268, 270
Ontario Provincial Police, 209-13, 216, 218-21, 226-28
open government, 15, 17, 38, 41, 46, 55, 75, 77, 82, 88-89, 109, 253, 303, 309, 329, 359-60
order-making powers, 17, 71, 79-82, 86, 108

policing of knowledge, 26, 235
political interference, 2, 36-39, 51, 57-58, 153, 294, 300, 316
politics of access, 1, 5, 7, 9, 17-18, 20-21, 118, 128, 315, 36, 37-46, 50-52, 55, 57, 63, 81, 107, 128, 136, 148, 157-60, 216, 227, 234, 280, 290, 299; and political leadership, 73, 91, 314
Prime Minister's Office (Canada), 35-37, 42, 51-52, 58, 62-63, 148, 338
Prince Edward Island, 10, 71-72, 77-79, 90, 240-41, 243, 245, 248, 304
prisons, 130, 170, 175, 182, 234-36, 250, 254
privacy, 9, 26, 56, 61, 64, 68, 77, 79, 88, 121, 150, 155, 183-84, 246, 262, 265, 274, 339, 346, 349, 360
Privacy Act (Canada), 143, 150, 153, 155-56, 183, 275
Privy Council Office (Canada), 35, 45, 53, 57-58, 59, 62, 148, 292-94, 302, 321, 331
Provincial Emergency Response Team (Ontario), 212, 221
public criminology, 370, 279
public health, 56, 60, 64, 309, 320, 324, 336
Public Safety Canada, 16, 184-85, 292
public sociology, 180

quasi exemptions, 16, 21, 26, 287, 288, 303-4, 307

Quebec, 11, 35, 71, 78-79, 82, 86-87, 200-1, 240, 243, 278

Rankin, Jim, 27, 306, 348, 370
red file process, 36-37
redaction, 3, 19, 20, 25, 126, 150, 153-55, 175, 218, 224-26, 246, 344, 351
Rees, Ann, 23, 57, 148, 299, 338
Reid, John, 40, 42, 60-61, 107-8, 146, 290, 296, 308
research methods, 2, 22, 142-43, 160, 169-70, 182, 209, 216, 221, 226, 239, 263, 352; historical, 195
review of access to information decisions, 77, 79
right to know, xii, 1, 3-4, 47, 54-55, 89, 109, 146, 287
Roberts, Alasdair, 2, 20, 51, 57, 62, 101, 111, 148, 295, 305, 327-28, 338
Royal Canadian Mounted Police (RCMP), 44, 97, 110, 115, 119, 122-25, 149-51, 172, 194-204, 205-6, 221, 275-78

Saskatchewan, 12, 71, 74, 76, 78, 83, 86, 243-44
Security Intelligence Review Committee (Canada), 103, 119

secrecy, 2, 7, 17, 38-40, 43, 45, 61, 64, 99, 103, 126, 145-46, 226, 246, 249, 296, 316; culture(s) of, 1, 18, 21, 54, 59, 107, 171
September 11, 2001, 15-16, 24, 61, 97-98, 100, 102, 105, 121, 125, 130, 202, 227, 277
surveillance, 57, 148, 222, 261, 263, 265, 278

Tactics and Rescue Unit (Ontario Provincial Police), 212, 221
techniques of opacity, 17, 20-21, 216, 236, 238, 241, 244-45
Togneri, Sébastien, 300
transparency, 3, 15, 17, 38, 46, 48-50, 53, 55, 70, 73, 74, 145, 209, 227, 317
Transport Canada, 98-100, 223, 292, 309, 325, 342
Treasury Board Secretariat (Canada), 19, 50, 60, 107, 291, 295, 299, 327, 329, 361

Vallance-Jones, Fred, 26, 336, 341-43
Video Monitoring Advisory Committee (Sudbury, ON), 267-68

Yukon, 13, 71, 77, 78, 237, 243, 307

Printed and bound in Canada by Friesens

Set in Futura Condensed and Warnock by Artegraphica Design Co. Ltd.

Copy editor: Francis Chow

Proofreader: Helen Godolphin